Grande Dame
Guignol Cinema

Grande Dame Guignol Cinema

A History of Hag Horror from Baby Jane *to Mother*

PETER SHELLEY

McFarland & Company, Inc., Publishers
Jefferson, North Carolina, and London

Acknowledgments

This book has taken two years to research and write, and could not have been accomplished without the guidance and support of my friend and fellow film buff, Barry Lowe. Additional thanks go to Julie Barkman, Katherine Boyd, Laraine Jones, Sharon McGregor, Hugh Monroe, Kath Perry, and Anita Plateris.

LIBRARY OF CONGRESS CATALOGUING-IN-PUBLICATION DATA

Shelley, Peter, 1962–
Grande Dame Giugnol cinema : a history
of hag horror from Baby Jane to Mother / Peter Shelley.
p.   cm.
Includes bibliographical references and index.

ISBN 978-0-7864-4569-1
softcover : 50# alkaline paper ∞

1. Horror films—History and criticism.   2. Women in motion pictures.   I. Title
PN1995.9.H6S47   2009   791.43'6164—dc22   2009030254

British Library cataloguing data are available

©2009 Peter Shelley. All rights reserved

No part of this book may be reproduced or transmitted in any form or by any means, electronic or mechanical, including photocopying or recording, or by any information storage and retrieval system, without permission in writing from the publisher.

On the cover: Joan Crawford and Bette Davis (as Baby Jane) in *What Ever Happened to Baby Jane?* (1962) (Warner Bros. Pictures/Photofest)

Manufactured in the United States of America

*McFarland & Company, Inc., Publishers
Box 611, Jefferson, North Carolina 28640
www.mcfarlandpub.com*

For Valmai Pears, my mother and first grande dame,
who encouraged my love of the movies

Table of Contents

Acknowledgments iv
Preface 1
Introduction 5

— THE FILMS —

"*What Ever Happened to Baby Jane?*" (1962) 21
Dead Ringer (1964) 32
Strait-Jacket (1964) 41
Lady in a Cage (1964) 49
Hush... Hush, Sweet Charlotte (1964) 56
Die! Die! My Darling! (1965) 66
The Night Walker (1965) 74
I Saw What You Did (1965) 81
The Nanny (1965) 87
Queen of Blood (1966) 93
The Witches (1966) 98
Games (1967) 103
Berserk! (1968) 109
The Savage Intruder (1968) 115
What Ever Happened to Aunt Alice? (1969) 123
Eye of the Cat (1969) 130
The Mad Room (1969) 137
That Cold Day in the Park (1969) 143
Trog (1970) 150
Flesh Feast (1970) 156
The Beast in the Cellar (1970) 161
Cry of the Banshee (1970) 167

What's the Matter with Helen? (1971) 173
Whoever Slew Auntie Roo? (1971) 181
Blood and Lace (1971) 187
The Baby (1973) 193
The Killing Kind (1973) 199
Night Watch (1973) 205
A Knife for the Ladies (1974) 211
Frightmare (1974) 216
Persecution (1974) 222
Homebodies (1974) 229
Ruby (1977) 236
Windows (1980) 244
The Fan (1981) 251
The Hunger (1983) 259
Night Warning (1983) 268
Epitaph (1987) 275
Misery (1990) 280
Bad Blood (1993) 289
Mommy (1994) 294
Mother (1996) 300
Mommy's Day (1996) 306
The Landlady (1997) 312
Inside (2007) 319

Bibliography 327
Index 329

Preface

The phenomenon is often commented on in horror film histories of the 1960s and 1970s, mostly in relation to the success of *What Ever Happened to Baby Jane?* (1962). It has been described as "Hag Horror," "Hagsploitation," "Psycho-Biddy Cinema," and most frequently, and the one I prefer, "Grande Dame Guignol." The nomenclature Grande Dame Guignol is used on the internet site *The Terror Trap*, and espoused by actor/playwright and film historian Charles Busch. Busch's play *Die, Mommie, Die*, in fact, was written as a tribute to the subgenre, and the film version, made in 2004, purposely references the style and content of these films. But as a film subgenre Grande Dame Guignol has not received specific literary collated coverage. This book is an attempt to do that.

Grande Dame Guignol is an amalgamation of two key and seemingly contradictory concepts—the grande dame and Grande Guignol. A grande dame is defined as an older woman of great dignity and prestige. A cultural and literary archetype, she is usually portrayed as a flamboyant woman prone to extravagant and eccentric fashion, such as feather boas, large hats, and excessive costume jewelry. She may be preoccupied with the concept of ladylike behavior, and expect all those around her to conform to her high standards of etiquette.

"Grande Guignol" is French for "big puppet show," coined by the Grande Guignol theatre company in Paris, founded by Oscar Metenier in 1895, around the time Georges Méliès started making films. Under the direction of Andre de Lorde, known as "the Prince of Terror," the company produced over one hundred plays written by de Lorde and based on the stories of his idol Edgar Allan Poe. These plays specialized in macabre shockers, and showed graphic violence, like ripped skin, gouged eyeballs, burning flesh, beheading, mutilation, acid-burning, dismemberment, and other psychological distress. These activities were used to explore themes of suffering, insanity, vengeance, and fear of the unknown. Actors judged the success of their productions by the number of spectators who fainted or vomited. The program usually began with a comic curtain-raiser, followed by two horror plays, and ended with a sex farce. The company peaked in popularity in the 1920s, but its reputation waned during World War II with the German occupation when the real horror of the Nazis engulfed Europe. Although the Nazis condemned the company as "degenerate art," their attendance is what alienated the French. After the war, the company produced detective stories, but these proved to be less popular, and the theatre closed in 1962—ironically, the year *What Ever Happened to Baby Jane?* was released. A few films had been made in Europe using Grande Guignol—*Mad Love* (1933) and *Eyes Without a Face* (1959)—but the trend entered the American mainstream in the 1960s with Grande Dame Guignol.

Grande Dame Guignol is a subgenre of the larger film genres of crime, drama, film-noir, horror, mystery, and thriller, often appearing with elements of melodrama, comedy, fantasy, and musicals. In his book *Hollywood in the Sixties*, John Baxter amusingly describes Grande Dame Guignol as "exercises in sado-gerontophilia" that celebrate "decrepitude," since they use older actresses in leading roles in horror movies when they were often no longer considered leading lady material. The actresses who were rediscovered as leading ladies include Elizabeth Ashley, Lauren Bacall, Elisabeth Bergner, Bette Davis, Joan Crawford, Tallulah Bankhead, Olivia De Havilland, Joan Fontaine, Miriam Hopkins, Veronica Lake, Piper Laurie, Florence Marly, Patty McCormack, Geraldine Page, Eleanor Parker, Ruth Roman, Ann Sothern, Barbara Stanwyck, Talia Shire, Susan Tyrrell, and Lana Turner. Some actresses, like Beatrice Dalle, Sandy Dennis, Catherine Deneuve, Debbie Reynolds, Simone Signoret, Elizabeth Taylor, and Shelley Winters, used the subgenre to continue as leading ladies. Others, who had rarely played leading roles and previously specialized in supporting roles, like Kathy Bates, Gloria Grahame, Sheila Keith, Diane Ladd, Ruth Raymond, and Flora Robson, also starred in films that fall into the subgenre.

Often, but not always, the actress playing a grande dame in Grande Dame Guignol had not worked for some time, or this role would be her last starring role. In other cases, it would either lead to a form of typecasting or rejuvenate the actress's career for a time in a fickle industry where the lifespan of an actress is usually five years. Some have criticized the Grande Dame Guignol films for being exploitative of their lead actresses,

Blanche Hudson (Joan Crawford) is ridiculed by her sister, Baby Jane Hudson (Bette Davis) in *What Ever Happened to Baby Jane?* (1962).

who had been accustomed to better material in their heydays, and who in these movies were purposely and perversely presented in an unflattering light. This criticism is not accurate. By definition, a star is someone who is extraordinary because they have the appeal and charisma required to be seen repeatedly, make an intimate connection with an unseen audience, and also add that little extra something to the roles they take on. In *The Star* (1952), it was said that stars are naughty, like children, but also appealing, like children. While it is true that work can be undertaken for financial considerations, so that an actor can keep working, they choose the best material offered them.

The argument that, by making a horror film, the starring actress is lowering her standards also carries an assumption that her earlier work was superior, when the reality is that a lot of the films made in the studio era were pretty silly and the products of a factory mentality, with the bottom line being the financial success of your last film. The idea that the actress colludes in presenting herself unflatteringly also assumes that she is foolish and desperate, which is not necessarily the case. Appearing in a Grande Dame Guignol film can be seen as an opportunity for acting, to present a character that is not normally associated with one's range. Such behavior is risky, because an actress can be judged as failing, but there is an inherent bravery in the intention. However, appearing in these films also shows that each actress had a precedent-setting role in her earlier work that gives her new role complexity and gives the audience another look, sometimes one last look, at her ability to fascinate us as a star.

The criteria I have used to qualify a film as Grande Dame Guignol is that it be a horror movie which uses grande guignol effects and stars an actress in a leading role playing a character with the airs and graces of a grande dame. Some of the horror films I considered had some but not all of these three elements, so they are not included. *Picture Mommy Dead* (1966), *Deadly Blessing* (1981), and *High Tension* (2003) all use grande guignol but have no grande dame. *The Night Digger* (1971), *Picnic at Hanging Rock* (1975), and *The Skeleton Key* (2005) have grande dames but no grande guignol. *The Anniversary* (1968) and *Notes on a Scandal* (2006) have a grande dame but are not horror movies. Other films, like *The Fiend* (1972), *Rosemary's Baby* (1968), *The Other* (1972), *Dear Dead Delilah* (1972), *Carrie* (1976), *Play Dead* (1985), *Flowers in the Attic* (1987), and *Sweeney Todd* (2007), are horror movies and have grande guignol, but their grande dames play supporting rather than leading roles. Joan Crawford in *I Saw What You Did* (1965), Florence Marly in *Queen of Blood* (1966), Elisabeth Bergner in *Cry of the Banshee* (1970), Sheila Keith in *Frightmare* (1974), and Delores Nascar in *Epitaph* (1987) all play essentially supporting roles, but their dames are so grande that I had to include them.

Since some of the films I have included are not available for viewing on DVD or video, I have used auctions and private film collectors to see them. That some of the movies may not be available, however, cannot be seen as a rationalization that they do not deserve exposure, since copyright or market considerations can stop a wide variety of films from commercial release. Most of the titles I cover here received theatrical releases, and although I am aware that the subgenre crossed over into productions made for television, I have limited my scope to feature films and some films that were released straight to video. I have watched all of the movies included in this book to provide my own observations as notes, including how some are only available in an altered form. *Eye of the Cat* (1969) is one such example, which was edited for television broadcasting, and I have used the plot description in the reviews of the original cinema release and the publicity pressbook to pinpoint any narrative differences.

Each film has its own chapter, and each chapter features a detailed filmography, including cast and crew credits, filming dates and locations (when known), a plot synopsis, information on any songs that appear in the film, details on DVD or video availability, release information and any significant awards given, and quotes from period and contemporary reviews. The credits for cast and crew have been taken from the film's actual screen credits, and augmented from sources like the *Internet Movie Database* and *Turner Classic Movies*. I have credited reviews with the names of the reviewer when possible, though some publications do not make this identification.

My notes on each film provide an analysis in terms of Grande Dame Guignol and its re-occurring motifs, its effectiveness as a horror film, and observations on narrative, filmmaking style and performance. I do not hesitate to highlight something I think is bad, but I also do not hesitate to praise good or provocative work, a lot of which I believe can be found in these movies. Chapters list the titles in chronological order, i.e., the progressive years that the films were released, although the release dates of some pictures are contentious — *The Savage Intruder* being a good example. I also include any behind-the-scenes information I could find from biographies of the cast and crew involved. I have also included the film's poster imagery and stills when I could obtain them (though some titles have no accompanying imagery, which I regret). Additionally, the book includes a bibliography for the materials I have sourced, for further reading. Like any work that attempts to cover a large volume of output, I am sure mistakes have crept in, and I welcome any corrections of fact.

While some dismiss Grande Dame Guignol as B-grade and embarrassing postscripts to the careers of the star actresses who appear in them, I challenge that opinion, particularly as the opinion is usually proffered by someone who has not actually watched the films in question. Although some were made with low budgets, that doesn't necessarily make them cheap in quality. The success of any film is dependant upon the talent and goodwill of those who create it. No one intentionally sets out to make a bad product or make themselves look ridiculous. Therefore, this intention must be honored by viewing and assessing the product with an open mind. Although naturally my reactions are subjective and reveal personal preferences, I have tried to set aside any preconceived notions to provide fair and balanced coverage.

Horror movies tend to get a bad rap in the universe of movie genres, as if making one requires less skill than, say, a comedy or a drama. There is an implication of inferiority and lowbrow appeal about them which I think only reveals a cinematic snobbery. Some critics tend to categorize the films under discussion as camp, the perverse enjoyment of something bad for humor, but I find this attitude minimizing and patronizing. I also find that it is often expressed by those who may have seen *What Ever Happened to Baby Jane?* but none of the other titles included in this book. For me the sign of good writing about films is that it compels one to see the movies under discussion. I hope my book does this for my readers.

Introduction

We generally think that a horror movie is successful if it has made us jump in our seats or even scream, since horror movies trade in fear and unease. They are a direct conduit to the unconscious and dream states, and exploit the primal emotion of fight or flight, except that we cannot flee because we are trapped in the cinema. But only if we want to be. The pleasure gleaned from horror movies is the safe and cathartic release of tension, and the comfort we take in being observers of someone else's terror. Like the genre of comedy, a good horror movie demands empathy in order to engender a response. Think of the shower scene from *Psycho* (1960) and how we are made to feel as if it is we who are being attacked. It confronts us with a nightmare, and reminds us of our vulnerability, our terror of the irrational and the unknown, our fear of death and dismemberment, and of man himself. Other horror movies confront fears of the forbidden, alienation, loss of identity and power, and sexuality.

Horror movies use the conventions of related genres, such as thriller, action and adventure, fantasy and science fiction, and up the ante. A world of normalcy is established so that it can be disturbed. Conflict is created between antagonists and protagonists. Chaos ensues as the body count steadily rises until the climactic finale, when someone must be defeated so that normalcy can be restored. When the antagonist is a creature of fantasy or ideology, the scenarios offer simplistic heroes and villains. Sometimes we can be made to empathize with the antagonist but usually we identify with the protagonist who is victimized. It is when the scenario deals with social realities that things can get complicated, and motives and empathies can be cross-wired. These secondary scenarios often reflect changes in the value system through which society is seen. Nowhere is this more interesting than in the representation of women as the antagonists of horror movies.

Although the horror genre wasn't officially born until the release of Tod Browning's *Dracula* (1931), earlier films that featured the stock conventions of horror movies (but were promoted as melodramas or "art" films) were being made from 1896, when Frenchman Georges Méliès started making short motion pictures. Women in these movies were initially seen as pillars of virtue, passive virgins who fell victim to a dominant male threat. This type of role became known as the damsel in distress or Woman in Peril. It was the ultimate representation of the male gaze, for which it is said the cinema was created, and a reflection of society's traditional view of women at the turn of the century.

The first radical departure from this treatment was the vamp or femme fatale (French for "fatal woman"). She was a female version of the male vampire, who had been celebrated by author Bram Stoker in his novel *Dracula* and filmed by F.W. Murnau as

Nosferatu (1922). The vampire was a Gothic creation inspired by folktales and a manifestation of the unknown, a malevolent carnivore and grotesque supernatural being who was the Satanic personification of evil. That this creature could have a female form made it seem even more evil, since women were meant to be nurturing creators of life. Mothers were not deemed sexually attractive, so the vamp was invented to be sexually alluring, seductive and dangerous to men. Closely tied to fears of the female witch, she is said to have the ability to entrance and hypnotize her male victim, achieving her hidden purpose by using the feminine wiles of beauty and charm. She tortures her lover, denying confirmation of her affection, and leaches his virility and independence so that he is driven to the point of exhaustive obsession and left a shell of his former self.

The vamp was also an archetypal character of literature and art, as well as being encapsulated in historical figures like Queen Cleopatra of Egypt and Mata Hari. Eve, Lilith, Delilah, and Salome came from the Bible. The Siren, the Sphinx, Circe, Helen of Troy, and Clytemnestra came from ancient Greek literature. The refrain of Rudyard Kipling's poem "The Vampire" became the film *A Fool There Was* (1915), which starred Theda Bara, who was the sexual counterpoint to actresses like Lillian Gish and Mary Pickford. As a predatory female, rather than being seen as a woman of free will, liberation, and unrestrained passion, her vamp is associated with misogyny—the fear and hatred of women. The vamp possessed a European exoticism not associated with American women, and, as an exaggeration of what a real woman is (as defined by the puritanical impulse) she was considered a freak. As such a monster, she needed to be punished for the threat she represented to the stable world of marriage, family and female submissiveness. If she was killed, her death was a warning to other women who dared to oppose the essential patriarchy of American society, and the presentation of women in successive horror movies would allow for morality plays on this theme.

That Theda Bara, whose character is known as "the Vampire" in *A Fool There Was*, is not literally punished remains acceptable, since we see evidence of her evil and our sympathy is with the male victim rather than the female antagonist. (Any woman who has to demand affection—"Kiss me, my fool"—doesn't deserve it). Treatments like these were used as sub-

Poster for *A Fool There Was* (1915).

tle and not so subtle propaganda to keep women in their place, since it was feared that female emotions were so dynamic that they had to be contained in order to protect the balance of the universe.

As the decades passed in film history, variations on the vamp would resurface, and it was rare that the female would triumph. Horror movies, more than any other genre, were the hardest on women, and titles like *Pandora's Box* (1928), *Dracula's Daughter* (1936), *Cat People* (1942), *I Walked with a Zombie* (1943), *Jungle Woman* (1944), *Cult of the Cobra* (1955), and *The She Creature* (1956) reinforced the idea of women's essential inferiority deeply ingrained in Western society. In her book *From Reverence to Rape*, Molly Haskell calls it "the Big Lie." A woman is least herself when demonstrating masculine imperatives, like driving to achieve and conquer, and most herself when following feminine instincts in loving a man or a child.

Horror movies were just as didactic in reinforcing the restrictions placed on the behavior of women imposed in 1934 by the Film Production Code as any other genre. A woman was punished for crime, sex and getting pregnant outside of marriage, adultery, divorce, leaving her husband, even getting a job. So just imagine what happened if she were a vampire. Any female who did not fit the mold or want to play the game was in for a hard time, and since so much of women's attractiveness to men was based on youth, the aging woman and her lack of appeal became fair game for ridicule. Being unmarried and sexually active once laid you open to being labeled a loose woman or "tramp." (Notice how close "tramp" is to "vamp.") Being an older woman who was unmarried and sexually frustrated was worse.

The career woman had been briefly accepted during World War II when the men were away fighting and industry needed women to take over male jobs, and this acceptance would re-emerge in the 1960s. However, in the 1950s, when women were shunted back to the kitchens and bedrooms, gender roles had become homogenized so that career and sexuality were subjugated to domesticity and motherhood. The 1950s also saw the popularity of Freudian psychology, presented in theatrical terms in the plays of Tennessee Williams, who often wrote about women who did not fit the status quo, like the faded Southern belle Blanche Dubois in *A Streetcar Named Desire*. The discontent these characters expressed in a society that did not want to listen came to be voiced in populist terms in the horror subgenre known as Grande Dame Guignol.

Hollywood's interest in female stars in leading roles dwindled when television had proved to be the rival that crippled the film studios, who no longer offered contracts to provide actors with regular work. Films like *The Misfits* (1961), and *Charade* (1963), and the later films *The Swimmer* (1968), *Finian's Rainbow* (1968), and *The Arrangement* (1969) all showed that an older man could still attract a leading role and a younger female romantic interest. Actors like Clark Gable, Gary Cooper, John Wayne, Spencer Tracy, Cary Grant, and James Stewart all played leading roles and remained top stars for as long as they wanted to. The actresses who secured leading parts were all in their twenties and thirties, however, with older actresses usually delegated to supporting roles. Some stars avoided this problem by working in television or the theatre, or simply not working at all. A few managed to overcome it by taking parts that led them to be seen in an unglamorous and unflattering light, something that would never have been tolerated during the golden years of the studio system.

Katharine Hepburn was the morphine addict Mary Tyrone in *Long Day's Journey into Night* (1962), before retiring temporarily to care for her sick lover Spencer Tracy.

Vivien Leigh was Karen Stone, a woman who hired gigolos for companions in *The Roman Spring of Mrs. Stone* (1961), and then the perverse tease Mary Treadwell of *Ship of Fools* (1965). After playing the psychopathic stage mother Rose Hovick in the musical *Gypsy* (1962), Rosalind Russell wore a pastel fright wig as Madame Rosepettle in *Oh Dad Poor Dad Mama's Hung You in the Closet and I'm Feeling So Sad* (1967), in what is ostensibly a comedy. Judy Garland played a teacher of disabled children in *A Child Is Waiting* (1961), and sank to almost self-parody as the blowsy singer Jenny Bowman in *I Could Go on Singing* (1963). Garland's withdrawal from the part of aging musical comedy star Helen Lawson in the outrageous *Valley of the Dolls* (1969) robbed us of seeing her have her wig ripped off in the film's bathroom showdown. Even the New York City sightings of retired screen legend Greta Garbo fed into the public's fascination with the fading beauty, a woman supposedly shunning the limelight while still seeking it with her daily walks.

It wasn't until Universal producer Ross Hunter started using former matinee queens in remakes of successful melodramas like *Portrait in Black* (1960) and *Back Street* (1961) that anyone thought to exploit the advanced end of the age range. John Baxter describes the creation of the Grande Dame Guignol as being due to a perception of the previously untapped box office potential of venerable ladies whose potential outran their looks. Ironically, the same lessening of censorship in the 1950s which allowed studios to exploit the sexual activities of the younger generation also allowed for interest in stars of middle-age or late middle-age. The success of these films can be attributed partly to older moviegoers feeling nostalgia for Hollywood of the past, but mostly to the new audience who was presumably unaware of the glorious past of the actresses they now saw as leading ladies. The cross-over appeal to the youth audience was often blatantly catered to in screenplays by juxtaposing the older woman with children and teenagers.

The role the actress plays in Grande Dame Guignol either presents her as a mentally unstable antagonist or as the Woman in Peril protagonist. The grande dame as unstable antagonist may pine for a lost youth and glory, or she may be trapped by idealized memories of childhood, with a trauma that haunts her past. She is akin to Miss Havisham in Charles Dickens's novel *Great Expectations*, her adult life wasted as she rots away in her unused wedding dress in her room. Like a ghost, the grande dame cannot rest until the unbalance of the universe is corrected. A refusal to accept reality and the natural process of life exemplifies the fear of aging and death, and implicitly a fear of women.

That there was no male version of the Grande Dame Guignol tells us that such an idea is less believable to screenwriters and directors. The grande dame as victimized protagonist is not necessarily unstable to begin with, though her mental state deteriorates as she is terrorized. She is the Woman in Peril at her most vulnerable, since youth has lessened her strengths, though having a star actress playing such a role gives her an automatic advantage over a non-star. But then that applies to the star playing the unstable antagonist, too. However, the most interesting of these films have characters that possess both these qualities.

An example of this is Bette Davis and Joan Crawford in *What Ever Happened to Baby Jane?* Initially we see Davis as the antagonist, tormenting her relatively normal but physically disabled protagonist sister Crawford. However, the climax reveals that Crawford became disabled when she tried to seek revenge on Davis when they were younger.

This plot twist makes us re-evaluate Crawford as an antagonist and the revelation turns Davis into a passive child, victimized and insane.

Before an analysis of four titles I consider seminal to the subgenre, which all explore the duplicity of the antagonist/protagonist, I make mention of *Arsenic and Old Lace* (1944). This film features the two aunts of Cary Grant who are serial killers, older women who are a threat to men (since all their victims are men). The picture is set at Halloween, and though the witch animation seen under the opening credits may be unconnected, it implies the aunts are witches. Their malevolence is diluted, given that the film is a comedy (black though it may be), with the accidental near-drinking of the aunts's poisoned elderberry wine used for repeated laughs. Director Frank Capra protects us from the sight of corpses by hiding them in dark interiors, and simultaneously suggesting worse than what we see. The aunts rationalize the killings as charity by helping lonely old men, who are attracted by their room-for-rent sign, "find peace." The aunts also hold funeral services for the dead, but the trophy cupboard containing the hats of the men they have murdered is unsettling. However, their madness is innocent compared to the stitch-faced sadist played by Raymond Massey, who has killed as many men as they have. The film ends with the aunts committed to an asylum, arranged by Grant, though we don't actually see them being taken away.

Sunset Boulevard (1950), directed by Billy Wilder, provides a similar ambiguous denouement for its murderous grande dame. It uses film noir style to tell the story of

Mr. Witherspoon (Edward Everett Horton) is about to drink the poisoned wine of Aunt Abby (Josephine Hull) and Aunt Martha (Jean Adair) in *Arsenic and Old Lace* (1944).

the 50-year-old, once-great silent film star Norma Desmond (Gloria Swanson), living in a rundown palazzo among the mementos of her past and plotting a "return" in her own adaptation of *Salome*. Her over-decorated house is an extension of her personality. Norma is wealthy and reclusive, delusional and tragic. Screenwriter Joe Gillis (William Holden) calls her a "cuckoo sleepwalker" whose only friends are former silent movie stars when he labels "waxworks." Desmond is a vamp with claw-like hands, a kinky cigarette holder, dark glasses, leopard-trimmed clothes, big jewelry, and turbans. Our first view of her is in long shot, behind blinds. Swanson was 51 at the time of filming and still beautiful, though Wilder films her in soft-focus close-ups. To undercut her, he makes Norma short-sighted, gives her childish handwriting, and makes her mouth tighten like a gangster when she becomes angry. Swanson's performance is larger-than-life, with oversized gestures and emotions suggesting silent movie acting, which relied on expression with the face and hands. When Joe says to Norma "You used to be big," and she replies, "I am big; it's the pictures that got small," we can see how right she is. Swanson shows us that Norma is a great actress and a great performer, attested by her effortless impersonation of Charlie Chaplin's Little Tramp, which recalls Swanson's beginnings in the Mack Sennett comedies.

Sunset Boulevard was Swanson's first film in nine years, after she had retired from the screen following a legendary run as a silent screen queen and the epitome of early Hollywood glamour. Swanson achieved stardom in the bedroom farces *Male and Female* (1919) and *The Affairs of Anatol* (1921), both directed by Cecil B. DeMille, and by the mid–20s began producing her own films, like *Sadie Thompson* (1928) and *The Trespasser* (1929). Her company ran into problems with director Erich von Stroheim's extravagant *Queen Kelly* (1928), which halted her career, as well as von Stroheim's. That Wilder would cast von Stroheim as Max, Norma's servant and humiliated first husband, is one of the many delicious Hollywood inside jokes he serves up.

Norma falls in love with Joe, whose age we don't learn, though Holden was 31 at the time. Holden's career had been in as much of a lull as Swanson's. After becoming a star with his first substantial feature role in *Golden Boy* (1939), he had become typecast as the boy next door, where Holden said he played "Smiling Jim." After fighting in World War II, he starred in several

Joe Gillis (William Holden), Norma Desmond (Gloria Swanson), and Max von Mayerling (Erich von Stroheim) in *Sunset Boulevard* (1950).

unremarkable films before being cast against type to play a psycho killer in *The Dark Past* (1949). 1950 would prove to be Holden's watershed year when he starred in two career landmarks, *Born Yesterday* and *Sunset Boulevard*.

Joe has driven into Norma's driveway, his car crippled by a blown tire, prefiguring the random and luckless way Janet Leigh will arrive at the Bates Motel in *Psycho*. What makes the relationship between Norma and Joe interesting is that it is one of mutual advantage. He becomes a kept man, and she gets a ghost-writer, as well as companionship and sex. Joe, as a failed writer, is matched with Norma, as a failed star, their situations exemplified by their respective cars. Joe can't afford the upkeep on his, and Norma owns a handmade 1932 Isotta Fraschini, which is kept on blocks in the garage. The opening scene in which Joe's dead body is discovered in the pool tells us where their relationship is headed, but it is only after Norma shoots him that she truly goes mad. That Norma is attracted to the story of *Salome* also warns us, since the character Norma longs to play ends up with John the Baptist's head on a platter. One feels sympathy for Norma at New Year's Eve, when Joe walks out on her and she attempts suicide. Joe's returning, after he hears of it, is evidence of some feeling and responsibility he has for her. Wilder brilliantly delays the reconciliatory embrace while Swanson sobs at midnight for fifty seconds as the orchestra plays "Auld Lang Sine."

Wilder parallels Norma and Joe's relationship with that of Joe and Betty Schaefer (Nancy Olson), a reader at Paramount, to show that the latter is just as manipulative. The 22-year-old Betty uses Joe to help her establish a screenwriting career, and he feeds off her enthusiasm to write. Joe only rejects Betty's romantic advances when his life with Norma is exposed, and his decision to abandon Norma is as much because she has cost him Betty as it is a rejection of the life she has given him. Norma's demands of Joe seem mild in the face of his cruelty to her—"playing hooky" to meet Betty, and confronting Norma with the truth about the fan letters Max has written, and the screen comeback. Norma is the antagonist as she holds power over Joe, but his resentment of it will make her his emotional victim—and a protagonist.

The film has baroque touches—the dead monkey and the ceremony of its last rites, the wheezing pipe organ, the rats in the empty pool, the tale of the maharaja who strangled himself with one of Norma's silk stockings, wrist cutting with a razor, the apparatus of Norma's makeover, the honeycomb tile pattern of Norma's dance floor that suggests a spider's web. When Joe tries to leave Norma the first time, his watch chain gets caught on the doorknob, showing that his exit will not be so easy. Wilder perversely has him reading the book *The Young Lions* in a scene where Norma wears a chin strap, and the tale of Betty getting her nose fixed in an effort to become an actress alludes to the vanity of all women. The famous end of the film, in which Norma descends her staircase as if it is the palace of the princess Salome, is described as a "mercy" for her, "as if her dream had enfolded her and the world had taken pity." She gets the attention of the Paramount newsreels, which are heartless about the misery of the famous, and she gets her close-up, even if it is out of focus. The police agree to this charade, since it will get Norma downstairs and presumably ready to be carted off to the nuthouse (though we aren't shown that). This grande dame appears to get away with murder, since she will end her life in a dream state of self-protecting dementia. If the theme of *Sunset Boulevard* is opportunism and its consequences, and how Hollywood exploits people, is Hollywood to blame for Joe's death and Norma's madness? Perhaps, but then this same corruption has redeeming qualities, since Norma murdering Joe also gives Max the chance to direct again.

The Star (1952) is written by Dale Eunson and Katherine Albert, and based on Joan Crawford. Eunson and Albert were long-time friends of Crawford. Albert was Joan's favorite fan magazine reporter, and in 1939 had written a novel, called *Remember Valerie March*, about a tough, ambitious and sexual tramp from Oklahoma who becomes a star. In the film, Bette Davis plays Margaret Elliot, a washed-up movie star whose age is not given, though Davis was 44 at the time. Margaret is said to be a former glamour queen who craves one good part to "put her back where she was." But she no longer has that "fresh dewy quality that the public wants." Someone called Barbara Lawrence is now the ideal, though the repeated images we get of Miss Lawrence show her styled to be another glamour queen, rather than the virginal type that "fresh and dewy" implies. When she finally appears, Miss Lawrence is revealed to be a just another bimbo. Margaret is the protagonist, but her self-destructive behavior will make her the antagonist too.

The film opens with Margaret in dark glasses passing the auction of her possessions, with a still of Bette in *Dark Victory* (1939) used as publicity. The auctioneer's cry of "going, going, gone" is a phrase Margaret will repeat to exemplify her career and mental deterioration. Margaret is said to have been "put out to pasture" and labeled box office poison after the failure of three pictures she had produced herself. Although her earlier pictures had people lining up around the block to see her, she says she was "sick of the tripe they were forcing me to play." She claims the big companies wouldn't give her three films a decent release, and that they "juggled the books," so she lost everything. The phrase "box office poison" is, of course, taken from Crawford's life, as she was so labeled in 1938 by Harry Brandt, owner of a small chain of movie houses who wrote an article in the *Independent Film Journal*. The article claimed that theatre owners were losing money with films featuring stars like Crawford, Katharine Hepburn, Marlene Dietrich, Garbo, and Mae West. The phrase would be memorably used in *Mommie Dearest* (1981), as Crawford, wearing a sequined evening gown, cuts down her rose garden.

That Margaret has won an Academy Award recognizes that she has more talent than just being a glamour girl, and Davis uses one of her own Oscars for her drunk driving scene. The drive has her act like a tour guide, where she points out the homes of such stars as Mitzi Gaynor and Jeanne Crain, as well as Barbara Lawrence. Gaynor and Crain are lightweight actresses, neither being Oscar winners or nominees, compared to Davis and Crawford, so the comparison speaks of the trend away from Margaret Elliot's ilk. Margaret's romantic interest in the film is her former co-

Poster for *The Star* (1952).

star, and presumed lover, Jim Johannsen (Sterling Hayden), who bails her out of jail following her arrest for drunk driving. He admonishes her for not being "a real woman" and "nothing but a career," though her daughter Gretchen (Natalie Wood) from a failed marriage proves he is wrong. A mechanic at a shipyard, Jim has abandoned the acting career Margaret had created for him and encourages her to also "stop chasing rainbows." It's telling that the title of the film they made together is "Faithless," since it is Jim who has no faith in Hollywood to provide a real life, and no faith in Margaret to be able to revive her career. Margaret had met Jim initially when he came to repair her bathhouse, and she cast him, a "nobody," to spite the profile actor who "wouldn't play horse to her Godiva."

Although Margaret Elliot is like Crawford on a superficial level, she is also a lot like Davis. Margaret is seen to have a sister and brother-in-law who expect a monthly check, and Bette looked after her mother and her sister. Davis had her own production company and produced *A Stolen Life* (1946), which was a hit. The end of Davis's long run as the top female star at Warner Bros. had come about because of the box office failure of her last three films there—*June Bride* and *Winter Meeting* (both 1948), and *Beyond the Forest* (1949) though Davis had asked to be released from her contract. The antidote to Crawford's "box office poison" was her agreeing to take a supporting role in *The Women* (1939), though she would be in trouble again soon after.

Davis brings her humor and physicality to the role, but she is essentially miscast in *The Star* because it is not conceivable that she would have a career based on glamour girl looks, an idea that is also reductive of Crawford. Margaret's attitude that she has been "managing directors for years," and she "knows what she's doing," is more Bette than Joan, as is her rude on-set behavior (though her "Bless you" is a direct quote from Crawford). The treatment also draws on the story of another troubled Hollywood star, Frances Farmer, when Margaret drives drunk, resists arrest, spends the night in jail, receives front page headlines ("Movie Star Jailed!"), and is considered an industry pariah. Margaret tries working in the May's Crenshaw department store, with the encouragement of Jim. However, she walks out after insulting "two old bags" that have recognized her and think it a disgrace that the store would employ a "jailbird." Like the prophetic moment in which Natalie Wood is warned not to fall overboard when sailing, the appeal of *The Star* is its behind-the-scenes look at Hollywood, as with *Sunset*.

The film's centerpiece is Margaret's screen test for "The Fatal Winter." Margaret had wanted to play the part of "the girl" who is 18. Now she is offered the part of the older sister, a 40-ish recluse who lives on a chicken farm, hasn't kept up her appearance and speaks in a sullen manner. The studio insists on Margaret making a test, much like Warner Bros. insisted on Crawford making a test for *Mildred Pierce* (1945), which is a humiliating idea for an established actress. Margaret agrees to it, and sees the idea of playing the older sister as a "challenge" and an "interesting experiment." Running lines with Jim, Margaret disregards the stage directions, and reports that the test director is from the stage and thinks he's slumming. She is made-up in character, wearing a shapeless old-lady dress and shawl, with her hair pinned up; but Margaret revolts. She redoes the make-up, costume and hair to look younger and sexier. Her plan is to be so good that the producer will want to cast her as the girl. She ignores the director, who sees that she is playing it "too light," by saying, "Women of 42 these days don't have to look ready for the old ladies home," and he films her, patronizingly commenting afterwards, "Your fans would love it."

Although the test has been presented to her as a mere formality, the decision is made that she is awful and no longer appropriate for the film. Davis's performance in the test recalls the broad femme fatale she played in *In This Our Life* (1942), and her big choices also prefigure her choices in *What Ever Happened to Baby Jane?* It's hard to call what she does bad acting; it's just Davis being Davis. Director Stuart Heisler focuses the camera on her reaction to the test as she watches it, since we have already seen Margaret film it. The scene culminates with her screaming "It's horrible. Shut up! You don't know anything" to her own filmed image before she falls to the floor sobbing. Margaret's ploy has backfired, and not even Davis's brilliance as an actress makes her believable as a woman 20 years younger than her real age, though the woman that *is* cast looks older than her.

The film's last scene, in which, at a party, Margaret rejects her Hollywood life and goes back to that offered by Jim, provides some sort of happy ending—except that the actress role in the screenplay she is offered is the same kind of actress that Margaret Elliot is. That she would reject such an offer, though the part is couched as a judgment of her, seems unbelievable. The film is to be called "Falling Star," and the actress is said to be a "simon-pure movie star, who's been on a sleigh ride, but she can't face the fact that it's over. Demanding, driven, ambitious. Her greatest tragedy is not being a woman." This confirms the sexism and double standards of the film and acting industry. Is a male actor who is said to be demanding, driven and ambitious not a real man? And even when Margaret goes to Jim, we have to wonder how long that will satisfy her. How long will it be before she is recognized again, and she defends herself with, "Yes, I am Margaret Elliot, and I intend to stay Margaret Elliot?" In a moment of panic, she had shoplifted a bottle of perfume, which turned out to be colored water. The jump to Baby Jane and other irrational behavior is not so hard to imagine.

Autumn Leaves (1956) stars Joan Crawford as Milly Wetherby, a lonely spinster typist, age undetermined, who falls in love with Burt Hanson, a schizophrenic 30-year-old Cliff Robertson, which also prefigures *What Ever Happened to Baby Jane?* in many ways (besides the fact that this is the first time Robert Aldrich directed Crawford). Though ostensibly a May–December drama, with Crawford as the older woman to Robertson's younger man, Aldrich uses film noir lighting and expressionist camera angles to darken the material. In his conversation with Aldrich in the book *Who the Devil Made It*, Peter Bogdanovich describes this film as a "weepie/creepie." The "autumn" leaves under the opening credits look like Rorschach blots, which tell us that the romance will have its psychological obstacles. The treatment's cruel twist of fate—delivering Crawford a lover who is mentally ill, supposedly scarred by the pseudo-incestuous affair of his wife with his father—is also a comment on the 1950s idea of the pathetic single older woman. Milly's condition in represented by the squeaking door of her bungalow, and she is said to be the "undefeated world's champ in believing in chiselers." She repeatedly rejects Burt's romantic overtures because she is troubled by the difference in their ages, urging him to find a girl "his own age."

However, Burt's response is that "young people are too young for me," citing a date who popped bubblegum, and another who is obsessed with Gregory Peck. Milly changes her mind about rejecting Burt's marriage proposal, ignoring her instincts, and we know that his cooing "I hope you'll never be sorry" will come back to haunt her. The film features a flashback to Crawford's youth, introduced by a concert pianist playing Chopin's "Fantasie Impromptu in C Sharp Minor," which was adapted into the popular song "I'm

Always Chasing Rainbows." The memory has Milly caring for a sick father and turning down a date. While the father tells her not to, she defends the decision with, "There's plenty of time." Aldrich's use of echoed voices, and playing Crawford's back to the camera, face unseen, tells us that Milly has sacrificed her youth; and this style of flashback will feature as prologues to *What Ever Happened to Baby Jane?*, and *Hush... Hush, Sweet Charlotte*. Although she admits to having family, Milly has moved away from them to come to Los Angeles and work from home. A pattern of self-exile is repeated to make the independent woman a loner, dependent upon charity from her employers. It is the casting of Crawford that subverts the stereotype.

Crawford's natural elegance and self-confidence would hardly seem to fit the ideal of a lonely spinster, although her mannish hairdo is daunting. Once you get past the notion that she would ever be unable to attract a man, one sees that the actress gives one of her best performances under Aldrich's direction. We see her in a bathing costume, and Crawford finally gets the beach scene—kissing her man as waves crash over them—that was denied her when she was fired from *From Here to Eternity* (1953). More in character is the fact that Milly is self-conscious about wearing the costume, and also a weak swimmer. The latter is in opposition to Crawford's earlier roles in which she was portrayed as a good athlete, or her body was otherwise shown off for us to see how she kept in shape ("for a woman her age"—unlike Davis, who lost her youthful slimness and job opportunities). The one concession to her age of 49 at the time of filming is how

Milly Wetherby (Joan Crawford) is threatened by her mentally disturbed husband, Bert Hanson (Cliff Robertson) in Autumn Leaves (1956).

her neck is often photographed in shadow, something which was also done for her in the later *Strait-Jacket* (1964) and *Berserk!* (1968).

The funniest scene of the film comes when Milly visits Burt's father, involving her reaction to his coming on to her, and his stated amazement at how Burt has attracted such a woman. The scene is also interesting in that the father suggests that Milly cares for Burt "like a mother," an idea that a psychiatrist will also have later. Aldrich adds horror movie music to the scene where Burt talks about his blocked memory of coming home early one day when married to his first wife, Virginia (that name is clearly meant to be ironic, given her affair) only to find her in bed with his father. Aldrich also gives Robertson a horror killer close-up, smiling as he overhears the father telling Milly, "The place for him is an institution." When Virginia visits Milly, Aldrich perversely has Crawford wearing a matronly housedress and no make-up to face the dewy 25-year-old Vera Miles. And when Milly visits Burt in the institution, the screenplay can't help but have Milly point out how pretty a nurse is, who also happens to be a younger woman.

A repeated motif in the film is being "born again." Burt tells Milly that he was born again when he met her, Burt uses this phrase again after he overhears Milly talking to his father; and the psychiatrist tells Milly that Burt needs to be born again to be cured. Presumably, Milly was also "born again" when she fell in love with Burt, since we assume it was her first real love. The film's happy ending suggests their love is reborn; but as soon as Burt becomes ill, Milly is reduced to being a caregiver again. Burt's schizophrenia is defined as a mental disorder, and Milly arranges for him to be forcibly committed for six months of treatment at a "sanatorium"—though not before the psychiatrist notes that Milly is his co-conspirator by her "mothering" of him in a co-dependent relationship. This makes Milly the protagonist/antagonist.

The film is notable among Crawford's vehicles of the 1950s for offering more depth than her other movies, and though Aldrich does provide some camp elements, the film in general has less camp appeal. Some humor arises from Milly's interactions with the psychiatrist. For instance, he adds, "Before you throw that ashtray at me," to one remark. In answer to Milly's, "In your world, everyone's crazy," he replies, "Since I don't know everyone in my world, I don't feel qualified to answer." The sobbing of Burt's retrogressive infantilism, his screams as he is taken away to be committed, and the montage of his shock treatment also prefigure the excesses of Bette Davis and *What Ever Happened to Baby Jane?* However, Aldrich gives Crawford an extreme close-up of a silent scream in the shock therapy montage, and a two minute monologue at the film's end, which is a tribute to her technique.

Psycho was made by Alfred Hitchcock in 1959 primarily as a low-budget horror movie to cash in on the wave of success that other companies at the time had achieved doing the same. However, what makes it relevant to the subgenre is Hitchcock's use of his leading lady, and the representation of Mother as an older woman and menacing character. Hitchcock's movies had been famous for the motif of the icy blonde female, conceited and aloof, who withholds sex and love. She is exquisitely beautiful, but frigid, snooty, uncaring. This archetype had been enacted by actresses like Anny Ondra in *Blackmail* (1929), Joan Barry in *Rich & Strange* (1931), Edna Best in *The Man Who Knew Too Much* (1934), Madeleine Carroll, Joan Fontaine, Grace Kelly, Kim Novak, Eva Marie Saint, and, later, Tippi Hedren. To destroy her complacency and emotional detachment, the blonde is punished, subjected to excruciating physical and psychological ordeals, like being chased, threatened, raped, and even killed. *The Lodger* (1927) features a serial killer who stalks blondes, and Tippi Hedren's attack by birds in the attic in *The Birds* (1963) is as vicious as the killing of Janet Leigh in the shower scene in *Psycho*. This woman is the antagonist to the male protagonist, though it is often the man who inflicts the punishment on the blonde because she has rejected him.

Although Hitchcock has been accused of misogyny, his films often centered on a female character, with the story told from her point of view, which demonstrated a sympathetic identification with the woman. The theme of the male's implication in the objectification and punishment of women finds its best expression in *Vertigo* (1958), which is thought of as Hitchcock's masterpiece. In *Vertigo* the male protagonist remakes a woman into the image of the woman he desires, an action which mirrors Hitchcock's own obsession with remaking his actresses into the blonde. In spite of the fact that Kim Novak is playing both the phantom ideal and the make-over victim, who is actually the same person attempting to deceive the protagonist, her humiliation still earns our sympathy. In opposition to the blonde, the brunette of his films is down-to-earth, unaffected, and even maternal, but she is rejected for being too available and possessive. In *Vertigo*, Barbara Bel Geddes would play this role, as would Kim Novak before her makeover. Hitchcock also uses the brunette for the secondary female character of the unattractive woman, although his instinctive alliance with the outsider (perhaps because of his personal body image) cannot prevent her from also being punished.

Hitchcock's mothers are equally unappealing, frequently depicted as intrusive and domineering, struggling with the films's protagonists, as seen in *Notorious* (1946), *Rope* (1948), *Strangers on a Train* (1951), *North by Northwest* (1959), *Psycho* and *The Birds*. *Rebecca* (1940) featured two older women who antagonized the protagonist: Florence Bates's Edythe Van Hopper and Judith Anderson's predatory and deadly Mrs. Danvers. *Strangers on a Train* features a memorable unintentional strangling of an older woman as a party game, in which the antagonist stares at a younger woman who reminds him of the woman he has actually strangled to death. *Shadow of a Doubt* (1943) is also noteworthy, since it features the "Merry Widow" killer, describing his victims as "faded, fat and greedy women" whose lifestyle improves once they become widows, but whose lives are considered expendable.

In *Psycho*, Janet Leigh is the leading lady, yet she is removed from the narrative one-third of the way into the film in an act of vengeance against the Hollywood star system. Although Leigh's hair is frosted blonde, her manner and personality is more the brunette, and her murder in the shower demands a shift in audience identification. Our first sight of Leigh's Marion Crane has her prone on a bed, sexualized in her bra and slip as her lover Sam (John Gavin) stands over her. She is in a relationship with someone who refuses to marry her because he is paying alimony for a wife living on the other side of the world. The price of sex is that women entrap men and steal their money (i.e., their genitals). The screenplay by Joseph Stefano introduces the theme of Mother as a woman disapproving of sex when Sam tells Marion that they must "turn Momma's picture to the wall" after a proposed family dinner. Hitchcock contrasts Marion's sexual availability with that of her co-worker Caroline (played by Hitchcock's daughter, Pat), who is married and not hit upon by Mr. Cassidy, he of the $40,000. Caroline's mother, too, is controlling, expressed by dialogue indicating she had given Caroline tranquilizers at her wedding, and that the mother has called Caroline to see if Caroline's husband Teddy had called her. Caroline's line to Marion, "He was flirting with you; he must have noticed my wedding ring," is the sad defense of a plain woman who cannot acknowledge her plainness. Mr. Cassidy is but one of the men we will see flirting with and harassing Marion.

When Marion wants to trade her car, Charlie the salesman patronizes her with, "Being a woman, you will do anything you have a mind to"; and her deceitful nature is shown in the way her image is reflected in mirrors. Charlie will say of her, "She looked like a wrong one," and Mr. Cassidy speaks of replacing the stolen money with "her fine soft flesh." The Bates Motel that she mistakenly drives into is a phallic symbol, the house erected on a hill above the hotel rooms; and Mother's ungenerous attitude toward Marion sharing a meal with her reflects her fear of a younger woman stealing Norman away from her. Norman spies on Marion undressing through a hole in the wall that is revealed after he removes a painting of "The Rape of the Sabine Women," and Marion's murder in the shower by knife is another phallic attack. The apparent woman-on-woman violence is the extreme demonstration of Hitchcock's pitting of women against each other as sexual competitors for the protagonist. After we see Norman dispose of Marion's body, we are shown a woman at Sam's hardware store buying insecticide, are introduced to Marion's sister Lila (Vera Miles), and learn she has been followed by a private investigator, Arbogast (Martin Balsam). In a montage of Arbogast looking for Marion at hotels, all the attendants are older women; and when Arbogast gets to Norman, he is told, "I'm not capable of being fooled. Not even by a woman." Hitchcock films Lila in shadow as she runs toward the camera to meet Sam, and when they go to report Arbogast's disappearance to the town sheriff, the sheriff's wife, Mrs. Chambers, whispers that Norman found his mother and her married lover dead together "in bed."

Poster for *Psycho* (1959).

Hitchcock has Lila drive the second act of the film, and although Miles's directness is funny, she does not have Janet Leigh's likeability. This compensatory dissatisfaction is appropriate for the narrative's younger sister, but also sways our sympathy and identification over to Norman, who becomes the new protagonist. But this identification will be shattered when it is revealed that Norman is Mother, and that Mother has taken over Norman's mind for good. The explanation by a psychiatrist of Norman's condition reinforces the cruelty of Marion stumbling into a psychological nightmare, emphasized by the smile on Mother's corpse in the fruit cellar. Norman was said to be already dangerously unbalanced, living with a clinging, demanding woman whom he considered having "thrown him over" for her married lover. After killing them both, Norman stole Mother's corpse; but he also needed to speak like her and dress up to be her—to give her half his life. It was the conflict in his schizophrenia that made the two personalities pathologically jealous, and what led Mother to kill Marion. Now that he had been caught, the conflict was over and the dominant personality is said to have won. However, if Norman is now all Mother, why would she want Norman to be "put away" for the crimes, when she is putting herself away? The easy answer is because we know Norman is crazy; but another response is that if we believe he is Mother and that she actually exists, then this is the worst thing a mother can do to her child. In this way, Mother kills both Marion and Norman.

Psycho proved to be a phenomenal financial success, if a mixed critical one. The stuffed birds, Norman's voyeurism and transvestism, and the dumping of bodies in the swamp all give the film gruesome touches, but it is the grande guignol slashing murders that will have the greatest resonance, introducing the slasher style to future horror movies. Although *Sunset Boulevard* and *The Star*, with their grande dames and their attempts at a return, will influence *What Ever Happened to Baby Jane?*, *Psycho* will add the low budget, the house setting, the contrast between the brightly lit outside world and the darkness of the interiors, the invalid woman, and the grande guignol. *Psycho* would also outdo every horror movie that came before it, pushing the horror genre into the mainstream and making it a more acceptable genre for actors and directors to be involved with.

The stage was set for the Grande Dame Guignol. Robert Aldrich, the director of *Autumn Leaves*, would make *What Ever Happened to Baby Jane?* as the first, but not the last, of its kind. A new subgenre was about to be born.

THE FILMS

What Ever Happened to Baby Jane? (1962)

Seven Arts Pictures/An Associates and Aldrich Production

CREDITS: *Producer/Director:* Robert Aldrich; *Executive Producer:* Kenneth Hyman; *Screenplay:* Lukas Heller, from the novel by Henry Farrell; *Photography:* Ernest Haller; *Music:* DeVol; *Editor:* Michael Luciano; *Art Director:* William Glasgow; *Set Decorator:* George Sawley; *Sound:* Jack Solomon; *Choreography:* Alex Romero; *Wardrobe:* Norma Koch; *Production Supervisor:* Jack R. Berne. B&W, 132 minutes. Filmed July 23–September 12, 1962, at the Raleigh Studios in Los Angeles and in Malibu, California.

SONG: "I've Written a Letter to Daddy" (Frank DeVol, Bob Merrill). Sung by Debbie Burton, Bette Davis.

CAST: Bette Davis (*Baby Jane Hudson*); Joan Crawford (*Blanche Hudson*); Victor Buono (*Edwin Flagg*); Wesley Addy (*Marty McDonald*); Julie Allred (*Baby Jane Hudson, in 1917*); Ann Barton (*Cora Hudson*); Marjorie Bennett (*Dehlia Flagg*); Robert Freed (*Ben Golden*); Anna Lee (*Mrs. Bates*); Maidie Norman (*Elvira Stitt*); Dave Willock (*Ray Hudson*); William Aldrich (*Lunch counter assistant at beach*); Ernest Anderson (*Ernie*); Russ Conway (*Police Officer*); Maxine Cooper (*Bank teller*); Robert Cornthwaite (*Dr. Shelby*); Michael Fox (*Motorcycle cop at beach*); Gina Gillespie (*Blanche Hudson, in 1917*); B. D. Merrill (*Liza Bates*); James Seay (*Police officer*); Bobs Watson (*Cop on street reading newspaper*); Don Ross; John Shay; Jon Shepodd; Peter Virgo.

VHS/DVD: DVD Warners Home Video, released October 1, 1997. Special Edition DVD Warner Home Video, released May 30, 2006.

Plot

In 1917 six-year-old Baby Jane Hudson is a successful child star in vaudeville whose income supports her whole family. By 1935, Jane has moved to Hollywood, and both she and her sister Blanche are movie stars, although Blanche is now the successful one and Jane a failure. After a party one night, there is an automobile accident at their house in which Blanche is crippled, and for which the alcoholic Jane is held responsible. As the years pass, the sisters become recluses, as Jane "retires" from her career to care for Blanche. Any pretense of harmony is shattered by a television retrospective of Blanche's old films, resulting in fan mail arriving at the house, which Jane resentfully throws in the trash. When she learns Blanche is planning to sell the house and perhaps place Jane in a home, Jane torments and progressively imprisons Blanche. Jane also plans a comeback and hires pianist Edwin Flagg to be her accompanist, scheming to dispose of Blanche so that she can have the house to herself to rehearse in. Jane fires Blanche's maid, Elvira, but when Elvira sneaks back to see Blanche and finds her bound and gagged, Jane kills her.

Upset by the murder, Jane sinks into drunkenness, missing a date with Edwin. When Edwin comes back again and confronts Jane, she tries to appease him with money. However, Blanche manages to knock over a table in her room with one freed hand, and the noise allows Edwin to discover her. Afraid that she is dying, Edwin runs away, and Jane drives Blanche to the beach to avoid being caught by the police, remembering that she used to rehearse on the beach as a child with her father. Blanche confesses she caused the accident when she had deliberately tried to run down Jane in retaliation for Jane's mocking behavior at the party that night. Jane avoided being hit by the car, and Blanche had snapped her spine, but she crawled in front of the car to make it look like she had been run down by Jane. Jane no longer harbors any resentment toward Blanche, and her mind returns to that of a child. She leaves Blanche to buy them ice-cream, and the police recognize the Hudson vintage car parked at the beach. They follow Jane, who dances for the gathering crowd, and then they find Blanche lying on the sand beyond.

Notes

This film has the distinction of being a beloved gay iconic title, which can be seen as both a compliment and perhaps something of a burden for film theorists, since a cult following suggests quality neglected by the mainstream, but also the derogatory implication of camp appreciation. However, for the purposes of this book, it meets the criteria of having not one but two grande dames in leading roles, grande guignol elements, and being a horror movie. That it is considered the first of the official Grande Dame Guignol titles is due to the fact that nothing quite like it had been made prior, although the seminal films—*Sunset Boulevard, The Star, Autumn Leaves,* and *Psycho* all helped lay the groundwork in terms of film history. While appearing to be a melodrama, the horror arises from psychological warfare in an atmosphere of Gothic regression, emphasized by Jane's make-up, and Blanche's invalidism. This environment of sibling rivalry and ancient grievances will be expressed in sadomasochism and emotional torment.

The action becomes progressively violent. A pet bird is taken from its cage and served on a plate, followed by a rat meeting the same fate, a slap, kicking, tying up and gagging, and culminating in a grande guignol murder with a hammer. As all this is acted upon Blanche, her isolation increases, moving from the loss of her pet, to no telephone, no buzzer, no food, no freedom, and, eventually, no life. As a horror movie, *What Ever Happened to Baby Jane?* is unusual, since its horror is minimal, and no blood is seen spilled. While the film's extraordinary casting and performances may be considered the reason for its appeal, there are other details—in the narrative and direction—that are equally worthy of note.

Robert Aldrich's production company had previously made the film noir *The Big Knife* (1956), the war drama *Attack* (1956), and the western *The Ride Back* (1957). Seven

Arts Pictures had previously made *The Roman Spring of Mrs. Stone* (1961) and *Gigot* (1962). Executive producer Kenneth Hyman had also previously made the horror titles *The Hound of the Baskervilles* (1959), *The Stranglers of Bombay* (1960), and *The Terror of the Tongs* (1961).

What Ever Happened to Baby Jane? begins with a black screen and the sound of crying, revealed to be a child crying at the sight of a pop-up toy that weeps tears. Crying is something that features repeatedly in the film to come, but the pop-up toy is interesting itself for the shock of the pop, and the unnatural and creepy way it cries. The screenplay offers two prologues, which delay the opening credits and also our view of the leading actresses. Such prologues are also a signature of Aldrich's. He would seem to be a surprising choice for a film about two women, since previously he had been known for male-orientated genre films like *Big Leaguer* (1953), *Apache* (1954), *Vera Cruz* (1954), and *Attack*, where women were relegated to supporting parts, if they appeared at all.

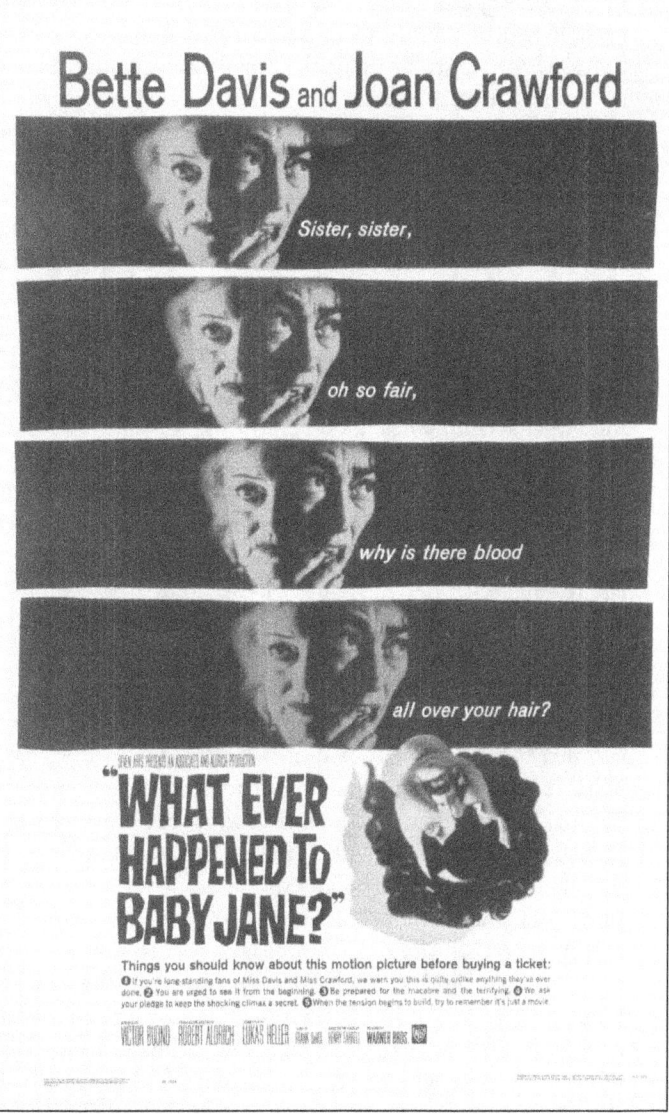

Poster for *What Ever Happened to Baby Jane?* (1962). The Baby Jane doll's hair is blonde and long in the film but black and short in the poster.

Kiss Me Deadly (1955) spoke of the legendary figures of Lot's Wife, Medusa, and Pandora in a pulp narrative that presented women as victims, whores, murderesses, or viragos. The sound under the opening credits of that film can be interpreted as a woman sobbing, catching her breath, or panting in sexual pleasure. Women screaming becomes a recurring motif, and it is remarked that they have "feline perception," and that "Dames are worse than flies." Aldrich spares us one act of violence against women—the sight of Christina Bailey (Cloris Leachman) being tortured with pliers—though she voices the writer Mickey Spillane's idea that women are the "incomplete sex." The climax is a perverse repeat of the fall from grace in the Garden of Eden, where a duplicitous woman unleashes an apocalyptic nuclear explosion that burns her alive and poisons Los Angeles, upping all the sadism and violence that has preceded it.

The Big Knife has Aldrich present the misogyny of writer Clifford Odets, who creates a succession of female characters whose only purpose is to be insulted by men. Aldrich's one concession to women's pictures was the Crawford vehicle *Autumn Leaves*, which is discussed in this book's Introduction as a seminal film.

In *Baby Jane*'s first prologue, the marketing of life-size Baby Jane dolls adds fetishism to Jane's vaudeville act, and the song she performs, "I've Written a Letter to Daddy," sexualizes the child. As the song has been requested by a boy, it also implies she has a strange youth appeal. Sung with the eerie vibrato adult voice of Debbie Burton, the cloying, sugary song is about Jane's devotion to a dead father, an odd choice since Jane's living father accompanies her on piano and joins her to dance. Their dance together further suggests an inappropriate relationship, since it poses them as a romantic couple, though, Jane, as the provider for her family, has, in effect, become an adult figure. Aldrich has Jane's hand-held letter fly over the audience, since it is attached to a string, to draw attention to the artifice, as does the way Jane is presented with a Baby Jane doll. His jump cut to Jane with her face against the doll's face only reinforces the strangeness, since, although the image is meant to show the doll's similarity to Jane, her stance also suggests a romantic attitude.

The illusion of Jane as a perfect child is broken backstage when she has a tantrum and is revealed to be a spoiled brat, though the staging and Aldrich's use of overdubbed comments by the assembled crowd makes it as false as the vaudeville act. This is the behavior that the adult Jane will continue with. The scene allows for a reversal of our feelings about Blanche. The initial shots of her watching Jane suggest her jealousy, with Jane as the protagonist. When their father turns against Blanche, and their mother comforts her with, "You're the lucky one. Someday it's going to be you getting all the attention," Blanche is the protagonist. But Blanche's "I won't forget" returns her to the role of antagonist. In the second prologue we are told that Blanche is "the biggest thing in movies today," and has a clause in her contract that the studio must make a picture with Jane for every one of Blanche's, which is evidence that Blanche has followed her mother's advice to "be kinder to Jane than she had been to her." This prologue begins with film of Jane, given as evidence that as an actress "she stinks"—in line with the idea that when the Hudson sisters were hired, the studio hired the "back end of the act" too.

The scenes we see are of Bette Davis in *Parachute Jumper* and *Ex-Lady* (both 1933), put together as if they were one picture. These films were made by Davis for Warner Bros. when the studio was trying to make her into a sexy blonde bombshell with peroxide hair, and before her break-out role in 1934's *Of Human Bondage* (though Davis was billed above the title for *Ex-Lady*). The footage has no context for us to consider her as good or bad, and the snippets are used in the same way the screen test was in *The Star*—for the effect it has on the person viewing. The little acting required of Davis here still underwhelms Ben Golden, who reacts with, "Boy, oh boy!" and eventually, "Kill it," yelled to the projectionist. Apart from this character's resemblance to Aldrich, the humor comes from his one observation of Jane's attempt at an accent: "She's got a southern accent like I got a southern accent." When the projectionist asks if he wants the picture again today, Golden replies, "I don't think anybody's ever gonna want that picture again." After the screening it is said that Jane is a "no-talent broad" with a drinking problem, which leads us to the nighttime accident scene. As in the flashback of *Autumn Leaves*, only the bodies of the Hudson sisters are revealed, though, unlike in *Autumn Leaves*, where Joan Crawford played herself at a younger age, these bodies are clearly not Davis and Crawford.

The car drives into a gate. After the accident, the voice we hear crying is presumably Blanche, since we learn later that Jane had fled. This makes the Baby Jane doll with the cracked skull seen on the ground misleading. The music by DeVol, using an arrangement of "I've Written a Letter to Daddy," under the opening credits is bombastic, with drums and regal horns that blare when the stars' names appear onscreen together. Davis and Crawford share equal billing, though Davis's name is to the left of Crawford's, thus getting preference, which Crawford acceded to since Davis plays the title character. When the film proper begins, the date is given as "Yesterday," a seemingly arbitrary way to add distance to what is about to occur. Crawford's period footage being from *Sadie McKee* (1934) is an interesting choice, since it is a film released close to the same year as those chosen for Davis. The difference between the films for the two actresses is that Crawford's was a star vehicle, made when she had been established as a star for six years. More of *Sadie McKee* is shown, though the dog food commercial that interrupts it is a sly comment on the priority of television.

That Crawford and Davis look nothing like sisters is a movie convention and acceptable, since seeing these two great stars together is so exciting. Jane's slouching walk and irritated manner are evidence of what is approximated as 30 years of servitude to Blanche, though the 1941 Lincoln convertible she drives is clearly evidence of a later purchase. Jane tells Blanche, "We're right back where we started," with Blanche totally dependent on Jane; but though she makes it sound like a position of empowerment, Jane clearly is not happy about it since she accuses Blanche of "stopping her from having friends." The responsibility is then part of her guilt complex, since she believes she crippled Blanche, and we learn later that the studio had hushed up the accident, sparing Jane from prosecution.

The house, an Italianate villa located in Hancock Park, the once fashionable district of Hollywood, is said to have been bought by Blanche in her Hollywood heyday, for the sisters to share. Baby Jane will tell Edwin Flagg that their father died young, but we do not learn of their mother's fate. Even so, they are single women alone, trapped together by guilt and obligation, with no sex life to speak of, though Jane was said to have been found in a hotel room with a strange man after the accident. The design of the house, with Blanche's room up a flight of stairs, seems a deliberate inconvenience, except that Jane's bedroom is also upstairs, though we rarely see her in it. The downstairs hallway has a connecting swinging door that squeaks, a reminder of the door of Crawford's bungalow in *Autumn Leaves*.

Jane's demonstrated ability to mimic Blanche's voice is a gift she uses to take advantage of Blanche, whose money is what the sisters live on. The "sick words" that Jane has scrawled over the envelope containing Blanche's fan mail is indicative of Jane's "sickness." Blanche's gradual disempowerment maintains her as the film's protagonist, even if Blanche's refusal to confront Jane directly implies a passive acceptance and allowance of Jane's behavior. Blanche does mention it obliquely when she admonishes, "You wouldn't do these awful things to me if I wasn't in this chair," but the increasing severity of Jane's torment indicates a growing impatience, and perhaps an aligned deterioration of the mind. Later Davis will reveal Jane's pathos, and the sympathy she receives will be similar to that afforded Norman Bates in *Psycho* (i.e., we don't want her to be caught). Jane's "sickness" could be alcoholism, since she drinks heavily, but the level of her venom towards Blanche suggests a mental disorder.

Jane, hearing her younger voice singing "I've Written a Letter to Daddy," is clearly delusional, and after the adult Jane sings some of the song, her look in the mirror and horrified scream is a step back to reality. When she hears the singing, Jane goes to a Baby Jane doll that she has in the room, and we later see that she has portraits of herself and sheet music in the house downstairs. Blanche, too, has a memento of her past in a painting of herself in her room above her bed, and the outmoded set decoration of the house is used as an extension of character. These imitations of *Sunset Boulevard*, and Blanche's imprisonment, are intercut with Jane's continued contact with the real world, whether it is with her neighbors, Edwin, or going to the bank and the offices of the *Hollywood Citizen News*. The revived interest in Blanche on television stands in marked contrast to Jane, who must ask at the *News* office, "Maybe you remember me?" and whose own celebrity is ignored by her preying neighbors who only want to meet Blanche.

French movie card for *What Ever Happened to Baby Jane?* (1962).

Jane will also have to ask Edwin, "Can you guess who I am?" That in her newspaper ad Jane calls herself an "established star" is reasonable, given her childhood, but that she needs an accompanist for "nightclub, personal appearances, etc." is a reach. The ad that Bette Davis placed in *Variety* after the picture was completed and before it was released, not knowing how the picture was going to be received, adds a delicious irony to this aspect of the film.

Edwin Flagg is introduced in a scene with his mother, Dehlia, foreshadowing a 1970 Diane Arbus photograph "A Jewish giant at home with his parents in the Bronx, N.Y.," where Buono, at 6'3", dwarfs Bennett. Dehlia's arthritis will prevent her from working for six months, or so she claims, but we get the feeling that Edwin is not the kind of son to provide for his mother, since he is infantilized by wearing pajamas, and because ultimately he abandons Jane and Blanche. Edwin uses a handkerchief, which is both the sign of an overweight person and the mark of a dandy. When Edwin comes to see Jane, Aldrich pans over the collection of sheet music, whose titles include

"She's Somebody's Little Girl," "I Wouldn't Trade My Daddy," and "I've Written a Letter to Daddy." Jane tells Edwin that her father said, "You can lose everything else, but you can't lose your talent," and the eerie voice of Jane as a child has fermented into the bad singing of Davis. Davis had sung in movies before. In *Dark Victory*, when drunk, she sang "Oh, Give Me Time for Tenderness," and in *Thank Your Lucky Stars* (1943) she performed "They're Either Too Young or Too Old," and was memorably man-handled by a jitterbug champion. Our reaction to Davis's singing here is filtered through Edwin's barely contained disdain, though Jane has her own look of disappointment when she first sees Edwin. Aldrich has Jane perform in a rehearsal room, with footlights. In her scenes with Buono, Davis's performance calms down, and for the first time we see a possibility for happiness for Jane, though we know what this means for Blanche.

Jane's killing of Elvira is presented as an act of self-defense, although Jane's imprisonment of Blanche could have been explained and forgiven of a more rational person. Aldrich begins the confrontation between Elvira and Jane by using the movie convention of showing Elvira at a bus stop, the bus passing, and then Elvira still at the stop (though this receives an extra kick by Elvira seeing Jane drive by). When Jane returns to find Elvira trying to get into Blanche's locked room, Aldrich presents Elvira as the stronger one, and Jane reverts to a childish obstinacy. It is telling that Jane only manages to overcome a greater antagonist by attacking Elvira from behind. However, Jane's regret afterwards, mixed with alcohol, indicates Jane has some sense of morality, and also an awareness of the consequences of her act, something that wasn't the case when Blanche was her victim. Although she will later deny responsibility to Blanche for the murder, it is apparent that performing it changes Jane, and begins a regression that will become complete at the beach.

The beach scene presents the Hudsons as famous and now notorious, yet still unnoticed by the crowds around them. Blanche's confession makes our feelings for Blanche ambivalent, because she has only now told Jane the truth; but the overlapping antagonist/protagonist component of Jane remains intact in light of her murder of Elvira. Thankfully, Jane's reaction to the revelation is not to attack Blanche again, but rather a relief that she no longer has to feel guilty; and her offer to get Blanche an ice-cream is both a demonstration of her acceptance and a childish denial. The crowd that forms around her on her return, when the police find her, recalls the end of *Sunset Boulevard*, even if Aldrich can't quite meet that level of irony. One waits for Jane to sing "I've Written a Letter to Daddy," since her rehearsal with Edwin has left us expecting a reprise, but instead she dances while holding the melting ice-creams. Whether Blanche survives is left unresolved, but since Jane has now been released from her curse, and Blanche's suffering has lessened, it doesn't seem to matter. Jane's regression complete, it would seem that any prosecution she is to face will be dismissed because of mental incompetence. The drums from the music of the opening credits are repeated for the tracking shot of the police finding Blanche, with the same arrangement of "I've Written a Letter to Daddy."

While the music under the opening credits and at the end of the film is effective, it is otherwise overdone, with the cartoony commentary on Edwin's first encounter with Jane particularly obvious. Throughout the movie Aldrich uses zooms for point-of-view emphasis, and cross-cutting to create suspense. Interestingly, he focuses the camera on Mrs. Bates in her scenes with Liza, presumably because the reaction shots are stronger than B. D. Merrill's performance. Aldrich uses a shock edit from Blanche talking about how "alive" Jane used to be, to Jane standing listening in the doorway. There is an amusing cut from Blanche's window to a street sign for Utter McKinley Undertaking. The sight of Edwin careening about the hallway in a wheelchair with a Baby Jane doll, recalling the removal of Elvira's corpse, is a bizarre image anyway, rationalized by his being drunk. Aldrich also draws a parallel between the relationship of Jane and Blanche, and that of Edwin and Dehlia, both seemingly unhealthy and grotesque.

The first prologue presents a flyer for Baby Jane's vaudeville act, subtitled "The Diminutive Darling Duse from Duluth." Jane's Duluth origins bring to mind the Midwestern background of Crawford, and Jane's "diminutiveness" recalls the small height of both Davis and Crawford in real life. Aldrich plays with our expectation of the appearance of the stars by the use of the prologues, with child substitutes, and then classic film footage, to tease and withhold. The narrative's establishment of the sister's rivalry also forecasts and exploits the known real-life history of Davis and Crawford. As the young Blanche and her mother look on as Jane performs, it's hard not to consider the absent fathers of both Davis and Crawford, and the sibling rivalry that existed between Davis's sister and Crawford's brother, which would re-emerge when both actresses were stars in Hollywood.

Our views of Crawford as Blanche and Davis as Jane are colored by the knowledge of what playing such parts meant to both actresses at this time in their careers. At the age of 54, Bette Davis was no longer the star she once had been. After the triumph of her Margot Channing in *All About Eve* (1950) she was again nominated for the Best Actress Academy Award for *The Star* (1952), but her output for the rest of the decade makes us understand why Davis herself referred to the 1950s as her "black period." In the 1940s, when she was the queen of Warner Bros., she made two or three films a year, but now the opportunities to play leading roles were significantly fewer.

The *Virgin Queen* (1955) and *Storm Center* (1956) came after three years of inactivity, and five years would pass before *Pocketful of Miracles* (1961), although in that time she played supporting roles in two 1959 films, *The Scapegoat* and *John Paul Jones*. Crawford, by comparison, at the age of 56 was doing better. She had been nominated for the Best Actress Academy Award for *Sudden Fear* (1952), and played leading roles in *Torch Song*, *Johnny Guitar* (1954), *Female on the Beach*, *Queen Bee* (1955), *Autumn Leaves* (1956), and *The Story of Esther Costello* (1957). Crawford, too, assayed in a supporting role in *The Best of Everything* (1959). *Baby Jane*, therefore, presented an opportunity for both actresses to play leads and finally co-star together. That the film was a horror picture was a first for both.

When we finally see them, we also see what they have sacrificed for the film. While Crawford has forgone the shadow over her neck used in *Autumn Leaves*, she compensates with the costuming of Norma Koch, which gives Blanche scarves for two of her three timeless classic robes. Crawford wears a bun hairpiece and false eyelashes, but otherwise is photographed without soft focus; and as the film progresses, she will appear gaunt from not eating. When Blanche is dying, Crawford has dark shadows under her eyes, and on the beach resembles the Greek actress Irene Pappas. Crawford also apparently lost weight by having to manipulate the wheelchair in character, and she incorporated her personal habit of knitting into her characterization of Blanche. She also smokes, whereas Davis does not (which is all the more surprising because Davis was a legendary smoker).

Davis as Jane used the dead white make-up she sported in *Mr. Skeffington* (1943), a heart-shaped beauty spot, kewpie-doll lipstick, and a blonde Mary Pickford wig with sausage-curls, said to have been worn by Crawford in *Our Blushing Brides* (1928). Jane looks like a dress-extra who kept her make-up on after hours, and simply added a new layer; but she also resembles a Japanese Noh figure. Davis's lack of vanity is ironic since she is playing a character that is vain, considering her make-up and what we presume is dyed hair. Davis's clothes are a mix of limp dresses, all caked in powder and perspiration, that seem to have been made around the time of the accident and bizarre, adult-size reproductions of Baby Jane stage outfits. The fur piece and wilted corsage she wears in public add a period flavor to the sheer blouses that expose her bra. Naturally, these kinds of clothes, and specifically the tight belts, only accentuate Jane's and Davis's thick waist.

Bette Davis and Joan Crawford in an advertisement for "What Ever Happened to Baby Jane?" (1962). Both actresses appear here as stars, as opposed to the hags they portray in the film.

Aldrich gives Crawford long reaction takes, something he doesn't do as much for Davis—perhaps because Blanche is the reactive character—and also presents the death of Elvira on Crawford's face. The rat scene has Aldrich showing Crawford crying and Davis cackling at the same time, with the overhead shot of Crawford endlessly circling in her wheelchair on homage to Lillian Gish in *Broken Blossoms* (1919). Some observers believe that Aldrich's stars merely played some version of their persona, Crawford the suffering stiff-upper-lipped martyr, and Davis the willful brazen virago. However, such a perspective reduces the complexity of their roles.

Davis's performance has been described as seriocomic blowsiness, and although she is perhaps the most stylized of the big female stars—Davis, Crawford, Hepburn, Garbo— she leavens her extreme theatrical choices and quirkiness with moments of preemptive stillness and deadpan reality. She also calibrates Jane's growing madness with a schizophrenic swing between child-like innocence and harridan retribution. One can sense

Davis's enjoyment of the part, since she hadn't had such a good one in such a long time. Crawford's acting, by comparison, is standard movie-acting, though it can have its own violent largeness, and she plays it straight. In the face of Davis's volcanic eruptions, Crawford has chosen to underplay, perhaps knowing she doesn't have the technique to match her. Crawford was needed to dub Jane's impersonation of Blanche's sweet, affected voice, an indication that Davis's voice is easier to parody, as evidenced by her popularity by female impersonators. However, Davis's use of smiling when she plays Blanche adds a sly reclaiming touch.

The film's surprising and phenomenal success upon release belies the difficulty Aldrich had in making it. He had bought the rights to the novel, which had been published in 1960, and optioned it as a project to be made by his own production company, with Davis and Crawford to co-star. Aldrich had enjoyed working with Crawford on *Autumn Leaves*, which was a critical and box office success, and she had told him of her long desire to work with Davis, encouraging him to find a suitable property. Co-starring projects had been proposed for Crawford and Davis when they were under contract to Warner Bros. at the same time in the 1940s, but none of these had been made. Both stars were prepared to lower their salaries in return for a percentage of the profits, but even that didn't help in getting a studio interested. Aldrich found that the project was not an easy sell because of the perceived diminished box office appeal of the actresses, even when combined in the one film. Aldrich would later say that the problem was that "the topic was perceived as controversial and not a built-in moneymaker, which would alienate portions of the public." Jack Warner was quoted as saying he "wouldn't give a plug nickel for either one of those old broads," but Aldrich piqued the interest of Seven Arts Pictures. Warner Bros. agreed to distribute the film, but wouldn't allow it to be made on the Warners lot, so interiors were filmed at a lot reserved for B westerns.

The production's budget of *Baby Jane* was low, at $980,000 (the budget of *Psycho* was, in comparison, $806,000), with a six-week shooting schedule, compared to an "A" Warner Bros. production like *Gypsy*, made at the same time, with a budget of $4 million and a 16-week shooting schedule. With his experience in independent film-making, Aldrich knew how to work pragmatically and with imagination, but such restrictions were new to both Davis and Crawford. The two screen divas were known for their outsized egos, mercurial temperaments and larger-than-life personalities, but they both knew that for them this was a timely opportunity.

The cinematographer, Ernest Haller, had photographed Davis in *Dangerous* (1935), *Jezebel* (1938), *Dark Victory* (1939), *All This, and Heaven Too* (1940), *The Bride Came C.O.D* (1941), *In This Our Life* (1942), *Mr. Skeffington* (1944), *Deception* (1946), *A Stolen Life* (1946), and *Winter Meeting* (1948). He had photographed Crawford in *Mildred Pierce* (1945) and *Humoresque* (1946). For the supporting cast, Peter Lawford was originally chosen to play Edwin Flagg, but then withdrew, so Aldrich hired Victor Buono, whom he had seen on the television series *The Untouchables*, and who had made his film debut in an uncredited part in *The Story of Ruth* (1960).

Release

Aldrich was able to preview the movie thirty days after filming was complete, and within eleven days of its release it recovered its production costs, eventually grossing $9 million. Tagline advertising for the film asked the question: "Sister, sister, oh so fair, why is there blood all over your hair?" and the poster included five points or "things you should know about this motion picture before buying a ticket." They are: 1) If you're long-standing fans of Miss Davis and Miss Crawford, we warn you this is quite unlike anything they've ever done; 2) You are urged to see it from the beginning; 3) Be prepared for the macabre and the terrifying; 4) We ask your pledge to keep the shocking climax a secret; and 5) When the tension begins to build, remember it's just a movie. The film was premiered on October 26, 1962, and released October 31, 1962. Davis would be nominated for the Best Actress Actor Academy Award and Buono for the Best Supporting Academy Award.

The film was remade as a made-for-TV movie in 1991, starring the real-life Redgrave sisters, Lyn and Vanessa. A stage musical treatment was produced in 2002, with libretto by Henry Farrell and music by Lee Pockriss.

Reviews

"Joan Crawford and Bette Davis make a couple of formidable freaks but this unique conjunction of the two one-time top-ranking stars does not afford either the opportunity to do more than wear grotesque costumes and make-up to look like witches and chew the scenery to shreds."—Bosley Crowther, *The New York Times*, November 7, 1962.

"...[A]n emotional toboggan ride, stopped by its horribly obvious outcome.... Davis quickly overcomes a viewer's earlier impatience, leaving one emotionally exhausted.... Miss Crawford gives a quiet, remarkably fine interpretation.... Once the inept draggy start is passed, the film's pace builds with ever-growing force."—*Variety*, October 31, 1962.

"In what may well be the year's scariest, funniest and most sophisticated chiller, Davis gives a performance that cannot be called great acting but is certainly Grande guignol. And Joan effectively plays the bitch to Bette's witch.... Aldrich knows just when to play his gargoyles for giggles."—*Time*, November 23, 1962.

"The main claim to fame of this luridly old-fashioned melodrama is the superbly uninhibited performances by Crawford and (especially) Davis.... Aldrich directs with a crude energy that is very effective but leaves no room for the ambivalences usual in his work."—Phil Hardy, *The Aurum Film Encyclopedia of Horror*.

Dead Ringer (1964)

Warner Bros. Pictures

CREDITS: *Director:* Paul Henried; *Producer:* William H. Wright; *Screenplay:* Albert Beich and Oscar Millard, from a story by Rian James; *Photography:* Ernest Haller; *Music:* Andre Previn; *Art Director:* Perry Ferguson; *Film Editor:* Folmar Blangsted; *Sound:* Robert B. Lee; *Set Decorator:* William Stevens; *Costumes:* Don Feld. *Make-up Supervisor:* Gordon Bau; *Supervising Hair:* Jean Burt Reilly; *Miss Davis's Make-up:* Gene Hibbs; *Miss Davis's Hairstyles:* Florence Guernsey. B&W, 115 minutes. Filmed August–September 1963 in Hollywood, and on location at the Greystone Park & Mansion in Beverly Hills.

CAST: Bette Davis (*Edith Phillips/Margaret DeLorca*); Karl Malden (*Sergeant Jim Hobson*); Peter Lawford (*Tony Collins*); Philip Carey (*Sergeant Hoag*); Jean Hagen (*Dede Marshall*); George Macready (*Paul Harrison*); Estelle Winwood (*Dona Anna*); George Chandler (*George, Chauffeur*); Mario Alcade (*Garcia*); Cyril Delevanti (*Henry, the Butler*); Monika Henried (*Janet*); Bert Remsen (*Daniel 'Dan' Lister, Bartender*); Charles Watts (*Apartment Manager*); Ken Lynch (*Captain Johnson*). *Uncredited:* Henry Beckman (*Prosecutor*); Perry Blackwell (*Piano Vocalist*); Charles E. Fredericks (*Tom Marshall*); Jon Lormer (*Alonzo*); Charles Meredith (*Defense Lawyer*); Bryan O'Byrne (*Mr. Beemas*); George Petrie (*Eddie Krauss*); Hazel Scott (*Bit part*); Claude Stroud (*Courtroom Witness*).

VHS/DVD: DVD Warners Home Video, released August 10, 2004.

Plot

After a separation of 18 years, poor Edith Philips meets her wealthy twin, Margaret, at the funeral of Frank de Lorca, Margaret's husband, whom Edith also loved. When Edith learns that Margaret had tricked the man into marriage, she lures Margaret to the apartment she keeps over her cocktail bar, signs her own name to a suicide note, and then shoots her sister. By stealing Margaret's life, Edith sacrifices her own romance with Sgt. Jim Hobson, who had promised marriage on his retirement. After changing clothes with the corpse, Edith moves into the de Lorca mansion and begins living her sister's life. The masquerade works until she meets Tony Collins, who is Margaret's lover. When he learns of the deception and threatens to blackmail her, Edith realizes that he and Margaret conspired to murder de Lorca. A fight ensues, and Tony is killed by Duke, the family's Great Dane. The police become suspicious and exhume the body of the dead husband. Arsenic is found, and Edith is arrested for murder.

Although she tries to convince Jim that she is really Edith, he refuses to believe her story, and she is sentenced to die in the gas chamber.

Notes

Another tale of sibling rivalry, this film returns Bette Davis to the kind of solo starring vehicle she had been handed when she was Queen of Warners. Aided by a music score by Andre Previn, which makes use of a deliciously baroque harpsichord, the screenplay races Davis from one crisis to the next, and offers a few grande guignol shocks along the way. Although *Dead Ringer* employed the hook of Davis playing twins—having two Bette Davises for the price of one—in reality, Davis only faced off against herself for the first third of the film. The fun of the remainder, provided you like Davis, is seeing her pretend to be someone she isn't, and seeing if she gets away with it. Another point of interest is the film's director, Paul Henreid, who had co-starred with Davis in *Now Voyager* (1942) and *Deception* (1946). Warner Bros. had wanted a television director who could complete the production quickly and under budget, and Davis proposed actor turned television director Henried, who had directed her in an episode of the television series *Alfred Hitchcock Presents* in 1959 called "Out There—Darkness." This episode had been shot by cinematographer Ernest Haller, who had lensed *Deception*, *A Stolen Life*, and *What Ever Happened to Baby Jane?* and would work on *Dead Ringer*.

Henried had directed previous films: the dramas *For Men Only* (1952), which he also starred in, and *A Woman's Devotion* (1956), in which he played a supporting role; and the crime dramas *Live Fast, Die Young* (1958), which featured twin sisters, and *Girls on the Loose* (1958). Producer William H. Wright had not made a horror movie before. He had produced Barbara Stanwyck's television anthology series, and had made the film noirs *Act of Violence* (1948), *Black Hand* (1950) and *The People Against O'Hara* (1951).

Playing twins was not new to Bette Davis, since she had done it before in *A Stolen Life*, the only film she had produced during her Warner Bros. heyday. That picture, directed by Curtis Bernhardt, is actually a template for *Dead Ringer* in terms of style and content. *A Stolen Life* had two cinematographers, Sol Polito and Ernest Haller, as well as a special effects team led by William McGann and E. Roy Davidson, all employed to create the illusion of Davis playing twin sisters. The film uses a double for Davis and split screen, but it also uses a matte for two impressive shots: a cigarette being lit as one sister sits in a high-backed chair and the other moves around it, and the sisters in profile as one's blouse collar is straightened by the other. Although the effects in *Dead Ringer* are less sophisticated, one can enjoy both films simply on a technical level, if one wishes to ignore the narrative. Character difference is presented in a more obvious way in the first film, where one sister is good and shy, and the other bad and prepared to steal the good twin's fiancé (and, implicitly, her life). Although Davis wears the same hairstyle for both sisters, the costuming is different, with the bad one dressed ironically in white. When Patricia, the bad sister pretends to be Kate, the good one, she is called "a very dangerous woman," and it is said of her, "She could worm the secrets right out of a sphinx."

Patricia is presented as a sexual predator by pursuing Bill (Glenn Ford), while Kate says that she can't fight for him because her sister "always gets ahead of her." Patricia confesses to Kate that she is "mad about him" in a scene where Davis wears no make-up as Kate. At the wedding of Bill and Patricia, Kate moves to avoid catching the bouquet. Kate's artist protégée, Karnock (Dale Clark), tells Kate that she is "stiff, ingrown, afraid, and not even a woman," and "not a ball of fire" because she retreats from his kiss. Kate humiliates herself by agreeing to model a negligee that Bill buys for Patricia. When they go sailing together, it is Kate who wants to go back when a storm comes up. Patricia insists on staying out for the excitement. After Patricia drowns, Kate then pretends to be Patricia, thinking it her "only chance of happiness," although such opportunism is out of character for her. Perhaps it is Patricia's wedding ring that Kate slips off Patricia when she goes under that causes her to become as "mad" as her sister. While Bill does not detect Patricia's deception, Karnock has an artist's insight, and tells the new Patricia that Kate had told him Patricia was prettier, but he thinks they look the same.

A Stolen Life differs from *Dead Ringer* in that the bad sister's death is an accident and not murder, and the good sister cannot make a go of her impersonation. *Dead Ringer* is especially frustrating since part of the pleasure derived from this kind of genre deceit is in the audience's curiosity about whether or not the ruse will be successful. We get the same plot devices: a usual drink, a dog that behaves differently toward each sister, a ploy to hide an ignorance of the geography of Patricia's house, the discovery that Patricia has been an unfaithful wife, a card left by Patricia's lover, and a meeting with the lover. However, there are differences too. Although Kate ends the relationship with Patricia's lover (who has animal trophies on his apartment walls) as Bill asks, Kate's anguish about her act makes her flee. Interestingly, she is caught leaving by Bill, and she tells him that he's been "the laughing stock of the whole town." Bill follows Kate, and they meet in a fog, which is romantic, dream-like, and creepy simultaneously. Bill reveals that he knew about Kate's pretence (not surprising, since Kate makes Patricia a homebody), and that "he fell in love with Patricia, but it was never right." At least this gives him some responsibility for rejecting Kate before, though he was supposedly duped by Patricia's evil. We know she's evil and not just bad, since her lover tells Kate that he had left his wife to be with Patricia, and that there were "others" with whom she had "interludes." One ends up not feeling so good about Kate either, since she'd rather have a man like Bill as her "grand passion" than be a "lonely third rate painter." As the music swells, he tells her, "Let's forget everything that's happened," which one would think is a hard ask. Since *A Stolen Life* shows us the events that causes Kate's suffering, it provides more back-story than *Dead Ringer*, thus giving us a greater appreciation of what is stolen, which is more like a couple of months than a life. It also gives Davis more room to explore two characters, though she still seems to have fun assaying both.

After *Dead Ringer*'s wonderful opening credits, Henreid gives us the sight of Davis looking relatively normal after the gargoyle histrionics of *Baby Jane*. The bus that drops off Edith at the Los Angeles Rosedale Cemetery recalls the bus that Elvira never caught in *What Ever Happened to Baby Jane?* Character and performance will differentiate the sisters in *Dead Ringer* more than in *A Stolen Life*, although make-up, costume and hair will assist. The black mourning attire and hat with a semi-opaque veil worn by Margaret also obscures the fact that she is played by Davis's stand-in, Connie Sezan. Although the film will use Davis's double for reverse shots, split screen is also employed, with the same high-backed chair effect seen in *A Stolen Life*. Davis as a sister is a concept carried over from *What Ever Happened to Baby Jane?* but it was also present in her first film, *The Bad Sister* (1931), as well as *The Sisters* (1938).

The life that Margaret, the thieving wealthy sister, leads is established by externals, like clothes, hair, make-up, residence, and behavior. In particular, when she is seen having a massage, this is recognized as being indicative of a frivolous woman who can indulge herself. The "good" poor sister, Edith, smokes, while Margaret, the "bad" one, does not. Margaret doesn't smoke because it is said to be bad for one's skin. (Having Edith smoke is also useful for Davis's acting, as she was a legendary film smoker. In fact, Davis smokes so much in this movie, it's as if she is making up for *What Ever Happened to Baby Jane?* where she didn't smoke at all.) The sister's relationship with the DeLorca dog, Duke, also polarizes them. Duke does not like Margaret, whereas he does Edith, and her empathy with the dog will be used to soften her character after she has committed murder. Margaret's charming manner is preferable to Edith's bitterness, even when Margaret slyly mocks Edith's dropping of a sprig of heather onto Frank's grave. (The sprig of heather will

Poster for *A Stolen Life* (1946), Bette Davis' earlier film about twin sisters that serves as a template for *Dead Ringer* (1964).

later be seen in the form of a broach Tony Collins gives Edith as Margaret, upon his return from Europe.) Edith's life had been "stolen" by Margaret after Edith had given Frank Margaret's address because "he wanted to do something nice," and he and Margaret had married. Margaret had perpetrated a lie about there being a child, making the marriage "necessary," though this doesn't lessen Frank's culpability in preferring Margaret over Edith. Clearly Margaret did betray her sister's trust by becoming interested in Frank, but was Edith so unappealing she couldn't find someone else? And the truth is that Edith *has* found someone else in Jim Hobson.

Edith tells Margaret that their father became a wino and was "taken away in a strait-jacket," which is a foreshadowing of both of their dark fates, and also a nod to Crawford's *Strait-Jacket* (1964). More effort is made to elicit sympathy for Edith when we go to her cocktail bar, where she is said to be a "soft touch" and downtrodden, since she is about to be evicted. Edith is so little concerned, however, that when the landlord gives her notice for being three months behind in rent, she is too preoccupied with a plan to revenge herself against Margaret to pay attention. Edith also hires a young pair of black musicians as a music combo, though we are told she cannot afford it. Edith will describe the room she has above the bar as "a dump," a reminder of her famous "What a dump" line from *Beyond the Forest* (1949). Although Jim is Edith's love interest, and gives her a present for her birthday, the relationship isn't presented as romantic. Jim later tells Edith as Margaret that it was "understood" that they would marry, though he had never asked her. So even with the love of a man who intends to marry her, Edith still prefers to reject him and abandon her own life and identity so that she can take over her sister's life. When Edith demands that Margaret visit her because she is aware of Margaret's lie, Edith changes her hair to resemble Margaret's. Edith changing into a dressing gown can be rationalized for comfort, though we know it is to make it easier for her to change into Margaret's clothes.

The confrontation allows Davis to play up Edith's anger and Margaret's vulnerability—all aided by her alternatively hateful and frightened eyes. The jazzy chaotic beat of the music combo in the bar provides suspense for the scene in which Edith shoots Margaret and changes clothes with her, with additional tension caused by the inopportune arrival of Jim. Henreid uses source music, like the combo, as much as silence. He uses Previn's score only sporadically for dramatic moments, and Previn's love theme for sentimental ones. Davis's singing of "Shuffle Off to Buffalo" to give the impression that both sisters are present in her apartment is a weak effort, yet Jim falls for it, and we get more of Davis's bad vocalization. Heinreid cuts away from the gun at Margaret's temple and back to the activity in the bar. Apparently Jack Warner wanted the film to contain a scene that rivaled the rat sequence in *What Ever Happened to Baby Jane?* and seeing the dead Margaret being undressed and having her hair combed back like Edith's is equally as humiliating and grotesque. Edith's physical suffering in completing the change makes us want to empathize with her, a woman who has killed. The idea that Edith would commit suicide is how the real Edith thinks she can get away with Margaret's murder, though Edith has been presented as too down-to-earth to kill herself. The earlier scene in which she had manically begged Jim to take her out provides the evidence of Edith's despair, yet we know it is based on fear of the idea of the murder she plans.

When Edith returns to Margaret's mansion, Henreid holds on her in close-up as she removes her veil in front of a waiting crowd, so that we wait to see if she is recognized as a fraud. Edith can explain any change in behavior, like her smoking, as the result of her grief over a dead husband and be believed, though her lower-class origins become clear when she becomes impatient with the servants. When Heinreid has Edith investigate a noise that turns out to be Duke in Frank's room, this exemplifies the classic horror movie convention of the Woman in Peril. Edith's cackle when she finds a birthday card from Margaret's lover recalls Baby Jane's cackle when she served Blanche the rat. When Margaret is called to identify Edith at the morgue, the image of Davis on the slab is perhaps one of the most unflattering shots of a female star in cinema history. Edith forsakes wearing the Margaret make-up in bed as a touch of anti–Hollywood realism, though the scarf she wears over the wig in bed later seems ridiculous, and Henreid shoots Davis in soft-focus close-ups. Margaret's best friend, Didi Marshall, gets a laugh when she says, "I think I'm still young enough to open a door myself," which references the pampered lifestyle of the wealthy and draws attention to the older age bracket of the film's cast. It also seems that Hagen, as a heavier woman, is cast opposite Davis to make Davis look thinner. Edith survives the "usual drink" and "safe combination" challenges, but the signature forgery receives a dramatic resolution when she deliberately

Edith deLorca (Bette Davis) undresses Margaret, the sister she has murdered in *Dead Ringer* (1964). The shot shows Davis's stand-in, Connie Sezan, as Margaret, with her face conveniently obscured.

burns her hand with a hot fireplace poker. Dressed in her scarf over the wig, and a black nightgown that makes Davis look like an old lady, Henreid gives her some anxious moments as we wait for the poker to heat. Heinreid cuts away from the poker in the fire to Davis's hand touching it, so we know that it is not really hot, and her scream of agony recalls her Baby Jane screams.

Edith learns that in his will Frank had bequeathed her $50,000, which means that she wouldn't have killed Margaret if she'd known. Additionally, Jim becomes a regular visitor at Margaret's, so Edith must pretend that she doesn't know him. Something else she doesn't know is that Margaret had a lover, and that their relationship is more sexual than what Edith had with Jim. The idea of an older woman and younger man being lovers was still quite taboo at the time, so this stands as another example of Margaret's adventurousness. It is when Tony observes Edith's prudery that he senses Edith has assumed Margaret's identity. We don't know if Tony catches on at Didi's party, since Peter Lawford's performance is rather vague, before he comes to Margaret's house, where he exposes Edith's charade. That scene begins with Tony telling her "You're not yourself," and him wondering if she's trying to "unload" him. Edith wears Capri pants and a low-cut blouse in this scene, the only outfit from Margaret's wardrobe that Davis doesn't appear comfortable in (which is pretty silly considering that both characters are played by the same actress).

It is the interruption of Jim in the scene that helps Tony put all the pieces together:

the twin sister who has committed suicide, Margaret being the last one to see her alive, Margaret smoking, her burned hand, Duke. Tony deliberately feeds Edith a fake memory and catches her out, then slaps her. Davis provides a series of entertaining screams when Edith is exposed, and our trepidation over her being caught is replaced by glee at her being exploited by someone better at deception than her. Tony's confession to Edith that he and Margaret poisoned Frank together reveals Margaret to be even worse than Edith imagined, though the fact that Duke hated Margaret is supposed to be an obvious clue. (Ironically, in *A Stolen Life*, the dog disliked the good sister, so she had to bribe it with food to make it tolerate her, in her guise as the bad sister.) Duke's throat-tearing bloody attack on Tony is appropriately ghastly, and practically unwatchable as grande guignol.

When Edith tries to convince Jim of who she really is, he tells her she couldn't be Edith "in a thousand years" because the Edith he knew was "sweet, gentle, and kind, and would never murder her sister." Edith dismisses it as a "lousy joke," and we don't really mind her being charged for a crime she didn't commit since she really is a murderer. The trial is presented via a montage of angled testimony superimposed over a long take of Davis reacting in close-up. Asked by Jim about her earlier confession, Edith accepts her fate by telling him that she is Margaret, and that Edith "would never have hurt a fly." This phrase was, of course, said by Mother as Norman Bates in *Psycho*. The original ending of the film saw Edith ascending her staircase, after her conversation with Jim, and Henry the butler asking what he should say at the trial, since he has known she is Edith all along. However, Warners insisted that Edith be punished for murdering Margaret, even if she is convicted of the wrong crime, so the trial montage and final scene with Jim were added. The additions may make Edith's fate clear, but the wonderful twist is apparent from the earlier scene with Jim, where Edith accepts that she is Margaret forever.

Dead Ringer is notable as the last film role in which Davis will have a romantic leading man (fittingly, she gets two). To play twins, the 55-year-old Davis uses her contemporary voice as Edith, as well as her own thinning hair, and dresses frumpily, apparently without a bra. For Margaret, who has married into Old California money, Davis pitches her voice higher, wears more stylish clothes, more make-up, and a wig that hides Gibb's face-lifting apparatus. The make-up used for Margaret, in particular, darkens the neck to make the face look lighter. It also creates a jaw line that is strong and firm, since Margaret is designed to look younger than Edith (as a wealthy woman she can afford to spend more on her appearance and skin). Gene Hibbs was brought in as a make-up consultant, since Davis would be playing women who were 10 years younger than her real age. Gibbs had worked with Marlene Dietrich, and perfected a non-surgical instant facelift by the use of lift tapes and rubber bands attached to the skin, with a wig covering the ears to hide the apparatus. This technique would help illustrate the difference between the sisters, particularly when shown from their back for over-the-shoulder shots.

By casting the same actress to play both sisters, Henreid puts a perverse spin on the protagonist/antagonist roles in the narrative that adds more complexion to the story than what's on offer in most Grande Dame Guignol features. That Edith's life is considered stolen by Margaret makes Edith the protagonist, and Edith's interest in the past defines her as a grande dame (even had she not been played by Davis). Margaret is Edith's antagonist; however, Edith's level of aggression and Margaret's vulnerability and willingness to make amends turn Margaret into the protagonist and Edith into the antagonist. Naturally, when Edith murders Margaret, Edith becomes the antagonist in extremis—but then she is also the protagonist in her struggle not to be revealed. The series of trials she endures to "play" Margaret—Duke, Jim, the safe combination, her signature, her friends, and Tony—all generate audience sympathy for Edith the protagonist. Tony's realization of Edith's act and his exploitation of her makes him the greater antagonist—but then Jim is also both antagonist and protagonist, as perhaps the one person who defends the memory of the original Edith. The narrative uses this later complication by having Edith admit her real identity to Jim when she faces arrest for the crime she didn't commit (which Margaret did). The film ends with an echo of this same issue, since Malden's face reflects the fact that Jim believes that the woman he has helped convict is actually Edith, as she had claimed but now denies.

French movie card for *Dead Ringer* (1964).

Dead Ringer was originally to have starred Lana Turner, who dropped out of the project because she didn't want to play identical twins, thinking that one edition of her gorgeous self was enough for the public. Jack Warner approached Davis, who had been cast in a supporting part as a madam in Robert Aldrich's western *4 for Texas* (1963), to replace her. As *Dead Ringer* was a leading role providing a double dose of Davis, and a Warner Bros. production to boot, Bette pulled out of the Aldrich film. The *Dead Ringer* script by Albert Beich and Oscar Millard was based on a story by Rian James called "Dead Pigeon," which had been made as a Mexican film, *The Other* (1946), directed by Roberto Gavaldon and starring Delores Del Rio. Rian James had written the story "Some Call I Love," which became the basis for the early Davis film *Parachute Jumper* (1933), and was featured in *What Ever Happened to Baby Jane?* Warners had wanted to remake *The Other* with Joan Crawford, apparently unconcerned about the release of *A Stolen Life* at the same time. Director Michael Curtiz was attached to the project; but although it was later proposed for actresses like Loretta Young, Susan Hayward, and Patricia Neal, he was never satisfied with the script, so the idea was shelved.

Release

February 19, 1964, with the taglines "Mirror, mirror, on the wall, now who's the fairest twin of all?" "What Bette Davis does to Bette Davis and to Karl Malden and Peter Lawford in Dead Ringer is just what 'Baby Jane' people will adore!" and "They were twins who once looked exactly alike until..."

Reviews

"Davis achieves good contrast in her dual portrayal and carries on gamely and with considerable histrionic relish.... If nothing else, twice as much lower case Bette Davis is better than none, though not clearly as good as one upper case Bette Davis."—*Variety*, dated February 5 1964.

"[Davis'] mammoth creation of a pair of murderous twin sisters not only galvanizes this silly little film, but it is great fun to watch.... It is sheer cinematic personality on the rampage, in a performance that, while hardly discreet, is certainly arresting."—Eugene Archer, *The New York Times*, February 20 1964.

"Exuberantly uncorseted, [Davis'] torso looks like a gunnysack full of galoshes. Coarsely cosmeticked, her face looks like a U-2 photograph of Utah. And her acting, as always, isn't really acting; it's shameless showing-off. But just try to look away."—*Time*, February 7, 1964.

Strait-Jacket (1964)

Columbia/William Castle Production

CREDITS: *Producer/Director:* William Castle; *Associate Producer:* Dona Holloway; *Screenplay:* Robert Bloch; *Photography:* Arthur Arling; *Music:* Van Alexander. *Production Designer:* Boris Leven; *Film Editor:* Edwin Bryant; *Set Decorator:* Frank Tuttle; *Miss Crawford's Make-up:* Monte Westmore; *Miss Crawford's Hair Styles:* Peggy Shannon. *Make-up:* Ben Lane; *Hair:* Virginia Jones; *Sound:* Lambert Day; *Special Effects:* Richard Albain. B&W, 89 minutes. Filmed in August 1963.

SONG: "There Goes That Song Again" (Jule Styne, Sammy Cahn)

CAST: Joan Crawford (*Lucy Harbin*); Diane Baker (*Carol Harbin*); Leif Erickson (*Bill Cutler*); Howard St. John (*Raymond Fields*); John Anthony Hayes (*Michael Fields*); Rochelle Hudson (*Emily Cutler*); George Kennedy (*Leo Krause*); Edith Atwater (*Mrs. Fields*); Mitchell Cox (*Dr. Anderson*). *Uncredited:* Lee Majors (*Frank Harbin*); Patricia Crest (*Stella Fulton*); Vicki Cos (*Carol Harbin, aged 3*); Patty Lee (*First little girl*); Laura Hess (*Second little girl*); Lyn Lundgren (*Beautician*); Robert Ward (*Shoe Clerk*); Howard Hoffman.

VHS/DVD: DVD Sony Pictures, released March 12, 2002.

Plot

Lucy Harbin returns unexpectedly to her farm in Danton after a trip out of town and discovers her husband in bed with his ex-girlfriend, Stella Fulton. Crazed, she grabs an axe and hacks the lovers to death in full view of her three-year-old daughter, Carol. Lucy is committed to an asylum, and her brother and sister-in-law take Carol and move west to another farm. Twenty years later Lucy is released from the asylum and comes to find her family. Carol, now a talented sculptress, is in love with wealthy young Michael Fields. The girl is anxious for her dowdy mother to look as she did 20 years earlier and persuades her to wear make-up, a black wig, youthful clothing, and jangling jewelry. Lucy behaves badly when she meets Michael; and the arrival of Dr. Anderson, the psychiatrist who treated her at the asylum, upsets her further. The doctor tells Carol that he thinks Lucy should return to the asylum, and he is about to tell Lucy when he is hacked to death in a farm building.

Later, Lucy tells Carol that the doctor left, but the girl finds the doctor's car and, suspecting that Lucy has reverted to violence, hides it. The next day Carol finds farmhand Leo Krause, having seen Carol's cover-up, repainting the car, which he claims as his. She fires him, but he refuses to leave. Lucy overhears the conversation, and Krause is later axed to death. That night Lucy meets Michael's parents, and she nervously reveals the couple's plans to wed. Mrs. Fields objects, and Lucy flies into a rage, vows that nothing will stop the marriage, and rushes from the house. Later that night Mr. Fields is chopped to death, and when his wife investigates the noise, a woman who appears to be Lucy attempts to kill her; but Lucy walks in and stops her. The look-alikes grapple until Lucy strips a mask and wig from the other woman, revealing it to be Carol, who had planned the deaths of her beau's parents even before Lucy's release. Carol has a complete breakdown and is committed to an asylum. Realizing that her own crime led to Carol's insanity, Lucy goes to care for her at the asylum

Notes

An entertaining serial killer grande guignol shocker about a grande dame trying to escape the past, *Strait-Jacket* is William Castle's graduation from "B" movie showman to "A" movie horror, complete with an "A" movie star. Castle had found success as the producer and director of low-budget "B" movies that employed outrageous audience participation gimmicks, such as fake skeletons in the cinema, quasi–3-D glasses making one able to "view" ghosts onscreen, and theater seats rigged with vibrating buzzers. His previous horror titles include *Macabre* (1958), *The Tingler* (1959), *House on Haunted Hill* (1959), *13 Ghosts* (1960), *Homicidal* (1961), *Mr. Sardonicus* (1961), *13 Frightened Girls* (1963), and *The Old Dark House* (1963), with associate producer Dona Holloway working on many of them. It is said that Castle had seen *What Ever Happened to Baby Jane?* fifteen times, and a dreamed of uniting Robert Bloch, the writer of the *Psycho* novel, and one of the stars of *What Ever Happened to Baby Jane?* in an "A" film about an axe murderer. His dream came true.

Strait-Jacket opens with a scream and a newspaper photograph of Joan Crawford yelling, a style that confirms Castle as a filmmaker who wants to grab his viewers' attention from the beginning (and is not above using exploitation and tawdriness to do so). Carol's narration follows, in a Robert Aldrich–style prologue, providing the exposition, with time being established via the song "There Goes That Song Again." The song is heard in a big band arrangement, although the clothes and hairstyles we will see do not reflect that period. Since Carol remembers things she didn't see, like her father meeting Stella at a bar, we have to question the truth of the memory, although it would be hard for Lucy to provide any reasonable rationale for such a violent act. Lucy's claim of being innocent when she is strait-jacketed is forgotten when she is released 20 years later, and behaves as if she were guilty. Frank's adultery is complimented by Carol's assertion that he only married Lucy for her money, although the farm shack they reside in seems to present them as poor, as does Lucy's cheap attire. That Frank is seven years younger than Lucy is an indication that she is different from the conventional woman who marries a man older than herself, that Frank may be a gold-digger, and certainly that an age difference in marriage can cause problems. Frank leaving his bedroom door open for Carol to see him with Stella, and the fact that he doesn't know Lucy well enough to realize she will return early to catch him, seals his fate.

Lucy is introduced in a shot that recalls the way Crawford's body was objectified in her entrance in *Rain* (1932), where her legs and arms are seen before her face. Lucy steps off a train, and the Watch Your Step sign tells us that she is entering a dangerous situation—and also that she is dangerous. Crawford smirks as she disembarks, and while the smirk may be in character, one feels it is also for the audience's first sight of her. Lucy wears a tight-fitting floral print dress, jangling bracelets, and an unflattering black wig with bangs that recalls the hairstyle she wore in *Mildred Pierce* (1945). Crawford, who was 58 in real life, ironically looks younger when she wears her hair grey-streaked as Lucy aged 49, as opposed to the woman of 29 in the flashback. Castle will occasionally shoot Crawford's close-ups with the flagged protective lighting of her face and neck Aldrich employed in *Autumn Leaves* (1956), but otherwise they are filmed in soft focus. He gives us a beautiful close-up of her looking into the window to see the lovers; and her discovery of the axe as mere happenstance soon gives way to the savagery with which she uses it. Though the beheadings are shown in shadow, as we see Lucy lunge at the bodies, again the camera position suggests it is a sight Carol could not have witnessed. Castle superimposes an extreme close-up of Carol over the grotesque image of Crawford yelling in the strait-jacket, and this close-up dissolves to the adult Carol. When we learn that Lucy is to be released and will arrive at the Cutler farm where Carol resides, Castle repeats the shot of Lucy disembarking from the train—but this time it is Lucy at age 49. The close-up of the grey-haired Crawford becomes a painting for the credit sequence, where title drawings of horror imagery recall those created by Irving Block for the title sequence of Crawford's film *The Caretakers* (1963).

Composer Van Alexander uses a child-like arrangement of "There Goes That Song Again" when Lucy meets Carol, and Crawford's tears are offset against Carol's stiffness. The issue of whether Lucy is capable of committing the same kind of axe murders again is answered in the narrative when it appears that she is, though the revulsion she expresses when she has to hold an axe clearly demonstrate her inability. Castle has Crawford shake as she holds the axe, recalling her long takes of slow reaction in *Sudden Fear* (1952), and Lucy gives a ghastly scream, with her hands over her mouth, when she sees a chicken beheaded. Lucy telling Carol that she hates to see anything caged (upon spotting the farm's chicken coop) is no surprise, and her concern over the "tidiness" of the pig pen recalls Crawford's private obsession with cleanliness. The bust Carol has sculpted of Lucy's head is a bust made of Crawford in the 1930s at MGM and provides a nice age-reflective moment, even if Carol's underhanded use of it to create a Lucy-mask shows the practical side to it.

When Carol takes Lucy to get a

Lucy Harbin (Joan Crawford) with her axe in *Strait-Jacket* (1964).

make-over, the taunting children's rhyme that Lucy hears is a deliberate appropriation of the famous Lizzie Borden ditty, with the name Lucy Harbin sounding similar to Lizzie Borden: "Lucy Harbin took an axe/Gave her husband 40 whacks/When she saw what she had done/She gave his girlfriend 41."

That it should be spoken by children seems too obvious in marking Carol as the creator; and since it sounds nothing like Diane Baker's voice, the idea of how she had it recorded remains amusingly obtuse. Castle also has the recording repeat phrases with emphasis—presumably arising from Lucy's disturbed perception—and because this is movie convention it doesn't strain belief too much. Lucy's make-over has her revert to how we saw her originally—wearing the same wig, bracelets, and a variation of the floral print dress. Although Lucy is at first upset by the sound of the bracelets, she accepts the look. With a boast, "When I look in the mirror it's hard to believe that twenty years have passed," Lucy's bravado is Crawford's expected self-confidence and sexual aggressiveness in reaction to the good looks of Michael. The scene in which a drunken Lucy puts her finger in Michael's mouth as she touches his lips is heightened by her playing the "There Goes That Song Again" on a record player—evidence of her actions' inappropriateness, as well as her psychological distress (although the intense look Crawford gives him is classic Crawford seductress). Lucy shows an awareness of her behavior, admitting, "When I put on those clothes, something happens to me," and unwittingly unravels her knitting as a reflection of her unraveling composure. This is reason enough for Dr. Anderson's intention to have her taken back to the asylum, her probation deemed to be a failure. Anderson also highlights the problem of the grande dame in Grande Dame Guignol: "She's trying to recapture her past; but for her, the past is dangerous."

Although the killing of Anderson initially seems perplexing, since it would seem that Carol as the killer would want Lucy to be taken away, her later confession that Michael's parents were the real targets rationalizes it. The scene of Anderson's axe murder conveniently has him reach for his pipe tobacco pouch on the chopping block to allow him to be beheaded. As with the murders of Frank and Stella, we are still spared the sight of his head being lopped off, though we do see him yelling as the axe falls, and this awareness is a progression that will lead to the sight of Krause's beheading. Krause's murder is preceded by an amusing bit of foreshadowing when a shirt sleeve on a clothesline gets wrapped around his neck, supposedly by the wind. That this happens in daylight subverts the horror movie convention of investigating a noise, though he will soon follow a closing door into darkness. After a door slams, Castle gives us the image of Krause looking at his own reflection in a mirror as he stands next to a carcass before moving into position to be beheaded. The obvious mannequin stand-in for Krause—as silly as the fake heads left in Lucy's bed—undermines the film's grande guignol, but Castle redeems himself with a cut to a large pig squealing when the axe connects.

The screenplay makes a Castle self-reference when Michael tells his parents that he and Carol are going to see a murder mystery at the drive-in, "nice and gory"—which also foreshadows the fate of Raymond. The scene in which Lucy, Carol and the Cutlers have dinner with the Fields begins ominously since Lucy is dressed in the clothes and wig that she knows changes her. Lucy's perception of the Fields' house dissolves into a high-angle shot of her in a small striped-wallpapered room, deliberately reminiscent of a padded cell, where Lucy wears only her slip. When the camera angle changes as Carol enters, we realize that this has been a distortion of reality by Lucy, and her being locked in is in opposition to the truth of Carol being locked out by the Fields, who refuse the idea of her marriage to Michael. The Fields state that their problem with Carol is that she is Lucy's daughter, but even before they know of Lucy's scandalous past they recognize Carol as coming from a class lower than theirs. A face-off between Lucy and Mrs. Fields is heightened by the masculine hostility of Edith Atwater (which matches Crawford's), and Lucy's touching of Mrs. Field being interpreted as entrapment. Lucy's fleeing sets up the Fields's as the next victims, once again with a misleading motivation established for Lucy. Castle employs suspense and red herring shocks that lead to Raymond's death, with a clock chime employed in the same way the pig squeal was for Krause. After what appears to be Raymond's head is revealed to be merely the shadow of a bust, the shower curtain in the bathroom becomes a macabre tease and an obvious nod to Bloch's *Psycho* (as is Mrs. Field, an older woman and a disapproving mother, opening it).

Poster for *Strait-Jacket* (1964).

In a narrative where coincidental absence has put the blame for the killings on Lucy and allowed Carol time to escape discovery, it is Lucy's convenient appearance that saves Mrs. Field—perversely, the most unlikable of all the victims—and allows for Carol's un-masking. One has to admire the wig that Carol has attached to the mask of Lucy as a one-piece construct. Though the two women together make a bizarre doubling, Baker's height over Crawford, even in high heels, gives away the charade. Carol's confession turning into a schizophrenic crying rant is juxtaposed with Lucy hugging a pillar and crying, and Castle superimposes Carol-as-a-girl witnessing the murders with Baker's meltdown. The last scene, with Lucy back to her grey-streaked hair and eerily calm, is the wrap-up in which Carol's modis operandi is explained. Her *Mildred Pierce*-ish self-sacrifice is quite ludicrous, with the cause of mental illness (Lucy) living with the result (Carol) in mutual misery, and Lucy giving up the freedom she has now earned. However, the head of the Columbia lady at her feet—an astonishing accomplishment of trademark violation—tells us that the film shouldn't be taken too seriously.

The film plays with our assumption of Lucy as the antagonist and Carol as the protagonist, although Lucy's "insanity" also makes her the protagonist. When we learn that Carol has been the antagonist all along, she also becomes a protagonist by virtue of being even more "insane" than Lucy. However, Lucy is more the grande dame, though Mrs. Fields certainly has similar qualities (though in a supporting role). Like her Blanche in *What Ever Happened to Baby Jane?* Lucy is a sad figure not only for the wasted years of her life, but also because she has no sex. What makes the scene with Michael so pathetic is that Lucy can only express sexual desire to a man that does not want her—or, rather, should not want her, since he is engaged. That doesn't mean that she isn't sexually desirable, but her sheltered life has limited her possibilities, which is why going to be with Carol at the end is repeating her imprisonment. Carol's tormenting of Lucy, and Crawford having to contend with the murderous intentions of a younger woman, will also feature in her future Grande Dame Guignol titles.

Crawford had returned to Grande Dame Guignol after playing a supporting role in *The Caretakers*, and *Strait-Jacket* confirms her fascination as a star. As a woman who has lived the last twenty years in an asylum, Crawford abandons her usual self-confidence and mellifluous voice to give Lucy a gentle fragility. While Lucy may have developed the skills necessary to survive in what she later admits was an environment of "pure hell," her reintroduction into normal society has reduced her to quivering fear. The rawness of her emotions will emerge when she becomes agitated, with even her voice going hoarse, though her self-confidence and sexuality will return when she wears the makeover clothes. The intensity of Lucy's interest in Michael in the scene in which she tries to seduce him resurfaces when Dr. Anderson visits. Castle gives Crawford a silent, long-take reaction to Anderson's question "Nervous?" culminating in her lighting a match on the revolving record, which stops it playing. Scenes like this demonstrate that Crawford is just as eloquent as Bette Davis in the use of her eyes.

While Crawford's performance as Lucy is unusual, she interacts well with Baker, who she had worked with in *The Best of Everything* (1959) and the made-for-TV movie *Della* (1964). Baker probably has the better part, since Carol has more depth than Lucy, though it is pleasing to see Crawford play irony after her somewhat humorless and tortured Blanche in *What Ever Happened to Baby Jane?* Baker's persona of a natural, down-to-earth brunette is therefore subverted when Carol reveals her agenda as a murderess, a woman who is just as willful as her mother and probably smarter—yet ultimately not smart enough.

Crawford was not originally cast as Lucy. After considering Grayson Hall, who had played the repressed lesbian Judith Fellowes in *The Night of the Iguana* (1964), Joan Blondell was cast. However, a grande guignol accident in which she walked through a pane of glass meant that Blondell had to withdraw from the film. Castle happened to meet Crawford at a Hollywood party and offered her the role. Crawford insisted on changes before she would accept, including her character's age changed from being in her 50s to her 40s. Crawford's production demands included a special dressing room supplied with brandy, vodka, and caviar; certain breaks during filming; that she could pick her cameraman, and had specified lighting; and script and cast approval.

Castle agreed to all of Crawford's demands. Like the sculptured head made at MGM, the film has other elements taken from Crawford's private life, including the product placement of a Pepsi six-pack as evidence of Crawford's alliance with the company; the casting of Mitchell Cox, who was vice-president of Pepsi Cola; Lucy's habit of knitting taken from Crawford's real-life hobby employed to calm nervous hands on movie sets; and the face of Frank cut out of photographs foreshadowing Crawford doing the same in *Mommie Dearest*. Additionally, the damaged relationship between Lucy and Carol recalls Crawford's infamous relationship with her adopted daughter Christina.

Anne Helm, who had recently played opposite Elvis Presley in *Follow That Dream* (1962), was originally cast as Carol. Once production began, however, Crawford found her unsatisfactory and asked that she be replaced, so Baker was brought in. Although Baker had played a duplicitous character in *Marnie*, Helm had a more voluptuous and explicitly sexual persona than Baker, and this may have been a reason that Crawford was unhappy, since she was known to be insecure about younger actresses in her films. Playing Lucy's husband Bill Cutler, Leif Erikson had been married to Frances Farmer when they were young contract players at Paramount in the 1930s, and the parallel between Farmer's real-life story and Lucy's commitment in an asylum is interesting.

Publicity portrait of Howard St. John and Diane Baker in *Strait-Jacket* (1964).

Release

Strait-Jacket was released on January 19, 1964, with the advertising taglines "Just keep saying to yourself: 'It's only a movie... It's only a movie... It's only a movie... It's only a... It's only... It's...,'" and "WARNING! Strait-Jacket vividly depicts axe murders!" Although Castle had planned to release the film without any gimmicks, he couldn't resist the thought of giving patrons their own plastic axes, complete with fake bloodstains. But the picture's real selling point was Crawford, who agreed to do personal appearances, which helped make it a huge hit.

Reviews

"...[S]everal of the characters and situations are awfully hokey and contrived. But whenever it's time to go chop-chop, *Strait-Jacket* is scary enough for anyone.... Crawford delivers an animated performance.... Some of Castle's direction is stiff and mechanical, but most of the murders are suspensefully and chillingly constructed"—*Variety*, December 5, 1963.

"The story is utterly invalid, psychologically and dramatically, and William Castle's direction and production are on the cheapest, sleaziest side. The only conceivable audience for this piece of melodramatic rot is those who have a taste for ghoulish violence and blunt shock-effected thrills."—Bosley Crowther, *The New York Times*, January 23, 1964.

"...[A] sanguinary shudder-show.... Yet despite foolish dialogue, blunt direction, and a fustian plot, there are moments of breath-stopping terror as the heads roll, at times almost literally." — *Time*, February 7, 1964.

"As empty of psychology as it is of wit or style, the film is of interest only in offering an absurd parody of Crawford's image and mannerisms." — Phil Hardy, *The Aurum Film Encyclopedia of Horror*.

Lady in a Cage (1964)

Paramount/Luther Davis Productions

CREDITS: *Director:* Walter Grauman; *Producer/Screenplay:* Luther Davis; *Photography:* Lee Garmes; *Music:* Paul Glass; *Production Designer:* Rudolph Sternald; *Art Direction:* Hal Perera, Rudolph Sternard; *Set Decoration:* Sam Comer, Joseph Kosh; *Sound:* Frank McWhorter, John Wilkinson. *Make-up:* Wally Westmore; *Hair:* Nelly Manley: *Original Paintings:* Martin Lowitz Galleries: *Editor:* Leon Barsha; *Special Photographic Effects:* Paul K. Lerpae. B&W, 94 minutes.

CAST: Olivia deHavilland (*Mrs. Cornelia Hilyard*); James Caan (*Randall Simpson O'Connell*); Jennifer Billingsley (*Elaine*); Rafael Campos (*Essie*); William Swan (*Malcolm Hilyard*); Charles Seel (*Mr. Paul*); Scatman Crothers (*Mr. Paul's assistant*); Jeff Corey (*George L. Brady Jr., aka Repent*); Ann Southern (*Sade*). Uncredited: Richard Kiel (*Mr. Paul's Strongman*); Ron Nyman (*Neighbor*).

VHS/DVD: DVD Paramount, released March 29, 2005.

Plot

Mrs. Hilyard is a wealthy widow and poet, who lives with her 29-year-old son Malcolm. She has had an elevator installed in her mansion to help her move between floors after suffering a broken hip. When Malcolm goes away for a summer weekend, a chain reaction of street accidents causes the electricity to go out, and Mrs. Hilyard becomes trapped in the elevator cage. She relies on an emergency alarm to attract attention, but the only response comes from an alcoholic derelict who ignores her pleas and steals some small items. The wino sells them to a fence and then visits the blowsy hustler Sade, attracting the attention of three young hoodlums, Randall, Elaine, and Bessie. The trio follows them back to the mansion and ransacks the house. Wanting no witnesses, they kill the wino and lock Sade in a closet. Randall then pulls himself up to the elevator and taunts Mrs. Hilyard with a note left by Malcolm threatening suicide because of her supposed domineering manner. When the invaders are side-tracked by their loot being taken by Mr. Paul, Mrs. Hilyard manages to throw herself out of the cage and crawl to the street. Caught by Randall, she gouges out his eyes. Elaine and Essie bring her back inside and then search for Mrs. Hilyard's safe, which Malcolm had mentioned in the letter. When Elaine and Essie abandon Randall, Mrs. Hilyard escapes again; in a struggle, Raandall is hit by a car. A crowd gathers, the police arrive to arrest the surviving intruders, and Mrs. Hilyard is finally safe.

Notes

A disturbing indictment of the amorality of 1964 American society, as well as a nightmare for those suffering from claustrophobia and vertigo, this film introduces Olivia deHavilland to the Grande Dame Guignol subgenre. While her performance can be faulted, there is no denying that every time the narrative moves away from her, the film suffers, which is also a criticism of the lack of audience empathy for the other characters. It is both a compliment and an insult to director Walter Grauman that *Lady in a Cage* is almost unbearable to watch. Although the film has some spectacular grande guignol, matters aren't helped by an overused musical score, quick edits and zooms, and a narrative that accumulates nihilistic opportunism to a sickening degree.

Grauman had previously made the war drama *633 Squadron* (1964), and the horror title *The Disembodied* (1957). *Lady in a Cage* is the first film produced by Luther Davis, and the only film his company would make. Lucas had not written a horror title before and was known as the screenwriter of titles like *The Hucksters* (1947), *A Lion Is in the Streets* (1953), and *Kismet* (1955).

The film uses a prison bar motif and discordant music over the credits to suggest entrapment, with the cars in heavy traffic representing both the industrialization of modern society and, with their beeping, people's impatience and insensitivity to the individual. Other images are used to reinforce this theme: a girl running her roller-skate over the leg of an unconscious man, a couple kissing in a car while an evangelist pontificates about evil on the radio, exploding garbage cans in the street, and a bleeding dog lying on the road seen and ignored by passing motorists. The exploding cans relate to the day being July 4, and people's agitation levels are raised because it is a hot day.

The camera enters the window of the three-storey house of Mrs. Hilyard (we never hear her called Cornelia), much as the camera crept through the window in the opening hotel scene of *Psycho*. Malcolm addressing a letter and calling his mother "darling" seems as jarring, as is mention of his "love notes" to her. The implication of Malcolm being gay, and his mother's responsibility for it, will be explored later in the film. Mrs. Hilyard's age, wealth and occupation present her as a grande dame, with deHavilland's screen history adding to her persona.

Malcolm's car hitting a ladder, initiating the accidents that cause the power outage is a clever comment on his carelessness and self-involvement. That the power goes out, just as Mrs. Hilyard enters her private elevator is fortuitous. Seeing that the air conditioning has turned off should have been a warning to her, but she still locks herself into the trap, as if she wants to be there. The portable transistor radio she holds reports that a woman's decapitated body has been found—another grande guignol touch—and the radio will figure in later.

The mirror on the button panel of the elevator's interior seems to exist for alternate views of deHavilland's face, and to support a star's vanity—as is the cleavage exposed by her diaphanous negligee. In an occasional narration, Mrs. Hilyard comments that she will never ignore an alarm bell again, recognizing that she herself has done so in the past. Her narration and speaking to herself are reasonably acceptable devices since, at this time, she has no one to exchange dialogue with, although a better filmmaker with a more expressive actress would have utilized silence and non-verbal communication to convey the same information. Brady's initial muteness is misleading, and Mrs. Hilyard gets a laugh when she comments, "I will build a small shrine to you" (if he helps her). His callous opportunism will only be the first of a succession of people to take advantage of someone in a weakened condition—stuck in an elevator with the brand name Safe-T (perhaps a too-heavy-handed irony).

The one-eye disability of pawnbroker Mr. Paul stands, somewhat perversely, as an outward illustration of his focus and greed in a universe where Mrs. Hilyard's broken hip and entrapment arouses no pity. Sade repeatedly refers to her fat in a self-deprecating manner, and her southern accent (unfortunate for an actress named Sothern!) does not make her equal opportunism and indifference any more appealing. The brunette Sothern here has the same dark shadows under her eyes as Brady, presumably to suggest that both are alcoholics, but she wears a tiara-style hair band as a mark of eccentricity.

The attack on Brady and Sade by Randall, Elaine and Essie creates ambiguous loyalties for the audience. This point is evidenced by the cut Sade sustains when pushed into a mirrored dressing table, with the stocking masks the three new arrivals wear distorting their faces. Mrs. Hilyard's plight is momentarily forgotten, as the Darwinian food chain has the younger and stronger beasts preying upon the weaker, using Sade as their "pickup truck" (with her hypocritically commenting on their "hardness").

Hoodlums Elaine (Jennifer Billingsley), Essie (Rafael Campos), and Randall (James Caan) confront looters George L. Brady Jr. (Jeff Corey) and Sade (Ann Sothern) in this lobby card for *Lady in a Cage* (1964).

The three are like an inverted version of the trio from *Rebel Without a Cause* (1954), united by amorality and narcissism. Caan's blatant imitation of Marlon Brando, complete with burping, is complemented by his hairy chest, tight jeans, and dead eyes. The bruise on Elaine's eye attests to Randall's brutishness, and an off-stage beating she receives implies that she likes it. She also dances to the sound of a music box, but in an inappropriate style to show how strange she is.

The initial encounter between Randall and Mrs. Hilyard includes a funny and revealing exchange:

> MRS. HILYARD: You're from an asylum?
> RANDALL: Asylum? Oh no, you don't. Reformatory. Work Farm. I been inside every way there is to be inside. I been some kind of inside since I was nine years old.
> MRS. HILYARD: Oh I see. You're one of the many bits of offal produced by the welfare state. You're what so much of my tax dollars goes for the care and feeding of.

The notion of the home invasion being apocalyptic is somewhat arch, with Randall's encounter with Mrs. Hilyard climaxing in her hysterical laughter as the radio speaks of "the man of tomorrow." However, Grauman showing Randall, Elaine, Essie and Sade all wearing stocking masks as they gaze at the trapped Mrs. Hilyard adds a sci-fi element to a Woman in Peril narrative.

The fate of Brady is determined by the nihilistic instincts of the trio—and his own culpability. Since he was the first to find Mrs. Hilyard and not help her, it is fitting that he should be stabbed to death, although Grauman stages it behind a chair so we see no blood. The anticipation of the murder being accompanied by the music of the music box remains unfulfilled when Paul Glass' music takes over. Brady being tormented before his stabbing is an attempt to create suspense, though the outcome is certain.

Sade's fate seems just as dim, particularly when her chance to escape is foiled by her own greed in wanting to take a share of the booty. The idea that the looters are "animals," as opposed to Mrs. Hilyard being a "thinking feeling human being," gets a spin with her "Stone Age, here I come" line when she detaches shards of metal to be used as weapons. Her reaction to Randall's repeated burps is "I think I'm going to be sick," which deHavilland delivers with amusing contempt, but Randall's response of "Watch the human being be sick in a cage" gets an undercutting laugh.

Grauman often cuts to life in the world outside the house to reinforce the claustrophobic horror within, where Mrs. Hilyard's offer of a bribe fails because it involves delayed gratification. However, an exchange between Randall and Elaine about what they could do with the money provides a telling remark. When she suggests they could have kids, he replies: "Kids of yours and mine? I wouldn't trust 'em with a dull kitchen knife. They'd cut us up the minute we closed our eyes."

Elaine does not disagree. When Randall joins Mrs. Hilyard in the elevator, his sexual attraction is cancelled by his admission of hatred toward his grandmother, equating her with an old and presumably sexless woman.

The idea of Malcolm being gay arises from his letter, the one he had addressed to "darling." The lines from the letter, "Release me from your generosity. Release me from your beauty. Release me from your love," are repeated, and make Mrs. Hilyard faint after she speaks to Randall while under the delusion that he is Malcolm. This threat is, of course, financial and emotional blackmail, and presents both son and mother as controlling and manipulative. The letter justifies Randall's physical mishandling of Mrs.

When Mrs. Hilyard (Olivia deHavilland) is trapped as the *Lady in a Cage* (1964), her house is looted.

Hilyard, whom he calls an "old crow," and the shards that bend as she attempts to stab him become metaphors for impotence. When Mr. Paul's strongman subdues the trio with brass knuckles, it is the third wave of parasitism which lessens the former greater threat, though again failing to assist Mrs. Hilyard. Once again the audience's empathies are complicated.

When the shards of metal are rejuvenated and used by Mrs. Hilyard to blind Randall, the Oedipus Rex analogy is not hard to spot, and the sight of Caan's bloodied eyes is saved for shock effect. What is interesting is the lack of empathy for Elaine and Essie, perhaps because both have suffered at Randall's hands. Mrs. Hilyard's second delusion about Randall as Malcolm is accompanied by the letter's "release" lines on the soundtrack—and a wavy effect on the screen—with her self-accusation that she is a "monster."

At the film's climax, although Grauman shows a driver screaming at Randall's bleeding eyes, he delays revealing if either Mrs. Hilyard or Randall has been hit by cars as they struggle and fall into traffic. We hear the sound of screeching tires before the camera finally shows her unharmed, as well as the gruesome sight of Randall's skull crushed under a wheel. The car that Elaine and Essie attempt to flee in striking the electricity line and restoring the power is pure irony, though Grauman offers too many shots of bystanders looking at Mrs. Hilyard as if she is deranged. A policeman covering her with a blanket is, finally, an act of compassion, and the last shot of her laughing at the water that drips from the air conditioner above her displays proof of the random luck that has saved her.

However, her inability to answer the telephone when Malcolm had sought her response to his threat may mean that her son is now dead; and in order to escape from the cage, she has undoubtedly broken something else when she fell. Mrs. Hilyard's days as a beleaguered protagonist may not be over—particularly since Sade is still in the house (the police have left only with Elaine and Essie). These concerns show a continuation of the problems that confront the grande dame in our world.

Apparently the part of Mrs. Hilyard was first offered to Joan Crawford, who turned it down. DeHavilland had won the Best Actress Academy Award twice, for *To Each His Own* (1946) and *The Heiress* (1949). Her last leading role had been in *Libel* (1959). She had played a supporting role in *Light in the Piazza* (1962), and worked sporadically in the 1950s, making six films during that decade.

The 47-year-old deHavilland's calibrated states of hope, disbelief, disappointment, frustration and fear are believable, and the role appears to displays her physicality, although her efforts to climb out of the cage hide her face, meaning that they may have involved a stunt double. DeHavilland allows herself to look unflattering as she perspires, has her face pressed against the wall and bars of the elevator, and suffers a cut hand; and Grauman uses extreme close-ups of her mouth as she screams for help. DeHavilland's recitation of the poem in voice-over results in a series of embarrassing "dramatic"

The progressive trauma of Olivia deHavilland is shown in this still for *Lady in a Cage* (1964).

face-pulling shots that read more as bad acting than her character's pretentiousness, though deHavilland's joy at finally getting the elevator gates open redeems her.

Release

The picture was released July 8, 1964, with an advertising tagline of "Do not see Lady in a Cage alone!" The film's controversial subject matter resulted in its being refused a cinema release in England, where it remained unavailable until 2000, and also its being banned in Finland.

Reviews

"[*Lady in a Cage*] adds Olivia deHavilland to the list of cinemactresses who would apparently rather be freaks than be forgotten ... a grande chance to go ape. Attagirl, Ollie."—*Time*, June 19, 1964.

"...[S]ordid, if suspenseful, exercise in aimless brutality.... A discerning viewer is left curious and repelled.... Olivia deHavilland as the trapped 'Lady' does project a sense of fear and self-appraisal ... a surface, somewhat obvious portrayal."—A. H. Weller, *The New York Times*, July 11, 1964.

"...[A] noxious, repulsive, grueling experience.... Davis's sensationalistically vulgar screenplay is haphazardly constructed, full of holes, sometimes pretentious and in bad taste.... [DeHavilland] gives one of those ranting, raving, wild-eyed performances often thought of as Academy Award orientated. [She] does about as well as possible under the dire circumstances."—*Variety* May 25, 1964.

Hush ... Hush, Sweet Charlotte (1964)
(aka *What Ever Happened to Cousin Charlotte?*)

20th Century–Fox/An Associates and Aldrich Company Production

CREDITS: *Producer/Director:* Robert Aldrich; *Associate Producer:* William Blake; *Screenplay:* Henry Farrell, Lukas Heller, from a story by Henry Farrell; *Photography:* Joseph Biroc; *Music:* DeVol; *Art Director:* William Glasgow*: Set Decorator:* Raphael Bretton; *Editor:* Michael Luciano; *Sound:* Herman Lewis, Bernard Fredericks; *Wardrobe:* Norma Koch; *Make-up:* Gene Hibbs; *Production Supervisor:* Jack R. Berne. B&W, 133 minutes. Filmed June 1, 1964–November 1964 at Baton Rouge and Burnside, Louisiana.

SONG: "Hush ... Hush, Sweet Charlotte" (Frank DeVol, Mack David). Sung by Bette Davis, Al Martino.

CAST: Bette Davis (*Charlotte Hollis*); Olivia deHavilland (*Miriam Deering*); Joseph Cotten (*Dr. Drew Bayliss*); Agnes Moorehead (*Velma Cruther*); Cecil Kellaway (*Harry Willis*); Victor Buono (*Sam Eugene "Big Sam" Hollis*); Wesley Addy (*Sheriff Luke Standish*); William Campbell (*Paul Marchand*); Bruce Dern (*John Mayhew*); Frank Ferguson (*Walter Blake*); George Kennedy (*Foreman*); Dave Willock (*Taxi driver*); John Megna (*New boy*); Percy Helton (*Mr. James*); Kelly Flynn (*Boy #2*); Michael Petit (*Gang leader*); Alida Aldrich (*Young girl*); Marianne Stewart (*Dora*); Kelly Aldrich (*Boy #3*); Mary Henderson (*Cleaning woman*); William Aldrich (*Boy dancer*); Lillian Randolph (*Cleaning woman*); Ellen Corby (*Lily*); Geraldine West (*Cleaning woman*); Carol De Lay (*Geraldine*); William Walker (*Joseph*); Helen Kleeb (*Martha*); Idell James (*Ginny Mae*); Teddy Buckner and His All Stars; Mary Astor (*Jewell Mayhew*). Uncredited: Robert Adler (*Mr. Howard*); Maye Henderson (*Cleaning woman*); Jerry Leggio (*Doctor*).

VHS/DVD: DVD 20th Century–Fox, released August 9, 2005.

Plot

In 1917, Sam Hollis tells the married John Mayhew that he has learned of his affair with Sam's daughter Charlotte, and of their plan to elope. Sam demands the elopement be cancelled, and John obliges, telling Charlotte in the summerhouse that night at a party at the Hollis estate. Left alone, John is murdered with an axe. Although she is not prosecuted, due to "lack of evidence," the blame still falls on Charlotte. Believing that Sam had killed John, Charlotte becomes a legendary recluse in the mansion, living alone with her housekeeper, Velma Cruther. In 1964 the Louisiana Highway Commission decides to build a road through her property, and her house is sold. Fighting against this progress, the deranged Charlotte enlists the assistance of her estranged cousin Miriam Deering, who had lived with Charlotte when they were girls. When Miriam arrives, she renews her friendship with former beau Drew Bayliss, who is Charlotte's doctor, but who jilted Miriam after the murder.

Charlotte becomes more emotionally disturbed, experiencing visions of John's disembodied hand and head, and the bloody axe that severed them. Harry Wills, a Lloyds of London insurance investigator, visits Charlotte, since he is curious as to why John's insurance was never claimed by his widow Jewell. Miriam fires Velma, who becomes suspicious of Miriam's true motives, and plans to move Charlotte out of the house and into an asylum. Velma returns to rescue Charlotte but is caught by Miriam, who hits her over the head with a chair, causing Velma to fall to her death. Continuing their plan to drive Charlotte over the edge, Miriam and Drew trick her into shooting Drew with a gun loaded with blanks, and Miriam helps Charlotte dispose of the body in a swamp. Drew's reappearance later reduces Charlotte to whimpering insanity. Believing Charlotte completely mad and secure in her room, Miriam and Drew go into the garden to discuss what they have done. As Miriam embraces Drew, she looks up to see Charlotte, who has overheard them, push a huge stone urn from the balcony above, crushing the two schemers to death. Later, as Charlotte is taken away by the authorities, Willis hands her an envelope from the now-dead Jewel containing her confession for the murder of John.

Notes

This follow-up to *What Ever Happened to Baby Jane?* is a bloated reprisal of the pivotal components of the earlier film, including director Robert Aldrich, but with a vital piece missing—Joan Crawford. Although an effort is made to surpass its predecessor in terms of grande dames and grande guignol with a southern locale added for florid exoticism, the new film cannot match the original's galvanic casting. Still, on its own terms, *Hush ... Hush, Sweet Charlotte* delivers as Grande Dame Guignol.

A severed hand and head, blood on the white dress of a virgin, a hand cut from shattered glass, a chair smashed over a head, a fall down a stairway (with the skull cracked on the last step), and an embracing couple crushed to death by a falling stone urn all provide the necessary gruesomeness. However, the narrative lacks the antagonist/protagonist dimension of responsibility for the characters the original possessed, since Charlotte is really only a victimized Woman in Peril. Aldrich had produced and directed the western *4 for Texas* (1963), which had been associate produced by William Blake, since *What Ever Happened to Baby Jane?*

Hush ... Hush, Sweet Charlotte opens in a *What Ever Happened to Baby Jane?*–style prologue with six shots of the Hollis house. Charlotte is seen in a painting that recalls the white dress Bette Davis wore in *Jezebel* (1938). In the summerhouse, her face is in shadow to conceal Davis's real age, and as a selective lighting state that Joseph Biroc will use in the film. The camera tracks behind a birdcage, bringing to mind the pet bird from *What Ever Happened to Baby Jane?* with the tweeting used to generate suspense and foreboding. Unlike Hitchcock, who informs the audience so that we have a first-person reaction, Aldrich withholds information so he can tease and misdirect. Charlotte's "I could kill you" foreshadows John's murder, his arm positioned as if expecting the hand to be chopped off, and his head stretched back in pain for the beheading that we aren't shown. The dance sequence is marred by extras with 1960s hairstyles, and a young blonde girl playing Charlotte's cousin Miriam lacks the pretence that is Olivia deHavilland. A portrait of the family shows Charlotte in white, brightly lit and touching the back of Sam's chair, in contrast to Miriam, who is in shadow in a dark plain dress, standing in the corner. When Charlotte appears at the dance, a blood stain on the front of her dress suggests the deflowering of a virgin, though she has presumably been cradling John's severed head in her lap. Unlike the first sight of Charlotte, this time it is obviously not Davis, with the stand-in's head and shoulders in shadow, and Davis's voice used. Wind chimes accompany Sam's advance on Charlotte.

Now in 1964, we see Sam's headstone in the graveyard next to the Hollis house, and note that he died in 1928, aged 45. Aldrich uses clock chimes and his signature overhead shot to demonstrate a person trapped when the new neighbor kid enters the house. When Charlotte appears, the sad, yearning tone she uses to call for John suggests that she is deluded but not crazed. Naturally, Charlotte's age is in counterpoint to the boy's, though she is dressed here to look attractive. Drew will describe her habit of sitting up every night waiting for John as how "innocent fancies become fixed delusions." The song from the music box, written by John for her, adds romanticism to Charlotte and her presence, and the music leads us into a gruesome nursery rhyme which has incorporated her legend. As Charlotte weeps, holding the box, a close-up of Davis is shown at the side of the film's opening credits, with the sweet string arrangement continuing the romantic idealization of her love. Aldrich gives her a necessary long take to cover the credits, but we shall see that these long takes will be standard for Davis's arias in the film.

The gun Charlotte fires at the bulldozer, and the stone urn she aims at the foreman, indicate her violent, impulsive reactions, and foreshadow the film's climax. Although Luke Standish says of Charlotte, "She's not really crazy; she just acts that way because people expect it of her," it is Velma's comment that Charlotte is "nothin' but a child" that seems more appropriate. Although Sam has left her wealthy, a woman who could live anywhere in the world "like a queen," Charlotte remains a helpless and pampered southern belle. The film may wish to make Charlotte a tragic figure because of what happened to John, and the conspiracy against her, but the adultery that is the basis for her love tarnishes its purity, even if she is thought to be virginal. Although Agnes Moorehead's performance suggests that Velma is as dotty as her employer, it is Velma's warning about cousin Miriam that should be believed. In some respects the highlight of the film is the clash between Velma and Miriam, since Velma is the role clearly meant to parallel that of Elvira in *What Ever Happened to Baby Jane?* who tragically underestimates the threat of the antagonist.

Charlotte watching Miriam's arrival behind the stone urns on the balcony is more foreshadowing, as is the plot point that only Drew received a telegram of her arrival. Joseph Cotten presents Drew as a rather seedy and faded beau whose faithless love had abandoned Miriam at the time of the murder/scandal, and whose grasping hold will eventually entrap her. Since she is the poor up-north relation who had to beg for everything she got, and who had snitched to Sam and Jewel Mayhew about Charlotte's affair with John, Aldrich gives deHavilland slow reactions to suggest her moral ambiguity. In *The*

Dark Mirror, as the murderous twin sister, deHavilland pulled a face to suggest evil, but here Aldrich has her portray anger in stillness and with a deadpan delivery.

The narrative repeats exposition for the mass audience during the dinner sequence, reminding us that Charlotte has to leave the house, with Drew delivering a funny line to Charlotte: "Anyone who knew you less well than I do might be forgiven for thinkin' you had a persecution complex." Of course, Charlotte *is* being persecuted, but not by whom she thinks. When Miriam observes afterward that Charlotte is "deranged," Drew responds, "Not to the extent of being committed." What makes the scene interesting is how Drew and Miriam's reaction to Charlotte's behavior can be interpreted in two ways—as simple observers, or, in retrospect, as conspirators judging her state of mind to determine the level of "treatment" they will apply. The same double meaning can be applied to Drew's act of giving Miriam

Poster for *Hush ... Hush, Sweet Charlotte* (1964).

a gun. Miriam's discovery of her slashed dress, via the creaking closet opening, is a standard of the Old Dark House subgenre, where a woman is frightened by the goings on in a haunted house. However, Miriam's duplicity in attempting to drive Charlotte mad to inherit her estate makes Miriam antagonist as well as protagonist.

The old pictures of Davis, deHavilland and Mary Astor in newspaper articles of the time are amusing period shots that lack the resonance of those of Victor Buono and Bruce Dern, who we know to be of a different generation. However, the tabloid magazine *Crimes of Passion*, with its headless and armless animation, is a nod to the grande guignol and, implicitly, the film's drive-in youth audience. When Miriam runs into Jewell Mayhew in the street, with Jewell still dressed in widow's black, Jewell's line that "Murder starts in the heart, and its first weapon is a vicious tongue" is both an attack on Miriam and on herself. Considering that Miriam has been blackmailing Jewell for years, leaving her penniless, Miriam's attempt at a sentimental reunion is perplexing (and further sabotaged by Astor's superior acting). DeHavilland even plays second fiddle to

Moorehead when Velma parodies Miriam's pretensions. The nastiness is extended to the crank notes that Charlotte produces, unaware that Miriam is the author, with the scene given a nice cap when Velma hands one note retrieved from the floor to Miriam with the word "Murderess." In a picture full of red herrings, this is yet another, since Miriam is not a murderess (yet, neither is she an innocent). The crank notes recall the fake fan mail from *Sunset Boulevard*, and Blanche's fan mail in *What Ever Happened to Baby Jane?* that Jane throws in the trash. Jewell's murder/scandal also recalls Astor's own scandals: the "purple diary"—supposedly evidence of her affair with playwright Charles Kaufman—used by her husband physician Franklyn Thorpse in a divorce hearing in 1936; and a 1951 suicide attempt.

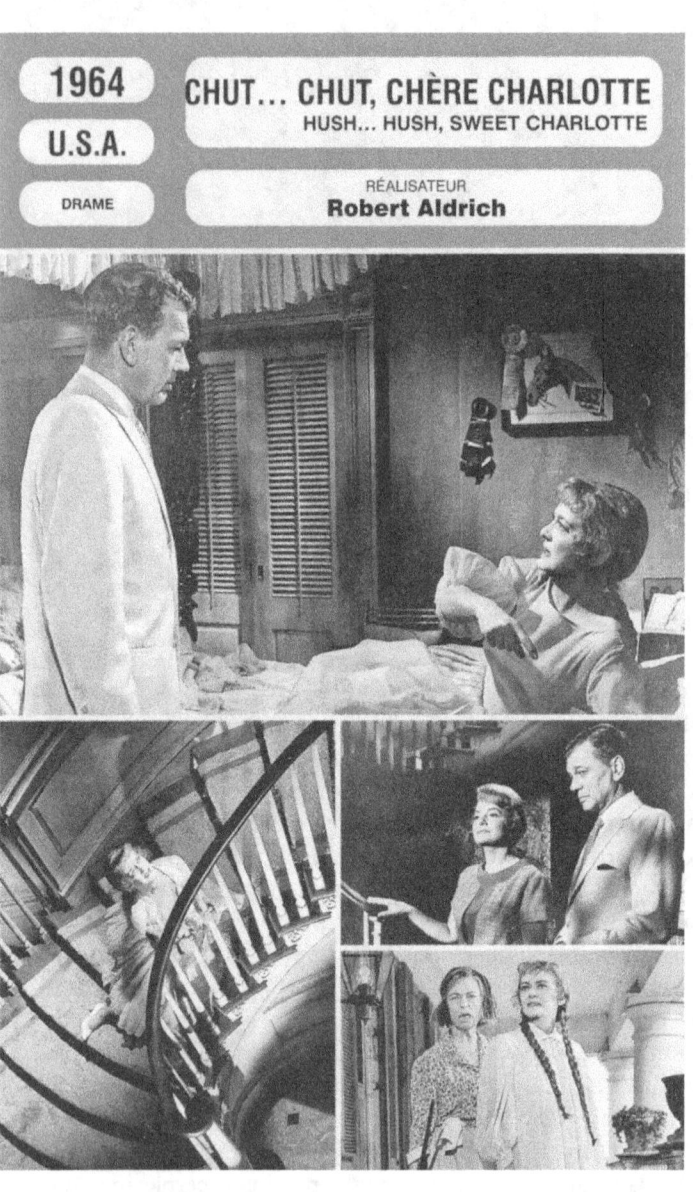

French movie card for *Hush ... Hush, Sweet Charlotte* (1964).

When Willis visits Jewell, she talks of herself as "ruined finery," and Astor's aging is rationalized by the fact that she plays a woman who is dying. When Miriam finds Charlotte singing John's song, Charlotte has a moment of clarity when she admits he is not returning. Then, speaking like a vampire, Charlotte confides that John's love is only real in the dark. However, her newfound peace is violated by a creaking door that reveals an axe and stump left for her to see. Miriam seems genuinely surprised by these fake supernatural tricks, so presumably they have been left by Drew. While Miriam's duplicity is still not confirmed, Aldrich uses the first of two beautiful images of deHavilland looking out into the night as dogs bark, her face distorted behind a lace curtain and frosted glass. When Willis comes to Charlotte, her reaction to his gentleness is to behave calmly, though this will soon evaporate when her music box is touched by women brought in to pack up the house. As if they have ESP, the black packers sense that Charlotte is not crazy—until she explodes at them. When a storm strikes that night, the thunder and lightning join the playing of the harpsichord and the voices calling out for Charlotte—all horror movie conventions. Charlotte's hand is cut by glass shards from the shattered mirrors in the music room, though she denies breaking them and claims to have seen Sam. Aldrich holds on Charlotte's surprised reaction to Paul Marchand at her door taking photographs, so that her face is a grimace and therefore perfect for his tabloid magazine. Then we see Miriam drop a fake head that resembles John's from a box she carries, outing her as someone trying to manipulate Charlotte, and Miriam and Drew's plot is disclosed.

While Aldrich uses some trick shots, like the fake train that leaves Hollisport station, he also employs unnecessary zooms (e.g., to show that Miriam has noticed that the drug vial is missing, he uses superimposition *and* a zoom). Velma's murder scene allows for a funny exchange between Miriam and Velma. When Miriam catches Velma dressing Charlotte to get her away, Miriam says, "You just can't keep hogs away from the trough." When Velma is pushed out of Charlotte's room, Velma observes, "You're finally showin' the right side of your face," as Miriam advances on her like a somnambulist. Before the push, a shot of a drugged Davis recalls the look on her face as the corpse of the murdered sister in *Dead Ringer*. Velma's extended death scene matches the excesses of Moorehead's performance. She has a chair thrown at her, falls down the stairs, and hits her head on the last step; and it's a nice touch to have Miriam afraid of retrieving the missing drug vial from Velma's hand. Velma's gruesome death also foreshadows Moorehead's own personal fate, where she and the principal cast of *The Conqueror* (1955) all contracted cancer from the radioactive dirt shipped in from an atom bomb test site in Nevada.

Charlotte's five-minute hallucination in the music room, a dreamlike Gothic dance macabre with ethereal music and expressionist imagery, is rather unbelievably, presented as being orchestrated by Miriam and Drew. Drew plays the harpsichord and mimes to Al Martino singing the title song in order to attract Charlotte. She goes to the harpsichord and finds a gun, presumably the gun Drew had given Miriam. The gun dissolves into a bouquet for her waking nightmare. Charlotte is back at the dance from the prologue for a stylized repeat of the original crime. In Hitchcock films like *Spellbound* (1944), *Vertigo* (1958), and *Marnie* (1964), characters need to recreate the stress of a drama so that they can be cured. However, this scenario supposedly has been orchestrated to push Charlotte over the edge—in spite of the fact that everyone thinks she's crazy anyway. Clearly the hallucination exists for its own sake, especially because it defies all logic for the conspirators to be able to anticipate Charlotte's reactions, since everything is presented from her point of view. John appears at the dance, where a gauze filter and a halo lights the brightest objects—the head and shoulders of the actors. A crowd of dancers wear blank masks, and the music swells. However, the music stops when Sam appears to frighten John away, and only wind chimes and footsteps are heard. John returns but dissolves into a figure without a head and a stump for a hand. Charlotte points the bouquet at him and fires, and the figure falls. Charlotte is distracted by the sound of mirrors shattering, and when she looks back, the scene dissolves back to the original lighting in the music room. Miriam appears and rolls the body over, and it is Drew. One can't help but question the timing of Drew appearing as himself, then changing into the headless one-handed figure, then switching back to himself again. Surely it would have been easier for them to just frame Charlotte for Velma's death?

Charlotte begging Miriam not to call the police recalls the similar scene between Crawford and Ann Blyth in *Mildred Pierce* (1945), and the slow turn Aldrich gives deHavilland when Charlotte offers her all her money is perhaps a little obvious. Aldrich redeems himself with an image of Davis and deHavilland in profile when a knock comes at the door, and the cross-cuts between Miriam trying to dismiss the visiting Willis, Drew's body falling over, and Charlotte's fear of being caught. Before the women drive Drew to a swamp, Aldrich repeats the shot of deHavilland at the window. Of course this narrative ploy has been appropriated from *Diabolique* (1955), where a murder is faked in order to scare a woman into having a heart attack. Although here Drew does not show us the technique that enables him to stay underwater without breathing, the appeal comes from watching Miriam play innocent and Charlotte guilty. The lush music that accompanies Miriam's victorious walk down the stairs and her preening in a mirror may indicate that she is celebrating too soon, and Charlotte's return to listen to Miriam and Drew is a plot contrivance that is justified by her reaction. At least it is finally cleared up who actually killed John Mayhew, even if Aldrich's long take on Charlotte's crushing of her conspirators is too much.

The wrap-up scene as a commercial necessity is reminiscent of the psychiatrist sequence in *Psycho*, with Aldrich shooting the three female gossips from unflattering angles. Although Charlotte is to be sent to the madhouse for killing Miriam and Drew, her manner is calm, and her leaving the music box behind is a sign of leaving behind the past. When she poses for Marchand this time, she is not a gargoyle, but rather a woman who has accepted her future. The business about Willis giving Charlotte the letter from Jewel is mere repetition, since we presume she had overheard Miriam's confession. Her exit begins like that of Norma Desmond in *Sunset Boulevard*, then, unfortunately, turns into something like Pollyanna, with the townspeople waving goodbye to her. Charlotte's fate is much too ambiguous for us to accept this kind of feel-good ending, underscored by Al Martino singing the title song yet again. As in *What Ever Happened to Baby Jane?* the music of DeVol throughout the film is too much, telegraphing our responses and overplaying the emotions, with even the title song performed too many times.

After *Dead Ringer*, Davis had played supporting parts in *The Empty Canvas* (1963) and *Where Love Has Gone* (1964), so it's good to see her back in a leading role. For the bulk of the film, wearing her long hair in braids with youthful bangs, the 56-year-old Davis's look here is more the grande dame gargoyle, and she looks feral when her long hair is let loose. She has fun with the southern accent, and is entertaining when she turns on Miriam, "her only kin," out of frustration, with her transition from anger to pathos recorded in one take. As previously stated, Aldrich favors Davis with long takes, in the much the same way he did Crawford in *What Ever Happened to Baby Jane?* since here Charlotte is the reactive character.

When Harry tells Charlotte that he saw her in London, we are reminded of Davis's own trip to London to flee from her Warners contract. Charlotte fainting allows for an unflattering shot of her, with the lines under her eyes and pocked skin of her cheeks in extreme close-up. Davis is so good at fear and panic, after Drew is supposedly killed, that deHavilland's impatience is believable, even if the eventual slapping and Miriam's spew of bile is rather labored (we just know that Crawford would have done it better).

Seeing Davis slapped and having Charlotte crawling down a staircase toward the zombified Drew, gasping and muttering, may be considered demeaning to such a great actress, but her decision not to spiral into total madness is a wise one, considering the retribution she administers soon after.

In a narrative that features four grande dames, Davis' usual large acting choices here are matched by the broad performances of Moorehead and Cotton, making Astor's scene with Cecil Kellaway, in comparison, a master class in understatement. Moorehead's choices also give the 48-year-old deHavilland more to play with than Miriam just being a sounding board for Charlotte, since Miriam is aware that Velma doesn't trust her. Moorehead and deHavilland actually make for better sparring partners than deHavilland and Davis. Cotten had been paired previously with Davis in *Beyond the Forest*, and was a real southerner, having been born in Virginia. He had played against the romantic leading man type in *Shadow of a Doubt* (1943), cast as a serial killer, and had appeared in Aldrich's *The Last Sunset* (1961). The 64-year-old Moorehead was perhaps the most visible of the cast members, thanks to her role as Endora on the television series *Bewitched*. She would be nominated for the Best Supporting Actress Academy Award for her performance in *Hush ... Hush, Sweet Charlotte*.

Since the film suffers from Crawford's absence, a history of the picture's production is necessary for context. After the success of *What Ever Happened to Baby Jane?* Davis and Crawford agreed to reunite for a sequel. Encouraged by Aldrich, the writer of *What Ever Happened to Baby Jane?* novelist Henry Farrell, penned a new story called "What Ever Happened to Cousin Charlotte?" Davis agreed to appear in it for more money, and if the title was changed to "Hush ... Hush, Sweet Charlotte," a line from the film. Crawford's condition was that her name come first in the credits, unlike in the first film where their names appeared side by side. Davis agreed to this. Because of the financial success of the first film, there was no need for a tight budget. Aldrich produced the picture, under his company and with the backing of 20th Century–Fox, on a budget of $1.3 million. Shooting began on location in Baton Rouge in the American South on June 4, 1964. Davis only played one scene with Crawford, where Davis watches her enter the antebellum mansion; otherwise they were never together. *Life* magazine sent a photographer to shoot a picture of them together, and they posed sitting on two gravestones, but the photo was never published. (This photograph is easily obtained online.) When the production went to Los Angeles for the studio interiors, a delay occurred when Davis was called away for re-shoots on *Where Love Has Gone*.

When Davis returned, Crawford checked into a hospital for pneumonia. Aldrich shot around her, and she would return but then leave again. Aldrich claimed that she had made herself sick worrying about Davis, since she felt he had a preference for Davis. Some thought that Crawford's absence was a ruse and she was, holding out for script changes, which had proved successful on *Johnny Guitar* (1954) and *Strait-Jacket*, where she had used her star power to alter the endings of the films in order to favor her. That Crawford's character would be killed by Davis in the narrative is something Crawford supposedly could not bear. With Crawford absent, the production closed down until the insurance company finally demanded she be replaced. Aldrich considered actresses like Loretta Young, Barbara Stanwyck, Katherine Hepburn and Vivien Leigh, as well as Ann Sheridan (whom he had originally wanted when the studio insisted on Crawford). Davis wanted Olivia deHavilland, who had just filmed *Lady in a Cage*.

DeHavilland is best remembered as the virtuous Melanie in *Gone with the Wind*

(1939), though she had played against type in *The Snake Pit* (1948) and *The Dark Mirror* (1946), her own version of *A Stolen Life*, as both the good and bad twin sisters. She had even sustained an unsympathetic role in her private life in the life-long feud with her actress sister Joan Fontaine. DeHavilland had also appeared with Davis in *It's Love I'm After* (1937), *The Private Lives of Elizabeth and Essex* (1939), and *In This Our Life* (1942); and in all three films they had been romantic rivals, though Davis was the bigger star. She had followed Davis's lead in suing her studio, Warner Bros., over the system that required suspension time be added to the length of a contract. Her fight kept her off the screen for three years, but she won the case, and the new law was named after her.

DeHavilland was reluctant to play an unsympathetic character, so Aldrich flew to Switzerland to convince her. It worked and she was cast, with production resumed on September 9. Not wanting to re-shoot the location exteriors, Aldrich used rear projection for deHavilland's scenes when a studio mock-up would not suffice. Aldrich would say deHavilland's casting that she was a better choice than Crawford because "we're not sure the butler did it. Anyone else steps out of the cab, you know the butler did it, and the story's over. The casting may have damaged the picture commercially, but it helped it enormously in believability." DeHavilland's favored persona was that of the mannered lady, and though this is a role Crawford aspired to, deHavilland's lesser technique gives

Miriam Deering (Olivia deHavilland) is hurt by the ridicule of her cousin, Charlotte Hollis (Bette Davis), in *Hush ... Hush, Sweet Charlotte* (1964).

Miriam's fake sincerity an edge. Being eight years younger than Davis and in trim physical shape, deHavilland also appropriated the glamour wardrobe that Crawford had wanted. However, the combination of deHavilland and Davis cannot match the combination of Davis and Crawford, since deHavilland lacks Crawford's iconic presence—a presence that would manifest itself in three future Grande Dame Guignols.

Release

December 24, 1964, for Academy Award consideration, then given a wider release in March 1965.

Reviews

"...[A] brilliant production right down the line.... There are moments when the going becomes complicated and overly contrived, however the spectator remains intent upon pic's unfoldment.... Davis's is an outgoing performance, and she plays it to the limit. DeHavilland is far more restrained but none the less effective dramatically in her offbeat role."—*Variety*, December 24, 1964.

"...[G]rossly contrived, purposely sadistic, and brutally sickening ... grisly pretentious, disgusting and profoundly annoying.... Davis accomplishes a straight melodramatic tour de force. Moorehead is allowed to get away with some of the broadest mugging and snarling ever done by a respectable actress ... deHavilland is closer to normal."—Bosley Crowther, *The New York Times*, March 4, 1965.

"DeHavilland flings away her composure but retains her chic. Mary Astor offers an ashen portrait of a woman who is not quite dead but already appears embalmed. Agnes Moorehead is a snarling, scratching sound-and-sight gag who seems determined to out-overact the best of them.... Davis's climactic staircase scene is a horrendous ham classic."—*Time*, March 19, 1965.

"Davis's control over the character's bewildering shifts of mood is a superb tour de force.... Aldrich's contribution to the Grande Guignol is mainly a matter of telegraphing the shocks and letting the ladies get on with it, but Biroc's camerawork is ravishing."—Phil Hardy, *The Aurum Film Encyclopedia of Horror*.

Die! Die! My Darling! (1965)
(aka *Fanatic*)

Hammer Films/Columbia Pictures Corporation

CREDITS: *Director:* Silvio Narizanno; *Producer:* Anthony Hinds; *Screenplay:* Richard Matheson, based on the novel *Nightmare* by Anne Blaisdell; *Photography:* Arthur Ibetson; *Music:* Wilfred Josephs; *Production Designer:* Peter Proud; *Production Manager:* George Fowler; *Editor:* John Dunsford; *Sound:* Ken Rawkins; *Make-up:* Roy Ashton, Richard Mills; *Hair:* Olga Angelinetta; *Wardrobe:* Mary Gibson. Color, 97 minutes. Produced at Associated British Studios, and filmed at Letchmore Heath, Hertfordshire, England.

CAST: Tallulah Bankhead (*Mrs. Trefoile*); Stefanie Powers (*Patricia Carroll*); Peter Vaughan (*Harry*); Maurice Kaufman (*Alan Glentower*); Yootha Joyce (*Anna*); Donald Sutherland (*Joseph*); Gwendolyn Watts (*Gloria*); Robert Dorning (*Ormsby*); Philip Gilbert (*Oscar*); Winifred Dennis (*Shopkeeper*); Diana King (*Woman Shopper*); *Uncredited*: Henry McGee (*Rector*).

VHS/DVD: DVD Sony Pictures, released August 12, 2003.

Plot

While visiting England, Patricia Carroll decides to visit the mother of her deceased ex-fiancé, Stephen Trefoile, at her desolate country home. Patricia endures the eccentricities of Mrs. Trefoile, a widow of 24 years and a religious fanatic living a puritan lifestyle. However, things change when Patricia confesses that she is now engaged to marry another man, Alan Glentower. Infuriated, Mrs. Trefoile imprisons Patricia in her attic, determined to cleanse her soul of sin. Progressively torturing Patricia, Mrs. Trefoile has her housekeeper Anna destroy Patricia's clothes, physically abuses her, and denies her food. Patricia escapes but is caught by Anna's husband, Harry, who is Mrs. Trefoile's only living relative, and brought back to the house. Thereafter, Mrs. Trefoile always has a gun with her when she speaks to Patricia. When Mrs. Trefoile catches Harry attempting to rape Patricia, Mrs. Trefoile shoots him.

When Anna sees Alan in the village asking after Mrs. Trefoile, she tells her employer, and they are prepared when Alan comes to the house. Moving Patricia to the cellar, where Mrs. Trefoile keeps a large painting of Stephen, she shows Patricia Harry's body as a warning. Growing progressively madder (she even hears what she imagines to be Stephen's voice), Mrs. Trefoile decides that Patricia must die. Seeing a piece of Patricia's jewelry worn by a barmaid at the local pub, Alan returns to the house. Anna and the grounds man, Joseph, fight him off until they realize that Mrs. Trefoile has lied about Harry having gone away on an errand. Joining forces with Alan, they interrupt Mrs. Trefoile just as she is about to cut Patricia's throat. Alan rescues Patricia, after a struggle with Mrs. Trefoile, during which her hand is cut by her own knife. Anna discovers Harry's body, and the next time we see Mrs. Trefoile she has a knife in her back.

Notes

A well written cat-and-mouse tale with grande guignol shock, blood-letting and a high quotient of female physical violence, *Die! Die! My Darling!* is the first Grande Dame Guignol in color. No doubt it was Silvio Narizanno's work in the theatre that helped him cast the extraordinary Tallulah Bankhead in her only title in the subgenre. However, while first-time film director Narizanno provides a classic sequence of grande dame misery, his use of music is too often obtrusive. Producer Anthony Hinds had previously made horror titles for Hammer Films. These include *The Quartermass Experiment* (1955), *X: The Unknown* (1956), *Horror of Dracula* (1958), *The Hound of the Baskervilles* (1959), *The Brides of Dracula* (1960), *The Curse of the Werewolf* (1961), *The Phantom of the Opera* (1962), *Paranoiac* (1963), and *The Evil of Frankenstein* (1964).

Die! Die! My Darling! features a credit sequence in which a cat in green tinted light chases a mouse in red tinted light. The mouse eventually gets away, though the cat seen holding the mouse by the tail, then eating, initially suggests the cat has won. This activity is symbolic of the narrative, where red will be described as "scarlet" and considered Satanic. The signs outside the property of "No admittance" and "No trade" warn us of the danger, as do the interior shadows, even in daytime. Although Mrs. Trefoile keeps a scrapbook of pictures of her younger self as an actress in her bedroom, the majority of the mementoes from her past are stored in the basement cellar, which will feature in the film's climax. Narizzano makes Harry's agenda quite clear when Harry affixes one of Mrs. Trefoile's glamour photographs to a can for target practice with his gun. Wearing widow's black, both for her husband and for Stephen (who is only seen in photographs and a painting), Mrs. Trefoile keeps Stephen's teddy bear in her bed.

Alan is against the idea of Patricia visiting Mrs. Trefoile, a stance that demonstrates his possessiveness and controlling nature, but also a reaction that will turn out to be prescient. The animal-print head scarf Patricia wears presents her as prey, which Narizzano suggests by showing Harry watching her while holding his gun when she arrives, and Harry's point of view of her legs, which also objectifies her comparative youthfulness. Anna, wearing a severe, mannish hairstyle, says nothing when she answers the door, which foreshadows her later brutish behavior and aligns her with the uber-servant Mrs. Danvers of Hitchcock's *Rebecca* (1940). Mrs. Trefoile is introduced with harpsichord music reminiscent of that heard in *Dead Ringer*, sitting in a large-backed cane chair of the kind seen in *Hush ... Hush, Sweet Charlotte*, wearing chained glasses. Any empathy with or compassion for her will soon disappear as she becomes the antagonist to Patricia's Woman in Peril protagonist. One could only consider Mrs. Trefoile a protagonist if one feels compassion for her deluded ideas of Stephen being a virgin and Patricia being "kept for the good of her soul," as one who must "sacrifice to be saved and be redeemed to decontaminate" Stephen. The battle between the two women can also be seen in terms of the older woman versus the younger woman, a theme found in *Strait-Jacket* and *Lady in a Cage*.

The madness of Mrs. Trefoile is calibrated with her grief and the denial of her former self, the ban on smoking, the limited diet, the removal of a telephone, and talking to Stephen (although Patricia also talks to herself, and we don't consider her deluded for doing so). Mrs. Trefoile rationalizes the denial of her past as a "harsh reminder of what I was and what I escaped," and this strategy includes removing all mirrors from the rooms. However, later we see that she has moments of weakness, during which she can access a mirror, lipstick, and alcohol in her bedroom closet. The long hours of home "service," in which extracts from the Bible are recited, gets a laugh when Patricia's stomach rumbles from hunger, though Patricia's revulsion at the eventual meal is predictable. Patricia's lipstick and red clothes will be seen as a sign of her "falling in error," and though the fact that Stefanie Powers has red hair is not commented on, it can't be seen as an asset to Mrs. Trefoile. The red interior of Patricia's suitcase can also be considered as a vaginal wall, since sexuality is another thing that Mrs. Trefoile denies herself, with her love of God as an alternative to any love interest. Narizanno uses horror movie conventions like the locked cellar, a ticking clock for suspense, and an image of Bankhead slowly closing a door in front of her when there is only the camera as witness. Mrs. Trefoile wears a black veil when she takes Patricia to church, and, as the only attendant, her disapproval of the presumably Anglican priest who has remarried, sets up the reason she will imprison Patricia. To Mrs. Trefoile, Patricia, though only his fiancée, was married to her son—forever—and Narizanno emphasizes her shocked reaction to Patricia telling her that she had intended to cancel the engagement with an extreme close-up of Bankhead's lip quivering

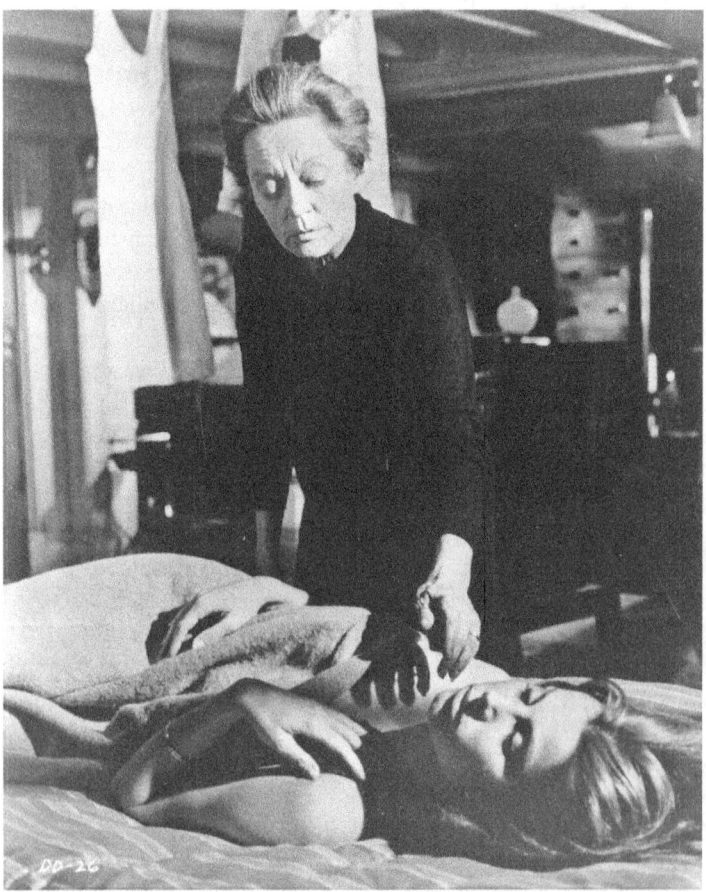

Mrs. Trefoile (Tallulah Bankead) is tempted to touch the sleeping Patricia Carroll (Stefanie Powers) in *Die! Die! My Darling!* (1965).

in rage. This image is then superimposed over a long shot of Powers running, with Patricia's freedom soon to be curtailed.

The ambiguous heavy breathing outside Patricia's door as she is locked in is revealed to be that of Mrs. Trefoile. Anna's thuggery receives a payoff with her pathetic admiration of Patricia's pink, feminine dress. Although it is never stated, it is presumed that the retarded Joseph is the offspring of Anna and Harry, and a sad indictment of their union. Patricia's music box, containing a broach that will appear later, recalls the music boxes of *Hush ... Hush, Sweet Charlotte* and *Lady in a Cage*, and the bars on the attic window where Patricia is imprisoned recalls those of Blanche's room in *What Ever Happened to Baby Jane?* Patricia's attempts to bribe first Harry, then Anna, fail, but the fact that both of them consider the offer tells us that their pay is minimal. Harry comments to Anna that Mrs. Trefoile "has had her foot on the back of my neck for sixteen years," while his sexual interest in Patricia and his gun are indications that they will have an eventual showdown. This complicates the Mrs. Trefoile-as-antagonist perception, since Harry is an opportunist to her antagonist, making it hard to determine which of the two is more sinister.

That the attic, equipped with bed and bathroom, was the room of Mr. Trefoile suggests that the marriage was less than satisfactory, and the cigarette Patricia smokes is one found there. The book she finds, *The Freedom of Religion*, presumably belongs to Mrs. Trefoile, which tells us that she spends time in the attic. It is an ironic title for the restrictions her form of religion demands, and that which she wishes to impose on Patri-

Patricia's suitcase is ransacked in *Die! Die! My Darling!* (1965).

cia. After a struggle, during which Patricia falls on scissors, Narizzano gives us the horror movie shot of her outstretched arm around a corner, and the image of Patricia in a sea of her ripped clothes. Mrs. Trefoile's fascination with Patricia's blood presents her as a vampire, and the sight of the scissors in Patricia's shoulder is our first grande guignol moment. The starved Patricia's realization of her desperation when she scrambles for a discarded potato skin foreshadows her attempt at escape, where the horror convention of a dangling sheet as rope is unseen outside the window where Anna and Harry quarrel. However, Patricia's discovery by Harry, wearing shaving cream that resembles drool, along with his giggling and ridicule of her, reinforces the cat-and-mouse imagery of the credits. The way he pulls her out of the lake and into a boat by her hair indicates his overpowering strength.

When Patricia is returned to the attic, a conversation takes place between her and Mrs. Trefoile during which only half of Bankhead's face is seen, framed by a curtained window, and only the top of Power's head and eyes are exposed as she hides behind a barricade. Mrs. Trefoile's threat to cut Patricia's face "so no man will want you," in order to force her to write a letter to Alan canceling their engagement, is the ultimate appeal to a woman's vanity. This vile demonstration of the jealousy of the older, less-attractive woman directed towards someone she sees as a romantic rival has a similar perverse tone to the cat-fighting between Anna and Patricia. Narizanno uses Harry's masturbatory jangling of keys against the banister as a signal of his approach to Patricia in the attic, who feigns desire for him as a ploy. The extreme close-ups of the eyes of both Powers and Vaughan attest to the intensity of their emotion, while Patricia's focus is on the keys to the car that she witnessed Harry parking. Harry's pushing of Patricia thrusts Powers at the camera, and it is only Mrs. Trefoile's entrance that saves Patricia from rape. Mrs. Trefoile's cream satin nightgown appears to be something from her glamorous, decadent past, but Harry calling her a "bloody old hag" reminds her of reality.

The anticipated showdown occurs when Harry follows Mrs. Trefoile to her cellar. Narizanno presents Harry as a horror movie victim who is shot by Mrs. Trefoile when he threatens her with a knife. The blood that trickles from his mouth is grande guignol. Her line, "He who sheddeth blood, so shall his blood be shed," will become prophetic to her fate, and her kissing his knife has the screen go scarlet. The blood on Mrs. Trefoile's hands recalls that of Lady Macbeth, which cannot be washed off, and although we presume it has come from her moving Harry's body, there is also a suggestion that she has deliberately cut herself. When she feeds Patricia at gunpoint, Mrs. Trefoile's eyes are black and red-lined, and Patricia's backfired attempt to give Joseph a postcard makes Mrs. Trefoile resort to physical violence, slapping and pulling Patricia's hair. Mrs. Trefoile showing Patricia the consequence of defying her is heightened by the running water on the green-faced corpse of Harry, and the pendulum light that recalls the cellar illumination of *Psycho*.

The quick thinking of Mrs. Trefoile is displayed when Alan visits the house, where the incriminating evidence of Patricia's headscarf is turned into an opportunity to have something she left behind returned to her. Patricia's apparent release from the cellar results in a tumble down the stairs, and the gruesome image of Powers' head hitting the banister is topped by Bankhead's reciting the film's title as her intention. Mrs. Trefoile dragging the unconscious Patricia into the cellar recalls Jane's dragging Blanche in *What Ever Happened to Baby Jane?* though, interestingly, she doesn't recoil from the red shirt Stephen wears in the painting in the cellar.

Narizanno uses a drumbeat for Mrs. Trefoile's attempt to slit Patricia's throat, intercutting between Alan and Anna. Anna's pain at the realization of being caught for what has been done to Patricia gives her character more depth, but her fear of Alan when he comes to the house is a surprise, given how easily she has controlled Patricia. Another surprise is Anna's shift of allegiance—before she is aware of Harry's death—when an exposed lie of Mrs. Trefoile enables her to help Alan. The blood smeared over Stephen's painting must come from Mrs. Trefoile, particularly after she repeats "They cut me" to him/it. The death of Mrs. Trefoile, when it is revealed that she has a knife in her back, presumably comes at the hands of Anna, who finds Harry's body, though this is not shown. That Mrs. Trefoile should be defeated by Anna, in spite of Anna's mixed feelings about her husband, both indicates how dangerous Anna is and the line that Mrs. Trefoile's madness has crossed.

Tallulah Bankhead was a beauty queen turned stage star who had bedazzled audiences in London and New York in the 1920s playing sophisticated bitches. She became more famous for her tempestuous personal life of hard drinking and uninhibited flamboyance than her acting performances. Tallulah's deep, raspy, sultry voice and theatrical habit of calling everyone "Daaahling" gave her an iconic camp distinction. She had played leading roles for Paramount Pictures in 1931 and 1932 in films like *Tarnished Lady*, *My Sin*, *The Cheat*, *Thunder Below*, *Devil and the Deep*, and, for MGM, *Faithless*. She disappeared from the screen until Alfred Hitchcock cast her in his *Lifeboat* (1944), and Otto Preminger cast her as Catherine the

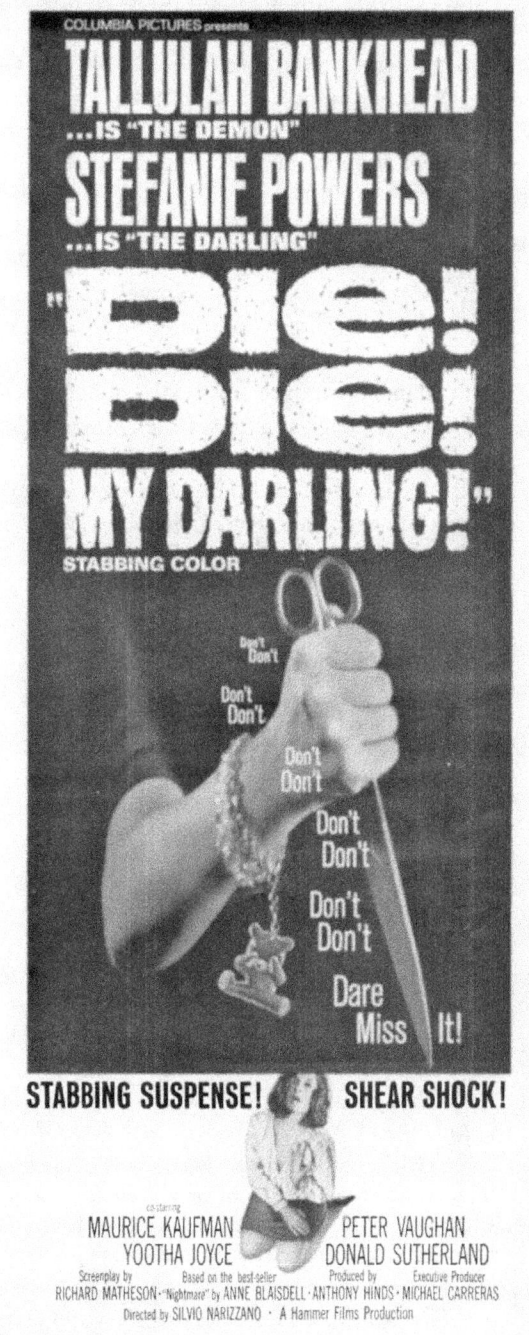

Poster for *Die! Die! My Darling!* (1965).

Great in *A Royal Scandal* (1945). *Die! Die! My Darling!* was Bankhead's first film role in twenty years. At 62 years of age, Bankhead appears with grey-streaked brown hair, which, for the most part, is kept pulled back in a bun (though it falls loose at night), and apparently no make-up, so that the age lines under her eyes and around her mouth can be seen. Bankhead is also photographed unflatteringly when she speaks to Patricia sitting on a bed, as Mrs. Trefoile is seen from below, standing over Patricia in anger, exposing her wrinkled neck.

With her distinctive slurred voice and her theatre and film background, Bankhead makes Mrs. Trefoile a grande dame; her line readings border on camp, but still remain realistic enough for her larger-than-life, loony character. She has an eerie moment when she stands behind Powers and, reaching around, touches Powers' face from behind, saying, "My poor Stephen's love." Followed by Harry, Mrs. Trefoile, her nightgown askew, exposing a shoulder, suggests both a pursued Woman in Peril and a seductive and deadly vamp. At one point Narizanno gives Bankhead a bravura opportunity to play a scene of grande dame misery. Appearing bravely with a sweaty face, she rolls on her bed in juvenile regression with Stephen's teddy bear, drinks, and applies lipstick from her secret closet, then smears the lipstick over her mouth as the music's shrieking strings recall Bernard Herrmann's score for the shower scene in *Psycho*.

When Patricia claims that Stephen was a suicide, driven to cause his own car crash death by Mrs. Trefoile, Bankhead's extra-slurred "Exactly why he what?" tells us that she is wounded. Bankhead also makes Mrs. Trefoile funny at times, as in her reaction to Alan's scarlet-colored car: "Filth. Corrupt."

The film gave Stefanie Powers her first leading role, since previously she had only played supporting parts, and she imbues Patricia's resistance with an amusing obstinacy that compensates for her occasional posturing. Powers was age 22 at the time of filming.

Release

May 19, 1965, in the U.S., with the tagline "She's One Mean Mother-in-Law!"

Reviews

"...[T]he camera excavates Tallulah's once-fabled beauty with indecent pleasure.... [It] makes no sense at all. But diehard dread addicts will appreciate that its settings look eerily authentic, its gore is in shivery color, and Tallulah spreads terror with explosive authority."—*Time*, April 2, 1965.

"Although she towers above the cast and story, Miss Bankhead's effort adds little to her record."—A. H. Weller, *The New York Times*, May 20, 1965.

"...[E]xpert thesping by Miss Bankhead could cause the release to take off with general audiences the way other horror pix with veteran actresses have done. Stefanie Powers does highly creditable job.... Narizanno's direction is imaginative in catching interplay of Bankhead's growing menace and Miss Powers's growing desperation and terror."—*Variety*, April 19, 1965.

"The mad Mrs. Trefoile is extravagantly played by a Bankhead determined to best Bette Davis's Baby Jane.... Powers's change from mild amusement to sheer terror and Bankhead's development from eccentricity to homicidal mania are handled with consummate skill by the two actresses. Unfortunately, Narizanno tends to lapse into gratuitous baroqueries."—Phil Hardy, *The Aurum Film Encyclopedia of Horror.*

"Bankhead's presence and Matheson's wry script make this a highly entertaining offering.... By turns humorous and frightening, Bankhead pulls out all the stops and gives an extraordinary performance.... Powers is also quite effective."—Gary A. Smith, *Uneasy Dreams: The Golden Age of British Horror Films, 1956–1976.*

The Night Walker (1965)

(aka *The Dream Killer*)

Universal

CREDITS: *Producer/Director:* William Castle; *Associate Producer:* Dona Holloway; *Screenplay:* Robert Bloch; *Photography:* Harold E. Stine; *Music:* Vic Mizzy; *Music Supervision:* Joseph Gershenson; *Art Directors:* Alexander Golitzen, Frank Arrigo; *Set Decoration:* John McCarthy, Julia Heron; *Sound:* Waldon O. Watson, David Moriarty; *Production Manager:* Herman Webber; *Editor:* Edwin H. Bryant; *Wardrobe:* Helen Colvig; *Make-up:* Bud Westmore; *Hair:* Larry Germain. B&W, 86 minutes. Filmed at Universal City.

CAST: Robert Taylor (*Barry Moreland*); Barbara Stanwyck (*Irene Trent*); Judith Meredith (*Joyce Holland*); Hayden Rorke (*Howard Trent*); Rochelle Hudson (*Hilda*); Marjorie Bennett (*Apartment complex manager*); Jess Barker (*Malone*); Tetsu Komai (*Gardener*); Lloyd Bochner (*the Dream, aka George Fuller*); *Uncredited*: Paulle Clark (*Pat*); Paul Frees (*Narrator*); Kathleen Mulqueen (*Customer*).

VHS/DVD: Not available on DVD. VHS: Universal Studios, released October 1, 1996.

Plot

Irene Trent's sleep-talking convinces her blind husband, Howard, that she is having an affair with another man. He suspects his attorney, Barry Morland, who denies the affair. After a quarrel with Howard, Irene leaves the house, and Howard is killed in an explosion in his laboratory. Unwilling to live in the house anymore, Irene moves into the apartment attached to the beauty shop she owns called "Irene's." Her dreams, in which she is visited by her imaginary lover, continue. One night he takes her to an apartment to drink champagne, and then to a wedding chapel peopled by wax dummies, where they marry. When the lover disappears, Howard takes his place, wanting to remarry Irene. Irene wakes up back in her bed but believes the nightmare really happened. She tells Barry about it, and once he gets past his initial notion that she is crazy, he helps her find both the apartment and the chapel. Although both locations have been emptied, Irene finds the wedding ring, supporting her claim. Barry thinks that George Fuller is behind it all.

Fuller is a private detective that Howard had hired to spy on Barry and Irene, and reveals himself to be the dream lover once Irene and Barry leave the chapel. Fuller is working with Irene's beautician, Joyce, who is also Fuller's wife, and who attempts to strangle Irene on his orders. A man who appears to be Howard arrives at the beauty shop while Irene is asleep and stabs Joyce. Barry believes that Howard is alive after an attempt is made on his life when he visits the Trent house, and persuades Irene to go back with him. Hearing gunshots and Barry calling out, Irene goes to the laboratory, where Barry removes the mask he has used to impersonate Howard. He explains that he murdered Howard, having first named himself as his beneficiary. Now, being blackmailed by Fuller, he has devised a plan with Fuller to drive Irene insane. When Barry attempts to stab Irene, he is shot and wounded by Fuller, who reveals himself to Irene as her dream lover and tells her how Barry had killed Joyce. Thinking Barry dead, Fuller moves to burn the house down with Irene in it, but Barry revives and a struggle ensues. Barry and George both fall through the gaping hole in the laboratory floor, leaving Irene alone and safe.

Notes

William Castle's second Grande Dame Guignol is a silly but fun second collaboration with writer Robert Bloch. Although basically a narrative about a Woman in Peril, the addition of dark romanticism, and the nuanced and anchoring performance of Bar-

Mexican lobby card for *The Night Walker* (1965).

bara Stanwyck, raise it above Castle's "B" movie sensibility. Castle's previous horror title was *Strait-Jacket* (on which Donna Holloway also served as associate producer).

The Night Walker begins with a brocaded book of dreams displayed under the opening credits. The narration about dreams that follows as a prologue features similar images of horror seen in *Strait-Jacket*: a flying young woman wearing a negligee; stars; multiple pairs of the same eyes; and a Salvador Dali–esque painting. The prologue climaxes with an isolated eye being held in a fist, and a woman screams as we are told, "When you dream, you become a night walker," as the camera lens closes around the eye. Howard's blindness presents him as a grotesque, using a cane (but not wearing dark glasses) and accompanied by harpsichord music. Harpsichord music was also heard in *Dead Ringer, Hush ... Hush, Sweet Charlotte,* and *Die! Die! My Darling!*—each time as an expression of, or to comment on, a sinister character. Interestingly, although Howard is disabled and a person that would ordinarily have our sympathy, the narrative establishes him as the antagonist to Irene's protagonist.

Howard compensates for his lack of sight by taping all of Irene's mutterings. As an act of empowerment, invasion of privacy, and paranoia, Howard also tapes all his conversations, and tape recordings will later be used in the film as devices of duplicity. The refusal of Howard to have a telephone in the house reads as odd (and recalls the lack of a phone in Mrs. Trefoile's house in *Die! Die! My Darling!*), but since a phone box stands just across the road, it may be an indication of his miserliness. The set decoration for the house resembles that of the Bates house in *Psycho*, and although the configuration is different, the same unwelcoming mustiness pervades the atmosphere.

Bloch stoops to writing lines like "You wanted to see me"—said to a blind man, but Castle uses the blindness to create Hitchcockian suspense (such as when Irene stands at the door, unbeknownst to Howard, as he speaks to Barry). This secret between Irene and Barry seems to support Howard's claim that they are having an affair, and Bloch plays with this assumption before revealing it to be false. Irene's dreams of a younger imaginary lover are the result of an unhappy marriage, but the prospect of three romantic interests is so unusual for a grande dame that we know the number will dwindle. A staircase confrontation with Howard is shot from a high angle, with him at the top and her at the bottom. Castle uses a patented Hitchcockian alternate point-of-view series of shots to get Howard down to Irene. Her insult "My dreams seem real because my life with you is a nightmare. My lover is only a dream, but he's still more of a man than you" may make Howard's attempt to hit her with his cane acceptable, though it is still a sign of his own viciousness.

Howard's retreat to his attic laboratory (its reason for existing is never explained) allows Castle to use smoke as a horror movie convention, as well as other tropes like the slow-closing door, the slamming and jammed door, interior shadows, the Woman in Peril investigating a noise, and the sudden hand on the shoulder. The assumption that the heat of the explosion has melted Howard away is gruesome, funny, and oddly satisfying, but the absence of a body allows for the possibility of escape and mendacity. Possibly brought on by her guilt, Irene's dream imagines her going to the laboratory after being awakened by the sound of Howard's cane. Her backing up to a hole in the floor, with a three-storey fall below, is another horror movie cliché, but the grande guignol burned face sported by Howard and Stanwyck's campy, deep-voiced screaming, make up for it.

Irene moving to the beauty shop she owns indicates that she is an independent woman, though we don't know how she happened to meet Howard or how long he has been blind. Barry shows her a photograph of Howard in which Howard is wearing dark glasses and smiling, which indicates he was once happy, or at least happy to be photographed. Our first impression of Joyce is ambiguous, since her look of surprise and smirking as she has her back to Irene can be interpreted as either genuine or sinister. However, the fact that she always has her hands in her dress pockets is a sign that she should not be trusted. When Joyce tells Irene, "You look tired," her emphasis on "tired" is a sign that Joyce represents the young antagonist to an older grande dame protagonist, as previously seen in *Strait-Jacket*, *Lady in a Cage*, and *Die! Die! My Darling!*

Irene's first apparent dream in the apartment begins with the sound of tapping on the door, which is similar to the sound of Howard's cane, and her dream lover is first shown in shadow. Castle gives Irene and the Dream a lush love theme, without harpsichord, that romanticizes the liaison, and then whirls the image to transition to daytime. Irene's meeting with Barry in a restaurant has Barry telling her how "very desirable" she is, but his suggestion that the dreaming is a sign of madness causes her to get up and walk into a waiter holding a flaming shishkabab. Irene's slapping of Barry, after he asks her if she killed Howard, is funny (and movie standard for the period—something Stanwyck was called upon to do often in her films). For her next dream, the Dream appears in the apartment without Irene letting him in, which is either a clue that he is real and part of a scheme, or dream shorthand. Bochner's arch playboy voice, though as distinctive as the voices of Taylor and Stanwyck, also adds an element of untrustworthiness which works against the intended romance.

Castle uses a subjective camera when the Dream takes Irene to another apartment—which is more appropriate, considering she should not be able to see herself in her own dream. The wedding chapel to which the Dream next takes Irene provides Castle with a scene of ultra contrivance that could only be accepted as a dream, even with Irene claiming later that the champagne she was given made her feel "dazed, as though it had been drugged." An overhead light fitted with burning candles that spins is a threat; organ music supplies a gothic touch; and mannequin "wax figures" stand as priest and witnesses. The mannequins recall those seen in *Hush ... Hush, Sweet Charlotte* and Castle's *Strait-Jacket*. Although Irene recognizes the falsity of what she sees, she still goes along with the marriage ceremony, where the priest's words come from a tape recorder, though she doesn't answer "I do" when asked, "Do you take this man?"

The Dream's disappearance, Howard's arrival (speaking with Bochner's voice), and the priest's repeat of the "dearly beloved" introduction indicates that the dream has become a nightmare. This time Irene answers "No!" to taking Howard as her husband, though since she has just been married, one would think that she would object on other grounds. Castle transitions with images of multiple twirling heads back to Irene in bed, where the Dream first came to her, and her cry of "I can't wake up" becomes camp because of Stanwyck's hysteria. Blochs script provides a funny line when Irene recounts the dream/nightmare to Barry, who asks, "You didn't, by any chance, dream the address."

The caged birds in the apartment of the manager recall the bird from *What Ever Happened to Baby Jane?* and the woman gets a laugh when she responds to Irene's story with, "I have dreams about a tall handsome man who takes me in his arms and we dance to the most beautiful music; and when I wake up in the morning, my feet hurt."

Irene's finding of the wedding ring in the chapel surprises Barry, and the appearance of the Dream (now known to be George Fuller) in daylight, and unseen by Irene and Barry, creates more Hitchcockian suspense. His telephone call to Joyce makes her involvement with "the plan" explicit, and the ticking clock that Barry hears at the Trent house is both a sign of its abandonment and a horror movie convention. Fuller's disposal of the mannequins down the hole in the laboratory supplies an initial shock effect, and his pulling the appendages off them has an unsettling implication.

Joyce massaging Irene culminates in Joyce applying a towel to relax Irene's jaw muscles — a rather ambiguous act that implies, though her revealed duplicity, strangulation. A black cat meowing in front of Irene's shop foreshadows Howard's arrival, with Joyce, as a woman investigating a noise, becoming a victim when she is stabbed in the back. Her attempt to retrieve the knife, and her inability to do so because of its placement, provides a gruesome grande guignol moment; and while Irene failing to help Joyce is disappointing, the cut telephone wire is even more so. Although Barry's ability to enter the shop makes him suspect, Taylor's performance makes the possibility that Howard is still alive believable.

The perverse length of time given to the unmasking of Barry in the film's climax, complete with the removal of false teeth and eyes, is appropriately grande guignol, as is George threatening Irene with a smoke funnel. The fall of Barry and George into a hole is a counterpoint to the falling stone urns of *Hush ... Hush, Sweet Charlotte*, and the

The blind Howard Trendt (Hayden Rorke) suspects his attorney Barry Moreland (Robert Taylor) of being his wife's lover in *The Night Walker* (1965).

sight of the corpses recalls that of the crushed Olivia deHavilland and Joseph Cotten. Castle ends the film with the sound of Irene's crying as the image retreats, surrounded by smoke, and the title "Pleasant dreams" appears. In the course of the narrative, the grande dame loses all three of her prospective lovers, though all three had their own agendas. Irene survives the attempts on her life and the attempts to drive her insane, and will inherit Howard's estate (though we haven't seen any evidence of her dependence upon it). However, Irene's continued sobbing may imply that she has been driven insane after all, and perhaps her life will not work out for her the way we hope. It is important to remember that she had created a dream lover, so perhaps this is an indication of her fragile state of mind. Only a sequel, which was never made, could address such concerns.

Barbara Stanwyck's last leading role had been in *Roustabout* (1964), although she had only appeared in one other film in the 1960s, *Walk on the Wild Side* (1962). Otherwise, she had worked on television, even starring in her own self-titled dramatic anthology series. Stanwyck had been married to Robert Taylor from 1939 to1951, and this gives Irene's relationship with Barry resonance, particularly in the way Barry ultimately betrays her. Lloyd Bochner is age 39 makes Stanwyck's Irene the older woman to her imagined dream lover.

When the material allows, Stanwyck gives a performance of subtlety and humor, moving from a Joan Crawford–esque seductive purr to a larger-than-life Bette Davis intensity, prone to hysterical outbursts. Her Irene has the neurosis of a woman living in an abusive relationship, the fear of a widow losing her mind, and a woman suffering from insomnia. However, this neurosis is balanced by audience empathy established by the actress' natural heartiness and likeability, although Stanwyck was capable of playing unlikable and wicked characters too. While Stanwyck can play women just as strong-willed as Davis or Crawford could, her ability to do comedy better than either of her peers sets her apart as the more versatile performer. Stanwyck playing anger often exposed her Brooklyn origins the way that Crawford's Midwestern accent could be heard (though here it is not as noticeable).

While her white hair appears to have some grey in the front, and the thinness of her face in close-up is the only evidence of her aging as a woman of 56, Castle occasionally uses the careful lighting that Crawford asked from him (and Robert Aldrich). Stanwyck's generally maintained attractiveness is appropriate for Irene as the owner of a beauty shop and a representative of her competence in managed beauty. Taylor, by comparison, looks tired, with lines under his eyes.

Irene Trent (Barbara Stanwyck) is romanced by her dream lover (Lloyd Bochner) in *The Night Walker* (1965).

Release

December 1964, with the tagline "Will it drive you to dream of things you're ashamed to admit!"

Reviews

"A lukewarm bloodbath, but it does afford veteran horrorist Barbara Stanwyck a chance to unleash her hysteria as of yore.... *Night Walker*'s real suspense, and perhaps the bizarre point of the entire show, lies in the tandem casting of Stanwyck and Taylor."—*Time*, February 5, 1965.

"Miss Stanwyck, silver-haired and seasoned, lends an air of dignity to the otherwise unbelievable woman in this totally unbelievable tale."—Bosley Crowther, *The New York Times*, Jan 21, 1965.

"...[A]ttains its goal as a chiller, but the unfolding is so complicated that audience frequently is lost. Film carries sufficient suspense and elements of shock.... Stanwyck scores as the weirdly perplexed widow who finds herself in horror situations, and Taylor is okay."—*Variety*, December 2, 1964.

"This ludicrously contrived shocker sees Castle once again trying to be Hitchcock.... Shoddy stuff despite Stanwyck's sterling performance."—Phil Hardy, *The Aurum Film Encyclopedia of Horror*.

I Saw What You Did (1965)

Universal

CREDITS: *Producer/Director:* William Castle; *Associate Producer:* Dona Holloway; *Screenplay:* William McGovern, from a novel by Ursula Curtiss; *Photography:* Joseph Biroc; *Music:* Van Alexander; *Art Directors:* Alexander Golitzen, Walter M. Simonds; *Set Decorators:* John McCarthy, George Milo; *Sound:* Waldon O. Watson, David Moriarty; *Production Manager:* John Morrison; *Editor:* Edwin H. Bryant; *Make-up:* Bud Westmore; *Hair:* Larry Germain. B&W, 82 minutes.

CAST: Andi Garrett (*Libby Mannering*); Sarah Lane (*Kit Austin*); Joan Crawford (*Amy Nelson*); John Ireland (*Steve Marak*); Leif Erickson (*David Mannering*); Sharyl Locke (*Tess Mannering*); Patricia Breslin (*Ellie Mannering*); John Archer (*John Austin*); John Crawford (*Trooper*); Joyce Meadows (*Judith Marak*); Uncredited: Douglas Evans (*Tom Ward*); Barbara Wilkin (*Mary Ward*).

VHS/DVD: DVD: Starz/Anchor Bay, released August 24, 1999.

Plot

Dave and Ellie Mannering, of Springton, California, are preparing to leave for an overnight business trip to Santa Barbara, 90 miles away, when they are informed that their babysitter is ill. They reluctantly leave the responsibility for the house and 9-year-old Tess to her teenaged sister Libby. Libby's friend Kit joins them, and they begin a telephone game in which they call people at random and ask silly questions. One of the numbers belongs to Steve Marak, whose wife Judith is about to leave him. Judith answers Libby's call and tries to get Steve out of the shower, but their continuing argument becomes so intense that he murders her. Steve takes the body into a wooded area and buries it. He returns to find Amy, his widowed neighbor (who is in love with him), waiting at the house. Libby calls Steve again, using the name Suzette, and says, "I saw what you did, and I know who you are." Steve begins to panic and tries to counter Libby's quips with his own questions concerning a rendezvous. Amy becomes jealous when she overhears the conversation and goes into the bathroom, where she finds Judith's bloody clothes and realizes what has happened. The girls, curious to see Steve, visit him, but Amy sends them away after pocketing their registration card. Steve kills Amy when she tries to blackmail him into living with her. Taking the card, he goes to the girls' home. Kit's father picks her up, and she eventually tells him the story. He calls the police, and they arrive at the Mannerings's home in time to shoot Steve before he strangles Libby.

Libby Mannering (Andi Garrett) and Kit Austin (Sarah Lane) look in the telephone book to find victims for their prank calls, as Tess Mannering (Sharyl Locke) watches in *I Saw What You Did* (1965).

Notes

William Castle's second film with Joan Crawford qualifies as Grande Dame Guignol despite the fact that Crawford plays a supporting role, since her impact is so powerful. Operating as a cautionary tale about the perils of teenagers making prank telephone calls while their parents are away, the narrative is weakened by the supporting characters being far more interesting than the leads, but redeemed by a shower sequence murder that is more horrifying than that of *Psycho*. Castle's previous horror title was *The Night Walker*, as was that of associate producer Dona Holloway.

Castle opens with the sound of someone dialing a telephone, and the split-screen image of Libby and Kit talking, each framed by circles so that the screen resembles a face with opening and closing eyes. He repeats this motif when he places eyes in the d's of the title word "Did." Castle establishes a playful, cartoonish tone with the Gidget-style silliness of the girls; some comic payoffs for their early prank calls; dog reaction shots; and the loud music of Van Alexander. The scenes that show the parents at their dinner differentiate between the attitudes of mother and father (Ellie is concerned, while Dave continues to make excuses not to go home). Since the girls are presented as the main characters, they are established as protagonists, although their immature behavior also makes them antagonists for their telephone victims. That they should unknowingly choose a murderer as one of their victims would seem to be poetic justice, even when Steve is established as a psychopath.

Castle uses mist around the Mannering farm, and slamming and stuck doors, as horror movie conventions before we get to the real horror of Steve's murder of Judith. Although Castle will try to return us to the original tone, the murder scene is so savage and shocking that this is simply not possible. Steve's psychosis is demonstrated by the mess he makes in the bathroom, slashing Judith's clothes presumably because she is leaving him. The fact that he takes a shower after his unseen fit tells us that he is insensitive at best. That Steve has a knife with him in the shower is hard to believe, unless he has been waiting for Judith, and the room's mess is designed to lure her in. The shower stabbing, during which he pulls Judith into the shower with him, goes *Psycho* one better, since he is naked and Judith is clothed, and both the attacker and the attacked are in the shower stall together. The repeated shots of the shower nozzle and the blood going down the drain are copied from the original, but Steve pushing Judith into the glass shower door is not, as it shatters and her dead body falls onto the floor.

Steve stops Amy from "straightening up" the bathroom by kissing her, giving her a misleading signal after she has called Judith a "childish, empty-headed little tramp," a description that she will repeat for Libby. Amy conveniently witnesses Steve packing a trunk into his car, presumably containing Judith. The transportation of the body recalls the same activities in *What Ever Happened to Baby Jane?* and *Hush ... Hush, Sweet Charlotte*. When Steve buries the body, although a threatening dog is initially a red herring, its owner as a witness will eventually get Steve caught by the police.

Steve's crime allows for the misinterpretation of Libby's refrain "I saw what you did, and I know who you are," though Amy is the more immediate problem. She insists on unlocking his house door for him, and tells him, "I'm giving the orders now." There is the implication that Steve was involved with Amy before he married Judith, and that Amy has been waiting for him, which has increased her frustration and longing. This frustration is expressed when the telephone rings while she is beseeching him, and she yells, "Let it ring!" at the second ring. That Libby calls herself Suzette on the phone and keeps hanging up on Steve is matched in its unbelievability by Libby's romantic idealization of the sound of Steve as "sexy" and "exciting," which makes the inevitable meeting a guaranteed disappointment for both of them. Before Amy listens to their conversation on Steve's extension, she has offered him her money, her frustration becoming desperation. However, Amy's instinct to look in the bathroom leads to her realization of Judith's murder, knowledge that will both empower and destroy her.

When Libby goes to Steve's house to see what he looks like, he sees her peaking through the window and assumes she is a burglar. However, the expectation of his chasing her with a knife remains unfulfilled, when Amy catches Libby, rather than Steve. The grande dame with an apparent younger female rival is a scenario repeated from *Strait-Jacket, Lady in a Cage, Die! Die! My Darling!* and *The Night Walker*. The confrontation reveals that Libby is no challenge to Amy, and Amy's victory enables Amy to confront Steve with what she knows. After Steve's amusing line "You wanna crack a whip, get yourself a dog," Amy delivers her ultimatum as a choice: "Life with me or no life at all," which he naturally sees as her trying to blackmail him into marriage. Amy has changed from being a protagonist to an antagonist, less sympathetic than a vicious mur-

Steve Marak (John Ireland) is not interested in the advances of Amy Nelson (Joan Crawford) in *I Saw What You Did* (1965).

derer because her love is about demands and control. Before Steve stabs Amy as she reaches to embrace him, she gives a pathetic rationale in "I had to do it this way." Although Steve is not concerned enough about Amy's death to even transport her body, her removal from the narrative is a blow that the film never recovers from, much the same way that Janet Leigh's death impacted *Psycho*.

Steve using the registration card to call Libby in advance, and her ease in informing a stranger of her parents' return the next day, allows for his advance. Castle gets a laugh from Steve using his handkerchief over the telephone receiver to muffle his voice. The highway patrol trooper that appears behind the stuck door of the barn when it is finally pulled open is another conventional shock effect, although it doesn't meet the expectation of Steve's arrival. Kit being picked up by her father sets up Libby as alone and more vulnerable, and the fact of Libby and Tess sharing a bed is rationalized by Tess' fear of the unknown. The dog Spot barking at Steve's arrival is another convention, and we get Steve's shock appearance after Tess goes to let the dog back inside the house. That Tess invites Steve in is evidence of a younger child's innocence (in her not recognizing his threat immediately), and Tess's lie to Kit earlier in the film about a phone call for her makes Libby's disbelief about Steve's presence understandable.

Steve hiding in the shadowed house interiors when Libby comes for him is an excessive suspense contrivance, though Steve's disempowerment as a threat is a welcome relief when he calls Libby "Just a kid." His overhearing her telephone conversation with Kit is acceptable, and even gets a laugh when Libby repeats, "I saw what you did, and I know who you are," as if Kit needed a reminder. However, the fact that she sees him listening at the window, and then calls the police, would seem a deliberate provocation. Castle gives Steve a horror movie monster reappearance when he crashes through the window. Having two people to chase when Libby and Tess are separated somewhat lessens his threat, although the knife thrown at Tess, which embeds itself in the front door, is a nice touch. Libby calling out to Tess in the mist, and telling her to get to the car, is another silly idea, since it enables the pursuer to locate and reunite the girls for his convenience. Thankfully, only Libby gets in the car, and Castle makes up for the stalled motor with another horror movie monster sight of Steve's hand appearing on the backseat. The end of the film offers the sped-up sound of talking, with an image of telephone wires, a recorded message ("Sorry you have reached a disconnected number"), and "The End" changed to "The End of the Line."

Joan Crawford was offered the role of Amy one month after having been fired from *Hush ... Hush, Sweet Charlotte*; she completed her scenes in four days. Her previous leading role had been in Castle's *Strait-Jacket*, and she was aged 59. Crawford and John Ireland had previously co-starred in *Queen Bee* (1955), where he played a man equally disinterested in her affections. Ireland plays Steve as stiff and emotionally inhibited, unromantic, intense, and frightening. Castle uses the same soft lighting on Crawford as he did in *Strait-Jacket*, with her neck photographed in shadow. Wearing a multi-tiered necklace that resembles an Aztec chest-plate, and an elaborately sculptured bouffant Marie Antoinette hairstyle, Crawford's face often features a severe expression that reveals Crawford's age, before she softens it with a smile.

Her mellifluous voice and self-confidence have returned, since Amy is in love with Steve, and Crawford emphasizes each word of "childish, empty-headed little tramp" as she throws clothes into Judith's unpacked suitcase. When Amy goes into the bathroom and sees

Poster for *I Saw What You Did* (1965).

the knife in the hamper and the smashed shower door, Crawford provides a realistic "Oh my god!" Amy's confrontation with Libby involves continuity goofs over Crawford's bouffant, since it becomes undone as Amy yells "Get outta here!" though it returns to its original sculptured perfection when Amy goes back into Steve's house. Amy's change of tact toward Libby—"Look, honey, you're too young"—offers perhaps Crawford's campiest line, and her death slide down Steve's body is punctuated by her sudden head turn to indicate the end of life.

Release

July 21, 1965, with the taglines "Fate dials the number ... terror answers the phone!" and "You may be the target ... of the next phone call..."

Reviews

"...[W]ell-produced well-acted entry in the suspense-terror field. Miss Crawford's role is well handled, and vital to the story. Slightest gesture or expression of this veteran conveys vivid emotion."—*Variety*, May 7, 1965.

"...[A] generally broad and belabored expansion of a nifty idea ... the picture would have brightened and chilled considerably more minus about half an hour, with the entire story held to the impressionable viewpoint of the youngsters. Unfortunately [Castle] dawdles the tempo. And the middle chapter involving Ireland and Miss Crawford is redundant."—Howard Thompson, *The New York Times*, July 22, 1965.

"*I Saw* delivers its message by telephone, and rings in some crude but effective suspense.... Joan is given big billing but has a small role, and soon both her number and her time are up. The plot perks right along without her.... Any who are hooked on horror shows will find every reason to haunt Castle's."—*Time*, July 30, 1965.

The Nanny (1965)

20th Century–Fox/A Seven Arts–Hammer Film production

CREDITS: *Director:* Seth Holt; *Producer:* Jimmy Sangster; *Screenplay:* Jimmy Sangster, based on the novel by Evelyn Piper; *Photography:* Harry Waxman; *Music:* Richard Rodney Bennett; *Production Designer:* Edward Carrick; *Production Manager:* George Fowler: *Editor:* Tom Simpson; *Sound:* Norman Coggs: *Make-up:* Tom Smith; *Hair:* A. G. Scott; *Wardrobe:* Rosemary Burrows. B&W, 93 minutes. Filmed June–July 1965 at Associated British Elstree Studios, Hertfordshire and London, England.

CAST: Bette Davis (*the Nanny*); Wendy Craig (*Virginia "Virgie" Fane*); Jill Bennett (*Aunt Pen*); James Villiers (*Bill Fane*); William Dix (*Joey Fane*); Pamela Franklin (*Bobbie Medman*); Jack Watling (*Dr. Medman*); Maurice Denham (*Dr. Beamaster*); Alfred Burke (*Dr. Wills*); Harry Fowler (*Milkman*); Angharad Aubrey (*Susy Fane*); Nora Gordon (*Mrs. Griggs*); Sandra Power (*Sarah*).

VHS/DVD: DVD: 20th Century–Fox, released April 8, 2008.

Plot

The unnamed Nanny has cared for Virginia Fane and her sister Penelope as children after their mother had died, although we don't know what happened to their father. Nanny has stayed to do the same for Virginia's children, as well as run the London apartment. Virginia is married to a Queens Messenger, Bill, who is a stern and distant father to Joey. Joey, now ten years old, is being released after spending two years in a school for disturbed children, having been placed there because of his implication in the drowning of his little sister, Susie. Joey refuses to have anything to do with Nanny, but finds an ally in Bobbie, the 14-year-old girl upstairs. After Bill is called away on business, Virginia suffers an attack of food poisoning that forces her to enter a hospital. Penelope, who has a heart condition after suffering from childhood rheumatism, comes to stay with Joey, since he refuses to be alone with Nanny. When Penelope sees Nanny loitering around Joey's room, she becomes convinced that Joey is telling the truth about his claim that Nanny had killed Susie. When Penelope has a heart attack while confronting Nanny, Nanny withholds her medicine and tells her story to the dying woman: the death of her own illegitimate daughter, Janet, had caused Nanny to leave the house and allowed Susie to fall accidentally into the bathtub. Not knowing the unconscious Susie was there, Nanny had filled the tub with water. After Penelope dies,

Nanny tries to drown Joey but finds that she cannot. As Joey and his mother are reunited at the hospital, Nanny packs her collection of photographs, presumably because she is leaving the household.

Notes

A creepy domestic drama that pits a child against a grande dame, this British horror movie has no specific grande guignol, but compensates with shocks and sadism. Starring Bette Davis in her fourth Grande Dame Guignol, the film explores the consequences of infantilism and the traumas of the past in a dysfunctional household.

Directed effectively by Seth Holt, with a pleasing use of silence and a mostly understated score, the film's best moments are the two deaths—no blood is seen, but their horror is still felt. Holt had previously made the horror title *Taste of Fear* (1961), again with producer Jimmy Sangster. *The Nanny* is based on a novel by Evelyn Piper, who had also written the novel on which *Bunny Like Is Missing* (1965) was based, another tale about mothers, children, and mental illness. Seven Arts Productions had not previously made any horror films but had produced such high-profile titles as *The Misfits* (1961), *West Side Story* (1961), *Lolita* (1962), and *Night of the Iguana* (1964). Sangster had also previously made the horror movies *Maniac* (1963) and *Nightmare* (1964).

The Nanny begins with the image of children in a park, playing on a horse-less carousel, while Nanny is seen feeding pigeons. The sweet music suggests that this nanny is just as sweet as Mary Poppins, with that 1964 film mentioned later in a sarcastic reference to Nanny. In her room, Nanny keeps

Japanese poster for *The Nanny* (1965).

photographs of children, including one of Virginia and Susie—but without Joey, the elder child. Our introduction to Virginia shows how she is afraid of Joey's return, and she provides the first of three flashbacks with Susie. This flashback has Virginia talking with Susie, and Holt uses an echoed voice to bring us back to the present. He films Wendy Craig in unflattering shots to expose Virginia as a hysteric. Later Nanny will say of Virginia that she is "little more than a child," a line used to describe Davis in *Hush ... Hush, Sweet Charlotte*, and we will see Nanny brushing Virginia's hair and spoon-feeding her. Virginia also drinks, which may contribute to her infantilism (the way it did for Baby Jane), with her regression a presumed consequence of Susie's death.

At the school, Dr. Beamaster tells us that Joey had been sent there because he would not eat or sleep, that he has a guilt complex from the death of Susie, and a "destructive inborn antipathy towards middle-aged women." Joey expresses this antipathy by pretending to hang himself for Mrs. Griggs, and the antipathy stems from his fear of Nanny. When Bill and Nanny come to collect Joey, Joey refuses to sit in the backseat of the car with her, and she makes apologies for his rudeness. At the apartment, Joey rejects the room she has prepared for him, insisting on having the spare room. He now insists on making his own bed, unpacking his clothes, and bathing himself, so that he has no need for her. Joey has brought some rope, which he will use to secure a cupboard against his room door at night to keep Nanny out. He also plays 1960s go-go music on a record player.

That both Virginia and Penelope have been disabled by having Nanny attend to them—Virginia psychologically and Penelope physically—tells us how dangerous Nanny is. Penelope's weak heart is an appropriation from *Diabolique*, and, as in that film, will be used against her. With sickness, death and abandonment facing him, it is little wonder that Joey has problems. Bill tells us Joey has never liked Nanny, and his subsequent behavior bears this out. Returning Joey home has only returned him to the cause of his anxiety, something which everyone seems to deny. Joey's refusal to eat the food Nanny cooks, believing she is trying to poison him, is a repeat of his previous behavior, and the battle between them will involve more food. Bill leaves for Beirut, his disinterest in his family apparent by his lack of sympathy for Virginia's emotionalism and his preference for "the club."

Bobbie's character is the only "normal" female character, but she is rather passive. The budding sexuality she expresses by allowing another neighbor to look up her dress is thankfully not explored with Joey, and she objects to him visiting her wearing only a towel. When Joey drops a flowerbox near the milkman, we get a laugh from the milkman calling Nanny "a silly old cow" for not accepting responsibility. The dropped flowerbox recalls the stone urns from *Hush ... Hush, Sweet Charlotte*. Since Joey appears to be the antagonistic character, Nanny is the apparent protagonist reacting to his aggression.

When Nanny offers Joey some hot chocolate, Holt supplies an extreme close-up of Joey's eyes. For the second Susie flashback, Holt shows us how Susie slipped into the bath and hit her head trying to retrieve her doll, which had fallen in, although the bathroom is too far away from where Joey is for him to have seen it. Holt doesn't show us Susie actually hitting her head, but the noise of contact is loud. Nanny turns on the water of the bath without looking, and returns, opening the shower curtain. *Psycho* has already warned us how dangerous bathrooms can be, and Holt cuts from Nanny opening the curtain to Joey telling the story to Bobbie.

Holt cuts from Bobbie and Joey opening a door to find Dr. Medman, to Nanny

Bill Fane (James Villiers) and Nanny (Bette Davis) see how Joey Fane (William Dix) refuses to eat in *The Nanny* (1965).

opening her door to face Joey and Dr. Medman. When Joey hits Nanny when she wants to bathe him, it is a physical advance on his previous verbal hostility. Penelope also rejects Nanny's offer to undress her for bed with, "I'm not my sister," though Penelope is just as disabled (made manifest the attack we have seen, during which Nanny had aided her). Holt foreshadows Penelope's next episode of heart distress by including a heartbeat on the soundtrack, which she awakens to. We don't know if this is her actual heart beating or some kind of premonition. The same ambiguity surrounds the sight of Nanny standing at Joey's closed door, holding a pillow (he is afraid of Nanny smothering him). Nanny's exposure of her involvement in Susie's death comes with a close-up of a shocked Davis, and Bennett's scream of "What happened in the bathroom?" provides the first real doubt about Nanny's sincerity. Penelope's inevitable attack is forewarned by Nanny's "Tea is bad for you late at night" and "Don't excite yourself." Holt gives Bennett a standard horror movie crawl on the floor in a desperate attempt to reach her medicine, but engenders a dark laugh when Nanny perversely follows and picks up the shoe Penelope has dropped.

The third Susie flashback shows Nanny being summoned by a doctor to a "not very choice" neighborhood where her daughter has died after a backstreet abortion. We don't know how old the daughter is, only that Nanny is "25 years too late," since she had been too busy looking after other people's children to care for her own illegitimate one. The doctor taunts Nanny with the grande guignol details of Janet's abortion before Nanny leaves to walk "for miles." Holt provides an out-of-focus close-up of Davis's face as Nanny walks, with Nanny saying the experience was "like a dream." This time, our first sight of Susie is face down in clear water with her doll in the bathtub. Holt cuts to Nanny entering the bathroom, but we see Susie alive, in soapy water, and without the doll. We hear Susie laughing before we see her, and Holt intercuts between the live Susie and the dead one. Nanny also sees both images, and tells Susie to "Stop playing tricks on your old Nanny." Since we know that Susie is dead, the flashback demonstrates Nanny's delusional denial.

With Penelope now seen in close-up—with dead eyes—Nanny's admission of trying to kill Joey because she couldn't have him tell on her is rationalized with "Being a nanny is based on trust." However, since Susie's death was an accident, and Holt doesn't show us Joey having seen Nanny bathing the corpse, her reasoning is faulty.

Now that we can believe Joey is innocent of Susie's death, and that he was telling the truth the whole time, our sympathies change, and Joey becomes the protagonist, with Nanny becoming his antagonist. Holt gives us another extreme close-up of Joey, but this time out of focus. When Joey hits his head on the windowsill as he attempts to run from Nanny, the blow recalls Susie's accident.

When Nanny carries the unconscious Joey to the bathroom, the loudness of the music emphasizes her menace (in a disappointingly obvious manner). When Nanny drops him face down into the water in the bathtub, Holt flashes back to the body of Susie in the same position, which causes Nanny to bring him back out of the water. This change of heart seems to result from the act of trying to drown Joey triggering her memory of the reality of Susie's death. While we don't see any direct retribution for Nanny, Dr. Medman does say that he doesn't know what will happen to her, and that she is "a sick woman." However, the unresolved treatment of Nanny makes it possible for this grande dame, whose photo collection infers a preoccupation with past lives, to move on to other households (though presumably without a satisfactory reference from the Fanes).

Greer Garson, who hadn't made a film since *Sunrise at Campobello* (1960), was originally cast in *The Nanny* but then changed her mind about doing it. 20th Century–Fox, who had just backed *Hush ... Hush, Sweet Charlotte*, suggested Davis, and she traveled to England to make the film at Elstree Studios. Davis was 57 at the time, and had last played a leading role in *Hush ... Hush, Sweet Charlotte*. As Nanny, Davis delivers a relatively restrained performance, using an English accent (though her New England origins make her usual speaking voice sound rather English anyway). Playing a paid employee whose level of

Nanny (Bette Davis) holds a pillow in *The Nanny* (1965).

emotional support is measured in terms of professionalism, Nanny hides her feelings behind smiles and the antiseptic authority of her role. As a reactive character, Davis uses her eyes more than words. The role also feeds off the idea of her as a homemaker in her private life, especially in the 1950s when she worked so little and was raising her daughter, B.D., and her adopted son Michael, while married to Gary Merrill. To this end Holt gives us an image of Davis in a rocking chair in profile, the reverse of Whistler's Mother.

As Nanny, Davis wears the dour attire of a spinster, with black dress and starched white collar, plus hat and gloves for her outside errands. Inside she wears the white apron of a servant. Her eyebrows are unplucked, and her hair is grey and wavy, with a bun on her neck, though she will also wear it in a long plait at night. Davis is lit so that a line runs from the left side of her mouth to her chin, to suggest her age and to show her as a woman who goes without protective make-up. In response to the sight of the doll left by Bobbie in the bathtub, she reacts with guttural moans rather than the expected screams. When Nanny refuses to give Penelope the medication, it recalls Davis in practically the same situation in *The Little Foxes* (1941), where she does nothing to help her dying husband. When Nanny goes to Joey's room, Davis's face in close-up and half in shadow is a standard horror movie image of an antagonist, with Davis's unwavering eyes used to focus her intent. When Nanny sinks to the floor and sobs, Davis's crying is almost a *What Ever Happened to Baby Jane?* cackle in it's extremity, and its touching quality reminds us of why Davis is such a star actress.

Release

October 27, 1965, with the taglines "Nanny wasn't responsible ... was she?" "Another memorable Davis portrait!" "She had been in the family for years. Then, two died mysteriously and two lived in terror!" and "Would you trust the nanny ... or the boy?"

Reviews

"A superior psycho-thriller ... with her usual professional know-how, Miss Davis plays comparatively pianissimo and wouldn't even get a malignant nod from Sweet Charlotte or Baby Jane. And it's all to the good of the film.... Her restrained yet compelling performance makes the whole thing jell."—*Variety*, October 13, 1965.

"With Bette Davis loose as 'The Nanny,' children better run for their little lives."—Howard Thompson, *The New York Times*, November 4, 1965.

"Having mopped up in three earlier blood-letters, moviedom's Ace Bogeywoman Bette Davis goes about her grisliness with quiet unruffled efficiency."—*Time*, October 29, 1965.

"Both script and direction revolve around Davis's performance which, for once, is understated and quietly effective."—Phil Hardy, *The Aurum Film Encyclopedia of Horror.*

"Filled with top notch performances by all involved. This is one of Hammer's most uncharacteristic productions and it also proved to be one of their most profitable."—Gary A. Smith, *Uneasy Dreams: The Golden Age of British Horror Films, 1956–1976.*

Queen of Blood (1966)
(aka *Flight to a Far Planet*; *Planet of Blood*; *Planet of Terror*; *Planet of Vampires*; *Space Vampires*; *The Green Woman*)

Cinema West Productions

CREDITS: *Director/Screenplay:* Curtis Harrington; *Producer:* George Edwards; *Associate Producer:* Stephanie Rothman; *Photography:* Vilis Lapenieks; *Music:* Leonard Morand; *Editor:* Leo Shreve; *Art Direction:* Albert Locatelli; *Set Decoration:* Leon Smith; *Wardrobe:* T. Glinkova; *Make-up:* William Condos; *Hair:* George Spier; *Production Manager:* Gary Kurtz; *Title Background Paintings:* John Cline; *Sound:* Harold Garver; *Sound Effects:* Nelson-Corso; *Special Effects:* Mikhail Karyukov. Color, 81 minutes.

CAST: John Saxon (*Allan Brenner*); Basil Rathbone (*Dr. Farraday*); Judi Meredith (*Laura James*); Dennis Hopper (*Paul Grant*); Florence Marly (*Alien Queen*); Robert Boon (*Anders Brockman*); Don Eitner (*Tony Barrata*); Virgil Frye; Robert Porter; Terry Lee; Forrest Ackerman.

VHS/DVD: Not available in either format.

Plot

In 1990 the International Institute of Space Technology has been investigating the possibility of life on the planets Venus and Mars. When the Astro Communications Unit receives a signal from a planet beyond Earth's solar system, the message is deciphered to mean that an ambassador is being sent to Earth. The aliens send an advance mechanical device that includes a video log of their flight plan, and which shows that they crash landed on Mars. When the signals stop, astronauts travel to the moon station Lunar 7 before boarding the ship Oceania 2 and heading to Mars. The ship lands safely on Mars, but sustained damage from a sunburst during the journey, and its fuel supply is depleted. Paul and Robert look for the marooned alien spaceship but find only one dead man aboard. They conclude that the others have boarded a rescue rocket. A second ship, Meteor, is sent to release a satellite that will locate the alien spaceship, with a rescue ship landing on Mars' moon Fobos. The Meteor astronauts, Tony and Allan, track the alien rocket on Fobos and discover the only inhabitant—a female humanoid. They bring her back to the rescue ship, but since it can only hold two passengers, Tony is left behind on Fobos to survive on emergency rations until Oceania 2 can return and collect him.

The rescue ship crashes in a dust storm, and Alan and the alien get out before the ship explodes. They are found and brought back to Oceania 2, which heads back to Lunar 7. The mute alien is a subject of fascination for the passengers, though, strangely, she refuses the food offered her and refuses to give a blood sample. When she is alone with Paul, she attacks and kills him, feeding on his blood. The other crew find Paul's dead body, then the alien sleeping as she digests the blood. They decide she must be fed the ship's supply of blood plasma in order to save themselves from ending up like Paul, and in order to deliver her alive. When the plasma runs out, the alien kills Robert. We see that she has the ability to hypnotize her victims, so they do not resist her.

With only Allan and Laura left, Allan ties the alien down, but she uses her eyes to burn through the restraints. Laura awakens when the alien begins to attack Allan and rescues him. When, during their struggle, Laura scratches the alien, she screams and runs away. She is found dead, having bled to death because she is a hemophiliac. Laura discovers that the alien has deposited eggs all over the ship, and Allan theorizes that she was the queen of a dying planet sent to Earth to find a new breeding ground. Although Allan wants to destroy the eggs, Laura stops him, since she has faith that they will be kept under control by Dr. Farraday. When the spaceship lands, Farraday is ecstatic about the find, and the eggs are taken. We see them vibrating, perhaps pulsating with blood and excitement about the new breeding ground they are about to enter.

Notes

This effort by Curtis Harrington, who would become the most prolific of the subgenre's directors, provides a grande dame in a supporting role to drive the narrative, much like the grande dame of *I Saw What You Did*. While the tale clearly influenced Ridley Scott's *Alien* (1979), Harrington cannot claim originality, since he himself recycled the plot and special effects footage from the Soviet production *Battle Beyond the Sun* (1960). *Queen of Blood* employs Hitchcockian suspense and a red color motif to present a vampiress, (prefiguring *The Hunger*). While the grande guignol here is limited to bloody wrists, and the horror is implied rather than overt, an interesting soundtrack and the restrained yet elegant directorial choices redeem the film's low-budget constraints.

Harrington had previously made the horror title *Night Tide* (1961), also featuring Dennis Hopper. Producer George Edwards had previously made the science fiction title *Voyage to the Prehistoric Planet* (1965), also directed by Harrington and associate produced by Stephanie Rothman. Rothman had earlier written and directed a horror title, *Blood Bath* (1966), which, oddly enough, incorporated footage from two Yugoslavian horror titles. *Queen of Blood* was the first production made by Cinema West Productions.

The paintings behind the opening credits convey an eerie and evocative alien presence, and recall the same device William Castle used for *Strait-Jacket* and *The Night Walker*. Discordant music, with strings reminiscent of Bernard Herrmann's score for *Psycho*, regal horns, the theremin, and an echo effect, add to the otherworldliness. The opening narration is acceptable for a sci-fi narrative of the future, and while only a viewing of *Battle Beyond the Sun* could determine what footage has been appropriated and what was new, Harrington's ingenuity does not make the differentiation too apparent. The snippets we get of the alien spaceship are dimly lit, obscuring clarity, with a pair of female hands grasping for controls or another alien as victim. This image establishes the female as powerful and potentially dangerous, prefiguring the alien queen and the struggle between her and Laura.

The echo heard during Dr. Farraday's speeches (without obvious benefit of a microphone) are clunky, and the alien video log that features an extreme close-up of the alien queen's eyes just before the crash on Mars is laughable in its assumption of dramatic editing. However, there is more ambiguity in the sight of the queen being fitted with a helmet, since it may also be a crown. At this stage we are unaware of the real agenda of the queen's mission, or even that she is a queen. Therefore, her sporadic appearances exist to tease us.

The Alien Queen (Forence Marly) intrigues astronaut Paul Grant (Dennis Hopper) in this lobby card for *Queen of Blood* (1966).

The main plot of the film is the romantic relationship between Allan and Laura, separated in space by differing missions. This scenario lacks the horror resonance of the alien situation, and the performances don't supply enough empathy for us to be too concerned about their fate.

Harrington occasionally uses zooms for emphasis, a post-modern technique that stands out in a film that is otherwise presented rather conventionally in terms of filmmaking. He also repeats a reaction shot of Laura (to the idea of Paul and Robert going in search of Allan and the alien) *three* times. The interior of the Oceania 2 features a repeated humming (which is either meant to be the sound of machinery or music) to add atmosphere. After the sunburst disturbance, Paul delivers a line that stands as one of two rare witticisms in the screenplay: "I've got a whole symphony in my ears, and it isn't Brahms."

The other is a comment of Dr. Farraday's, made when Alan and Tony insist on going in the Meteor (with a chance they will not be able to make it back): "You're either fools, or very brave men."

The red light of Mars fits in with the red color motif of the film. Other reds include a dust storm, the throbbing light of the room in which the queen is kept on the Oceania 2, the eggs, the queen's leotard, lipstick and bloodshot eyes, and, of course, blood. The discovery of the queen on the rocket ship is presented when the astronauts activate a light sensor that casts her shadow. She is then seen in long shot, again in shadow, framed in a doorway, her pose an indication of her gender. These portentous images combine sexuality and vulnerability with her monstrousness, so that she is both antagonist and protagonist—like other grande dames in Grande Dame Guignol.

The absence of Tony, off collecting soil samples, serves as a narrative red herring and padding, although it does offer a payoff when we are led to believe that he is to die by volunteering his seat on the rescue ship for the queen. However, the scene in which the queen meets the crew of the Oceania 2 more than compensates, particularly in the pan Harrington provides: Her seductive smile as she looks at each man in turn vanishes when she finally sees Laura. The antagonism between the queen, as an older woman, and Laura recalls similar antagonisms in *Strait-Jacket*, *Die! Die! My Darling!*, *The Night Walker*, and *I Saw What You Did*. The queen's refusal to eat prefigures her hunger for blood, as her refusal to give a blood sample prefigures her death (with Robert theorizing that she must have a "low pain threshold").

The queen's attack on Paul is portrayed via suggestion, with one hand on his back, her eyes turn white, and our view of the queen makes it appear as if she's kissing him. The way her other hand moves up his chest, as if it is a fin, adds an element of creepiness and confirms her being less human than her apparent lover. The blood we see on his wrist is matched by the blood on her mouth, with a smear off her lips adding a touch of barbarism. Robert gives a speech to defend her behavior, which sounds both reasonable and naive:

How can you expect her to conform to our ideas of proper behavior? She's not necessarily aware that she's done wrong. Wrong, from our point of view, that is.

Amusingly, Robert becomes her next victim.

The idea that her race is technologically but not morally advanced, since they feed as vampires, is an interesting one. The queen's disinterest in attacking Laura may also have a rationale in that she needs someone to get her back to Earth, and it may be that her Amazonian world values women more than men, which the images from the alien spaceship implied. The queen's attack on Robert shows her advancing on him, recalling Norma Desmond's advance toward the camera at the end of *Sunset Boulevard*. However, Harrington cross-cuts to Robert's reaction in order to give a staccato impression of the queen's movement. He also uses extreme close-ups of her mouth and eyes, which work to make her both a femme fatale and a monster.

The queen's attack on Allan begins with her shadow passing the sleeping Laura, although Laura seemingly has the intuition to awaken and save Allan. Harrington uses a Hitchcockian suspense device when Laura looks for the queen by alternating points of view of her looking with what she sees. This scene also serves to make Laura Woman in Peril, responding to something and investigating. Strange sound effects are heard—the sound of the queen feeding from Allan's wrist, and a close-up of the queen with bloodied teeth, is pure vampire cinema. Lighting also makes the queen's normally red leotard look flesh-like, as if she is naked. Interestingly, we don't see Laura's struggle with the alien, only the resultant blood of the queen. Her scream is,

The Alien Queen (Florence Marly) attacks Allan Brenner (John Saxon) in *Queen of Blood* (1966).

of course, the only sound we hear her make, and, as such, it is effectively disturbing. Allan's theory that she died because she was a hemophiliac—perhaps confirming her royalty—recalls the hemophilia of Alexei Romanov. The throbbing of the eggs seen at the end, which Harrington repeats as the film's final shot, is both sexual and squirm-inducing.

Florence Marly, as the alien queen, was 46 at the time of filming. She had last played a leading role in the Japanese crime drama *Tokyo File 22* (1951), and had played opposite Humphrey Bogart in the American thriller *Tokyo Joe* (1949). That Marly gets above-the-title credit for her supporting role is only natural, since she plays the title character. Although she has no lines as the alien, her muteness conveys the queen's exoticism and menace perhaps better than if she had spoken. The kinkiness of her skintight red costume receives a boost by the greenness of her skin color and the white bouffant she wears as a hairstyle. Harrington exposes the lines under Marly's eyes and gives her one soft-focus close-up (when Robert assumes that her green skin is due to a high chloroform content).

Release

March 2, 1966, with the tagline "Hideous beyond belief with an Inhuman Craving."

Reviews

"Eerie space opera.... Best thing is the bizarre climax, if you can wait that long."—Leonard Maltin, *2009 Movie Guide*.

"To make up for a small budget Harrington utilizes color to good advantage and emphasizes character rather than effect."—John Stanley, *Creature Features*.

"The stock footage looks great. Early scenes are a little dramatically hesitant, but once it settles down into horror mode, [it] gains impetus. Harrington constantly aims for an atmosphere of otherworldly weirdness. He is considerably aided by the spookily unearthly presence of Marly."—Richard Scheib, *The Science Fiction, Horror and Fantasy Movie Review*.

The Witches (1966)

(aka *The Devil's Own*)

20th Century–Fox/A Seven Arts–Hammer Film production

CREDITS: *Director:* Cyril Frankel; *Producer:* Anthony Nelson Keys; *Screenplay:* Nigel Kneale, based on the novel *The Devil's Own* by Peter Curtis; *Photography:* Arthur Grant; *Music:* Richard Rodney Bennett; *Production Design:* Bernard Robinson; *Choreography:* Denys Palmer; *Production Manager:* Charles Permane; *Editor:* Chris Barnes; *Art Director:* Don Mingaye; *Sound:* Ken Rawkins; *Make-up:* George Partleton*: Hair:* Freida Steiger; *Wardrobe:* Harry Haynes. Color, 90 minutes. Filmed at Bray Studios, with exteriors at Hambledon, England.

CAST: Joan Fontaine (*Gwen Mayfield*); Kay Walsh (*Stephanie Bax*); Alec McGowen (*Alan Bax*); Duncan Lamont (*Bob Curd*); Gwen Ffrangcon-Davies (*Granny Rigg*); John Collin (*Dowsett*); Ingrid Brett (*Linda Rigg*); Leonard Rossiter (*Dr. Wallis*); Michelle Dotrice (*Valerie Creek*); Carmel McSharry (*Mrs. Dowsett*); Martin Stephens (*Ronnie Dowsett*); Ann Bell (*Sally Benson*); Viola Keats (*Mrs. Curd*); Shelagh Fraser (*Mrs. Creek*); Bryan Marshall (*Tom*). Uncredited: Yemi Ajibade (*Mark*); Kitty Atwood (*Mrs. McDowall*); John Barrett (*Mr. Glass*); Roy Desmond (*Dancer*); Catherine Finn (*Nurse*); Prudence Hyman (*Stephanie's Maid*); Lizbeth Kent (*First Villager*); Artro Morris (*Porter*); Willie Payne (*Adam*); Charles Rea (*Police Sergeant*); Ken Robson (*Dancer*); Brian Todd (*Dancer*); Don Vernon (*Dancer*); Rudolph Walker (*Mark*); Terry Williams (*Dancer*).

VHS/DVD: DVD: Starz/Anchor Bay, released July 25, 2000.

Plot

While teaching at a mission school in central Africa, Gwen Mayfield is subjected to a traumatic encounter with a voodoo witch doctor and suffers a nervous breakdown. Seemingly recovered, she returns to England and is hired by Alan Bax to be the new headmistress of the Heddaby village private school. It soon becomes apparent that Heddaby is an odd place where inbreeding has dulled the intellect of the residents. Alan and his journalist sister Stephanie are the exceptions. Gwen notices that the villagers frown upon the budding relationship between two of her students, 14-year-old Linda Rigg and Ronnie Dowsett, and can't understand why. When Ronnie is taken ill, Gwen believes that a voodoo doll she has found is responsible. Going to visit Ronnie, she meets Ronnie's mother, who has Gwen drop her off at the home of Granny Rigg. When Ronnie's father tells Gwen that Ronnie and Ronnie's mother have left town, Gwen tells him that she thinks his wife and Granny came to some arrangement. Angry, Ronnie's father goes to confront Granny, but is discovered drowned the next day.

When Gwen goes to the local pond where the dead man had been found, she sees bare footprints in the mud. However, a herd of sheep attacks her and destroys the evidence. Gwen tells Stephanie that she suspects the village houses a witches coven, and that she intends to tell what she knows at the inquest the following day. That night, the same witch doctor mask that terrified her in Africa appears in her room, and she collapses. Waking up at a nursing home, Gwen has lost her memory, and it is only the sight of a doll brought by another patient's visitor that brings it back. She runs away before she is moved to another home, and is picked up by the village's butcher. Brought to Stephanie's house, Gwen soon realizes that she is Stephanie's prisoner. Stephanie confides in Gwen that she is the head of the coven, and plans to sacrifice Linda as a virgin in order to immortalize herself. Forcibly initiated into the coven, Gwen witnesses the preparatory ritual by the coven members. When Linda is summoned, Gwen urges someone to stop the killing, but everyone else is in a trance. Just as Stephanie is about to stab Linda, Gwen cuts herself with a knife and spills it on Stephanie, recalling Stephanie's warning that "If blood is spilled the power turns against the seeker and destroys him." Stephanie dies, and the villagers trances are broken. Afterwards we see that Alan has connected his beloved organ music to the school's loud speakers, with the approval of Gwen, who has decided to remain as headmistress of the school.

Notes

A mostly well-directed Grande Dame Guignol with two grande dames, this film features a classic animal attack sequence but climaxes in a seven-minute witches coven ritual that goes over the top. Starring Joan Fontaine as a traumatized Woman in Peril, the narrative places a stranger in an even stranger town, and delays the blood spillage until the end. Cyril Frankel had had an undistinguished career as a British director, and had previously worked on the television series *Gideon's Way* and *The Baron*. Producer Anthony Nelson had made the B-drama *Never Take Sweets from a Stranger* (1960) with Frankel, and many horror titles for Hammer Films, including *Horror of Dracula* (1958), *The Mummy* (1959), *The Stranglers of Bombay* (1960), *The Terror of the Tongs* (1961), *The Gorgon* (1964), *The Reptile* (1966), and *Rasputin the Mad Monk* (1966).

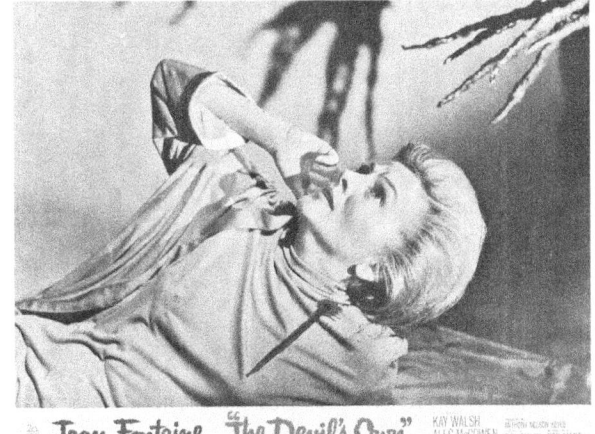

Gwen Mayfield (Joan Fontaine) is attacked by an African witchdoctor in this lobby card scene from *The Witches* (1966); aka *The Devils Own*.

The opening shot of *The Witches* shows a voodoo doll placed in front of a seemingly idyllic and isolated landscape. To the sound of drumbeats, colored feathers and the giant tribal mask of a witchdoctor appear (to be seen later in the film). The pre-credit sequence acts as a prologue that recalls those of Robert Aldrich and William Castle, designed to present the trauma that the grande dame must endure and overcome. Here Gwen is established as the narrative's protagonist, with the red smoke under the credits suggesting that her troubles are not over. Her nervousness during the job interview should give Alan pause about her "full recovery," but since he is a man who failed the entrance examination for priesthood but still likes to wear the collar, he is no person to cast the first stone.

Gwen's attraction to a cat suggests she is a spinster, and the narrative uses her love for her students as a substitute for a romantic interest. The organ music that Alan likes provides a gothic touch, with him being a failed priest adding to his strangeness. The church being "damaged" and having not been repaired hints at the villagers' Satanism, as does the observation that the children are inbred. A rabbit skinned by the butcher, Bob Curd, and the hand of Linda placed (off-screen) in a washing mangle are initial gruesome touches before the climactic grande guignol. Gwen being the only adult that supports the love between Linda and Ronnie indicates both her romanticism, and her status as an Other. The idea that the cat is stalking Gwen seems ridiculous, but it garners a payoff at the climax when she releases it from its entrapment in the doll sack.

Witchcraft is described by Stephanie as an activity taken up by older women as a sex substitute, a "secret power when normal powers are failing." Stephanie's seeming alliance with Gwen is a refreshing narrative touch, given how she is later revealed to be an antagonist. The fortuitous removal of the footprints from the mud when Gwen is attacked by the herd of sheep, and Stephanie's proximity afterwards, suggest that Stephanie set them off. This scene is perhaps the most effective in the film, even though sheep may not appear to be the most aggressive or dangerous of animals; the sight of a star of the caliber of Joan Fontaine falling into the mud generates quite a shock.

As to how Stephanie managed to obtain the same giant mask from the opening scene in Africa in order to give Gwen a relapse is perhaps a plot contrivance, but the narrative jump to presumably months into the future is a pleasing one.

Alan Bax (Alec McGowan) receives a mysterious package from Granny Rigg (Gwen Ffrangcon Davies) as Gwen Mayfield (Joan Fontaine) looks on in this lobby card for *The Witches* (1966).

Frankel begins Gwen's stay in the "nursing home" with an out-of-focus shot of a swinging light, reminiscent of the swinging bulb in *Psycho*. Gwen's room having bars on the window recalls *What Ever Happened To Baby Jane?* In a film of relatively subtle horror convention effects, Frankel uses repeated zooms in the scene where the sight of the doll returns Gwen's lost memory, and a close-up of Fontaine's face in profile as she slowly opens a door. The appearance of Dr. Wallis becomes that of a suspicious menace rather than a caring physician, since the film has made us empathize with Gwen from the beginning. Frankel utilizes an Hitchcockian suspense device by allowing the audience to see Gwen regain her memory before the other characters become aware of it.

Gwen's escape from the nursing home turns comical when the driver of the truck she hitches a ride with fails to notice her crouching down to avoid being spotted as they leave the grounds. Frankel uses obvious rear-projection for the scene in which Gwen is picked up on the road by Bob Curd, which makes it seem like a re-shoot. When Gwen returns to Heddaby, Stephanie's confiding of her identity and intention to Gwen is rationalized because Gwen is considered her intellectual equal. This attitude makes Stephanie a narrative antagonist but still remarkably likeable, even if her ambitions are considered "insane." Stephanie's killing of Linda is to make Stephanie young again, so that she can live "a second lifetime." A 14th century book by Dr. Johann Wordsworth is to be used as a Latin incantation to "release the power," and an ancient Mexican blade will be the sacrificial knife. The naive assumption that Gwen will not reveal Stephanie's murder is made even before she is forced to become one of the coven, although her initial imprisonment recalls other prisoners in *What Ever Happened to Baby Jane?*, *Lady in a Cage*, and *Die! Die! My Darling!* Stephanie wanting Gwen to witness the murder can be viewed as providing her the opportunity to stop it. Even though Gwen has expressed her disapproval to Stephanie, Stephanie's perceived alliance with Gwen is further evidence of her isolation. The sight of the cat squirming in the doll sack, with a photograph of Linda on its face, is also a symbol of Gwen and the hypnotized Linda.

Stephanie in pagan attire and red dress, and wearing a horned headpiece with candle-holders, stands in contrast to the white sheath worn by Gwen. Gwen's head is pushed down for her initiation in extreme supplication, a reminder of who is in control. The coven's meeting scene, in which the witches pour lemon juice over themselves, eat worms, dance and have an orgy, is naturally laughable until it is time for Linda to be killed. Gwen repeats Stephanie's warning that "If blood is spilled the

Bottom: Gwen Mayfield (Joan Fontaine) sees the dagger that Stephanie Bax (Kay Walsh) will bring into play in *The Witches* (1966).

power turns against the seeker and destroys him," as she cuts herself. That no one stops Gwen can be rationalized by the general trance and Stephanie's focus on Linda. Gwen uses Stephanie's own evil to kill her; and the antagonistic grande dame is defeated by the protagonistic grande dame, leaving only one grande dame in the village.

Joan Fontaine had not played a leading role in a film since *A Certain Smile* (1958), though she had played supporting parts in *Voyage to the Bottom of the Sea* (1961) and *Tender Is the Night* (1962). *The Witches* would be her last film role. Having found the novel *The Devil's Own*, she purchased the film rights and brought it to Hammer Film Productions as a starring vehicle. Although she does not receive screen credit as such, Fontaine is said to be the film's co-producer, something which her autobiography does not make apparent. Fontaine provides a warmth and sensitivity to Gwen, and also plays well off the 54-year-old Kay Walsh's witty and robust Stephanie. As in the two films she made for Alfred Hitchcock — *Rebecca* (1940) and *Suspicion* (1941), for which she won the Best Actress Academy Award — her Gwen demonstrates that she has the intelligence to be aware of danger and the courage to defend herself.

At 49 years of age, Fontaine wears her strawberry-blonde hair in a short bouffant style, combed off her forehead, although she will use a headband, and it will be flattened when she is in bed and in distress. The dark roots of her hair are apparent, her eyebrows are black, and while she is occasionally lit with a shadow on her neck, her make-up gives her face a definite paleness. The husky lower register of her voice suggests a sophistication and sensuality that the whispering virginal upper register does not, and she uses an English accent. Gwen's initiation scene, with Fontaine on her knees and head bowed, casts her in a pose just as undignified as her falling into the mud during the sheep attack.

Release

February 1967, with the taglines "What do The Devil's Own do after dark?" and "A stranger in town that has lost its mind.... If she's not careful, she may lose hers too!"

Reviews

"Miss Fontaine performs sensibly, her eyebrows never arched higher and for jolly good reason ... *The Devil's Own* is devilishly good, whether or not you believe in witchcraft."— Howard Thompson, *The New York Times*, March 19, 1967.

"...[S]ome unintentional yocks creep into the situation not designed for them.... An amiable, if somewhat tepid drama.... Miss Fontaine looks delightful and brings a sensitive air to her thesping, but there's not enough fiber in her role to give her full scope."— *Variety*, November 22, 1966.

"The first three quarters are very engrossing. The final quarter deteriorates somewhat when the sacrificial ritual begins to resemble a jazz dance class filled with particularly untalented students."— Gary A. Smith, *Uneasy Dreams: The Golden Age of British Horror Films, 1956–1976*.

"[A] conventional, less resonant treatment of the witchcraft motif, with a script that trades on the usual racist and sexist stereotypes.... Walsh gives a powerful performance."— Phil Hardy, *The Aurum Film Encyclopedia of Horror*.

Games (1967)

Universal

CREDITS: *Director:* Curtis Harrington; *Producer:* George Edwards; *Associate Producer:* John W. Hyde; *Screenplay:* Gene Kearney, based on a story by Curtis Harrington and George Edwards; *Photography:* William A. Fraker; *Music:* Samuel Matlovsky; *Art Director:* Alexander Golitzen, William D. DeCinces; *Set Decorator:* John McCarthy, James H. Biggs; *Sound:* Waldon O. Watson, Robert R. Bertrand; *Production Manager/Assistant Director:* Hal W. Polaire; *Editor:* Douglas Stewart; *Makeup:* Bud Westmore; *Hair:* Larry Germain; *Visual Consultant/Costume Design:* Morton Haack. Color, 100 minutes.

CAST: Simone Signoret (*Lisa Schindler*); James Caan (*Paul Montgomery*); Katharine Ross (*Jennifer Montgomery*); Don Stroud (*Norman*); Kent Smith (*Harry Gordon*); Estelle Winwood (*Miss Beattie*); Marjorie Bennett (*Nora*); Ian Wolfe (*Dr. Edwards*); Antony Eustrel (*Winthrop*); Eloise Hardt (*Celia*); George Furth (*Terry*); Peter Brocco (*Count*); William O'Connell (*Party Guest*); Ena Hartman (*Party Guest*); Joanne Medley (*Party Guest*); Jeff Scott (*Party Guest*); Carmen Phillips (*Holly*); Edra Gale (*Party Guest*); Rachel Rosenthal (*Party Guest*); Luana Anders (*Party Guest*); Robert Aiken (*Party Guest*); Max Lewin (*Party Guest*); Florence Marly (*Baroness*); Carl Guttenberger (*Arthur*); Pitt Herbert (*Pharmacist*); Stuart Nisbet (*Detective*); Kendrick Huxham (*Bookseller*); Richard Guizon (*Masseur*).

VHS/DVD: Not available on DVD. VHS: Good Times Home Video, released May 10, 1995.

Plot

Manhattan socialites Paul and Jennifer Montgomery own a vast art collection and entertain their friends with novel parlor games. One day a cosmetics saleswoman, Lisa Schindler, arrives at their apartment, pretending that she knows a friend of Jennifer's. When Lisa's lie is exposed, she collapses, and the Montgomerys agree to let her stay with them until she recovers. When Paul and Jennifer introduce Lisa to their games, Lisa ups the stakes by giving them a pair of guns. When the guns are used in a game with delivery boy Norman, things go wrong and it appears that he is killed. Paul and Jennifer try to hide the murder, fearful that Lisa will report them or, worse, blackmail them. Paul encases the body in plaster so that it appears as an art object, but Lisa, who is also a medium, has the sense of a disturbed spirit.

When Lisa uses a crystal ball to summon up the spirits, Jennifer has a vision of

Norman with one eye bloodied from the bullet. Paul accuses Lisa of upsetting Jennifer unnecessarily and orders her to leave—the same day the plaster sculpture is shipped off. Alone, Jennifer has another vision of Norman, who pursues her; she shoots him. When Paul returns, he calls the police to report the murder, and the mute Jennifer is taken away. After selling the collection, Paul celebrates with Lisa, who has been his business partner in robbing Jennifer. As they drink champagne together, Paul realizes too late that Lisa has poisoned him. With Paul dead, Lisa takes all the profits and moves on to her next victim.

Notes

A colorful if studied horror film, this is the second Grande Dame Guignol from director Curtis Harrington. Although Harrington may overuse horror movie conventions, the narrative—in which pretence turns to murderous imperatives, and an older scheming grande dame is pitted against a younger Woman in Peril—redeems him. Harrington had previously directed *Queen of Blood*, with *Games* being his first big-budget studio film. Producer George Edwards had produced the horror title *The Navy vs. the Night Monsters* (1966) prior to *Queen of Blood* for Harrington. *Games* was the first film made by assistant producer John W. Hyde.

Games opens with the child-like sound of a music box, and Tarot cards and colored dots under the credits. A red dot explodes on the eye of a white skeleton that appears next to Curtis Harrington's name, and we shall see how a bleeding eye will feature in the narrative. The New York apartment of the Montgomerys introduces Paul and Jennifer as wealthy, with pop-art paintings, a fun-house mirror in the hallway, and a gargoyle on the newel post of their stairs. The demonstration of the "life-giving power of galvanic electricity" at the party shows the indolent rich's penchant for game playing, and conjures up images of the electric "creation" scene from *Frankenstein* (1931), another Universal picture.

The soft focus photography on Marjorie Bennett as the Montgomerys' maid foreshadows that used on older actress Simone Signoret as Lisa. The Montgomerys' party also features the "Turnpike" pinball machine, which employs the sound of a driving car, and scores points for "Serious Injuries," "Fatalities," "Pedestrians," and "Innocent Bystanders." A win is indicated by the sound of a woman's scream, a message of "You're Dead, Man!" and the image of a skeleton's head in a red glow. This image is superimposed over Jennifer's face as she deconstructs her look by removing false eyelashes and a wig. Although the skeleton image can be seen as foreshadowing her demise, it also creates a false expectation, which is something Harrington will do often. The party guests are also used to juxtapose the older with the younger, in the same way Harrington will use Ross to parallel Signoret.

Paul's kissing Jennifer as she wears his false mustache suggests a sexual kinkiness and depravity that will be borne out in his scheme to rob her of her money, while the photographic clutter on their bedside table indicates Jennifer's possibly unhealthy attachment to the past. Lisa's appearance coincides, somewhat obviously, with Jennifer pricking her finger on a rose thorn, although no explanation is given for why Lisa's German character has a French accent (apart from the fact that Signoret is German but was raised in France).

With the duplicitous Lisa standing before a double mirror, Harrington places Jennifer in between the two images of Signoret in a visual comment on the age disparity between the two women. Signoret's jowly neck is exposed next to Ross's lineless 27-year-old youthfulness; and Lisa being revealed as a liar who has gained entry to another home to sell her goods should warn Jennifer about her mercenary nature. Lisa's breathlessness and collapse will be diagnosed as "heat frustration," which may be a polite way of blaming her matronly weight (we will later learn that she needed to become a houseguest to carry out her and Paul's nefarious plan). Lisa's weight, the way she slurps wine, her taking excessive sugar for her tea, and her smoking are all used as characterization. Without any romance, the grande dame is reduced to being a horror movie antagonist, though Lisa's deadliness is underrated by Paul. Lisa as the older grande dame is also presented

Poster for *Games* (1967).

as a dangerous threat to the younger female in a scenario familiar from *Strait-Jacket*, *I Saw What You Did*, *Berserk*, *Lady in a Cage*, *Die! Die! My Darling!*, *The Night Walker*, and *The Witches*.

Harrington employs the horror movie convention of thunder and lightning during the arrival of Lisa's trunk, and the ominous perspective showing Lisa and Jennifer from outside a window as it rains is repeated for a shot of Lisa holding a gun. The feather boa that Lisa gives Jennifer is something associated with drag queens and gender play, as well as being a phallic symbol. Lisa wearing Paul's robe is both a sign of their unrevealed alliance and another gender-swapping touch. Lisa makes the observation that the Montgomerys' juvenile penny arcade and game room involve lower stakes than what interests her—particularly after her husband has been killed playing a game of Russian roulette with her. The music is heavy-handed, but Harrington provides an out-of-frame gunshot to intimate that Lisa has killed herself, and uses a similar high-backed cane chair to that seen in *Hush ... Hush, Sweet Charlotte* and *Die! Die! My Darling!* The gameplaying challenge is met by Paul and Jennifer when they make Lisa think he has slapped Jennifer, and Lisa and Jennifer fool Paul with the idea that she is having an affair with Norman. Organ music, masks, smoke and candles are used when they enact a gothic attempt to stab Jennifer with a blade, fortuitously interrupted by Jennifer's lawyer, Harry, who delivers the amusing line, "I'm sorry to intrude on such conventional affairs." Interestingly, while the masks of Jennifer and Lisa are pretty, Paul's is grotesque.

Paul aiming a gun at Norman through a window begins the scene that will set the scheme against Jennifer in motion. Norman's whistling of the song "London Bridge" is used to identify his presence, and will later be used to trick Jennifer (as well as being utilized by Paul as a sardonic perception of victory). Jennifer's youthful sexual desirability is employed to "tease" Norman into a trap that supposedly goes wrong when Lisa's guns are mixed up and blanks are replaced with real bullets. Paul "accidentally" shooting Norman in the eye reminds us of the red dot on the skeleton's face in the opening credits (as well as Caan being blinded in *Lady in a Cage*).

The blood from the eye is prime grande guignol, as is Norman's blood splattering on Paul's hands and forehead. The dripping blood from the sheet that enfolds Norman's body is a stock horror convention, and Paul's line that if Lisa found out "She'd bleed us dry" is both obvious and prophetic. Paul supposedly encasing Norman's body in plaster offers up more grande guignol, but a close-up of blood-tinged water from the sheet in a washing machine lacks the same ghoulish resonance. Harrington gives Ross an extended grainy close-up, perhaps to absorb the horror of Norman as an art piece, then raises the possibility of Norman still being alive in a scene in which groceries are delivered but the face of the delivery man remains obscured by the grocery bag.

Harrington uses a catalogue of horror conventions for the Woman in Peril set pieces: a closing door, Jennifer opening a door and light falling on her, blood spots on the bathroom floor, Jennifer investigating a sound, a clock ticking and chiming, a dripping tap, the cat knocking over a flowerpot, wind chimes, the lowering of the servants elevator, and a barking dog. The cat smelling the feet of the stature is a red herring, and the ringing telephone is also used to establish alibis for both Paul and Lisa. Lisa in shadow and holding the crystal ball we have seen her purchase presents her as a monster "feeling an uneasy spirit," with the statue again used as a red herring. When Jennifer knocks the ball from

Jennifer Montgomery (Katherine Ross) and Paul Montgomery (James Caan) are surprised to see that their house guest, Lisa Schindler (Simone Signoret), has a gun in *Games* (1967).

Lisa's hands, it rolls toward a boot, revealing Norman alive with a bleeding eye. Since Jennifer is the only witness to this image, the assumption is made that it is a vision (though later it will be revealed to have been the real Norman). Harrington employs the slow turning of a door knob as another horror convention, and the shipping of the statue in a wooden cage recalls Olivia deHavilland in *Lady in a Cage*.

Jennifer equates the statue with her vision of Norman, so its removal gives the expectation of the threat removed, though Lisa's leaving seems a far greater removal of threat. However, Jennifer being watched by an unknown person from an upstairs window tells us that she is not as alone as she thought. Harrington uses wind chimes, a ringing telephone, and an image of Ross behind patterned glass to show something is still wrong. Again he piles on the conventions: the Universal horror movie *Dracula* (1931) on television, a blackout, lit candles, footsteps, blood drops, the "London Bridge" whistling, and a hand on an opening door. When Jennifer is in the stalled servant's elevator, she becomes another *Lady in a Cage* (but at least the telephone is unplugged rather than the wire having been cut).

The blood stains on Norman's body offer more grande guignol, and it is Jennifer's presumed insanity which stops her from commenting on Paul's removing the fake bleeding eye from Norman's corpse or calling the police on him (behavior similar to Joseph Cotten deconstructing for the deranged Bette Davis in *Hush ... Hush, Sweet Charlotte*). Paul only incriminates himself when he is safe from retribution, with Jennifer's incapacity making him her guardian and benefactor. The wind chimes are used again for Lisa's return, and the music of her running her finger around a champagne glass when Paul is poisoned by her is perhaps the most effective of all the film's sound effects. The circus-type music that accompanies Lisa's exit signifies the triumph of the evil grande dame, who is also revealed to be a serial killer when she takes a postcard from the apartment to find her next victims, as The Tarot card of "Justice" shown under the end credits adds a touch of irony.

The soft focus close-ups used for Signoret, at 45 years old, stand as counterpoint to the way Estelle Winwood (as an eccentric, cat-owning spinster with ribbons in her hair) is photographed without any effort to conceal her age. However, Signoret's clumsy way of collapsing, and her obvious acting, do make one regret such a casting choice. Harrington had devised the film as a starring vehicle for Marlene Dietrich, who hadn't made a movie since *Judgment at Nuremburg* (1961), but the studios thought her no longer able to draw audiences. Dietrich may have supplied a hint of sexual desirability and sexual interest between Lisa and Paul, which Signoret does not, thereby giving the grande dame a love interest.

Signoret had attained international film

Lisa Schindler (Simone Signoret), a grande dame doubly dangerous with a gun, in *Games* (1967).

stardom by winning the Best Actress Academy Award for *Room at the Top* (1959), but was also known as the conniving mistress of *Les Diaboliques* (1955). After her Oscar win, she had played a supporting part in *Ship of Fools* (1965), worked in France and England, and had last played a leading role in *The Deadly Affair* (1966). Since Signoret is an actress, the idea of Lisa as a former actress passes muster. While it would have been easier to believe that Dietrich and not Signoret would have a possessive husband, Signoret provides an amusing spin on how her guns are "old but valuable." Lisa's feather boa would also have had a more resonant association with Dietrich, based on the use of same in the latter's Hollywood films. Even though Dietrich is a stylized performer, it is doubtful that she would have stooped to the flashing eyes that Signoret employs for reading tarot cards or summoning Norman's spirit. However, for Lisa's return to toast the success of the scheme, an effort is made to give Signoret a more glamorous look, complete with white fur.

Release

September 17, 1967, with the taglines "Where the Normal is Not and the Bizarre Is," "Passion wears a mask of terror in this strangest of all games!" and "Playing Games Can Be Dangerous!"

Reviews

"Old Pro Signoret walks handsomely through her part. Youngsters James Caan and Katharine Ross walk woodenly through theirs.... About the only fun in *Games* is the eye-beguiling set and what must be the most blood-drenched elevator between Fifth and Madison."—*Time*, September 22, 1967.

"Harrington is not a particularly original director but he is exuberant, delighting in all the old tricks of the mystery film genre.... [A] strong, enigmatically humoress performance from Simone Signoret who gives authority to the eerie make-believe."—Bosley Crowther, *The New York Times*, September 18, 1967.

" ...[A] low-key suspenser with more appeal to the intellect than to the emotions.... Miss Signoret caroms between a former lady of great elegance to a sleazy hausfrau.... Three stars are competent."—*Variety*, September 13 1967.

"Harrington directs the hash of horror standbys with a good deal of verve and flair, but it disappoints after the subtle ambiguities of the first half."—Phil Hardy, *The Aurum Film Encyclopedia of Horror*.

Berserk! (1968)

(aka *Circus of Terror*; *Circus of Blood*)

Columbia Pictures Corporation

CREDITS: *Director:* Jim O'Connolly; *Producer:* Herman Cohen; *Associate Producer:* Robert Sterne; *Screenplay:* Aben Kandel, Herman Cohen; *Photography:* Desmond Dickinson; *Music:* Patrick John Scott; *Editor:* Raymond Poulton; *Art Director:* Maurice Pelling; *Production Manager:* Laurie Greenwood; *Wardrobe:* Jay Hutchinson Scott; *Hair:* Pearl Tifaldi; *Make-up:* George Partleton; *Set Dresser:* Helen Thomas; *Sound:* Mike Le Mare. Color, 96 minutes. Filmed at Shepperton Studios in England, and on location at the Billy Smart Circus.

SONG: "It Might Be Me" (Patrick John Scott). Sung by Circus ensemble.

CAST: Joan Crawford (*Monica Rivers*); Ty Hardin (*Frank Hawkins*); Diana Dors (*Matilda*); Michael Gough (*Dorando*); Judy Geeson (*Angela Rivers*); Robert Hardy (*Superintendent Brooks*); Geoffrey Keen (*Commissioner Dalby*); Sydney Tafler (*Harrison Liston*); George Claydon (*Bruno*); Philip Madoc (*Lazlo*); Ambrosine Phillpotts (*Miss Burrows*); Peter Burton (*Gustavo*); Thomas Cimarro (*Gaspar*); Golda Casimir (*Romy, The Bearded Lady*); Ted Lune (*Skeleton Man*); Milton Reid (*Strong Man*); Mariane Stone (*Wanda*); Miki Iveria (*Gypsy Fortune Teller*); Howard Goorney (*Emil*); Reginald Marsh (*Sgt. Hutchins*); Bryan Pringle (*Constable Bradford*); Uncredited: Robert Rowland (*Big Top Ticket Holder*).

VHS/DVD: Not available on DVD. VHS: Sony Pictures, released June 21, 1994.

Plot

At a performance of the Great Rivers Circus, tightrope walker Gaspar's high-wire is tampered with, and he is strangled. This murder is the first in a series of killings that plague the circus, which travels to England. The owner and ringmaster, Monica Rivers, is delighted at the increase in box office the tragedy has incurred, but her business partner, Dorando, is not and wants to leave. When Frank Hawkins appears to apply for Gaspar's job, he is hired; he also begins a romance with Monica. When Dorando is killed, Scotland Yard sends Superintendent Brooks to investigate the cases, just as Monica's daughter, Angela, returns to the circus after having been expelled from her private school. Matilda, the wife of Lazlo the Illusionist, suspects Monica of being the killer and warns Frank against her while at the same time trying to seduce him. Frank rejects Matilda's advances; and then she is killed when the safety device on Lazlo's sawing act malfunctions.

Frank asks Monica to accept him as her new business partner, and she agrees, although Angela thinks Monica is too old for Frank. When the circus comes to London, there is a party where Angela becomes upset when she hears about Monica's plans to go away with Frank. During the next performance, Angela appears in Gustavo's knife-throwing act, then throws a knife into Frank's back, during *his* act. He falls to his death onto a bed of spikes, and Angela attempts to stab Monica, blaming her for the death of her father, who had been killed in the circus. Stopped by Brooks, Angela escapes and is struck by lightning outside the big top.

Notes

Joan Crawford's fourth Grande Dame Guignol is a circus film in which grande guignol murders are enacted by a serial killer. While director Jim O'Connolly includes footage of animal acts that feel like filler, and the narrative slows down for the inevitable police procedural, the picture does feature the older grande dame pitted against two younger women. O'Connolly had written the screenplay for the horror movie *The Night Caller* (1965), and had previously directed crime titles.

Herman Cohen had produced and written the horror titles *I Was a Teenage Werewolf* (1957*)*, *I Was a Teenage Frankenstein* (1957), *Blood of Dracula* (1957), *How to Make a Monster* (1958), *Horrors of the Black Museum* (1959), *The Headless Ghost* (1959), *Konga* (1961), and *Black Zoo* (1963). He was a contemporary of Roger Corman and William Castle as a horror movie visionary, and his taste catered to the bloodlust and baser impulses of audiences. Although he is not as well-remembered today as Corman and Castle, Cohen led the way for the slasher films of the 1980s, and had the business sense to change the title of his film from *Circus of Blood* to *Berserk*—so that it piggybacked onto the still-lingering *Psycho* craze. Associate producer Robert Sterne had previously made the horror titles *The Black Torment* (1964) and *Repulsion* (1965).

Angela Rivers (Judy Geeson), Frank Hawkins (Ty Hardin), Monica Rivers (Joan Crawford), and Matilda (Diana Dors) face off in *Berserk!* (1968).

The hanging death of Gaspar seems contrived in the way the broken wire wraps around his neck, but O'Connolly uses the swinging body as a wipe over the title credits. Monica is seen as tough in the way she scares away a photographer who wants to shoot Gaspar's body, and she is called "inhuman" by Dorando for counting box office receipts rather than grieving. When he places his hand on her papers to get her attention, she hits it with her fist, which also suggests the controlling aspect of her romantic relationship with him (she later rebuffs his advances). When Monica interviews for a replacement act, she says she doesn't want "broken-down has-beens," but rather "something fresh, a new face," which she gets with Frank. This age discrimination foreshadows her relationship with Frank, who after some initial resistance—"Leave the comedy to Bruno and the rest of the clowns"—becomes her new love interest, although we never see them kiss. Their age difference is only mentioned later by Angela, to whom it is pointed out that *Frank* doesn't think Monica is too old for him.

Frank's romanticism is represented by the fact that Hardin often appears bare-chested, and his masculinity is enhanced by a quick temper (evinced when he punches a prospective agent who doesn't respect the idea that "he doesn't like to be touched"). Later Brooks will reveal that Frank had been found not-guilty of having killed a man in Canada, since his violence was determined to be self-defense. His kinkiness is suggested by the hood he wears in his act (clearly used to conceal Hardin's stunt double) and the steel bayonets that lay on the ground sixty feet below his wire (which will eventually impale him). Frank's interest in being Monica's business partner works against his romanticism and indicates another agenda, which will be punished by death in the same way that her previous business partners were.

When Dorando follows Frank, Dorando passes a painting of an angry-looking clown, which foreshadows his murder. He conveniently stands in front of a hole in the canvas that allows a spike to be hammered into his head, a contrivance that is soon forgiven because the sight of the spike protruding from his skull is so perfectly grande guignol. Monica is seen walking toward Dorando's trailer after his death to create suspicion in a film with multiple suspects, and burns Dorando's contract (an act that is never explained). We may wonder why Monica hasn't heard Dorando's scream when we see her walking nearby immediately after the killing, though Frank later admits that he had seen her sneak out from his bed. The growl of the lions that accompanies Monica and Bruno as they go to Dorando is said to indicate that the lions "smell blood," which is as mercenary as Monica saying, "Murder is good for business."

Some amusing dialogue is offered when, at a group meeting of the circus staff, someone asks the clairvoyant, "What do the stars, your crystal ball and the tea leaves tell you?" and she replies, "They tell me to mind my own business." Romy, the Bearded Lady also gets in on the act, answering accusations by saying: "How could I get away with murder? I'm the easiest one in the whole circus to identify. You see my beard before you see me."

The introduction of Brooks to investigate the killings adds a camp element. He is not outed as being gay, but he does wear a boutonnière, is said to have a "fetish for dressing smartly," and is warned by his Commissioner to "leave your expensive feathers in their moth-proof containers." This garners a payoff when, upon his arrival, he steps in elephant excrement.

Matilda is Monica's sexual rival for Frank, something which Monica acknowledges when she calls her "attractive, in a common sort of way." When Matilda makes advances towards Frank, he rebuffs her with "I hope the timing in your act is better than here," and "You're peddling your merchandise at the wrong booth." Thankfully, the narrative allows Frank to enjoy kissing Matilda before he rejects her, adding some ambiguity. However, the way she is thrown out of his trailer, and the resulting catfight with Wanda, who laughs at her, are unnecessarily demeaning to her.

Angela arrives more than half way into the narrative, which dilutes the believability of her later confessing to being the killer. In a scenario that foreshadows that of Christina in *Mommie Dearest*, Angela has been expelled from the Fenmore School for Young Ladies for "smoking, imitating teachers, and other pranks, resisting all discipline and supervision." Monica herself admits that Angela has a "knack for causing trouble," something Angela will blame on Monica's prioritizing of the traveling circus before her daughter, and will use as a rationale to kill. The troubled relationship between mother and daughter recalls *Strait-Jacket* and *Mildred Pierce*. One can even make a symbolic Hitchcockian comparison between Angela's natural blonde hair color and the dyed redness of Monica's. The battle between the older grande dame and her two younger rivals (Angela *and* Monica, who's also blonde) recalls the older woman/younger woman equation from *Strait-Jacket*, *I Saw What You Did*, *Lady in a Cage*, *Die! Die! My Darling!*, *The Night Walker*, *The Witches*, and *Games*.

The scene in which the dwarf Bruno's enlarged shadow follows Monica, which culminates in the camera creeping up behind her and Bruno placing his hand on her shoulder, is a standard horror movie Woman in Peril scene. Bruno being half the size of Monica adds a humorous spin to this encounter.

Matilda's murder is telegraphed by the argument she has with Monica (who takes issue with Matilda telling Brooks she thinks Monica is the killer). Mathilda's death also provides another gruesome grande guignol killing, although only Matilda's scream of realization is shown, with none of the blood that accompanied Dorando's death. A police analysis of the crime scene reveals that Monica's husband was a trapeze artist in the circus who was accidentally killed six years previously (and we also see a poster for Pepsi—a Crawford product placement).

Before the circus opens in London, Monica discovers that Angela has joined the knife-throwing act of Gustavo, and warns: "The hazards of the act are nothing compared to the dangers built into Gustavo, who thinks he's a throwback to Casanova and Don Juan."

Monica Rivers (Joan Crawford) and Frank Hawkins (Ty Hardin) dance while Angela Rivers (Judy Geeson) watches in the background in *Berserk!* (1968).

O'Connolly includes stock footage in a montage of the circus being constructed. This is not nearly so arbitrary as the audience reaction shots and extended footage of animal acts that may be necessary for a circus film but still feel like filler (no matter how clever the animals are or how plebeian the audience is meant to be as they eat ice-cream and popcorn).

A pre-opening party song, "It Might Be Me," is performed as a musical comedy number, shot in a style different from the rest of the film. An opening night parade inexplicably includes someone dressed in a Batman costume. O'Connolly edits in close-ups of all the remaining suspects watching Angela in the knife throwing act (a red herring ruse, since Angela is the killer), which he repeats with Frank's act. Another red herring is tossed out when Frank initially slips from the high wire, but the fact he is not wearing his usual hood foreshadows his fate. Angela's revealing herself is somewhat obfuscated by her being on the high wire when she throws the knife that makes Frank fall, but her running to Monica on the ground and confession are standard movie conventions used to explain motivation before she attempts to kill Monica.

Angela's fate remains somewhat ambiguous when lightning strikes and a pole falls near where she is running, though the dramatic lightning strike recalls that which kills the murderous daughter, Rhoda, in *The Bad Seed* (1956). Even if Angela recovers, the police will ensure that she is prosecuted for her crimes, and the threat of the real antagonist is removed. However, the death of Frank also removes Monica's love interest, although she retains her position of power in the circus — perhaps until a new high wire act is hired.

Joan Crawford had not made a film since *I Saw What You Did*. She brings her strength and authority to Monica, and her glamour and sense of irony rationalizes the love affair between a woman and a man 25 years younger than she. In one scene, dialogue-free Crawford stands with her hand on her hip, demonstrating her sensual nature and self-confidence; and throughout the film she provides surprising laughter and lightness in her line-readings to offset her other, more severe reactions.

As a color film, *Berserk* is rarity in the Crawford canon, since she was previously only seen in color in a sequence of *The Ice Follies of 1939* (1939), *Torch Song* (1953), *Johnny Guitar* (1954), and *The Best of Everything*. The Edith Head–designed black leotard that Monica wears shows off Crawford's still-shapely legs, and her wardrobe is all earth tones—dark green, orange, and tan/brown. The orange dress coat that accompanies the black tights, and an orange cape, are designed to match her red hair color, which she wears in a sculpted bun pulled back from her forehead. Even when her hair is loose, Monica still has her forehead exposed, which only emphasizes the largeness of Crawford's head compared to the size of her body. Crawford's neck in close-ups is photographed in shadow,

Poster for *Berserk!* (1968).

as it was in *Autumn Leaves, Strait-Jacket,* and *I Saw What You Did,* to protect her age, which was now 62. When Angela is told that Monica "has the gift of eternal youth," we can appreciate how Crawford must have loved this line.

It was said that Crawford's drinking had made her an unbankable risk for the American studios' moneymen, so she sought work overseas and found her way to producer Herman Cohen. Supposedly Cohen's ground rule for working with Crawford was that there would be no drinking without his permission, and no drinking at all before noon; and to hold her to her agreement, he kept her flask in his jacket pocket. Crawford's daughter, Christina, had wanted to play her daughter onscreen, an idea Crawford senior vetoed.

Release

January 11, 1968, with the taglines, "Your front row seat to murder!" and "The motion picture that pits steel weapons against steel nerves!!!"

Reviews

"O'Connolly is no Hitchcock. What drains the picture of merit and real persuasiveness is the round-up of bloodless characterizations, a petty and conniving gang of meanies. Even a last-minute, mother-love injection doesn't thaw Miss Crawford's portrayal of a ruthless iceberg, who, one feels, gets what she deserves."—Howard Thompson, *The New York Times,* January 11, 1968.

"Story is full of holes, but it makes no difference ... an old fashioned thriller with more circus entertainment than plot or thrill, but it's got the name, the promotion, and the non sophisticated audience appeal that makes this type of entertainment."—*Variety,* December 9, 1967.

"Joan Crawford still has as pretty a set of gams as any actress in films. She displays them right up to the pelvis in the costume she wears as ring mistress and owner of an English circus, in which a killer at large perpetrates a parlay of improbable murders."—*Time,* January 19, 1968.

"A badly scripted shocker designed as a vehicle for Joan Crawford.... That the homicidal maniac turns out to be Crawford's daughter merely confirms that the movie's central fantasy is the anxiety generated by the figure of the sexually threatening mother, an image tailor-made for the star."—Phil Hardy, *The Aurum Film Encyclopedia of Horror.*

"Crawford is indecorously showcased as the sexy romantic lead.... The scenes where she is drooled over by both Michael Gough and Ty Hardin are horrific indeed! ... The revelation of the killer's identity is terribly contrived and completely illogical."—Gary A. Smith, *Uneasy Dreams: The Golden Age of British Horror Films, 1956–1976.*

The Savage Intruder (1968)
(aka *Hollywood Horror House*; *The Comeback*)

William Burton, Congdon Films, Inc.

CREDITS: *Producer/Director/Screenplay:* Donald Wolfe; *Associate Producer:* Ann May; *Photography:* John A. Morrill; *Music:* Stu Phillips; *Editor:* Hartwig Deeb; *Production Design:* Normand Houle; *Set Decorator:* Coke Willis; *Sound:* Rod Sutton, Jim Contreras: *Make-up Supervision:* Lou Lane; *Hair Dresser:* Gretchen Moon; *Wardrobe:* Ruth Foster; *Miss Hopkins's Gowns:* Treva; *Production Manager:* Bill Brown; *Special Photographic Effects:* F Stop. Color, 100 minutes. Filmed in Hollywood at the Norma Talmadge Estate.

SONG: "Taking a Chance on Love" (Vernon Duke, John Latouche and Ted Fetter), special arrangement by Dave Roberts. Sung by Miriam Hopkins.

CAST: Miriam Hopkins (*Katharine Packard*); John David Garfield (*Vic Vallance*); Gale Sondergaard (*Leslie Blair*); Florence Lake (*Mildred*); Lester Mathews (*Ira Jaffe*); Riza Royce (*Mrs. Jaffe*); Joe Besser (*Bus Driver*); Minta Durfee (*Guest*); Virginia Wing (*Greta*); Charles Martin (*Doctor*); Sydelle Guardino (*Mother*); Richard Guardino (*Young Vic*); Jason Johnson (*Josef*); Bill Welsh (*TV Announcer*); Dorothy Kingston (*1st Victim*); Parke McAllister (*Newscaster*); The Synergy Trust (*Party Characters*); Katina Garner (*Blonde*); J. B. Larson (*Percy*); Bud Douglas (*Midget*); Phyllis Selznick (*Girl Friend*).

VHS/DVD: Not available on DVD. VHS Unicorn Video, released February 14, 1989.

Plot

Vic Vallance is a nurse and psychopathic serial killer of middle-aged women in Hollywood who has been traumatized by childhood abandonment by his alcoholic and promiscuous mother. After dispatching a woman he has followed from a bar, he arrives at the house of the reclusive and alcoholic former actress Katharine Packard. Katharine has broken her left leg falling down the staircase of her mansion while drunk, and is confined to a wheelchair. Hired to care for Katharine, Vic befriends the servant Greta and begins an affair. Greta's revulsion at Vic's apparent romantic interest in Katharine makes her threaten to leave the house, which forces Vic to kill her. After killing Katharine's other (old) servants, Leslie and Mildred, Vic imprisons Katharine in her own home. When Katharine tries to dismiss Vic, he kills her too, and uses one of

Katharine's look-alike mannequins as a replacement companion in the now empty mansion.

Notes

The only Grande Dame Guignol made by Miriam Hopkins, this film has garnered fascination because of its obscurity. While easily dismissed as slasher-style exploitation, the film actually has merit. The evocative use of the Hollywood sign, pleasing deployment of music and silence, and good performances all compensate for the sillier aspects of the production. While the narrative slows down when the grande dame is imprisoned in her room, pacing picks up again when the serial killer antagonist commits his murders. *The Savage Intruder* is the only film to date directed by Donald Wolfe, who also wrote the screenplay and produced. It is also the only title made under Congdon Films, and the only title made by associate producer Ann May.

The Savage Intruder begins with twirling classic glamour pictures of Hopkins superimposed over the Hollywood premiere at Grauman's Chinese Theatre of "The Dancing Cavalier" (created for 1952's *Singing in the Rain*), stock footage of parties and film production, and champagne being poured into a glass. All this excitement fades away to the sight of the Hollywood sign in the Hollywood Hills, dilapidated and punctured by bullet holes, the metallic letters creaking in the wind. Wolfe shows that while the illusion of perfection can be sustained in a long shot, a close-up will expose reality, age, and vulnerability. The sound of a dog barking precedes the sight of a dismembered head and hands under the sign (presumably Vic's latest victim). The flies that buzz around the dead flesh demonstrate the grande guignol sadism of the murders, and the parasitism in nature foreshadows Vic's relationship with Katharine.

Wolfe cuts from the corpse to a bar where a television newscast reports the discovery, and where we see Vic's next unnamed victim drinking. A moralist might contend that this marks her as a loser, and Wolfe perversely has her walk past a beauty shop when she leaves to underscore her age and need for beautification. Vic is shown pursuing her via the horror movie convention of the camera revealing only his white trouser-clad legs, with the music of Stu Phillips employing a drumbeat to up the suspense. The notion of the victim as a drunkard is reinforced when she sits at her mirrored dressing table and drinks. Vic's ease with which he breaks into her house will extend to his ease in killing her (aided by his youthful advantage and assumed sobriety). The electric knife he uses to cut her hand adds a modern element to his weaponry, with his plugging into her electricity supply symbolic of a further personal violation. However, his change to a butcher's knife to kill her is a return to the more effective and traditional method, with Wolfe showing blood splattered on a toilet (a horror convention) as a way to imply rather than show the murder. The murder recalls the shower sequence of *Psycho* in its use of a knife and the prominence of a toilet (associated with Marion Crane's failed attempt to flush away the evidence of her crime).

Vic's face is revealed as he rides the Movieland Tour Bus, leading him to the home of Katharine, his white nurse's pants identifying him as the killer. The use of white is appropriate for someone who presents himself as a nurse, as is the white color of Katharine's mansion appropriate for her comparative innocence. The hippie headband Vic wears confirms his youthfulness, and the fact that he refashions it as a tie indicates that he is aware of the social obligation of the role he is about to play. The bus driver describes Katharine as "retired," and the fact that the bus stops in front of her house indicate an existing interest in Katharine, even if said interest borders on the ghoulish. The little girl vomiting when the bus stops to see the view of the gated property (and to allow Vic to disembark) reflects the tackiness of the tour, the insensitivity of the patrons, and both Vic and Katharine's sickness. Since Vic arrives before Katharine breaks her leg and has need of a nurse, it would seem that Vic is a Charles Manson-ish figure, a person of ambition with violence as the only means to satisfy it.

Katharine is introduced by period photographs of her younger self, and her voice is heard as she speaks on the telephone. Her handling of the phone is unrealistic, which alludes to the delusion she is having about hosting a party, a delusion Wolfe reinforces by including false group murmurings on the soundtrack.

Poster for *The Savage Intruder* (1968).

Katharine's reference to a drink before she makes her entrance as "one more glass of personality" is a sign of her insecurity and alcoholism, so that her tumble down the staircase undercuts the glamour and elegance she has tried to establish for her phantom guests. Her wig coming off as she falls is the final indignity. The resulting broken left leg leaves her in a cast, reliant upon crutches and a wheelchair to move, and making her even more vulnerable.

Vic's entry into the house is presented ambiguously. Although we are told that a nurse has been hired for Katharine, none specifically attends. This allows for the assumption that Vic is the expected nurse, and gives him the opportunity he has been waiting for. Vic's entry to the grounds shows the neglected swimming pool full of dirty water, with leaves floating on the surface. That it does have water in it is a small improvement on the state of Norma Desmond's pool in *Sunset Boulevard*; and Katharine having a larger staff than Norma indicates that Katharine is not as isolated (though her clothes and the playing of melodramatic mood music in her room indicate otherwise).

Vic telling Mildred the housekeeper that he is "Laurel N. Hardy" shows that he is anarchic, and therefore not to be trusted, but the laugh comes more from her not getting the joke. If the joke isn't enough, John David Garfield's uncanny vocal resemblance to his father, and the obnoxiousness of Garfield's persona, should serve as sufficient warning. Mildred's remarked antipathy to the "callowness" of the new Hollywood stars, and her calling present-day youth "self-centered animals," defines her generation. Her words recall the use of the word "animal" in *Lady in a Cage* and *Games*, and they also seal her fate.

A conversation between Vic and Greta in the kitchen displays a bizarre humpty-dumpty egg timer that will later feature in the plot, and brings a laugh:

> GRETA: She [Katharine] is unhappy because she didn't have enough success. But we should all be grateful for what we have.
> VIC: Thanks for the advice. I'll remember that the next time someone hands me a bedpan.

Katharine being a widow offers some explanation for her reclusiveness, and it is interesting that all her servants are female. Her sexual deprivation is typical of the grande dame in Grande Dame Guignol. Since Vic is a younger man, the possibility of him becoming a love interest for Katharine is present, particularly since their initial mutual dislike parallels that fiction often used in movies as a romantic device for people to overcome and eventually fall in love. However, us knowing that Vic is a killer, and the difference in their ages, make any potential romance seem doomed. Vic takes a drug kept in his box of knives, and hallucinates a flashback in which Wolfe opens with the child Vic walking down a hallway of psychedelic-colored and geometric-designed boxes. The orgy taking place behind a door is photographed with a distorted lens to turn the participants, which include Vic's mother, into grotesques. A raised axe, a dismembered arm, and blood pouring from a vodka bottle add grande guignol fuel to the fire. His mother drinking Vodka will prove prophetic for Katharine, who favors the same.

Vic's opening of the locked "heart of the house" is an example of his intrusiveness and boldness, and also allows us to see the Katharine-clone mannequins who wear the costumes from her past. Vic's confession to Greta that his mother was "a lush who slept around, ran off with a pimp, and put me in a foster home" rationalizes his rage against middle-aged women, which is how we are meant to see Katharine. Katharine also being a drinker makes the idea of romance between Vic and her even more unlikely, and foreshadows his use of the vodka against her.

Katharine's obvious interest in Vic is introduced by her (badly) singing "Taking a Chance on Love"; and Wolfe provides a montage of Vic buying clothes on credit, though he is alone, which differs from a similar scenario in *Sunset Boulevard*. The *Sunset Boulevard* connection continues when Katharine sits with Vic as they watch one of her old films, which is actually Hopkins' *Wise Girl* (1937). The scene shown from *Wise Girl* is an interesting choice, since in it, Hopkins's character is repeatedly interrupted having a bath, showing her exposed and violated. *The Savage Intruder* having been filmed at the Norma Talmadge estate invites comparison between Katharine and Talmadge, an actress in silent films whose career ended with the coming of sound. (Talmadge's New Jersey accent didn't match her persona of "The Lady of the Great Indoors," as she was known.) The movie clip establishes that Katharine was a star of talkies, but, unlike Talmadge, who ran her own production company, there is no suggestion that Katharine had the same. Thus she was an actress dependent upon others for employment, which makes the expiry of her career more pathetic than tragic.

Wolfe cuts from the image of the young Hopkins to flashes of contemporary images on the wall of a bar where Vic and Greta are drinking, and the lively youth culture stands in opposition to the stagnancy of life in their employment environment. Close-ups of Greta laughing are inter-cut with the same contemporary images on the wall. Wolfe segues to the resultant scene of Vic and Greta having sex, but presents it as a series of photographs—capturing the event for prosperity like one of Katharine's films, although the images are tinted green. He then cuts to the sight of Katharine's back being massaged to reinforce the difference between Greta's young flesh and Katharine's older flesh. Katharine's infatuation with Vic echoes *Sunset Boulevard* when he is seen shirtless and using the now clean swimming pool (although, like in the scene where he buys clothes, she is not with him, preferring to observe him from her balcony). Her new happiness inspires Katharine to have a *real* gathering, at which all the guests are her contemporaries. (This will later be mirrored when a youthful gang invades the house.) Wolfe emphasizes the age and disinterest of the attendants by having one snore at dinner.

When Greta tells Vic that she is pregnant (in seemingly record time), as well as voicing her distaste for Vic's interest in Katharine, he states that his agenda with her is strictly a financial one. It is interesting that when Greta decides to leave the house she doesn't think to warn Katharine about Vic. Greta becomes the Woman in Peril when she wanders the darkened house with a flashlight, looking for Vic, with the vibrations of a chandelier (a horror movie convention) generating unease. The rolling of the dropped flashlight when she is axed recalls the swinging light bulb in the cellar from *Psycho*, this time revealing her hacked and mutilated body. The image of the fingers of a dismembered hand moving echoes the flashback to Vic's mother's murder, and when Greta's fingers stop moving, an indication that her death has come.

Vic wears red pants—as opposed to his standard white—when he buries Greta in the flowerbed, as if he is stained by her blood. When Leslie, confronts him by the flowerbed, her question "Are you burying your conscience" shows that Leslie is not aware of what he really *has* buried. Greta's jealousy towards Katharine as a love interest for Vic represents Vic's first obstacle. The antipathy that Leslie and Mildred feel towards him will later make them additional antagonists in a scenario in which he is the clear antagonist of the household and Katharine the protagonist. That the audience should not want Vic to be stopped is the complication of the antagonist/protagonist equation that is typical of Grande Dame Guignol.

Katharine's night out on the Sunset Strip with Vic leads to a youth party where she offers an amusing response to an offer made by a munchkin:

> MUNCHKIN: Coke, speed, smack, grass or acid?
> KATHARINE: The only trips I take are to Europe.

The party's gay admirers of Katharine fondle her hair and clothes, but when she is seen on Santa's float as the Queen of the Christmas Parade on Hollywood Boulevard, she makes a comment to a TV interviewer about how the Boulevard is being overrun with "queers."

The white sheath Katherine wears, with ostrich feather collar and sleeve trims, present her as a caged exotic bird when Vic locks her in her bedroom. The horror movie cliché of Katharine discovering that her telephone has been disconnected is redeemed somewhat by Wolfe first showing us Vic disconnecting it. Katharine, as a grande dame imprisoned in her own house, recalls Crawford in *What Ever Happened to Baby Jane?*

and deHavilland in *Lady in a Cage*, and, as a prisoner, Stephanie Powers in *Die! Die! My Darling!* Vic's repeatedly injecting her with vodka, then force feeding her drink in a toast to "lonely rich old bags," offers further humiliation. His insisting she sing "Taking a Chance on Love" as she is inebriated is sadistic retribution for her infatuation with him. Wolfe employs an extreme close-up of Vic's eye to reveal his threat—and, implicitly, his own drug addiction. Katharine's pathetic cry of "I don't want to die!" leads to another of Vic's flashbacks, where the image of blood pouring out of a bottle is used again. This is the last we see of Katharine.

The trunk that Vic removes from Katharine's room carries the implication that she is inside it, much like the basket that held the seemingly dead body in *Les Diaboliques*. The buzzer rigged to be activated by the egg timer in Katharine's bedroom is to give the impression that she is still alive, and recalls Crawford's buzzer in *What Ever Happened to Baby Jane?* Wolfe uses ticking clocks as a horror convention, and also to heighten specific noises in the house when Leslie repeats Greta's searching of dark rooms with a flashlight. Leslie's searching the grounds at night allows for wind and a banging shutter to be added for atmospheric affect. Wolfe also spares us music, so that silence can be used to create tension. In these scenes Sondergaard's hair is long and loose, when previously she has worn it in a bun, which only emphasizes the unprotected way she is photographed to appear haggard. The look also recalls Crawford in *What Ever Happened to Baby Jane?*

Leslie shining a flashlight on the glass case that had housed two of Katharine mannequins, but that now only has one, makes us think of the missing Katharine. It also foreshadows a mannequin becoming her substitute, so that Vic seen in bed with one is not so startling as it might have otherwise been. When Leslie is attacked by Vic with a syringe, which would seem to be a change of modus operandi, Wolfe cuts from her scream to a screaming kettle in the kitchen. The slight suggestion had been made that Leslie harbored lesbian feelings toward Katharine by her slapping Vic when he told her that he "serves all her [Katharine's] corpulent needs," though this confrontation occurred just when Leslie was about to open the box of knives in his room.

Vic talking to the mannequin, who has false eyelashes and lipstick, in Katharine's wheelchair gets a laugh—as the mannequin also wears a cast, the way Katharine did. That Vic would prefer a mannequin to Katharine, who he has buried in the flowerbed with Greta, is a rejection of real women in favor of a passive and mute appropriation. Wolfe cuts from Vic kissing the mannequin in close-up to a close-up of the boy Vic in the multicolored op-art geometric pattern of the flashback, with thunder and lightning employed as a horror movie convention before the murder of Mildred. Wolfe teases us with Mildred going into a walk-in closet and not being attacked until she leaves. With Greta, Katharine, Leslie and Mildred all murdered, Vic has the house to himself. He has eliminated all the females in his life. The laughing face of Vic's mother in the last of the flashbacks is superimposed over the mannequin, which recalls Mother in *Psycho* and Hitchcock's superimposing a skeleton face over Anthony Perkins's face at the end of that film. Wolfe ends his picture with a reprise of "Taking a Chance on Love" that Vic whistles as he wheels the mannequin in the wheelchair, and the image is multiplied in a glass reflection as the white mansion is seen from a distance.

Miriam Hopkins was age 66 at the time of filming. Her last leading role had been in *Old Acquaintance* (1943). Since then she had been featured in supporting parts, notably in *The Children's Hour* (1961), *Fanny Hill* (1964), and *The Chase* (1964). Hopkins casting in *The Children's Hour* is remarkable, since she had appeared as one of the leads in the original version of the Lillian Hellman play *These Three* (1936), both films having been directed by William Wyler.

Hopkins had played a similar type of character as Katharine Packard in an episode of the TV science fiction anthology series *The Outer Limits* entitled "Don't Open Till Doomsday" in 1964. As aged and demented bride Mary Kry, abandoned on her honeymoon in 1929, she has waited thirty-five years for her groom to come back to her. Ironically, the director of photography, Conrad Hall, would not use his legendary soft focus lens on her and relentlessly exposed Hopkins's 61-year-old wrinkles. Wearing a black wig, heavy eye shadow, false eyelashes, a pearl necklace, a ratty feather boa, and a shimmery, black, knee-length flapper dress with knee-high gartered stockings, Hopkins looked grotesque but still managed to be funny. Her character proved to be as malevolent as the alien who had kidnapped her husband, with Hopkins willing to sacrifice anyone in exchange for her principled man, who refused to help the alien rejoin others of its kind to annihilate the universe.

Hopkins was known for a non-naturalistic theatrical acting style bordering on ham, which fits her Katharine, who is an obvious soul-sister of Norma Desmond. This extravagance of choice makes her Katharine amusing, though Hopkins can't quite bring off the vulnerability, since her brittleness exists to conceal it. Katharine's use of a stiff platinum wig and a white ball gown are evidence of her need for dressing up to entertain, even when the wig is far less flattering than her real hair, seen later. Additionally, Wolfe photographs Hopkins so that we are aware of her lack of height. Katharine's false eyelashes, silver nail polish and make-up for the party are kept for her ordinary day application, and this constancy shows that she is always artificial and conscious of her appearance.

When Vic meets Katharine she sports her natural blonde hair, though, the lines on her neck and Hopkins's fleshiness are apparent. In the massage scene, Hopkins breasts are visible under her loose robe; and when Katharine stands up next to Vic, we see that she is only half his height. (While Garfield's height is not documented, Hopkins was known to be only 5'2".) Such exposure can either be interpreted as bravery or foolishness on the part of an actress in her 60s. Hopkins receives an unflattering close-up for Katharine's repeated scream at Vic to "Get out!" in a film where she has few close-ups. His punching her into unconsciousness is a shock, and as demeaning as Crawford being kicked by Davis in *What Ever Happened to Baby Jane?* and Fontaine in the mud in *The Witches*.

Release

The release date of *The Savage Intruder* is unclear, as there are no reviews in either *Variety* or *The New York Times*. For the purposes of this book, I have dated the film with a 1968 release, since that is the year most commonly given. However, the film apparently was re-released in 1973, 1975 and 1977 under the titles *The Comeback* and *Hollywood Horror House*. Also, since Miriam Hopkins died in 1972, it is assumed that the film was originally released prior to her death. As *The Savage Intruder*, the film used the taglines, "A new high in Terror and Shock!" and "She loved and trusted him until he cut off her head."

Reviews

"Deliciously seedy and sadistic, with wild LSD flashbacks, convincing bloodshed and a near-nude scene from aging star Miriam Hopkins.... Too sluggishly paced to be a lost classic, nonetheless an unsettling obscurity that might be worth a look for its period atmosphere and nasty disposition."—Fred Beldin, *All Movie Guide*.

"Despite Wolfe's inconsistent handling of the material and the film's minuscule budget, *Savage Intruder* has some interesting things to say about the decadence of late–1960s Hollywood.... Unfortunately, the whole production cries out for some serious editing and faster pacing to make the suspense more compelling."—Danny Fortune, *Alternative Film Guide*.

"Gruesome thriller, which borrows from *Night Must Fall* and *Sunset Boulevard*, and is inept when it is not unpleasant."—David Gritten, *Halliwell's Film Guide*

"...[O]dd, critically neglected retake on the classic *Sunset Boulevard*.... Rarely screened, this has disappeared from release, although the film itself has no reputation."—Robert Cettl, *Serial Killer Cinema*.

What Ever Happened to Aunt Alice? (1969)

MGM/Associates and Aldrich Production/ABC/Palomar Pictures

CREDITS: *Director:* Lee H. Katzin; *Producer:* Robert Aldrich; *Executive Producer:* Peter Nelson; *Screenplay:* Theodore Apstein, from the novel *The Forbidden Garden*, by Ursula Curtiss; *Photography:* Joseph Biroc; *Music:* Gerald Fried; *Editor:* Frank J. Urioste; *Art Director:* William Glasgow; *Set Decorator:* John W. Brown; *Production Supervisor:* Fred Miern; *Unit Manager:* Eddie Saeta; *Sound:* Dick Church; *Make-up:* Bill Turner; *Hair:* Jean Austin; *Wardrobe:* Renie. Color, 101 minutes. Filmed October 23, 1968–January 5, 1969, at the Aldrich Studios, Los Angeles, California, and on location in Tucson, Arizona.

CAST: Geraldine Page (*Mrs. Claire Marrable*); Ruth Gordon (*Mrs. Alice Dimmock*); Rosemary Forsyth (*Harriet Vaughn*); Robert Fuller (*Mike Darrah*); Mildred Dunnock (*Miss Edna Tinsley*); Joan Huntington (*Julia Lawson*); Peter Brandon (*George Lawson*); Michael Barbera (*Jim Vaughan*); Peter Bonerz (*Mr. Bentley*); Richard Angarola (*Sheriff Armijo*); Claire Kelly (*Elva*); Valerie Allen (*Dottie*); Martin Garralaga (*Juan*); Jack Bannon (*Olin*); Seth Riggs (*Warren*); Lou Kane (*Telephone Man*); Spike (*Chloe*); Howard Wright (*Mourner*); Uncredited: Jess Riggle (*Cab driver*).

VHS/DVD: DVD: Starz/Anchor Bay, July 11, 2000. Re-released by MGM November 2, 2004.

Plot

When Claire Marrable's husband dies she learns that he has left her penniless. She moves to the desert of Tucson, Arizona, and attempts to keep up a grand lifestyle by murdering her housekeepers for their money and burying them under pine trees in her garden. When Alice Dimmock applies for the housekeeper position, it is because she had been the housekeeper of Edna Tinsley, who was the last of Claire's victims. Claire finds Alice to be the most pleasing of all her companions, but things change when Claire spots Alice befriending their neighbor, Harriet Vaughn. Harriet also receives the romantic attentions of Alice's nephew, racing car builder Mike Darrah, who aids Alice's investigation. When Claire announces that she and Alice are taking a day trip to New Mexico, she catches Alice in a lie and plans to kill her.

Mike discovers that Miss Tinsley had withdrawn all her savings before disappearing, and warns Alice of the danger. Before Alice can get away, Claire confronts her, and a fight ensues. Beating Alice unconscious, Claire puts her in a car, which she sinks in a nearby lake. Before Alice's death, she had warned Claire that she had told someone else about her suspicions. Figuring Alice's confidant is Harriet, Claire drugs her and her son, Jim, and sets fire to their house. Suspecting Claire has killed his Aunt Alice, Mike goes to the police. The next morning Claire awakens to see that her garden of corpses has been unearthed, and that Harriet and Jim have survived, having been saved by Mike. She learns that her husband's stamp album, which she thought worthless, is actually worth $100,000, and, recognizing the irony, laughs hysterically.

Notes

A Grande Dame Guignol enlivened by an outrageous performance by Geraldine Page, this cat-and-mouse tale about a serial killer of older women pits one grande dame against another. While the narrative becomes sidetracked in a romantic subplot, the femme battles (that prefigure *The Baby*) and director Lee H. Katzin's penchant for ghoulishness still satisfy. Produced by Robert Aldrich, the director of *What Ever Happened to Baby Jane?* and *Hush ... Hush, Sweet Charlotte*, the film was begun with Bernard Girard as director, who was replaced after four weeks. Girard had made *The Mad Room*. Katzin's only previous film had been the western *Heaven with a Gun* (1969); otherwise he had worked in television on such series as *The Rat Patrol*, *Hondo*, and *Mission Impossible*. Executive producer Peter Nelson had previously made the Elvis Presley drama *Wild in the Country* (1961).

The film is obviously titled to be associated with *What Ever Happened to Baby Jane?* though it is not an appropriate moniker. Something does eventually happen to Aunt Alice in the narrative, but she is not presented as the unbalanced antagonist Baby Jane Hudson was. The better question would have been "What Ever Happened to Aunt Claire?" since the root of her madness is not identified (even if the antagonism—as opportunism—is). Her fear of poverty, and the scorching sun and dry winds of the desert, turn Claire Marrable into a vampire who kills at night. Claire's grey hair indicates that her youth has gone, and her choice of victims reveals her sadism and hatred of womankind.

The film opens with a shot of flowers at Joseph Marrable's funeral, with organ music playing on the soundtrack. Claire is first seen in shadow, then from behind, her face obscured by a black veil similar to that worn by Margaret DeLorca in *Dead Ringer*. Claire's obvious lack of grief will be rationalized at the end of the film when she admits that she hated her husband. Her pleasurable expression, her greater interest in collecting the flowers then grieving, and the *Psycho*-like strings of the music all contribute to the idea that her attitude here is abnormal. The music for the film also prefigures that in *The Baby*, since it is by the same composer. Additionally, it uses rearranged versions of the same opening music, with a cello and an arrangement for French love songs indicating Claire's adolescent notion of romance. Her grande dame affectation, as a woman who pretentiously sips Grande Marnier liqueurs, also conceals dangerous and violent impulses.

Katzin cuts from Claire's devastation upon hearing of her pennilessness to her planning to attack her companion, Rose Hull, who we are to assume is the first victim. The burial is grande guignol—a form of being buried alive—with the grande dame down on her hands and knees doing the hard work that murder often requires.

Later Claire will speak of the "courage" it takes to kill, but we feel that Alice is closer to the truth when she says that all it takes is "nerve and cruelty." Since Rose is introduced and eliminated in this one scene, and we have learned of Claire's need for money, our empathy is with the killer, so we recognize Claire as protagonist *and* antagonist. The personality of her next victim, Edna Tinsley, is established when we see her willingness to demean herself before Claire's arrogant imperialism and insults. Claire's reluctance to burn Edna's Bible along with her clothes indicates that Claire can be intimidated (and the Bible will become a plot point).

When Claire is surrounded by men at a party, the potential for a love interest in undercut by the idea

Poster for *What Ever Happened to Aunt Alice?* (1969).

that her appeal is her acquired wealth. Her temporary need for a wheelchair recalls the wheelchairs in *What Ever Happened to Baby Jane?* and *The Savage Intruder*. Harriet is used to parallel two widows, with Harriet disinterested in the advances of Mike, although the subplot of their romance only pays off when he rescues her from Claire's murder attempt. Since Harriet does not represent a younger antagonist, like so many younger women do in Grande Dame Guignol, she can only be a protagonistic Woman in Peril. Like the Harriet/Mike romance, in narrative terms the appearances of George Lawson, and particularly Julia Lawson, are even more disposable. When Joan comments that Claire has had rotten luck with housekeepers, Claire replies, "Actually, I think I've done rather well," with her smiling face dissolving to the arrival of Alice.

Although Alice could be seen as an antagonist to Claire's protagonist, her overwhelming likeability defuses the notion of Alice's deceit, thereby displacing the audience's established empathy and making Claire more the antagonist. The intrusion of a stray dog, Chloe, which Claire calls a "tramp," provides Claire with a funny line with additional subtext: "I have not taken loving and diligent care of my garden to have it wrecked by this vagrant bitch." The subtext relates to Claire's preference for housekeeper-companions with "savings and no one in the world." Alice having a nephew will prove to be Claire's downfall, though it will not save Alice.

Claire's paranoid jealousy of Alice's friendship with Harriet can be rationalized by her reasonable fear of disclosure, which will later make her attack Harriet. Katzin shows Claire in shadow, her back to the camera, watching Alice enter the house after talking to Harriet. The bars on the windows of Claire's house recall the bars on the house in *What Ever Happened to Baby Jane?* Claire's entering a teenage girls' competition, "How I Lured My Most Recent Boyfriend," to win prize money points up her duplicity and avarice. Claire as a serial killer grande dame recalls the Simone Signoret's serial killer in *Games*. Claire's first attempt to kill Chloe is thwarted when the dog snarls, forcing Claire to retreat. This foreshadows Claire's second murder attempt and demonstrates that there are more vicious animals than her.

Alice's appreciation of Claire's "gracious way of life" may be a ruse to ingratiate herself with Claire, but it also provides the groundwork for Claire to later comment that she enjoys Alice's company and regrets having to kill her. The argument they have, when Alice's "Irish temper" fires up and she "raises her voice" in reaction to Claire's complaint over a late dinner, displays their clash over the time to satisfy separate agendas. As to why Alice bitters the pheasant she serves Claire remains a mystery, though Alice does seem to want to throw suspicion on George, who had given her the fowl. Claire's talk of "the courage to kill" is the deluded mind's rationale for murder—an attempt to give a mercenary act some grandeur—and an idea that the film's ironic denouement will expose as that of desperation.

Claire's startled cough at the revelation of Alice's $40,000 savings ($40,000 was the amount Marion Crane stole in *Psycho*) is perhaps too obvious a reaction, as is the dripping tap and the snooping that leads Claire to catch Alice in a lie. The top of Claire's head and eyes seen from behind a chair; an extreme close-up of her eyes; and an extended close-up of her watching Alice as the record player winds down are all effective in presenting Claire as a threat. Claire's laugh when Alice's real grey hair is revealed is a good example of grande dame oneupmanship. The ominous opening of a door, with the intruding feet revealed to be those belonging to Alice and not Claire, works against the horror convention; though the expectation that warm milk will be used to scald is fulfilled.

The final confrontation between the two women reveals the fact that Edna Tinsley was Alice's companion, which implies that Alice has abandoned her own gracious life to investigate Edna's dis-

Claire Marrable (Geraldine Page) and Alice Dimmock (Ruth Gordon) in *What Ever Happened to Aunt Alice?* (1969).

appearance. The physical confrontation would seem mismatched because of Gordon's greater age, and Katzin initially emphasizes Alice's vulnerability by placing Claire in shadow, making her a horror movie monster. While the prospect of seeing two women physically grapple is acceptable for the genre, the narrative provides a surprise when Alice refuses to hit the prone Claire with a wooden statue and thus claim victory. This establishes Alice's moral superiority and humanity, qualities which are not always advantageous in a horror movie. Alice's foolishness in turning her back on Claire, who we know can fight dirty, is rewarded with Alice being strangled with the telephone cord and then hit with the receiver. Claire's throwaway line that the phone is "dead" is black comedy, since our protagonist has been defeated. But Katzin's subsequent cut to Claire's secret graveyard under the pine trees as Paige laughs is cleverly misleading, since Alice is not yet dead.

Alice unconscious in a wheelchair recalls the unconscious Elvira and Blanche in wheelchairs in *What Ever Happened to Baby Jane?* and the women together in a car recalls Davis and Crawford in *What Ever Happened to Baby Jane?*—as well as Davis and deHavilland in *Hush ... Hush, Sweet Charlotte*. The idea of Claire being unable to get out of the car, which is rolling into the lake, provides suspense (and the car being pushed into the lake recalls the cars in the swamp in *Psycho*). This time, however, the victim is alive, and we see her underwater. Claire's laughter marks a sardonic end to our hopes that Alice will survive. While we know that Alice has told Mike her suspicion that Claire is a killer, her telling Claire that "she told" is also a pathetic attempt to save her life. That Claire would assume the person told is Harriet is something Alice may have been able to predict, considering what a small circle of acquaintances they have, but we still don't blame Alice for Harriet's attack.

Claire Marrable (Geraldine Page) attacks with a spade in *What Ever Happened to Aunt Alice?* (1969).

Chloe's barking shows that she has escaped from the fire. The close-up of Claire looking out her window to what is revealed to be her uprooted pine trees, and then closing the curtain in front of her face, is both a horror convention and an example of Page's silent expressiveness. Claire's laughter ends the film when she proposes herself as a companion with the line, "After all, I'd make a handsome pine tree." Such a closing sidesteps camp, however, by the inclusion of Page's tears and a final feeling of empathy for her situation as the defeated antagonist and the trapped protagonist.

Geraldine Page was 44 at the time of filming, and Ruth Gordon was 72. Page had last played a leading role in *Dear Heart* (1964). Better known as a Broadway actress, Page was nominated for the Best Actress Academy Award for *Summer and Smoke* (1961) and *Sweet Bird of Youth* (1962), two parts she had played on stage. She was also nominated for Best Supporting Actress for

Hondo (1953) and *You're a Big Boy Now* (1966). She would eventually win the Best Actress Oscar for *The Trip to Bountiful* (1985).

Ruth Gordon came to *What Ever Happened to Aunt Alice?* after having won the Best Supporting Actress Academy Award for *Rosemary's Baby* (1968). Her last leading role had been in *Dr. Ehrlich's Magic Bullet* (1940). Apart from her role the same year in *Abe Lincoln in Illinois*, she was only featured in supporting roles. This would change when she later played the lead in the cult favorite *Harold and Maude* (1971). Ironically, her early life story was told in *The Actress* (1953), but by this time Gordon was too old to play herself. She found a second career as a Broadway playwright, and returned to Hollywood, with her husband Garson Kanin, as a screenwriter for films starring Katharine Hepburn and Spencer Tracy. Gordon was cast as Alice over Helen Hayes, who hadn't made a film since *Anastasia* (1956) but who was four years younger. Hayes would go on to win the Best Supporting Actress Academy Award for *Airport* the next year.

Page's Method-acting mannerisms and her theatrical intonation are perfect for Claire's grande dame, who is both patronizingly funny and frightening. When Claire learns of her seeming destitution, Page retreats from the camera's stare like a wounded animal. Her face crumbling with disappointment and fear, she finally turns away, with one hand spread like a claw. Katzin photographs Page unflatteringly, her hair grey and disheveled. When Claire wears Alice's wig, Page momentarily looks younger, though strands of Claire's grey hair peek out from underneath. Page's laughter over a shot of the pine trees in her garden is used as a motif through the film, and she is wonderful at delivering lines that are only partially witty on their own.

When Alice refuses to hit the prone Claire in the fight scene, Page's reaction in close-up suggests Claire's amusement and insanity, as does her laughter at the denouement. Gordon's inventive and eccentric performance creates a fascinating counterpoint to Page's outrageous technique, with the strawberry-blonde hair Gordon sports later revealed to be a wig. While the wig is a character choice for Alice, it cannot be credited as an effort made to conceal her age, since the wrinkles around Gordon's mouth are readily apparent.

Release

July 23, 1969, in New York, and August 20, 1969, in general, with the taglines, "A horrific tale ... with grave consequences!" "What makes her garden grow ... wouldn't you like to know!" and "Whatever happened to Aunt Alice was more terrifying than what happened to Baby Jane."

Reviews

"[A]n amusingly baroque horror story told by a master mysogynist [Aldrich].... Miss Page touches everything with a sense of inspired madness. And if you demand parody, there's always the busy performance of Ruth Gordon, wearing a curly red wig and looking like a crazy, animated peanut."—Vincent Canby, *The New York Times*, July 24, 1969.

"Fresh story, using old-hat scare tricks that still work, and top direction combine with highly skilled acting.... Miss Page delivers a bravura performance. Miss Gordon, working crisply, offers a remarkable portrait of a brave woman. The two ladies play off each other relentlessly and audience reaps the reward."—*Variety*, July 16, 1969.

"Not particularly well directed, but admirably uncluttered and done with ghoulish relish, the film boasts fine camerawork by Biroc, who makes a memorable image of Page's garden blooming in the Arizona desert, each tree fertilized by a body beneath."—Phil Hardy, *The Aurum Film Encyclopedia of Horror*.

Eye of the Cat (1969)
(aka *Wylie*)

Universal/Joseph L. Schenck Enterprise Production

CREDITS: *Director:* David Lowell Rich; *Producers:* Bernard Schwartz, Phillip Hazelton; *Screenplay:* Joseph Stefano; *Photography:* Russell Metty, Ellsworth Fredericks; *Music:* Lalo Schifrin; *Editor:* J. Terry Williams; *Art Directors:* Alexander Golitzen, William D. DeCinces; *Set Decoration:* John McCarthy, John Austin; *Sound:* Waldon O. Watson, Frank H. Wilkinson; *Production Manager:* Henry Kline; *Make-up:* Bud Westmore; *Hair:* Larry Germain; *Wardrobe:* Edith Head; *Animal Trainer:* Ray Berwick. Color, 102 minutes. Filmed in San Francisco.

CAST: Michael Sarazzin (*Wylie*); Gayle Hunnicutt (*Kassia Lancaster*); Eleanor Parker (*Aunt Danny*); Tim Henry (*Luke*); Laurence Naismith (*Dr. Mills*); Jennifer Leak (*Poor Dear*); Linden Chiles (*Tendetto*); Mark Herron (*Bellemondo*); Annabelle Garth (*Socialite*); "Tullia" The Cat.

VHS/DVD: No current release in either format.

Plot

Aunt Danny is a wealthy San Francisco dowager who is dying from emphysema. On a trip to her beauty parlor, Bellemondo's, a cat hides in her limousine, causing her to have an attack. As a witness to the attack, beautician Kassia Lancaster devises a scheme to steal Danny's fortune, and finds Danny's estranged nephew Wylie to help her. When Kassia gives Wylie a make-over, they are interrupted by the same cat, which sets off Wylie's ailurophobia (a fear of cats). After reuniting with his brother Luke at Danny's, Wylie discovers that the house is overrun with cats, and that Danny has made them the heirs to her estate. Danny agrees to remove the cats and change her will to make Wylie her heir, whom she favors over Luke. Danny is nearly killed in an incident when her electronic wheelchair short circuits and she rolls down a hill, only to be saved by Luke at the last minute before the chair is crushed by street traffic.

After the new will is signed, Kassia and Wylie plan to murder Danny; however, the return of one cat stops Kassia from turning off Danny's oxygen supply. When the cat goes to Wylie, shock and fear sends him into a coma. Luke places Wylie's body in the cellar, hoping that he will die of fright, since Luke is revealed to be Kassia's real boyfriend. While Luke turns off Danny's oxygen, the cat stalks Kassia, forcing her up a ladder in the conservatory garden. Kassia falls to her death when the cat attacks. When Luke hears her scream, he finds Danny also in the conservatory, who informs him that Wylie had brought her there to save her from Kassia and Luke. Wylie reappears to say goodbye to Luke and Danny, and leaves the house.

Notes

A Grande Dame Guignol written by Joseph Stefano which has more talk than action (and little blood), this film by David Lowell Rich only sporadically succeeds as a horror movie. While the narrative limits the grande dame by making her a Woman in Peril, she does have an unhealthy fixation on one of her Cain-and-Abel nephews. And then there's the classic sequence of her rolling down a steep San Francisco hill in a wheelchair. The picture also pits the grande dame against a younger rival, a scenario repeated from *Strait-Jacket, I Saw What You Did, Lady in a Cage, Die! Die! My Darling! The Night Walker, The Witches, Games,* and *Berserk*.

David Lowell Rich had directed a lot of television, and although he had not done a horror title, he had made *Madame X* (1966), *Rosie!* (1967), *A Lovely Way to Die* (1968), and *Three Guns for Texas* (1968). Joseph L. Schenck Enterprises had previously made the science fiction adventure *Journey to the Center of the Earth* (1959), and the drama *Rage* (1966). *Eye of the Cat* would be its last production. Producers Bernard Schwartz and Philip Hazelton had previously produced the horror title *The Shuttered Room* (1967).

The film opens with the animation of a walking white cat superimposed over the street where Danny lives, which is intercut with a marmalade-colored cat seen entering the house and wandering the rooms. Observation will be a recurring motif in the narrative, whether by cats or humans. Director David Rich uses split-screen and triple-screen images to provide alternate perspectives on the same activity, such as Danny leaving the house and being driven by Luke to Bellemondo's. The split-screen effects are an example of Rich's postmodern film effects, which also include jump and flash cuts, zooms, extreme close-ups, and a ghostly image distortion for a flashback scene. That the marmalade cat will sneak into the car and follow Danny into the room where her hair is being done shows the animal's agility, intrusiveness, and danger. An irony involving Danny's affection for the cats is that their fur is counterproduc-

Poster for *Eye of the Cat* (1969).

tive to her health, since she uses a wheelchair and oxygen (both in the backseat of her limousine and in an oxygen tent in bed at night).

When Danny experiences her attack, she drops a necklace with a cameo, which springs open to show a photograph of Wylie (and which will be stolen by Kassia). Danny's gasping for breath is grande guignol, and Rich has her fall toward the camera, with an extreme close-up of the dark interior of her mouth transitioning to a black screen. A cat seen in shadow before it enters is a horror movie convention, and Rich uses it when Kassia gives Wylie a make-over. Kassia's objectification of Wylie's body, although it can be rationalized as professionalism, foreshadows the fact that she cannot be trusted. The eye-dropper she uses on him continues the metaphor of watching, and underscores the idea that she will deceive him (i.e., she wants him to see her in a way that is not the truth).

We are told that Danny considers Wylie "the prince of her soul," and that he had run away from her after stealing $5,000. Kassia's assumption that Wylie would agree to her scheme is based on him being a thief. Wylie and Kassia, then, are established as co-conspirators and double antagonists to Danny's protagonist. Wylie's fear of cats is introduced when he hears the sound of the marmalade cat purring, which Wylie calls a "death rattle." He recounts a childhood trauma in which a black cat climbed onto his crib and placed its mouth over his to "suck the breath out of the baby's mouth." Rich employs flash-cuts and a close-up of the black cat advancing in slow motion for the flashback.

The hiss of the oxygen tent in Danny's room accompanies our introduction to her, with the hiss recalling that of a cat. Wylie's discovery of Danny's one hundred cats is supplemented by her cat statues, showing how Danny's interest is also a fetish. The grande dame is defined by the size of her house, her wealth, and her obsession with Wylie. One thing that makes Danny different from other grande dames is that, aside from the fact that she's dying, she is not particularly preoccupied with her youth. Her decision to take in one hundred stray cats to be the "heirs" to her fortune (before Wylie returns to claim it) also attests to her perceived isolation. The revelation that Danny hates Luke, who lives with her as a companion, because she favors the absent Wylie indicates her great need for love.

Wylie (Michael Sarazzin) and his Aunt Danny (Eleanor Parker) in *Eye of the Cat* (1969).

Luke makes an interesting comment on Wylie's running away, after Wylie had earlier called him Danny's "slave": "He runs away to prove he's free and always comes back because he's convinced he's not."

A dialogue exchange between Wylie and Kassia foreshadows Kassia's demise and adds some wit to the screenplay:

> WYLIE: It's not a good idea to take cats lightly.
> KASSIA: That depends on whether you're a man or a mouse.

The greenhouse conservatory, with its wild and overgrown plants, recalls the garden of Violet Venable in Tennessee Williams's play *Suddenly Last Summer*, and the rain-ruined curtains will become significant during the climax. In the park scene, Danny's ingratitude and bias becomes apparent when she sees Wylie and dismisses Luke with the camp line, "This moment's not for sharing." The book Wylie reads when he is alone is called "Knowing Yourself," another Stefano joke in a narrative full of deception.

Danny being willing to sacrifice her cats for Wylie is a testament to her love for him. In contrast, the disposable love she has for the cats is reiterated when she removes, and presumably kills, the kittens that Luke has missed in his sweep of the house. Rich makes the sight of the cats running for food as they are lured by Luke into Danny's limousine horrifying in its domestic context. When Danny calls her lawyer to rewrite her will, her line, "Impossible isn't a word I retain you to use," sums up her haughtiness and demanding need for control.

The network television version of *Eye of the Cat* supposedly used outtakes and added new scenes filmed by persons unknown in 1971. While the plot descriptions in period reviews of the film and the pressbook suggest that the bulk of the narrative has been retained, and only the last thirty minutes were affected, there are elements in the edited version that still allude to the original intent. In regards of the marmalade cat, ambiguity arises due to the fact we do not know whether the cat has stayed behind or has returned. The re-edited film shows this one cat as being the only returning feline, as opposed to all the cats that returned in the original edit of the film. However, since the marmalade cat will feature in the wheelchair-rolling-down-the-hill scene, it is possible that this cat originally stayed behind, while the rest of the felines returned for the climax.

Wylie holding his breath under water in the bath shows his resilience after the cat trauma. Luke dries Wylie with a towel in a brotherly yet homoerotic fashion, while dialogue reveals that it was Luke who stole the money from Danny's strongbox for Wylie. An exchange between Danny and Luke after Danny has suffered another attack from the excitement of Wylie racing her about in her wheelchair in the conservatory offers more Stefano wordplay and double meanings (predicated upon Luke being aware of Kassia and Wylie's apparent plot):

> LUKE: I hope they do kill you.
> DANNY: What are you talking about?
> LUKE: Your lungs, of course. What did you think I was talking about?

Wylie calls Danny a "dirty old man" for her interest in Luke's sex life, although we know that she has a greater interest in Wylie's sexuality. The romantic montage that Rich provides of Wylie and Kassia driving, walking, and sailing in Sausalito feels like unnecessary filler. However, it does contain one interesting plot point, when Kassia admits that she has fallen in love with Wylie, as opposed to her previous opportunistic use of him. The youth ship party that follows features marijuana smoking and sitar playing, and another blackly funny Stefano line when a man tells a woman in passing, "Isn't it about time that you stopped talking about dying and started doing something about it?"

The comment reminds us of the black but *un*funny plan Kassia has instigated, so the party culminating in a catfight between her and Wylie's former girlfriend, Poor Dear, is appropriate. As ugly as catfighting is to witness (where women brawl like men), the term "catfight" is particularly apt for the context of this film. The fight being an amusement for male onlookers also adds a sexual undercurrent, and can be paralleled to the antagonism between Kassia and Danny (the older grande dame threatened by a younger rival).

Throughout the film, Rich gives equal time to shots of the marmalade cat watching as he does of Kassia observing, thereby comparing their focus and determination (although the re-edited version of the film gives the cat the advantage). These scenes in which the camera elegantly pans around the multi-leveled interior of the house are reminiscent of theatre, though with minimal dialogue and music.

The wheelchair-rolling-down-the-hill sequence is the highlight of the film, and begins with Danny on the street and the short-circuiting of the chair's electrical control. As we have not seen anyone tamper with the chair, this is presented as fortuitous. The appearance of the marmalade cat is just as fateful, as it keeps Wylie away and unable to help her. When the cat jumps into her lap, Danny loses her grip on the brickwork she had been holding onto for support. The cat jumps at Wylie as Danny's chair rolls backwards, and her nightmarish descent is filmed in slow motion. The efforts to rescue her seem unwarranted, and Luke's actions seem mystifying, given his real agenda (while Wylie's actions are revealing of his).

An exchange between Dr. Mills and Danny following the incident, after he has sedated her, features more Stefano wordplay:

> Dr. Mills: Let the dreams come.
> Danny: They're going to murder me!
> Dr. Mills: No one has ever been murdered by a dream.

The slap that Wylie gives Kassia when she threatens to turn off Danny's air supply reveals Wylie's true intention, although it doesn't stop Kassia from trying anyway. Rich has Hunnicutt stand behind a lamp so that the light underneath Kassia's face in close-up makes her look evil as she watches Danny, with the hiss of the air again used as a conventional device of suspense. Danny under the oxygen tent is both grande guignol and a romantic view of isolation, since Rich photographs Eleanor Parker looking very beautiful behind the tent's filter. The marmalade cat's growl at Kassia as she approaches Danny signals the point of the film where the one hundred cats may have originally appeared, given that Danny's room is where we first saw them. However, a scratch from the one cat is enough to stop Kassia, and we get repeat of a cat traumatizing Wylie when the marmalade cat goes to him.

Luke scares the cat away from Wylie, but not before Wylie goes into catatonic shock, captured by Rich in close-up. The shock being fake would make more sense considering the film's ending. (If the shock is real, we presume that the marmalade cat's actions have reversed Wylie's condition. Rich doesn't let on.)

Luke's sudden kissing of Kassia reveals his involvement with her, expressed before the apparently enfeebled Wylie. Dr. Mills has conveniently told Luke of a patient of his with a similar catalepsy as Wylie's, who has died of fright brought on by claustrophobia after being locked in a broom closet. Rich shows us Wylie's cataleptic point of view using an out-of-focus camera, recalling the ghostly images of the flashback to Wylie's father's funeral.

Eye of the Cat (1969)

While Luke deals with Wylie, Rich intercuts to the cat (or cats) dealing with Kassia. Hunnicutt's reaction shots suggest that she is chased by a horde of felines not the single marmalade cat we are shown, and the idea of only one cat forcing her to climb a ladder is preposterous. The fall to her death has been foreshadowed by the earlier sight of Luke using the ladder to remove the ruined curtains, so that now Kassia has less to hold onto. Her losing her grip also recalls Danny losing her grip in the wheelchair-rolling-down-the-hill sequence. Luke's discovery of Danny in the conservatory is a thriller shock, as is Wylie's reappearance. Although we are to believe that Wylie has lost his fear, Danny's line that "the cats are everywhere" implies that she thinks he is still susceptible to them. Her comment is also another indication of the original intent to include one hundred cats. The film lacks a satisfying denouement, unless we are supposed to feel that Luke being left with Danny in mutual misery is some sort of poetic justice.

The film's publicity pressbook includes two stills from what are presumably scenes deleted from the existing available copy of the film. One shows Kassia being frightened by a black cat that leaps on her to grab the food she is carrying. The other shows Kassia bloodied and "apparently attacked by some of the more than 50 felines living there." In the photo, four black cats can be seen behind Kassia as she walks away from the staircase, pursued by the animals. This still in particular confirms the notion that all the cats returned for the climactic attack on Kassia, although other pressbook imagery indicates that only the marmalade cat followed her up the ladder.

Eleanor Parker was 46 at the time of filming. Her last leading role had been in the comedy *Panic Button* (1964), and she had been playing supporting parts, most notably in *The Sound of Music* (1965). Parker had been nominated three times for the Best Actress Academy Award—for *Caged* (1950), *Detective Story* (1951), and *Interrupted Melody* (1955)—but had never won.

In her wheelchair, Parker recalls Joan Crawford in *What Ever Happened to Baby Jane?* Ruth Gordon in *What Ever Happened to Aunt Alice?* and Miriam Hop-

This faux-newspaper article from the *Eye of the Cat* pressbook features an image of Kassia (Gayle Hunnicutt) pursued by cats in a scene missing from the available version of the film *Eye of the Cat* (1969).

kins in *The Savage Intruder*. Known for an acting style that verges on over-acting, Parker makes Danny's improper obsession with a man half her age (and her nephew, to boot) believable in her *Sunset Boulevard*/Norma Desmond–style grasping and casual cruelty. Although Danny isn't the most empathetic of the big-screen grande dames, it's a shame Parker doesn't make us care more about Danny's plight, since this is a woman suffering (and who's also wanted dead by everyone around her—apart from her cats). It's frustrating that the screenplay fails to offer more about Danny's past, since the possibility of her being an incestuous mistress holds such potential.

Parker abandons her usual blonde hair to appear as a brunette, sporting a long black witch's hairstyle and false black eyelashes. The dark hair sets off her pale skin (possibly made even paler because her character is a recluse). The lines on her neck are exposed by the collars of the clothes she wears, which include the fur borders of a pink, floor-length nightgown that echoes the fur of her cats. Rich makes no attempt to conceal Parker's age, except in two key scenes. When Danny overhears Kassia and Wylie talking about the murder plan in the conservatory, Rich photographs Parker with shadowed lines on her face—presumably shadows from tree branches, but also to indicate foreboding. The semi-shadow on her face when Wylie leaves, where only her forehead and eyes are illuminated, suggests the sadness of her loss and perhaps the sinister retribution she will inflict on Luke.

Release

June 18, 1969, with the taglines, "Terror that takes you beyond any fear you've ever known," and "Terror that tears the screams right out of your throat!"

Reviews

"...[D]irection creates electric tension and real horror. However, the scenario drops the cats about mid-point, then drags the animals back for a climax that is as hokey as it is horrible."—Howard Thompson, *The New York Times*, June 19, 1969.

"Pic has a few good jolts, successful buildups, and good looking people, but stilted dialogue and plot shot through with holes keep mystery at a minimum, suspense overdue.... Parker struggles valiantly in an ill-defined role."—*Variety*, June 2, 1969.

"Rich is no Hitchcock, and though extravagantly enjoyable with excellent performances, the film never quite brings off its notion of the house as a family hell in which the characters are trapped by the grim charade of their own devising."—Phil Hardy, *The Aurum Film Encyclopedia of Horror*.

The Mad Room (1969)

Columbia Pictures

CREW: *Director:* Bernard Girard; *Producer:* Norman Maurer; *Screenplay:* Bernard Girard and A.Z. Martin, based on a screenplay by Reginald Denham and Garrett Fort, which was based on the play *Ladies in Retirement* by Reginald Denham and Edward Percy; *Photography:* Harry Stradling, Jr; *Editor:* Pat Somerset; *Art Direction:* Sydney Z. Litwack; *Set Decoration:* Sid Clifford; *Sound:* James Z. Flaster, Arthur Piantadosi; *Music:* Dave Grusin; *Wardrobe:* Moss Marby; *Hair:* Virginia Jones*: Make-up:* Ben Lane. Color, 92 minutes. Filmed in Vancouver, British Columbia.

SONGS: "Open My Eyes" and "Wildwood Blues" (both by Nazz).

CAST: Stella Stevens (*Ellen Hardy*); Shelley Winters (*Mrs. Gladys Armstrong*); Skip Ward (*Sam Aller*); Carol Cole (*Chris*); Severn Darden (*Nate*); Beverly Garland (*Mrs. Racine*); Michael Burns (*George*); Jenifer Bishop (*Mrs. Sally Ericson*); Gloria Manon (*Edna*); Lloyd Haynes (*Dr. Marion Kincaid*) ; Barbara Sammeth (*Mandy*); Lou Kane (*Armand Racine*); Uncredited: Allen Pinson (*Security Guard*); Emil Sitka.

VHS/DVD: No current release in either format.

Plot

Ellen Hardy is the companion to Mrs. Gladys Armstrong, a wealthy widow who lives with her stepson, Sam Aller, and her maid-secretary, Chris, in a mansion on Vancouver Island, Canada. Mrs. Armstrong is building a museum on the property as a tribute to her husband. Ellen and Sam are preparing to marry when Ellen learns that her eighteen-year-old brother, George, and sixteen-year-old sister, Mandy, are to be released from the Hospital for Mental Ills in Ontario where they have been confined for years. At six and four, they were the prime suspects in the butcher knife–slaying of their sleeping parents, but it was never determined which of the two was responsible. Claiming that the teenagers are staying with an uncle who recently died, Mrs. Armstrong invites Ellen to move them into the mansion. George and Mandy tell Ellen that they need a "mad room" where they can go to let off steam, and Ellen secretly lets them use an attic study which Mrs. Armstrong has kept locked since her husband's death.

When Mrs. Armstrong discovers the "mad room," and Ellen tells her about the children's past, she is unnerved. That night Ellen finds Mrs. Armstrong hacked to death.

The children first suspect each other, but they finally realize that Ellen has committed both the present *and* the past murders. To cover up the crime, Ellen disposes of Mrs. Armstrong's corpse in a dam and plants evidence indicating that the death was accidental. At a committee meeting of museum fundraisers at the mansion, the wife of Mrs. Armstrong's masseur, Armand, claims that the missing Mrs. Armstrong has run away with her husband. This provides Ellen with a convenient explanation for Mrs. Armstrong's absence. Unbeknownst to Ellen, however, Major, the family dog, has carried off one of Mrs. Armstrong's severed hands. Ellen sees Major with the hand, and Sam sees Ellen butchering the troublesome hound in the mansion basement with one of Mr. Armstrong's sabers. Caught, Ellen sits on the floor and cries "Forgive them," still trying to blame others for her actions.

Notes

Ladies in Retirement (1941) was a melodrama and not a horror movie, and *The Mad Room* cannot be viewed as a remake since it alters the source material considerably. The original film had already altered the set-up by casting the twenty-three-year-old Ida Lupino as Ellen at forty (who was sixty in the play). *The Mad Room* turns the original old sisters into younger male and female teenagers, thereby making Ellen the older character, although she is still young herself. The new film's Ellen is both guilty of the crime that her brother and sister have been committed for, and guilty of the murder she blames on them after their release. The original presented the two siblings as mad, but did not implicate Ellen in their crime or have the sisters kill the mistress of the house to which they had come. It also made more of the resistance of the house's owner to the sisters' presence, whereas this new version does not, though her murder implies that this would be forthcoming.

Additionally, the original included characters who investigated the murder, which are not present in the new version, and the consequences of Ellen's crime were more apparent when she fled the home to turn herself over to the police. Here Ellen does not admit to what she has done, or even leave the home. However, the idea of the murdered mistress being a grande dame is maintained, with Shelley Winters making her first in a series of Grande Dame Guignol appearances. While *The Mad Room* offers some grande guignol, the film is less effective once the grande dame is removed from the narrative, since Stella Stevens lacks the charisma as a performer to match or replace Winters. Although the director, Bernard Girard, repeatedly uses the device of overlapping dialogue (which director Robert Altman would make popular in the 1970s), the film in general is harmed by the intrusive music score of Dave Gruisin.

Bernard Girard had last directed the crime drama *Dead Heat on a Merry-Go-Round* (1966). He had not directed a horror movie before, but he had helmed episodes of the television anthology series *The Alfred Hitchcock Hour*, *The Twilight Zone*, and *Alfred Hitchcock Presents*. Producer Norman Maurer had previously made films with the Three Stooges, as well as the romantic comedy *Who's Minding the Mint?* (1967).

The opening credits of *The Mad Room* utilize newspaper headlines about the murders the children are accused of, after blood-spattered wildflowers are shown on the door and walls of the parent's home, as well as a bloody and lifeless arm. Girard has the red "m" of the title's "Room" drip to suggest blood, and uses red as the color of Sam's car and Chris's nightgown. When Ellen is first seen, she is running across a bridge in an extreme long shot. Her pastel-colored Baby Jane–ish dresses, kewpie-doll make-up, and sculpted blonde hair all give the impression of a person who is hiding something. This duplicity is reinforced by the way Girard favors the back of Ellen's head, and the way she is photographed in pieces (e.g., in one scene only half of her is seen in a mirror, while all of George and Mandy are on view). After Ellen and Sam make love in the grass, the builder Nate tells Sam, "You look all petered out"—a sly use of the colloquialism of "peter" for penis.

The sight of Gladys receiving a massage, with Winter's back flesh exposed, recalls the massage scenes with Bette Davis in *Dead Ringer* and Miriam Hopkins in *The Savage Intruder*. The inference that Gladys is having an affair with Armand gives her some grande dame sexuality and a love interest that is refreshing for the subgenre. Although Gladys has invited George and Mandy to her house, Gladys is presented as the film's protagonist to their perceived antagonism, with Ellen an antagonist by her family relation. When Ellen goes to see George and Mandy in the asylum, Girard shows empty swings swinging in a park, a colored mobile of pointing hands (in a narrative where a dismembered hand will feature), and the odd sight of the other children running in a circle as if they are trapped. Gladys's language defines her character as a grande dame when she orders Nate out of the house to "feed him" (i.e., to give him orders), as does her comment to Ellen:

> You know, Ellen, I always thought that you would give me credit for sensing falsehood. But then again, I never did actually think that you would give me reason to distrust you.

Gladys' drinking from a balloon glass of brandy before bed is a sign of pretentiousness, and Chris reveals how Gladys wears false teeth (that we never see evidence of), which she keeps in a glass of water, and how water once dripped from them as Gladys smiled at her. Gladys's enjoyment of dog-racing receives a perverse spin in the way she keeps her dog tied up and half-starved, with the image of one dog growling and foaming more potent than the human killings in the film. This mistreatment of dogs will come back to bite Gladys when Major refuses to stay and protect her from the perceived threat of the guests in her house, after she had earlier chased the dog out of the house. Consequently, Major's taking her dismembered hand—twice—is a funny, macabre revenge upon her. Interestingly, Major's murder, which Girard films with an out-of-focus lens, is the only one we are witness to.

Winters gives Gladys

Lobby card for *The Mad Room* (1969): Ellen Hardy (Stella Stevens) and Gladys Armstrong (Shelley Winters).

both a shrewish yell and breathless intonation. Girard presents her as a horror movie monster when she stands at the top of the stairs as Ellen ascends, with the camera below Ellen to show how overpowering Gladys is. Previous to this confrontation, Girard had shown Gladys to be the Woman in Peril by the low and high camera angles he used to photograph her as she walked down a semi-lit corridor to the "mad room."

Ellen's confession to Gladys about her childhood is undermined by the music which accompanies it. Girard provides a ghostly flashback of Ellen at fourteen at the time of her parents' murder, during which she wears her blonde hair in curlers. Ellen confiding that her mother didn't enjoy being pregnant and hated her three children emphasizes a lack of the maternal instinct, which can also be applied to Gladys, who has no children and is suspicious of Ellen's motives for concealing her siblings from Sam. The toys that were burned to keep the children warm represent the destruction of their childhood and a reason for Ellen, as the eldest child, to resent the parents enough to kill them.

Girard shows Chris playing rock music in her room when Gladys's murder occurs, although only the aftermath is shown (and even that is partly obscured). The music would have muffled Gladys's presumed cries and vocal attempts to identify her attacker. Mandy smearing blood from the walls all over herself seems an odd reaction (though perhaps not—if one considers her a child already traumatized by the murder of her parents). When George accuses Mandy of being Gladys's killer, the extended fight between Ellen and George is also accompanied by rock music. Ellen's battle to overcome George's strength in her ultra-feminine dress adds comic and sexual components to the struggle.

When Ellen talks to George and Mandy after the fight, her statements are unconvincing, which is either a comment on Stevens's performance or an intimation that Ellen killed Gladys. If we are to blame Ellen for murdering Gladys, this would establish her as the younger antagonist to Gladys's older grande dame, a pattern that had been seen in *Strait-Jacket, Lady in a Cage, Die! Die My Darling! The Night Walker, I Saw What You Did, Games, Berserk,* and *Eye of the Cat.* This younger-woman-versus-older-woman equation is further highlighted by the even younger ages of George and Mandy.

The women's committee at the mansion restores the grande dame quotient, with Sally's voice sounding like Gladys.' Girard presents the gathering as a group of gargoyles, all greedily eating and talking at once, and all wearing ridiculous society hats. Mrs. Racine's drunken speech receives a great payoff when she goes to the bathroom and throws down the bottle she is drinking from. A piece of the glass is used to cut her wrist, another off-camera act of violence. The nighttime removal of Gladys's body by Ellen and George is supplemented by the patterned shadow on Ellen's car, and Glady's body falling down the dam almost looks like animation, with Winters given an upside-down close-up

George (Michael Burns) and Mandy (Barbara Sammeth) in shadowed profile in *The Mad Room* (1969).

behind churning water. This disposal of a body recalls similar actions in *What Ever Happened to Baby Jane?*, *Hush ... Hush, Sweet Charlotte*, *I Saw What You Did*, *Games*, and *The Savage Intruder*.

Ellen painting wildflowers in the bathroom with Mrs. Racine's blood links Ellen to the murder of her parents, and Girard places Stevens in the center of one wildflower on the mirror as Ellen sings a child's wildflower song (unidentified). This act establishes Ellen as the antagonist to George and Mandy's nominal protagonists, although neither Girard nor the audience has invested George or Mandy with any sympathy up until the point we realize that they have been wrongfully committed. George had been established as a horny teenager, ogling the legs of women and looking up their dresses during the boat trip to the mansion. However, the expected rape in his pursuit of Chris fails to materialize. Although George's burgeoning relationship with Chris is meant to make him more acces-

Gladys Armstrong (Shelley Winters) as grande dame Woman in Peril in *The Mad Room* (1969).

sible their resultant romance becomes a plot distraction. Mandy is more unlikable, and rather tomboyish, in comparison to Ellen's cartoony girlishness. Ellen's wildflower paintings also parallel the scenario they have created for Glady's fall into the dam, where, before, she had been painting alongside it. If we believe that George and Mandy did not kill their parents, and that Ellen did, then there really is no other suspect in the killing of Gladys. But her murder remains unsolved.

Shelley Winters had been working steadily in the 1960s, having won the Best Supporting Actress Oscars for *The Diary of Anne Frank* (1959) and *A Patch of Blue* (1965). Her last leading role had been in the comedy *Buona Sera, Mrs. Campbell* (1968), and she was age 48 at the time of filming *The Mad Room*.

Release

New York: April 30, 1969; USA: May 1, 1969, with the tagline, "Forgive Them. Forgive Them. Forgive Them"

Reviews

"...[A] weak story which has actually all been seen before, and in most cases better developed ... any astute filmgoer will perceive the twist long before it comes.... Miss Winters knows just how to throw away a line and give it the right touch of humor."—*Variety*, March 12, 1969.

"...[A] fine suspense-shocker ... a dandy chiller that is original, civilized, well played, exquisitely directed and scenic. Threading it all is a current of electric tension that triggers a jolting surprise and a hair-raising postcript.... [Girard] has given real horror a new look it has long deserved."—Howard Thompson, *The New York Times*, May 1, 1969.

"Tasteless remake of *Ladies in Retirement*, in the brutalized vein which audiences are supposed by producers to want. In modern dress and sharp locations, it succeeds only in being nauseating."—David Gritten, *Halliwell's Film Guide*.

"American Gothic: a remake of *Ladies in Retirement*, rather disastrously renovated for contemporary consumption.... Skeletons in the cupboard, hacked-up bodies, and severed hands still can't make it anything more than routine."—*Time Out Film Guide*.

That Cold Day in the Park (1969)

Commonwealth United Entertainment

CREDITS: *Director:* Robert Altman; *Producers:* Donald Factor, Leon Mirell; *Associate Producer:* Robert Eggenweiler; *Screenplay:* Gillian Freeman, based on a novel by Richard Miles; *Photography:* Laszlo Kovacs; *Music:* Johnny Mandel; *Editor:* Danford B. Greene; *Art Decorator:* Leon Ericksen; *Production Executive:* James Margellos; *Sound:* John H. W. Gusselle; *Make-up:* Phyllis Newman; *Wardrobe:* Ilse Richter; *Hair:* Salli Bailey. Color, 113 minutes. Filmed at Panorama Studios, Vancouver, Canada.

CAST: Sandy Dennis (*Frances Austen*); Michael Burns (*the Boy*); Susanne Benton (*Nina*); John Garfield Jr. (*Nicky*); Luana Anders (*Sylvia*); Edward Greenhalgh (*Dr. Charles Stevenson*); Doris Hickingham (*Mrs. Edory*); Frank Wade (*Mr. Edory*); Alicia Ammon (*Mrs. Pitt*); Rae Brown (*Mrs. Parnell*); Lloyd Berry (*Mr. Parnell*); Linda Sorenson (*the Prostitute*); Michael Murphy (*the Rounder*).

VHS/DVD: DVD released by Force Video on March, 15 2004, in the United Kingdom. VHS edition released by Republic Pictures in the USA on January 1, 1998.

Plot

Frances Austen lives in the Vancouver apartment of her deceased mother and continues to socialize with her mother's aged friends. At lunch one day she becomes preoccupied with a young man sitting on a park bench who she sees from her window. When it begins to rain, Frances goes to him and invites him to dry off in her apartment. Accepting wordlessly, he goes with Frances. She runs him a bath, feeds him, and plays music for his entertainment. All this time the boy does not speak. She asks him to sleep over in her spare room, since his clothes will not dry until the morning. He stays, and she locks his door. The next morning Frances serves him breakfast, then leaves to buy him new clothes, while the boy explores her apartment. That night the boy climbs out the window and down the fire escape. He returns to his parents' house, and then visits the houseboat where his sister Nina lives. Smoking marijuana and eating hash cookies, the boy talks about Frances. He is grateful that, thanks to her, he now has his own room and bed.

The boy returns to Frances's apartment and gives her some of the hash cookies. They get stoned together, though Frances is unaware of the cookies' ingredients, and play blind man's bluff. When Frances goes to a gynecologist and then goes bowling with her friends, Nina visits the boy at the apartment, taking a bath of her own. Frances returns with Charles, who tells her of his romantic interest. Assuming the boy is the lump in his bed, Frances confesses how she is lonely but that she is not attracted to Charles. She asks the boy to make love to her and screams in horror when she discovers that the boy has hidden toys in his bed to make it appear he is sleeping. Meanwhile, the boy fights with Nina and Nicky at a restaurant, and returns to Frances. While he bathes, she nails his window shut. He finally speaks, telling her that he will find a way to get out, and that he will not make love to her. Determined not to lose him, Frances goes barhopping in search of a companion. Assisted by the friend of a prostitute she had approached, Frances hires Sylvia to accompany Frances. However, in a fit of jealousy, Frances kills Sylvia. The boy hides from her, but Frances finds him and kisses him as he cries, aware that he is now her prisoner.

Notes

A mood piece that climaxes in grande guignol, this film features perhaps the youngest of the grande dames in Grande Dame Guignol. An early film by director Robert Altman, it features elements like overlapping dialogue, hand-held and out-of-focus camerawork, zooms, and the unconventional framing that will stamp his later work. While it lacks the gruesomeness of other horror titles in the subgenre, it does present the necessary moral ambiguities and divided audience empathy.

After making a lot of television and short films, Altman's only previous feature was the science fiction thriller *Countdown* (1968). *That Cold Day in the Park* is the first film for producers Donald Factor and Leon Mirell. Associate producer Robert Eggenweiler had previously made the dramas *The Bigamist* (1953) and *Private Hell 36* (1954), with Ida Lupino, and the western *The Halliday Brand* (1957).

We first see Frances walking home through the park purposefully and humorlessly, ignoring the Boy who sits on the bench. This indifference is repeated in her silence towards Mr. Parnell, who greets her at her door, and is indicative of grande dame behavior. Frances wears a black dress, black gloves, and a brown coat, and her hair is sculpted and worn up. Although Sandy Dennis is only 31, Frances becomes a grande dame by behaving as her deceased mother—becoming a hag by association. Altman also continuously draws parallels between Frances and other women to highlight how much older she presents in attitude and appearance. The way the

Frances Austen (Sandy Dennis) and the Boy (Michael Burns) in *That Cold Day in the Park* (1969).

Boy crosses his arms in his white jacket conjures images of a strait-jacket, which prefigures his entrapment (and recalls *Strait-Jacket*).

Uncle David's sneeze at lunch draws Frances's attention to the Boy in the rain, and her guest's fear of him indicates their conservative nature. While Frances's willingness to let him into her home shows greater tolerance, the head scarf she wears under her umbrella when she beckons to him is a reminder of her repressed nature. The mother and daughter lunch guests mirror the perceived relationship Frances had with her mother, where the mother is childish and spiteful in taking a seat that the daughter was about to sit on. Additionally, the daughter is a woman much older than Frances, although their behavior and friendship aligns them as contemporaries. The cockney accent of the mother, and the photograph of the Queen on the wall, indicate that Frances is of English origin, which Dennis's accent also suggests.

While Nina will later comment on the Boy's "number" of not speaking, Frances's assumption that he is mute is a natural one when he does not answer her. She is right when she points out that she is perceived as talking a lot because he does not talk at all, but this also presents the stereotype of the lonely spinster starved for attention. Her way of asking him a question and then controlling him shows her treating him like a child, possibly in the same way that Frances treated her "senile" mother. However, the Boy becomes complicit in his treatment by not objecting to it. This complicity creates the moral ambiguity of Frances's character, in that she is both protagonist and antagonist. The Boy shares the same moral ambiguity, which colors his final entrapment.

The yellow/green interior color of Frances's apartment is a reflection of the green and brown color scheme of her clothes. It also suggests aging and sickness, as represented by Frances's mother and herself. Frances looking at the Boy's reflection in her bathroom mirror is an indication of her sexual interest, and the voyeurism prefigures Sylvia's procurement. Altman will often present Frances in mirrored reflections, sometimes distorted in glass walls, representing her duplicity. The Boy's body is objectified more than Frances,' with his walking around the apartment naked when she is out signifying his youth and sensuality. Additionally, the conflict between the perceived older woman and a younger person recalls *Strait-Jacket*, *Lady in a Cage*, *Die! Die My Darling!*, *The Night Walker*, *I Saw What You Did*, *The Nanny*, *Queen of Blood*, *Games*, *Berserk!*, *Eye of the Cat*, and *The Mad Room*.

Frances turning off the television that the Boy watches as he plays her organ comes off as not only controlling of him (by not asking his permission), but also as controlling his excess. That she has had to take a course in music appreciation, and spends thirty to sixty minutes a day listening to music, are more examples of the artificial pleasure she takes from life. The exuberance and campery of the Boy's dance to the music suggests he is faking muteness, with the dance seen as both funny and seductive to her. He is naked under the blanket, and Frances's smiling pleasure at him is due to his dancing and the exposure of his body. The hot water bottle that she provides for his bed receives a payoff when he discovers the water the morning after, but its warm liquid comfort is another antiquated old-person's device.

When Frances makes the offer for him to stay, she is seen in shadow, like a horror movie monster, and Altman suggests her vampirism by having Dennis wear her hair down at night. The Boy's awareness of Frances locking the spare room door the morning after should signal to him that she is untrustworthy; and this is the first of many opportunities that he does not take to flee from her when he can. This behavior makes the Boy implicit in his own entrapment.

The issue of Frances buying him new clothes and discarding his existing ones remains an unresolved plot point. Although we see him recover his shoes, which have been damaged in her oven, we don't see him retrieve his clothes. While he apparently prefers to wear no clothes in the apartment, and one can assume that the clothes Frances buys for him are of better quality than his own, we don't see what Frances does with his original garb. This is more of the Boy's opportunism, which is also evident from his appropriating Parnell's jacket. Frances's promise that he can take the new clothes with him when he goes continues the mixed messages she delivers to him given the fact she locks him in the spare room. (Her shopping trip points up a continuity error, since the time it takes her to shop is not covered by the Boy's activities in the apartment.)

Altman demonstrates the Boy's disconnection from his family by presenting him returning with an exterior shot that pans up and down the house as the Boy presumably travels. The Boy's behavior of entering without knocking is a display of insensitive casualness. Nina and Nicky's permissive sex and drug use stands in contrast to the lack of sex and social puritanism of Frances. Although Frances will indulge in the hash-laced cookies, albeit unknowingly, she herself is not necessarily presented as a prude, considering her willingness to hire Sylvia.

When we hear the Boy speak to Nina, it comes as no surprise, since his behavior with Frances has suggested fakery. Interestingly, he says that he left Frances because he "got tired of not talking," as if not talking was as frustrating as Frances's continual talk in trying to get him to answer her. He denies the claim that Frances is an old lady who has "picked him up," although Nina and Nicky's assumption is that only an old lady would do so. Nina's reveal that the Boy has been doing his silent number since he was a kid presents him as a veteran manipulator, but also as someone who may be equally as lonely as Frances.

The Boy's return to Frances is indicative of the better lifestyle she offers, with Mrs. Parnell's disapproval presenting her with the attitude that Frances's older friends, and presumably her mother, would have towards him. Mrs. Parnell, as an employee Frances has inherited from her mother, exists as another mother figure that Frances partially resents and can control. The wine and fruit Frances serves with the burned cookies is her attempt to disguise their tacky nature, indicated by how Mrs. Parnell points out that someone has tried to scrape the burned bits away. The hash cookies provide some insight into Frances' character, since she becomes playful when stoned, although her scaring the Boy into playing blind man's bluff can also be seen as unleashing her potential antagonism.

The hallucinogenic music in this scene adds both strangeness and a child-like quality that applies to both characters, where the score had previously romanticized Frances to some degree. Her kissing the Boy after he ties on the tie is presented as casual, impulsive, due to the drugs, and non-sexual. Frances still wearing her red bathrobe recalls the Boy only wearing a blanket during the dance scene. Altman again presents her as a vampire by showing her shadow searching for the Boy, her hand outstretched like *Nosferatu*. The game of blinds man's buff, a game of sense-deprivation, is heightened by the Boy's non-talking, with a harmonica (rather than a voice) used to attract the one who is blinded. The game ends with a long shot of Frances alone and unable to find the Boy, although whether he has left the apartment again is not revealed.

Frances going to see the gynecologist because she is "going to be married" is another plot point left unexplained, although Altman uses the other women in the waiting room, and their overlapping dialogue, as comparison with Frances. The chattering of the women about sex parallels Frances's perceived chattering to the Boy. Altman distances us further by shooting the scenes from an exterior point of view, with the camera behind blinds. Frances closing the blinds when she is to undress allows for a scene button, as much as the Boy hanging a dress up at the houseboat to block our view of Nina's lovemaking.

Nina visiting the Boy at Frances' apartment is a surprise, since we wonder how she acquired the address, particularly since she enters through a window from the fire escape. The bath scene recalls the bath scene from *Lady in a Cage*, when Nina has the Boy join her. Nina's incestuous feelings toward her brother may partly explain his silent behavior, and receives a pay-

Poster for *That Cold Day in the Park* (1969).

off when the expected kiss becomes a laugh when she points out the sleep in his eyes.

Altman intercuts the dialogue scene in which Charles's proposes with more footage of Frances's doctor's examination, for obscure reasons, though it does spare us Charles's embarrassment at Frances's rejection of him. The narrative might have been more interesting had Frances found Charlie appealing, but the treatment is more pre-occupied with Frances's interest in the Boy, and negating the sexual appeal of older men and women. The scene where the Boy has left toys in his bed to fool Frances into thinking he is there only works because of her scream of realization at the end. It's hard to believe that he would not respond to her attempted seduction if he were there, so the reveal of the toys comes as no surprise. It's equally hard to believe that she did not recognize the toys when she turned on the bedside lamp before her kiss.

Frances's monologue delivered to what she thinks is the Boy includes a confession that she was little company for her mother, and that she finds Charlie and old people "disgusting." The repeat of this word sets herself up to be rejected by the Boy, as her "I want you to make love to me" will be repeated at film's end for horror impact. Seen half in shadow, Frances again seems vampiric, with the excessive scream of her perceived humiliation making her appear even more monstrous.

The Boy's last trek outside has him in a restaurant with Nina and Nicky, where he comments that Frances "makes a big deal out of sex." While this comment may be true of her, it's something that he can't really know at this time since he wasn't there to hear her bedside monologue. His seeing the bed made, with the toys on top, is another warning to him that she has discovered his ploy, yet still he stays with her. That Frances does not mention the ploy or his absence warns us that she will do something to retaliate, which she does. The hammering of the nails into the window is heard but not seen, and Altman uses fast cuts when the Boy sees the nails, the only time he does so in the film.

When the Boy confronts Frances and finally speaks, she does not react. His remarks are interesting, and are as follows:

> Don't think I can't get out of here. And if you think by keeping me here I'm gonna get in bed with you or anything like that, you're wrong. If I want a girl or anything I'll just go out and get one myself. And I might not come back.

His looking at knives before he chooses a hatchet to try and remove the nails is a funny grande guignol choice of weaponry, with the hatchet recalling the axes of *Strait-Jacket*, *Hush ... Hush, Sweet Charlotte*, and *The Savage Intruder*. Frances's apology to him creates an expectation that she will let him go—an expectation thwarted when she locks him in afterwards. However, the fact that she goes out to find him a girl is a sign that she has heard at least part of what he has said.

The grotesque beehive sported by the prostitute at the bar may be period hairstyle, but it presents her as a freak, so that her calling Frances a pervert becomes amusing. The room where Sylvia is found is remarkable for the background presentation of two lesbians, one femme and one masculine. The silence between Frances and Sylvia in the taxi on the way back to her apartment creates tension, with Altman using the ticking on the meter as an Ingmar Bergman–ish, ticking-clock device. Of course, the ticking tells us that Sylvia's time is running out, since we know the dangerous situation she is being led into.

Sylvia scores a laugh from her line "Are you looking at us, lady?" after Frances leaves her with the Boy, and her greater interest in him leads to his assumed impotence. That the Boy is not attracted to Sylvia is not only ironic, but an indication of the doomed nature of Frances's effort. The rattling of the bed springs that accompanies their attempt at sex adds humor. It's not the rattling, however, that draws Frances back to the room. Rather, her curiosity, which turns to deadly jealousy, provides ambiguity. Altman's dark lighting of the scene makes us initially think that Frances has joined in, and it is the Boy's resistance and his turning on a light that reveals the knife Frances has used to kill Sylvia.

Frances Austen (Sandy Dennis), the youngest grande dame in Grande Dame Guignol, in *That Cold Day in the Park* (1969).

The Boy's run from the room creates the expectation of his escape from the apartment, but, oddly, he doesn't go to a door. Rather, his attempt to hide seems a stunned reaction to the violence, and Frances finding him is no surprise. Altman uses what sounds like an overdub of her line "I want you to make love to me" as the darkness of her head blocks the camera's view of the Boy crying. Frances's tenderness is also part derangement, since she tells him that she has asked Sylvia to leave—though he knows Sylvia is dead. The music repeats the combination of child-like innocence and creepy horror, with Frances presented as a triumphant trapper.

Sandy Dennis had last played a leading role in *Sweet November* (1968), and had won the Best Supporting Actress Academy Award for *Who's Afraid of Virginia Woolf?* (1966). Although Altman manages to restrain Dennis's method mannerisms, they add an appropriate oddness to the character of Frances, as well as making her a touching, if pathetic, figure. Dennis inspires sympathy in spite of her controlling behavior and unrequited desire. She uses a stillness, somewhat like that of Bette Davis, before she strikes, adding more danger to her violence. However, this stillness can also be interpreted as a kind of emotional retardation, exemplified in the scene in which she fails to react to the Boy finally breaking his silence and speaking to her. Dennis also makes Frances rather poetic in her physicality when stoned.

Release

June 8, 1969, with the tagline, "How far will a woman go ... to possess a 19 year-old boy?"

Reviews

"Dennis is strikingly effective, if her character's veering into madness is a bit abrupt. Michael Burns is good as the cherubic youth.... [The screenplay] waters down interesting personal relations, turning the denouement into Grande guignol, rather than perceptive dramatic and psychological progression."—*Variety*, May 27, 1969.

"[S]ick, tedious, over baked and inane psychosexual nonsense.... In neither the screenplay nor the direction is there any shading of sensitivity or warmth bestowed on these singularly unappealing characters, least of all the psychotic heroine played by Miss Dennis like a nasal-voiced, computer."—Howard Thompson, *The New York Times*, June 9, 1969.

"...[P]retty well done ... [it] doesn't declare itself as a horror film until too late, and the audience is already lost.... Dennis supplies a convincing portrait of the repressed, sex-obsessed spinster. Burns is adequate as the boy."—Roger Ebert, *Chicago Sun–Times*, July 22, 1969.

"There may be something in the film medium itself that works against these stories of obsessional incarceration: we in the audience are trapped along with the prisoner, and we long to get away. One can admire this film for its craftsmanship: it has a cold brilliance. But that's all."—Pauline Kael, *5001 Nights at the Movies*.

Trog (1970)

Warner Bros.

CREDITS: *Director:* Freddie Francis; *Producer:* Herman Cohen; *Associate Producer:* Harry Woolveridge; *Screenplay:* Aben Kandel, based on an original story by Peter Bryan and John Gilling; *Photography:* Desmond Dickinson; *Music:* John Scott; *Editor:* Oswald Hafenrichter; *Art Director:* Geoffrey Tozer; *Trog Design:* Charles Parker; *Production Manager:* Eddie Dorian; *Wardrobe:* Ron Deck; *Make-up:* Jim Evans; *Hair:* Pearl Tipaldi; *Set Dresser:* Helen Thomas; *Sound:* Michael Redbourne. Color, 91 minutes. Filmed at Bray Studios, Windsor, Berke, England.

CAST: Joan Crawford (*Dr. Brockton*); Michael Gough (*Sam Murdoch*); Bernard Kay (*Inspector Greenham*); Kim Braden (*Anne Brockton*); David Griffin (*Malcolm Travers*); John Hamill (*Cliff*); Thorley Walters (*Magistrate*); Jack May (*Dr. Selbourne*); Geoffrey Chase (*Bill*); Robert Hutton (*Dr. Richard Warren*); Simon Lack (*Colonel Vickers*); David Warbrook (*Alan Davis*); Chloe Franks (*Little Girl*); Maurice Good (*Reporter*); Joe Cornelius (*Trog*); Uncredited: John Baker (*Anesthetist*); Golda Casimir (*Professor*); Herman Cohen (*Bartender*); John D. Collins (*TV Crewman Watching Monitor*); Shirley Cooklin (*Little Girl's Mother*); Robert Crewdson (*Dr. Pierre Duval*); Pat Gorman (*Army Officer*); Brian Grellis (*John Dennis*); Paul Hansard (*Dr. Kurtlimer*); Bartlett Mullins (*Butcher*); Rona Newton-John (*Reporter*); Cleo Sylvestre (*Nurse*).

VHS/DVD: DVD: Warner Home Video, June 26, 2007.

Plot

While exploring a new fissure in an underground cave off the local English moors, students Malcolm, Cliff, and Bill come upon an ape-like creature. When Bill is killed, the other two report the incident to anthropologist Dr. Brockton of the Brockton Research Center, author of *Social Structures in Primates*. The police remain skeptical, even after Dr. Brockton takes a photograph of the beast, which she believes is a troglodyte—a 10-million-year-old missing link between man and ape. When the police go to the cave, the creature appears and attacks the cameras of the reporters there to cover the wild story. Dr. Brockton shoots the creature with a tranquilizer gun and takes it to her laboratory, dubbing it "Trog." She begins a training program for Trog, to "unlock the secrets of human behavior." However, during a ball-retrieving game on the grounds, a local dog is killed by Trog.

A Court of Enquiry investigates the community's concerns about Trog, with calls for it to be destroyed spurred on by local land developer Sam Murdoch. Although her case is damaged by evidence from a co-worker, Dr. Selborne, Dr. Brockton presents the testimony of international scientists who witnessed the surgery that implanted a transmitter into Trog's chest, allowing him to speak. After Sam's disruptions result in his ejection from the Court, he breaks into the Center and frees Trog. However, Trog kills Sam, then goes on a rampage in the town, killing three men. Trog also kidnaps a child, who he takes back to his cave. The Army is called in, but Dr. Brockton sneaks into the cave before they enter. She persuades Trog to give her the child and brings her back outside, but cannot persuade the soldiers to let Trog go. They enter and, finding Trog, shoot. Trog falls and is impaled on a stalagmite. Dr. Brockton leaves the site, saddened by the loss of the creature she has grown fond of.

Notes

This unintentionally funny and outlandish sci-fi shocker posits a grande dame as love interest for an antagonistic prehistoric creature, which is a rather bizarre comment on the desirability of leading ladies of a certain age. Trog is also Joan Crawford's second Grande Dame Guignol picture for producer Herman Cohen, her fifth Grande Dame Guignol overall, and her last feature. Although the grande guignol is limited to one scene, its hideousness makes up for the rather juvenile antics that pass for horror by director Freddie Francis.

Francis had previously directed the horror titles *The Brain* (1962), *Paranoiac* (1963), *Nightmare* (1964), *The Evil of Frankenstein* (1964), *Dr. Terror's House of Horrors* (1965), *The Skull* (1965), *The Psychopath* (1966), *The Deadly Bees* (1967), *They Came from Beyond Space* (1967), *Torture Garden* (1967), *Dracula Has Risen from the Grave* (1968), and *Mumsy, Nanny, Sonny and Girly* (1969). Herman Cohen had previously produced *Berserk!* with Crawford. *Trog* is the first film made by associate producer Harry Woolveridge.

Francis uses horror movie conventions to create foreboding and shock effects, although the rocks that falls onto the student scientists as they descend into the cave, and the figure that stalks Bill, are both ambiguously presented. The design of the cave features stalactites and stalagmites, the latter used in a death scene à la *Berserk!* The appearance of a lizard is used as a red herring, the camera creeps up behind Bill to surprise him, and a scream is deprived of it's sound when the film cuts to the waiting Malcolm. The line "It's your funeral," spoken by Malcolm to Cliff and Bill as they venture further than Malcolm cares to, is unnecessarily obvious. When Dr. Brockton takes a photograph of Trog, we see her from Trog's point of view, holding the camera. Francis then cuts to the image of Trog that she has photographed in a freeze-frame, then to Inspector Greenham looking at the photograph. (A discrepancy later arises when Trog recoils from some television lights and goes wild when photographed with a flash camera—after having shown no apprehension when confronted with a flashlight upon his initial discovery.)

Considering Trog is a man wearing an ape's head and a fur chest piece, what redeems the concept and gives it some reality is the fact that Trog is a man and not an animal, and that Joe Cornelius's eyes can be seen behind the Trog mask. When the television crew invades the cave, Trog conveniently appears to be filmed. The onlookers predictably scream and disperse when Trog ventures outside, and Trog naturally has to attack a cameraman who gets too close. When Dr. Brockton appears to fire repeated tranquilizer darts, Trog's advance is only halted when he is close to her, increasing his potential threat against her. Anne's line, "For a senior citizen, he certainly has a marvelous appetite," is a somewhat amusing reference to Trog being 10 million years old. Dr. Brockton theorizes that his existence is the result of being frozen during the ice age and recently thawed out to be reborn.

After a comment that Trog seems docile, a photographer's flash enrages him; while the resentment of Sam Murdoch matches Trog's anger. If Trog begins as the film's antagonist, then Sam's antipathy for him and Dr. Brockton makes him equally antagonistic, and subsequently make Trog the protagonist in reaction. Dr. Brockton shares this ambiguous stance, since she oscillates from protagonist to antagonist as the one who cares for Trog the most (an American in an English town) and being perceived as a mad scientist with Frankenstein-like ambitions.

Dr. Brockton's notion that Trog has the mentality of a "backward child" allows her to devise the training program, which includes playing music, color differentiation, throwing and retrieving a ball, and winding a doll. The blonde doll that he reacts to lovingly foreshadows the little blonde girl he takes back with him to his cave. Dr. Brockton's treatment of Trog evokes Crawford's behavior toward the deaf girl in *The Story of Esther Costello* (1957), and the grande dame with the child recalls *The Nanny*. Dr. Brockton's affection for Trog is expressed by her repeatedly caressing his face, which reinforces him as her love interest. Their relationship even becomes touching when Trog reaches out for her pink scarf and she gives it to him to wear. Although Dr. Brockton has a daughter, Anne, we don't learn what became of the doctor's husband, or if she was even married, since it appears her career is her priority.

The dog that Trog kills being attracted by a ball foreshadows Trog later being attracted by a ball in a children's playground. The film that Dr. Brockton shows to her international colleagues consists of footage from the film we have seen without being aware of a camera recording the activity; and the Court of Enquiry seems only to exist for Sam to continually interrupt the proceedings. Thankfully, Michael Gough is so funny as Sam that we welcome his every appearance, especially when he uses the sexist men-are-superior argument to persuade Dr. Selbourne to testify against Dr. Brockton. Trog's "memory" of his origins consists of four minutes of tinted footage of stop-motion dinosaur figures fighting before being killed by a volcanic eruption, taken from *The Animal World* (1956), with special effects by Ray Harryhausen and Willis H. O'Brien.

Dr. Brockton (Joan Crawford) with a caged Trog (John Cornelius) in *Trog* (1970).

Upon breaking into the Centre, Sam delivers an amusing line to Trog: "Missing link; if that's what you are, you *should* be missing." Of course, his releasing Trog results in Sam's own death. The killing is presented in long shot, near Sam's car and a close-up of Sam's bloody face strikes home when Trog puts his body inside the car. Sam's body sets off the car horn, the sound of which immobilizes Trog, who is only released when Dr. Brockton turns it off. Trog's rampage through the town recalls that of the monster in *Frankenstein* (1931), and his killing of the butcher by hanging him on a meat hook provides the grand guignol image of blood dripping onto the floor and the hook seen through the butcher's neck. Other attacks involve less guignol devices, such as being cut by glass and burned alive, with Francis using the stalled-car convention to generate suspense.

Trog meeting the little girl is shown by her accidentally sliding down a slippery dip into his arms as he waits at the bottom, and Francis repeats the child-like music we had heard when Trog was playing with the doll in the laboratory. The taking of the girl also invokes *Frankenstein*, in which the Monster plays with a little girl before unintentionally killing her. That Trog should be gentle in his treatment of the girl before—when he first sees her he tenderly strokes her face, and he handles her carefully when he puts her on the ground at the entrance to his cave—help make Trog a sympathetic figure.

The ridiculously outsized military on hand at the climax to deal with one troglodyte is matched by the ludicrous ease in which Dr. Brockton enters the cave against their wishes, not to mention their poor aim when they try to shoot Trog. A continuity goof shows Dr. Brockton's coiffure outside the cave to be loose and windswept, while for the interiors her hair is much more proper and controlled. Francis has Dr. Brockton leave the site after she brushes away the reporter that she had been happy to talk with when Trog was first discovered. This rudeness is presumably based on her grief over the loss of the man she loves, although she does not witness Trog's death. What is more frustrating is something that Francis could not know at the time—that this exit would be Crawford's last on film. Perhaps if he did, he would have let the walk continue longer, though it does seem sadly ironic that a woman with such an iconic face should have it hidden in her final shot.

Freddie Francis would claim that by the time he made this film, Joan Crawford had "gone past it" and could no longer remember lines. He was forced to use idiots cards, and was obliged to keep the camera relatively immobile in order for her to have an unobstructed view of them. He also claims that the footage from *The Animal World* was used to pad out the running time because of the slowing of the shooting schedule resulting

Dr. Brockton (Joan Crawford) in *Trog* (1970).

from Crawford's dialogue difficulties. Even so, at 64 years old, Joan Crawford invests the silliness with conviction and restraint, though she does give the occasional yell when provoked.

When the distraught mother of the kidnapped girl is abusing Dr. Brockton, Crawford keeps her eyes downcast and makes no reply. Francis saves his close-ups of Crawford for the climax, perhaps because only here we do see in her face the ravages of time, as the shots lack the shadowy lighting that could hide her age. Otherwise, her hair is a strawberry-blonde, and she looks quite jaunty in her grey pants suit for the scenes in the cave. For the scene in which she operates on Trog, she wears green scrubs and a green cap, with a white mask that covers her nose and mouth so that only her eyes are seen, making her look as youthful as she did in the 1940s.

Release

Premiered September 1970, released October 24, 1970, with the taglines, "FOUND: One missing link—and all the terror that goes with it!" and "Here comes Trog. You'll laugh at yourself for being so scared ... but don't laugh at Trog!"

Reviews

"There is a rudimentary virtue in *Trog* in that it proves that Joan Crawford is grimly working at her craft.... Thanks to a script that makes everything vapidly obvious from the start, *Trog* is no more exciting or scientific than the antics of a rambunctious kid in a progressive school."—A.H. Weller, *The New York Times*, October 29, 1970.

"Trog carries enough exploitable elements to score nicely in its intended market where contrivance, a bit of corn and an imaginative premise spell b.o. coin.... Freddie Francis's direction maintains a fast and often suspenseful pace.... Miss C is okay in her characterization, but principal interest rests on the monster."—*Variety*, September 16, 1970.

"...The motifs of the noble savage versus both the positive and the negative aspects of civilization remain undeveloped and lack conviction under Francis's routine direction.... Crawford in one of her few sympathetic roles at the end of her career."—Phil Hardy, *The Aurum Film Encyclopedia of Horror*.

Poster for *Trog* (1970).

Trog (1970)

"This may well be the silliest film to come out of Britain's 'Golden Age.' Once again Herman Cohen exploits Joan Crawford in one of his ridiculous shockers.... Crawford plays her part with utmost sincerity, which couldn't have been easy.... Gough's performance is wildly unhinged."—Gary A. Smith, *Uneasy Dreams: The Golden Age of British Horror Films, 1956–1976.*

Flesh Feast (1970)

(aka *Time Is Terror*)

Viking International Pictures

CREW: *Director:* Brad F. Grinter; *Producers:* Brad F. Grinter, Veronica Lake; *Screenplay:* Thomas B. Casey, Brad F. Grinter; *Photography:* Thomas B. Casey; *Set Design:* Robert Moulet; *Production Design:* Harry Kerwin; *Production Manager:* Harry Kerwin; *Sound:* Duke McGrath; *Special Effects:* Doug Hobart; *Make-up:* Bill Rogers, Gaye Doucette; *Wardrobe:* Candy Twitty; *Hair:* HeadHunter, Miami Beach. Color, 72 minutes. Filmed in Miami, Florida.

CAST: Veronica Lake (*Dr. Elaine Frederick*); Phil Philbin (*Ed Casey*); Doug Foster (*Carl Schumann*); Harry Kerwin (*Dan Carter*); Brad Townes (*Tyler*); Martha Mischon (*Virginia Day*); Dete Parsons (*Sharon*); Heather Hughes (*Kristine*), Dian Wilhite (*Nurse*); Yanka Mann (*Miss Powell*); Craig McConnel (*Father*); Chris Martell (*Max Bauer*); Bill Rogers (*José*); Otto Schlesinger (*Benito*); Eleanor Vale (*Mrs. Lustig*); Kay Tremblay (*Woman in Park*); Monica Dagovitz (*Nurse*); Debbie Kuhn (*Nurse*); Bill Kuhn (*Ilan*).

VHS/DVD: Not available on either format.

Plot

Dan Carter, a newspaper reporter, is murdered at the Miami airport after he was seen following Carl Schumann. Schumann is involved with a group of South American revolutionaries and Dr. Elaine Frederick, who has been experimenting with a youth restoration process which uses a special breed of flesh-eating maggots. As a cover for her work, Dr. Frederick also rents rooms in her mansion to nurses, but is unaware that Kristine, one of her tenants, is actually a detective working in league with Ed Casey, Dan's editor. The mansion is soon invaded by a security team, there at the behest of their mysterious "commander," and who bring the aged Max Bauer to be subjected to Dr. Frederick's experimental treatment. When the process appears to be a success, they send word for their commander to come. When Dr. Frederick sees that a corpse Kristine has secured from the hospital where she works is no longer appealing to the maggots, Dr. Frederick realizes that the maggots are only effective when they have fed on recently-dead flesh. Max is killed by Jose, one of the security team, after Max has raped and killed the nurse Sharon, whom Jose has fallen in love with. As the Commander arrives for his treatment, his guards discover Max's body in the mansion's garden and kill Carl, as Kristine and Ed arrive at the house. Meanwhile, in Dr. Frederick's laboratory, the Commander is revealed to be the aged Adolf Hitler. Strapping him down to an operating table, she tells him of her mother, who was experimented on with maggots at the Ravensbruck concentration camp. Laughing, she salutes "Heil Hitler," and proceeds to torture him with flesh-eating maggots.

Notes

The poor production values of this film are of the lowest quality in all of Grande Dame Guignol cinema, which is a shame, since the reappearance of Veronica Lake after nineteen years off the screen marks one of the longest periods of absence a leading lady has endured in the sub-genre. Although it features some worthy grande guignol, and climaxes in a truly horrific fashion, one's interest is soon extinguished by a confusing narrative that poses more questions than it answers. Then there's the disappointing camerawork and direction. The film is the first directorial effort by Brad F. Grinter, who had previously acted (uncredited) in *Death Curse of Tartu* (1966), and had a supporting role in *Scream, Baby, Scream* (1969), both independent horror movies filmed in Florida (as this film would be). 1970 was a comparatively good year for Grinter as an actor, having three films released. This is the first production by Viking International Pictures, and the only film made to date by producer V. L. Grinter, presumably a relative of the director.

Grinter employs a Robert Aldrich–style opening credit delay until after the initial murder, but also fake-sounding background noise for the airport and what appears to be dubbing for the actors. The

Poster for *Flesh Feast* (1970).

double pursuit of characters suggests a promising narrative, and when Grinter has dialogue from the newspaper office overlap the visual at the airport, we're not sure whether it's innovative or inept. The contrivance of the murderer changing into a cleaner's outfit in order to appear inconspicuous suggests the latter. That there is a uniform available, let alone one that fits, is contrived convenience. We get a laugh from the killer cleaner when he backs up to the telephone stall where his victim waits, mopping all the while, and then produces a weapon with which to stab his victim to death. The obvious (and uncredited) music screams "murder," though Grinter's use of music will improve when we get to Dr. Frederick's maggot lab, accompanied by an appealing sci-fi theme.

The line that Dr. Frederick has "set up a lab for secret experiments" and "then advertised for nurses" gets another laugh. Interestingly, Dr. Frederick is both protagonist and antagonist; and the idea of Kristine and Sharon as antagonists pitted against her recalls the older woman/younger woman dynamic of *Strait-Jacket*, *Lady in a Cage*, *Die! Die My Darling!*, *The Night Walker*, *I Saw What You Did*, *Queen of Blood*, *Games*, *Berserk!*, *Eye of the Cat*, and *The Mad Room*.

The maggot lab's lights, which are more like a changing, multi-colored projection on the wall, are said to be "colors of the spectrum that affect the larvae." When Gayle (played by an actress not specifically identified) drinks a glass of whisky to cope with the current war news involving her boyfriend, it is a presumed nod to the Vietnam era in which the film was made. One of the film's many odd notions is the idea that Ed would assist Kristine (a character who virtually disappears a third of the way into the film) in stealing body parts for Dr. Frederick.

Grinter favors static long takes of seated characters spouting exposition. He uses the most basic camerawork, with the camera locked down on the person speaking. The majority of the film's "action" takes place at the mansion, with the airport, the hospital exterior, the newspaper office, and the amputation location as exceptions. The corpse in the wheelchair that Kristine steals recalls the wheelchairs in *What Ever Happened to Baby Jane?*, *What Ever Happened to Aunt Alice?*, and *The Savage Intruder*. Grinter gets a laugh from the comic interruptions Kristine experiences while moving the body from the hospital to a waiting van, even if the idea of doing so in daylight seems unnecessarily risky. When the corpse has a leg sawn off, the disturbing sound of the saw compensates for the lack of blood (presumably the blood has solidified in the frozen corpse). Another laugh comes from Carl's disgust at the sight of the flesh-eating maggots, when Dr. Frederick wryly notes, "I never said the process was pretty."

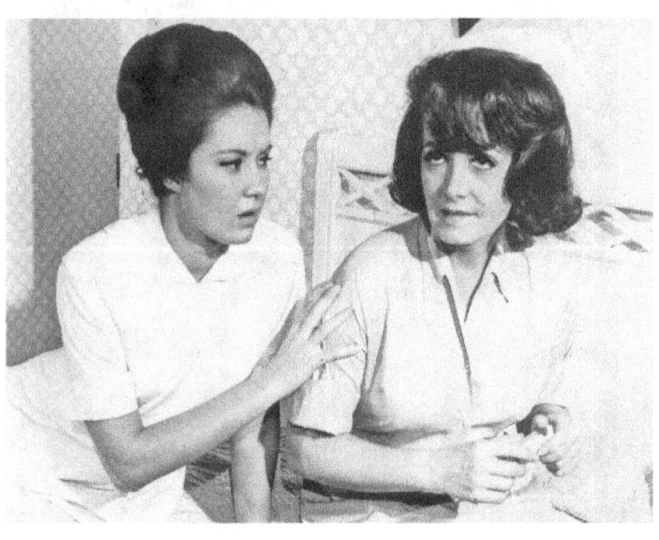

Sharon (Dete Parsons) comforts Gayle (unidentified actress) in *Flesh Feast* (1970).

The aging make-up on

Max Bauer is pretty unconvincing, foreshadowing that on "Hitler" at the climax—a sign of the film's budgetary limitations (as is the overuse of the house). Amusingly, when Max is unbandaged after his treatment, his grey hair has regained its color, a dye job we have not been privy to (and presumably not performed by the maggots themselves).

Although it ends in another murder, the subplot romance between Sharon and Jose reads as superfluous (but it does provide a parallel to that of Dr. Frederick and Carl). While Sharon's killing can be explained by strangulation, that of Max by Jose is less clear. Although having two fresh corpses would seem to be the answer to Dr. Frederick's concerns, she isn't made aware of either death.

The Commander's German accent is perhaps a too-obvious indication of his identity, which is kept from us when only his legs are seen arriving (with accompanying walking stick), and he is subsequently filmed only from behind. Grinter shoots Lake in close-up for the climax, something he had not often done previously in the film, and the sight of the maggots on Hitler's face as he yells in pain is true grande guignol. The film ends with Dr. Frederick's laughter, with her "Heil Hitler" used as an echo.

Lake was age 50 at the time of filming; her last leading role had been in *Isn't It Romantic* (1948). She had left Hollywood because of personal problems. In the 1950s Lake had been arrested several times for public drunkenness and disorderly conduct, and was found to be working as a barmaid. She had a supporting role in a Canadian film, *Footsteps in the Snow* (1966), and published an autobiography entitled *Veronica*. She would use the proceeds to make *Flesh Feast*.

Our first view of Lake shows us the back of her black-turbaned head. The turban recalls that worn by Norma Desmond in *Sunset Boulevard*, as will the matching long black gloves we later see. Lake's character fits the grande dame mold because of the actress' lengthy absence and reappearance, although her back-story, which rationalizes, revenge adds a preoccupation with the past. Dr. Frederick's sleeveless black dress and gloves worn under a white lab coat are soon replaced by pastel-colored outfits, which reinforce her femininity. Lake's display of anger is believable, and she uses her husky voice for some breathiness in her intonation. Although the plot is ridiculous, and, as one of the film's producers, she must take responsibility for the quality of the film, Lake doesn't embarrass herself entirely in her performance. She even employs a raised eyebrow for arch irony. However, the negative reception the film received surely contributed to her never working again.

Release

Said to have been filmed in 1967, the exact release date in 1970 is not known. The taglines include, "Morbid horror in vivid COLOR," "Living bodies used for the most vile experiment ever devised!" "Creeping, crawling, flesh-eating maggots!" and "Living bodies used for the most vile experiments ever devised by the mind of a madwoman."

Reviews

"Cheaply made and in one or two scenes extremely gruesome."—Phil Hardy, *The Aurum Film Encyclopedia of Horror.*

"It is anybody's guess what possessed Lake to choose such a dire and impoverished production for a comeback, let alone to act as producer. The climax does offer the mildly fascinating spectacle of her going bonkers but it comes without the layer of self-conscious freakshow appeal."—Richard Scheib, *The Science Fiction, Horror and Fantasy Movie Review.*

"Bomb. Embarrassing, amateurish gorefest."—Leonard Maltin, *2009 Movie Guide.*

"A bad film ... [it] has a better reputation than it deserves.... It lacks both the wit and talent to be good camp, and the courage to wallow in its own bad taste. What's left is flat, boring, and lifeless."—Rob Wrigley, *Classic Horror-com.*

The Beast in the Cellar (1970)
(aka *Are You Dying, Young Man?*; *Young Man, I Think You're Dying*)

Tigon Pictures/Leander Films

CREDITS: *Director/Screenplay:* James Kelly; *Producer:* Graham Harris; *Associate Producer:* Christopher Neame; *Executive Producer:* Tony Tenser; *Music:* Tony Macaulay; *Photography:* Harry Waxman, Desmond Dickinson; *Editor:* Nicholas Napier-Bell; *Art Direction:* Roger King; *Unit Manager:* Caroline Langley; *Make-up:* W.T. Partleton; *Hair:* Olga Angelinetta; *Wardrobe:* Mary Gibson; *Sound:* Tony Dawe. Color, 101/88 minutes. Filmed at Pinewood Studios in England, on location on the Pinewood lot in Buckinghamshire, and in Sussex at the Bluebell Railway.

SONG: "She Works in a Woman's Way" (Tony Macaulay, Barry Mason), sung by Tony Burrows with the Edison Lighthouse.

CAST: Beryl Reid (*Ellie Ballantyne*); Flora Robson (*Joyce Ballantyne*); Tessa Wyatt (*Joanna Sutherland*); John Hamill (*Cpl. Alan Marlow*); T. P. McKenna (*Detective Chief Superintendent Paddick*); David Dodimead (*Dr. Spencer*); John Kelland (*Sergeant Young*); Christopher Chittell (*Baker*); Vernon Dobtcheff (*Sir Bernard Newsmith*); Anthony Heaton (*Anderson*); Peter Craze (*Roy*); Anabel Littledale (*Gloria*); Dafydd Havard (*Stephen Ballantyne*); Gail Lidstone (*Young Ellie*); Elizabeth Choice (*Young Joyce*); Merlin Ward (*Young Stephen*); Howard Rawlinson (*Young Soldier*); Roberta Tovey (*Paper Girl*); Robert Wilde (*Soldier in NAAFI*); Reg Lever (*Ambulance Man*).

VHS/DVD: Not available on DVD. VHS: Warner Home Video, released May 3, 1989.

Plot

Police investigate the murder of several soldiers in uniform around the small Lancashire town of Littlemeer. Two elderly sisters, Joyce and Ellie Ballantyne, have lived in their house since birth, and fear that something they keep bricked up in the cellar may be responsible. When they discover that it has managed to burrow out, they try to seal off the exit hole. Joyce injures her ankle in the process and is bed-bound. A home-help nurse is sent to tend to her, but as Ellie learns of more killings, she decides to defy Joyce's wishes and inform the police. When they arrive, Ellie tells of how their father returned from World War I shell-shocked and transformed into an abuser. He particularly hated their younger brother Stephen, since his birth resulted in the death of their mother. After their father died, Stephen had wanted to enlist in World War II, but the sisters drugged and bricked him up in the cellar to prevent a repetition of the same horrors. Having now escaped after thirty years, it is believed that the mad Stephen is the killer. The police track him with dogs, forcing him back home. When he finds the sisters in Joyce's bedroom, he attacks. He is shot in time by Alan Marlow, who had been visiting. With the dead Stephen cradled in Ellie's arms, Joyce says that is was "all done for him."

Notes

Starring 67-year-old Flora Robson in a rare leading role, this film is a rather tame horror piece that plays more like a stage play than a motion picture, and is marred by an obtrusive and obvious horror movie music score. It features two grande dames as sisters with a secret from their past, and a series of slashing murders that provide the necessary grande guignol. This is the first film directed by James Kelly, who wrote the horror movie *Doctor Blood's Coffin* (1961). *The Beast in the Cellar* was the first film to be produced by Graham Harris, the first for Leander Films, and the first of associate producer Christopher Neame. Neame is the son of director Ronald Neame, who had made *The Prime of Miss Jean Brodie* (1969). Executive producer Tony Tenser, under Tigon Pictures, had previously made the horror titles *Curse of the Crimson Altar* (1968), *The Blood Beast Terror* (1968), *Witchfinder General* (1968), and *The Haunted House of Horror* (1969).

A pre-credit scene of army tank maneuvers has one of them breaking down at night on the moors under a full moon. Any horror movie fan can tell you that this is not good. The resultant attack on a soldier, complete with animal sounds and blood flying from the slashing, suggest the culprit may be a werewolf. The attack is shown from the attacker's point of view, perspective that will be repeated in later attacks. The music under the credit sequence, featuring a yellow full moon in an orange sky, is a relief from the attack's generic horror movie quality. This transition from inspiration to obviousness will continue through the film. After the credits, the screaming of the woman as she finds the victim's body heralds another horror movie convention. What distinguishes the scene in which the police examine the crime scene is

Ellie Ballantyne (Beryl Reid) and Joyce Ballantyne (Flora Robson) shine a flashlight into the cellar in *The Beast in the Cellar* (1970).

the fact that the corpse is never shown, capped by Alan running away to vomit upon seeing it. The severity of the attack, described as "brutal and vicious," coupled with the claw marks on the body, lead the police to consider a leopard as the culprit.

Joyce's introduction shows her tending to a cage of guinea pigs, with the cage recalling the birds in *What Ever Happened to Baby Jane?* and *The Night Walker*, the cages of *Lady in a Cage* and *Trog*, and the prisons of *Strait-Jacket, Lady in a Cage, Die! Die My Darling!, The Night Walker, I Saw What You Did, Games, Berserk!*, and *Eye of the Cat*. The animals she keeps being guinea pigs reflects what she has done to Stephen by locking him up in the cellar. When Joyce is told of the attack, she seems to know immediately that it has been done by Stephen. She dresses in her father's army coat and hat, and, taking a flashlight, presumably heads for the cellar. Why Joyce wears these clothes is never addressed but she will don the same attire for the film's climax. However, the mouth organ and drums in the score provide an obvious military motif. In contrast, composer Tony Macaulay gives Ellie's entrance a lushly romantic sound, which will correspond to the character differences between the sisters. Sisters were featured as grande dames in *What Ever Happened to Baby Jane?*, *Dead Ringer*, and, less pointedly, *The Mad Room*, with only the Hudson sisters of *Baby Jane* able to be equated with the isolation and co-dependence of the Ballantynes.

Ellie's yelling is explained by her deafness, and she is presented as the emotional, sentimental optimist (compared to Joyce's practical, bitter pessimist). Although Joyce accuses Ellie of not facing reality, Joyce is just as deluded in thinking that what they have done to Stephen is "all for him." The opposing attitudes of the sisters relates to the contexts of their father and Stephen, one being an aggressive antagonist and the other a passive protagonist who becomes an antagonist out of madness. Kelly gives the painting of the father its own special light (and the military music each time it is seen), and each sister has a turn speaking to it, which is a non-naturalistic theatrical device.

The sisters are presented as the film's protagonists who have committed an act of antagonism. Audience empathy is divided when Stephen returns to them for the climax, like the divided sympathy that other grande dames in Grande Dame Guignol engender. Joyce's sacrifice of a love life and marriage is compared to Ellie never having had the same chances, with Ellie's interest in Alan recognized by Joyce as being a love interest, unrequited though it may be. Although the narrative's repeated visits by Alan are explained by his performing daily errands for the isolated women, his character is used to provide updated exposition. The soldier who has been killed is revealed to be age nineteen. This is significant, since both Joyce and Ellie are old women who have both misspent their youth as soldiers guarding Stephen, who was imprisoned at age nineteen.

Stephen's attack on Roy in the barn consists of expressionistic blood spatters and Gloria's eyes in extreme close-up. The rats we hear in the cellar indicate both the squalor of Stephen's living conditions and a horror movie atmospheric convention. A later shot of a rocking horse in the cellar would seem to be a token acknowledgement of Stephen's comparative youth, though it could also suggest that the cellar was used as a storage area. The investigation of the grounds gets Joyce and Ellie out of the static interior stage-type scenes, even if the music overdoes the suspense element (anticipating a shock appearance by Stephen). Joyce's sprained ankle drives her back inside, though Kelly does intercut between the arrival of Joanna, and Ellie burying the bicycle victim.

Ellie's burying of the body recalls *What Ever Happened to Aunt Alice?* and *The Sav-*

age Intruder, just as her dragging the corpse to the grave recalls the disposal of bodies in *What Ever Happened to Baby Jane?*, *Hush ... Hush, Sweet Charlotte*, *I Saw What You Did*, and *The Mad Room*. The bed-bound Joyce recalls Crawford in *What Ever Happened to Baby Jane?*, Eleanor Parker in *Eye of the Cat*, and Miriam Hopkins in *The Savage Intruder*.

During Joanna's search for an entry to the house, the swinging shed door is employed as a horror movie convention, as much as the darkness in which Ellie does her burying. The screaming of an oversexed cat is used to differentiate between the youthful nurse and the aged spinster. When Ellie has to pop the eye of the victim back into its eye socket before she buries him, it provides a moment of grande guignol squeamishness, even if the moment is clearly an insert performed by a hand that is probably not Reid's.

Kelly photographs Joyce unflatteringly in close-up in bed, with the lines under her eyes apparently due to guilt-based insomnia, although he does present a virtuosic shot when Ellie enters the bedroom at one point. We see the sisters in what is revealed to be a mirrored reflection when the camera pans across the room to show the reverse view of them.

The scene in which a patrol officer is killed begins with the song "She Works in a Woman's Way" played in an army bar sporting a Mother's Day banner, and the song's lyrics describe the difference between a girl and a woman. This age commentary again draws attention to the advanced age and lack of sexual appeal of the sisters, with Kelly sparing us any sight of blood during the murder and simply having the victim look toward the camera. When Joanna speaks of the murders, Kelly focuses the camera on Ellie as she stops drinking tea in reaction to what she hears.

Ellie's reveal to the police about their father and Stephen occupies fifteen minutes of screen time. Her monologue is intercut with point-of-view flashbacks, drawings of World War I action, and a flashback of the father's arrival at a train station (with one of his young girls running from him in horror). Kelly also intercuts Ellie's story with shots of the police tracking dogs chasing Stephen, whose breathing is heard on the soundtrack, and Joyce out of bed and listening to Ellie. The use of the dogs seems premature, since this occurs before the police interview Ellie; however, we presume that her unheard initial telephone call to them was enough to implicate Stephen. Her story includes how Stephen was brought home from boarding school after their father had died, to be "the man of the

Ellie Ballantyne (Beryl Reid) disposes of the body of a victim of *The Beast in the Cellar* (1970).

house" (although he was younger than the sisters). When it is revealed that Joyce is the one who objected to Stephen going off to fight in World War II, Joyce speaks to herself as if to Stephen, her face photographed half in shadow.

When another flashback is intercut to show the older siblings and Stephen being drugged, doubles for Joyce and Ellie are shot in profile to hide their faces. Interestingly, Ellie is presented as the more sexually available sister, compared to the drably dressed Joyce, which contradicts Ellie's earlier comment about her not having Joyce's romantic chances. The idea that what was done to Stephen was "best for him" is repeated, as it will be yet again when the film ends.

Poster for *The Beast in the Cellar* (1970).

After Ellie's story, we get a storm as a horror movie convention—wind, rain, thunder and lightning—all foreshadowing Stephen's return. Ellie's previously disclosed fear of nighttime storms becomes her fear of Stephen, who arrives with a subjective point of view of him going upstairs to Joyce's to room. His labored breathing but inability to speak, long hair and fingernails, and eyes photographed in extreme close-up all present him as a deranged antagonist. His death is portrayed in a rather muddled way, however. We see him reach for the medals on Joyce's army coat, but Ellie claims that he only wanted a drawing of their father that Joyce has beside her bed, an idea seemingly confirmed by his scratching at the drawing.

The death of Stephen removes the antagonist from the grande dames; however, we imagine that they will have to accept responsibility for creating the monster that has committed the murders. The idea that Stephen is so mad that he harbors only resentment toward soldiers who represent his father, rather than his sisters who have locked him up, is hard to believe. The narrative doesn't really give Stephen any opportunity to earn our sympathies, which he surely deserves.

While Flora Robson gives Joyce dignity, and Beryl Reid delivers Ellie's monologue superbly, their performances in general are less resonant than other grande dames because of the limitations of the narrative. As characters, both sisters are reactive and become Women in Peril due to the circumstances at the climax. If we had seen either of them suffer some retribution for their heinous behavior, or even some remorse (rather than the implied concurrence of their last lines), then the film might be more satisfying.

After having played supporting parts, Beryl Reid scored a leading role in *The Killing of Sister George* (1968), reprising her Tony Award–winning Broadway success, and had just played a lead in *Entertaining Mr. Sloane* (1970). Having been typecast as a slightly tipsy, slightly mad older woman, Reid was the first cast of the two leading ladies, and was 50 at the time of *The Beast in the Cellar*. Flora Robson had last played a leading role in the British film *Innocent Sinners* (1958).

Release

April 14, 1971, with the tagline, "A chill-filled festival of horror!" Because of the lack of confidence the producers had in their product, it was released on a double bill with *Blood on Satans's Claw*. The original UK cinema version cut the scene with Roy and Gloria in the barn, removing the shot of Roy pulling down Gloria's panties and Gloria undoing Roy's trouser buttons. It also reduced the amount of blood spatter shown.

Reviews

"It looks and sounds as if it might have first been planned as a bad play for the ladies who rattle teacups during London matinees.... The ladies spend most of their time in the parlor drinking tea and talking the plot over and out."—Vincent Canby, *The New York Times*, April 15, 1971.

"The mechanics of suspense are deployed with routine efficiency ... but the atmosphere is dissipated by the labored performances, a badly constructed script which pointlessly elaborates the simplest encounters and the perfunctory introduction of sniggering bawdiness in the barn to boost the picture's box office appeal."—Phil Hardy, *The Aurum Film Encyclopedia of Horror*.

"Slow moving with some jarring gore effects, [it] simply does not pay off after the extended buildup."—Gary A. Smith, *Uneasy Dreams: The Golden Age of British Horror Films, 1956–1976*.

"Idiotically boring farrago, totally lacking in suspense and wasting good talent."—David Gritten, *Halliwell's Film Guide*.

Cry of the Banshee (1970)

American International Productions

CREDITS: *Director/Executive Producer:* Gordon Hessler; *Producer:* Louis M. Heyward; *Associate Producer:* Clifford Parkes; *Screenplay:* Tim Kelly & Christopher Wicking, based on a story by Tim Kelly; *Photography:* John Coquillon; *Music:* Wilfred Josephs; *Editor:* Oswald Hafenrichter; *Production Design/Art Direction:* George Provis; *Set Decoration:* Scott Slimon; *Make-up:* Tom Smith & Betty Blattner; *Hair:* Ivy Emmerton; *Sound:* Kevin Sutton; *Wardrobe:* Dora Lloyd; *Titles:* Terry Gilliam. Color, 91 minutes. Filmed on location in Middlesex, England, at the mansion of William S. Gilbert, of Gilbert and Sullivan fame.

CAST: Vincent Price (*Lord Edward Whitman*); Essy Persson (*Lady Patricia Whitman*); Hugh Griffith (*Mickey*); Patrick Mower (*Roderick*); Hilary Dwyer (*Maureen Whitman*); Carl Rigg (*Harry Whitman*); Stephen Chase (*Sean Whitman*); Marshall Jones (*Father Tom*); Andrew McCulloch (*Bully Boy*); Michael Elphick (*Burke*); Pamela Farbrother (*Margaret Donald*); Quinn O'Hara (*Maggie*); Jan Rossini (*Bess*); Sally Geeson (*Sarah*); Robert Hutton (*Party Guest*); Godfrey James (*Head Villager*); Gertan Klauber (*Tavern Keeper*); Peter Benson (*Brander, the Major-domo*); Guy Deghy (*Party Guest*); Richard Everett (*Timothy*); Louis Selwyn (*Apprentice*); Mickey Baker (*Shepherd*); Ann Barrass (*Villager*); Jane Deady (*Naked Girl*); Carol Desmond (*Girl*); Joyce Mandre (*Party Guest*); Pamela Moiseiwitsch (*Maid*); Elisabeth Bergner (*Oona*); Nancy Meckler, Hugh Portnow, Stephen Rea, Maurice Colbourne, Dinah Stabb, Tony Sibbald, Neil Johnston, Rowan Wylie, Tim Thomas, Ron Sahewk, Maya Roth, Philly Howell, Guy Pierce (*Villagers*).

VHS/DVD: DVD: MGM (Video & DVD), released April 15, 2003.

Plot

Lord Edward Whitman, a 16th-century magistrate in England, goes on a quest to find witches in his village, and punishes any woman he fears is a threat to his authority. This mistrust of women extends to Edward's son, Sean, who is a rapist. At the local inn, Sean's rape of a new maid is interrupted by the appearance of Maggie, a charm seller. When Sean attacks Maggie, she tells him of Oona, the leader of a cult of Druids who worship at the ruined church. Whitman instigates an attack on Oona's family, killing several of her children but sparing her life. Oona swears revenge, placing a curse on the Whitman household, and summons an avenger, whose power she can bend to her will. Oona calls her command over this spirit "Sidhe," whereby the summoned banshee is like a werewolf, a union of man and wolf. Roderick, the Whitmans' stud groom, responds to the summons, compelled to do so by the power of the medallion he wears. Roderick is also the lover of Edward's daughter, Maureen, as well as a companion to Edward's disturbed wife, Patricia. Roderick has demonstrated a power over animals, rescuing a village girl from a mad dog, which Father Tom attributes to Roderick's medallion.

When Sean is riding one night near the ruined church, he is attacked and killed by Roderick in the form of a banshee. Since Oona cannot be found, Edward orders that female villagers be tortured in order to extract information about her, although this fails to provide any insights. Oona summons Roderick to kill Patricia, but his murder of Maureen is halted when Edward's son, Harry, and Father Tom find Oona, who is subsequently killed by Harry. Roderick tells Maureen that Oona's curse has been broken, but when she takes him to Edward, Roderick transforms into the banshee again. Maureen shoots Roderick to save her father, and Edward decides to leave the village. Stopping at Roderick's gravesite, Edward discovers that the coffin is empty. Roderick has not been killed, and when Edward goes to tell Harry and Maureen, he finds them both dead in the carriage. The coachman reveals himself to be Roderick and rides off with Lord Whitman inside, thus completing Oona's revenge.

Notes

Like *I Saw What You Did*, this film qualifies as Grande Dame Guignol in spite of the fact that the grande dame only has a supporting role because she is so important to the narrative. While it features a lot of grande guignol, the film also offers some disturbing misogyny, pedestrian horror, and direction that focuses on seeming irrelevancies. Director Gordon Hessler had previously made the horror titles *The Woman Who Wouldn't Die* (1964, aka *Catacombs*), *The Oblong Box* (1969, which he also produced), and *Scream and Scream Again* (1970).

The film includes a pre-credit quote from Edgar Allan Poe, alluding to the shriek of the banshee to come, although the shrieks can also apply to the numerous women who are tortured, raped, and killed during the narrative. Under the credits are cartoon images of flying beasts, created by Terry Gilliam and reminiscent of his designs for the television comedy series *Monty Python's Flying Circus*. The first live-action image is of a branding iron in the shape the letter "H" (for heretic), used to burn the flesh of Margaret Donald, who is accused of witchcraft by association. The burning flesh and the whipping she will receive in the street are both grande guignol, with the branding recalling Cecil B DeMille's *The Cheat* (1915). Although the punishment may be period-accurate, as is the general attitude towards women, the choice of Hessler to expose her breasts when she is being locked into the stocks reads as unnecessarily exploitative.

The killing of sheep by a mad dog is a red-herring, although it does reveal Roderick's ability to tame wild beasts. The dog's bark, which initially sounds dubbed, will later be appropriated by the human banshee. The scene in which two children are brought to Edward is really only worthwhile to demonstrate the family's sense of entitlement to cruelty, though Edward being stabbed in the neck with a fork shows that he is not invincible. The attack on Edward being enacted by a female is quite pleasing, and matches up with Patricia's leaving the scene in disgust. Hessler uses a dog's howl to stop the torment of the girl, as a foreshadowing of the fear the banshee will incur, and as one of the few occasions for a respite from the mistreatment of women. Sean's rape of Patricia is supposedly excused by the fact that she is his stepmother, and that she would prefer the advances of a younger man. Hessler presents Patricia's reactions ambiguously, so that one could interpret her anguish as pleasure. He repeats the dog's howl in daytime as an indication that not all horrors occur at night, with the Whitman house described as "cursed" and the Whitman children as "seeds of evil" even before Oona enters the scenario.

The inn scene begins with a song about the loss of maidenhead and the maiden's revenge on her abuser by using a knife to take a man's maidenhead, although the closest the narrative will get to such equal-opportunity violation is the curse's elimination of Edward's offspring. The interruption of Sean's attempted rape of the maid will see a grisly payoff

Poster for *Cry of the Banshee* (1970).

when she is later burned alive by Edward. The narrative repeats Sean's humiliation technique for both the maid and Maggie, and Hessler again exposing the actress' breasts. These scenes, along with the rape of Patricia, indicate that Hessler was aiming his film at an audience that wants sex and not horror. This notion is reinforced by the ritual dance of Oona's "children," where flesh is apparent under white clothing. The dance recalls the coven ritual of *The Witches*, and the white clothes are juxtaposed with the red uniforms of the invading soldiers who catch the children in nets and use axes on them. Although no blood is seen, the axes recall those from *Strait-Jacket*, and Hessler gives Bergner a long close-up of her reaction, with a superimposition of day turning into night.

When Oona pronounces her curse and summons the avenger, Hessler adds the horror movie convention of thunder and lightning. He presents Oona as a grande dame, with her children at her feet repeating her name. Since Edward behaves so reprehensibly, one cannot consider him the film's protagonist. This makes it easier to consider Oona as such, although she is Edward's antagonist.

Sean's death obscures our view of the banshee, and we only see the results of the face slashing, which adds to the mystery of whether or not Roderick is responsible. The decision not to show the creature is a convention used by filmmakers like Val Lewton, who did so when working on low budgets and with the insight that an unseen suggested menace is far more frightening than men in full view. The repeat of the human-sounding dog howl also implies that the mad dog may be responsible, with Sean's companions abandoning him to his fate by withholding his horse as a sign of their infantile irresponsibility.

When the mad dog is hunted down and killed, Hessler shows a gun aimed at the camera, the smoke of the explosion, and the head of the dog on a spike. This subjective camera technique is also used in other scenes. Patricia's mad scene goes on too long, an example of the self-indulgent overemphasis Hessler gives to lesser incidents. However, it does suggest the idea that perhaps Roderick's counsel is what is disturbing her, since she is the next victim. Edward's line that he should have killed Oona and not shown her mercy doesn't match the presumption that it was the mad dog that has killed Sean. We aren't shown the soldiers returning to the church and being unable to locate Oona, or the sight of Oona hiding to avoid retribution. When she is found by Harry and Father Tom in a moment of remarkable coincidence, it would appear that she has remained within the underground area of a previously unexplored open tomb.

Harry's resistance to the torture of Margaret by Burke seems to exist only to allow for their extended fight scene, another indulgence of Hessler's, though the fire used on Margaret leads to Oona's line, "Born in fire, dies in fire." This line will be the key to killing the banshee, though Edward tragically does not heed it. Oona's use of voodoo dolls that approximate Sean, Patricia, and Maureen recalls the voodoo of *The Witches*. Only the untimely killing of Oona deprives us of seeing the Edward doll. Patricia's death scene maintains the mystery by keeping the banshee in shadow, with her calling out Roderick's name failing to give the game away because of their close association. Her investigating a noise makes her a Woman in Peril, and the blood spatter during her attack makes her murder more gruesome and resonant, though again Hessler goes on for too long.

Lord Edward Whitman (Vincent Price), Sean Whitman (Stephen Chase), and courtroom soldier (actor unidentified) in *Cry of the Banshee* (1970).

Edward asking about the paid mourners at Patricia's funeral engenders some amusement, though the sight of her whitened hair in the coffin provokes a gothic shock. It is this transformation that convinces Edward that witchcraft is responsible, though since the mad dog is dead, it is easy to rule him out for a second murder. Edward's decision to kill villagers until information about Oona is forthcoming seems a terrible misuse of his power—and ultimately misguided, since the killing of the maid from the inn doesn't help him. Maureen's attack also presents her as a Woman in Peril investigating a noise, though her going to Roderick as the killer is a clever narrative touch, after Roderick has been imprisoned by Edward for being caught in bed with her. It is ironic that Roderick should be punished for the lesser offence, since he has killed Sean and Patricia, and it is only the fortuitous killing of Oona by Harry that allows Maureen to survive.

As Edward had pointed out after his attack on Oona's children, one wonders why she didn't use her powers to defend herself, since here, too, Harry's cutting of her throat is easily accomplished.

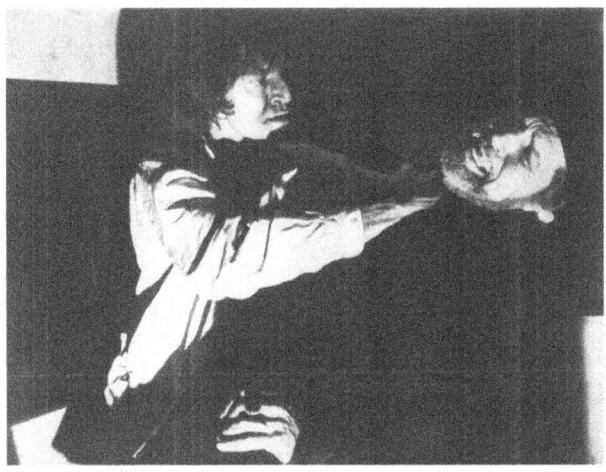

The possessed Roderick (Patrick Mower) attacks Lord Edward Whitman (Vincent Price) in *Cry of the Banshee* (1970).

Although Oona's death recalls Joan Crawford's turn of the head when she died in *I Saw What You Did*, Oona does get to predict that the Whitman curse will live on. Just how that will work is not made clear, since none of her children are seen to continue the summoning ritual, and it doesn't explain why Roderick still transforms when he attacks Edward. Roderick's confession to Maureen that the "power is no longer over him" doesn't seem to concern her, considering that he is admitting to having killed Sean and Patricia. Perhaps this is because she loves him more than she loved her brother and stepmother. Hessler uses tilted camera angles when Edward is alone in his castle, with the sound of the banshee heard on the soundtrack. The extended double strangulation between Edward and Roderick seems silly, even if we finally get to see Roderick's werewolf make-up as the banshee.

Roderick's gory head blasting is more grand guignol, though we see how easily his face recovers for the closing coach ride; and the serene faces of the dead Harry and Maureen provide momentary surprise. The narrative's ending denies us the sight of Edward's physical punishment, though his being kidnapped by his nemesis provides a gothic resonance, as if simply slaughtering him is insufficient retribution for his deeds.

Elisabeth Bergner was age 72 at the time of filming. She had last played a leading role in the German film *The Happy Years of the Thorwalds* (1962) but had not played the lead in an English language film since *Paris Calling* (1941). Wearing black under her white witch's sheath, Bergner's Oona wears her medium-length hair in a tussled, wild style. It is unfortunate that she happens to resemble and sound like Essy Persson who plays Patricia, unless this is deliberate. Bergner's performance is competent if not legendary.

Release

January 1970, with the tagline, "Edgar Allan Poe probes new depths of TERROR!"

Reviews

"The film is only mildly diverting.... After an absence of three decades Miss Bergner's screen appearance is only slightly startling."—A. H. Weiler, *The New York Times*, December 17, 1970.

"[A] slickly produced and photographed programmer.... Hessler evokes a heavy brooding sense of evil, getting thoroughly convincing performances from players exceptionally well cast physically.... However, the scenes in which Bergner calls forth her avenger from beyond are strangely lacking in impact and drama..."—*Variety*, August 5, 1970.

"Only in the location scenes does Hessler create a sense of haunting evil. Elsewhere the film exploits whatever opportunities for violence are provided by its theme.... Only those who remember Bergner's sugary performances of the late twenties and early thirties will appreciate the nicely sacrilegious aspect of casting her as Oona and cutting her throat."—Phil Hardy, *The Aurum Film Encyclopedia of Horror*.

"The production is well mounted due in no small part to the use of opulent costumes which were left over from the big-budget historical film *Anne of the Thousand Days*.... Vincent Price is given little to do here, other than to act unpleasant, but his presence is always welcome."—Gary A. Smith, *Uneasy Dreams: The Golden Age of British Horror Films, 1956–1976*.

What's the Matter with Helen? (1971)
(aka *The Best of Friends*; *The Box Step*)

Martin Ransohoff Presents/Filmways Pictures/Raymax Production

CREDITS: *Director:* Curtis Harrington; *Producer:* George Edwards; *Executive Producer:* Edward S. Feldman; *Associate Producer:* James C. Pratt; *Screenplay:* Henry Farrell; *Music:* David Raksin; *Photography:* Lucien Ballard; *Editor:* William H. Reynolds; *Art Direction:* Eugene Lourie; *Set Decoration:* Jerry Wunderlich; *Wardrobe:* Morton Haack; *Hair:* Sydney Guilaroff; *Make-up:* William Tuttle; *Sound:* Al Overton Jr.; *Musical Numbers Staging and Choreography:* Tony Charmoli. Color, 101 minutes.

SONGS: "Goody, Goody" (Matty Malneck), sung by Debbie Reynolds; "Animal Crackers in My Soup" (Ray Henderson, Irving Caesar, Ted Koehler), sung by Samee Lee Jones; "Nasty Man" (Ray Henderson, Jack Yellen, Irving Caesar), sung by Robbi Morgan.

CAST: Debbie Reynolds (*Adelle Bruckner Stuart*); Shelley Winters (*Helen Hill Martin*); Dennis Weaver (*Lincoln "Linc" Palmer*); Michael Mac Liammoir (*Hamilton Starr*); Agnes Moorehead (*Sister Alma*); Helene Winston (*Mrs. Greenbaum*); Peggy Rea (*Mrs. Schultz*); Logan Ramsey (*Detective Sergeant West*); Swen Swenson (*the Gigolo*); Timothy Carey (*the Tramp*); Samee Lee Jones (*Winona Palmer*); Robbi Morgan (*Rosalie Greenbaum*); Paulle Clark (*Mrs. Plumb*); Yvette Vickers (*Mrs. Barker*); Molly Dodd (*Mrs. Rigg*); Debbie Van Den Houton (*Sue Anne Schultz*); Teresa De Rose (*Donna Plumb*); Pamelyn Ferdin (*Kiddy M.C.*); Allen Pinson (*the Man*); James Dobson (*Cab Driver*); Sadie Delfino (*the Little Lady*); Tammy Lee, Sharon Hisamoto, Stacey Hollow, Marcia Garcia, Bambi Meyers, Roxane Meyers, Vicki Schreck, Keri Shuttleton, Shawn Steinmann, Madelon Tupper, Sian Winship (*Adelle's Kiddystars*); Uncredited: Peter Brocco (*Old Man*); Gary Combs (*Matt Hill*); Annette Davis (*Spinster*); Douglas Deane (*Fanatical Man*); Minta Durfee (*Old Lady*); Helene Heigh (*Widow*); Peggy Patten (*Ellie Banner*); Harry Stanton (*Malcolm Hays*); Peggy Walton-Walker (*Young Girl*).

VHS/DVD: DVD: MGM (Video and DVD), released August 27, 2002.

Plot

In Braddock, Iowa, in the 1930s, dance instructor Adelle Bruckner and her accompanist, Helen Hill, become pariahs when their sons are sentenced to life in prison for the murder of Ellie Banner. After a man telephones them at the school and threatens them, they decide to move to Hollywood, California, and start new lives. At Adelle's Academy of Dance they train little girls, while stage mothers eagerly await the appearance of talent scouts. Since Adelle has dyed her hair to resemble Jean Harlow, she convinces Helen to also undergo a make-over, and cuts her hair. The sight of the scissors makes Helen recall the death of her husband Matt, mangled by plow blades when he lost control of the horses pulling the farm equipment. Actor Hamilton Starr comes to the academy to offer his services as an elocution teacher, and even though Helen takes an instant dislike to him, Adelle hires him.

Texan Lincoln Palmer, the divorced wealthy father of Adelle's student Winona, comes to watch his daughter rehearse and begins an affair with Adelle. As Helen begins to decorate the dance studio for an upcoming recital, Adelle informs her that Linc has rented a real theater for the event. Backstage at the recital, Helen has visions of the bloodied faces of Ellie Banner and Matt, and her screaming ruins the show. Helen goes into the cellar and finds that the cardboard cutout of Adelle used to advertise the studio has been mutilated. That night, when Linc picks up Adelle for a date, he shows her a newspaper clipping he received in the mail about the Banner murder. When Helen refuses a letter addressed to her old name, Adelle accuses Helen of sending herself the letter to cover the fact that Helen had sent Adelle the clipping. Helen denies doing so, but Adelle orders her to move out. After Adelle leaves with Linc the following evening, Helen is packing her suitcase when a man enters the house and ascends the stairs, asking if she received his letter. Panicked, Helen pushes the man down the stairs to his death. Returning to the studio, Adelle is shocked to find a dead body in the hallway. When she finds a letter he was carrying, notifying Helen that she has inherited money from a relative, Adelle helps dispose of the body without notifying the police. In the pouring rain, the women lug the body to a construction site across the street and dump it into an open trench.

The body is found by the police the next day. While Adelle sleeps that night, Helen listens to Sister Alma on the radio, who exhorts all sinners to confess their mistakes to God. When Adelle awakens and finds Helen gone, and hears Sister Alma on the radio, she realizes that Helen has gone to the sister's church and hurries to stop her. Adelle arrives as Helen approaches Sister Alma and begs to confess. Not interested in Helen's confession, Sister Alma dismisses her, causing Helen to become hysterical. Adelle grabs the raving woman and hustles her home, where Helen blames Adelle for her anguish because she stopped Sister Alma from granting her absolution from her sins. That night, Linc proposes to Adelle, and she accepts. Adelle arrives home to find the walls spattered with blood, and discovers that Helen has slaughtered the pet rabbits she had lovingly raised, in order to free them. Helen also admits that she pushed her husband in front of the plow to stop his constant sexual advances. Adelle tries to humor Helen, promising to contact Sister Alma for her. When Adelle mentions that she and Linc are getting married, Helen stabs her to death. Soon after, Detective Sergeant West from Braddock arrives. He shows Helen a photo of the man they found in the trench, identifying him as Ellie Banner's lover, who was seeking revenge on the mothers of Ellie's killers. After West leaves, Helen runs to tell the news to Adelle. When Linc comes to collect Adelle for their wedding, he finds Helen playing "Goody Goody" on the piano and Adelle's corpse, dressed in her dancing costume, propped up on the stage.

Notes

While this film features a grande dame in Shelley Winters (in her second Grande Dame Guignol), and plenty of grande guignol effects, as a horror movie it is weakened by poor pacing and a subplot that distracts from the main conflict. After the considerable technique director Curtis Harrington showed in *Games*, his approach here seems much more subdued and conservative. It's all the more disappointing because the screenplay by Henry Farrell, who wrote *What Ever Happened to Baby Jane?* and *Hush ... Hush, Sweet Charlotte*, continues the thread of women entangled in the complications of the protagonist/antagonist equation. Moving from sisters to cousins to co-workers and mothers of a pair of murderers, Farrell here presents his recognizable archetypes. One is sexually repressed, the other sexually active, with an attendant man of indeterminate sexuality. Both women are haunted by their pasts, since they blame themselves for the heinous action of their sons, and are social antagonists by association. While the narrative seemingly presents only one of them as preoccupied and "crazy," the other's attempts to run away from the situation only leads her to become inescapably and mortally confronted by it. That the women will turn on each other is expected. That it takes so long for it to happen is a frustration.

Martin Ransohoff and Filmways Pictures had previously made the horror titles *The Fearless Vampire Killers* (1967) and *Eye of the Devil* (1966). Raymax Productions had previously produced the television series *The Debbie Reynolds Show* and two television specials for Debbie Reynolds. *What's the Matter with Helen?* was the first film made by executive producer Edward S. Feldman, and the first horror title made by associate producer James C. Pratt. It is director Curtis Harrington's third Grande Dame Guignol.

Harrington opens with a Hearst Metrotone Newsreel of Franklin D. and Eleanor Roosevelt to provide period ambiance before we see a sepia-colored recreation of the mothers fleeing a courthouse. The transparent jigsaw puzzle pieces that cover their faces under the credits never finish creating a total image to conceal them, as if to show how they cannot escape their predicament and that there will be no easy solution to their problem. The crime scene photographs of the murdered woman shows her bloodied corpse, and also her resemblance to Adelle. This resemblance is a plot point later discussed when Helen tells Adelle that the murder of the woman who was the same age as themselves was clearly the son's "substitute revenge." The stones thrown at the women as they are led to a taxi, and the cut on Helen's hand (said to have come from a knife by someone in the crowd) makes the women seem vulnerable to attack. The brightly lit interiors of the Iowa studio are complimented by Harrington's use of a red flashing fluorescent light on the women's faces, which alternates showing youthful and aged appearances. The cardboard cut-out of Adelle is used for the transition between cities, but will also be used later as a plot point, as will the particular costume she wears in it. The cut-out also presents Adelle as the profile member of the team, though hair, costume and make-up already differentiate her character.

Adelle's confession that her husband "took a powder" from their marriage, and that work meant that she neglected her son, who now refuses to answer her letters, is used to rationalize her guilt and moral responsibility. Helen similarly rationalizes the guilt she carries over her son witnessing the death of his father, and his idea that Helen could have rescued him from the blades of the plough. Since we never hear the defense offered by the boys for their crime, and only know their attitudes from their mothers' point of view, these casual explanations may be questionable. However, as the sons do not appear as characters in the narrative, it is only the mothers' point of view that is important. Since both of the killers are males who have killed a female, and the threatening telephone caller is also male, Helen's line, "Men can be lower than the angels," gets a resonant laugh. The telephone caller alters the empathy equation and changes the women into protagonists.

The women teaching prepubescent children to dance is their own form of motherhood substitution, without providing counsel on the perils of fame and public attention. Along with the stage mothers, Adelle and Helen traffic in the exploitation of sexualized children, with the popularity of child film star Shirley Temple described as "the cat's meow." Hamilton Starr's entrances are filmed like he is a horror movie monster, whether as a shock or prefigured by shadow. Although Helen's fear of him is initially an expression of her insecurity, it will later prove to be justified. Starr's homosexuality can be inferred from his theatrical flamboyance, although Adelle is equally flamboyant, and how his references for the job include female movie stars like Constance Bennett and Kay Francis. However, this sexual preference is pure conjecture, and contradicted by his later sexual advances toward Helen. Helen being presented as unattractive makes Hamilton's potential interest in her odd, and this is why it is easy to misinterpret his initial response to her as disdain.

Adelle's beauty is presented as more period-appealing, even if her stylized femininity is as much a cartoon woman as Stella Stevens was in *The Mad Room*. Adelle's "Goody Goody" tap dance can be interpreted as a seduction of Linc, even though her students and their mothers also witness it. His response to her provides a perverse twist in the tango scene by the fact that he has paid the Gigolo to dance with Adelle, as if another man is his sexual substitute. Fritz Weaver's Texan accent also unintentionally emasculates Linc, as does Linc's promoting his daughter as a Shirley Temple clone. The caged birds in his house recall *What Ever Happened to Baby Jane?* and *The Night Walker*. Helen, by contrast, has white rabbits as her love interest, which may not be as pathetic at it seems as a love interest for a grande dame.

The Academy revue features three acts, including "Animal Crackers in My Soup," which was sung by Temple in *Curly Top* (1935), and "Nasty Man," which was sung by Alice Faye in *George White's Scandals* (1934). These scenes go on far too long, and Harrington only occasionally cuts to backstage activity. His insertion of the entire performance recalls the extended animal acts featured in *Berserk!*, which also offered context but still seemed like filler. Thankfully, the sight of a fan reminds Helen of the

Hamilton Starr (Michael Mac Liammoir) is found snooping by Helen Hill (Shelley Winters) and Adelle Bruckner (Debbie Reynolds) in *What's the Matter with Helen?* (1971).

plough blades, and her visions and screaming pull the focus backstage. Perversely, Farrell has one of the children being too fat for her costume, with her having to be cut out of it. Starr brandishing scissors then adds to Helen's mania, since it was the sight of Adelle's scissors (when cutting her hair) that made Helen initially flash back to the plough accident. Adelle's anger at Helen, who "bitched up my one big moment," is an indication that Adelle is really an amateur for placing so much importance on her appearance in the revue, which is meant to celebrate her students. Adelle is also presented as self-absorbed and careless for repeatedly leaving the front door to the Academy open, allowing the Man to enter.

Helen is the Woman in Peril when she walks through the darkened Academy to discover the stabbed cardboard cut-out of Adelle and what seem like blood smears. Helen's idea of "someone out there seeking revenge" is more horror movie convention, and a continuation of the idea that the antagonist is an external threat. Helen smelling Adelle's clothes can be interpreted many ways, but the slow-motion camerawork that Harrington employs for the Man's fall down the stairs can only be interpreted as obvious. Thunder, the quick edits, the superimposing of Matt's bloody face over the Man's, blood from the Man's head, and the loud music all continue the obviousness. Adelle's violence is expressed when she slaps Helen with the letter the Man was carrying—in the same impulsive way Adelle had grabbed Helen's shoulders during the scene in which she accused Adelle of only being interested in Linc for his money.

The disposal of the Man's body (in the worksite's trench) recalls similar events in *What Ever Happened to Baby Jane?*, *Hush ... Hush, Sweet Charlotte*, and *The Mad Room*. The rain is a nice touch, and the ground had been laid earlier so to speak, when Adelle noticed the worksite across from the Academy. What makes this event so interesting for the narrative is that the Man's murder reunites the women, although in an entrapped way. By killing what appears to be an innocent man, Helen becomes an antagonist, but since we don't want the pair to be caught, they both remain protagonists.

Sister Alma's church being called "The Haven of the Open Hand" is an amusing reference to Helen's hand being cut at the start of the film, and Alma's cutting rejection of Helen will hurt just as much. Alma anointing her followers with oil "for everlasting youth" is a comment of the appeal of youth among her older congregation, with Agnes Moorehead's dyed red hair another sign of youth appropriation. Alma's refusal to listen to Helen's confession is funny—"I offered you my blessing, but you refused it"—and the slap that Adelle gives Helen also gets a laugh thanks to Alma's reaction: "You only did what had to be done, sister. God has forgiven you."

Adelle's view that she only wants Helen to stay until she is well enough to leave repeats Adelle's rejection of Helen. It confirms Helen as the antagonist to Adelle's protagonist, a position that she will embrace at the film's climax. The white rose that Hamilton gives Helen contains a thorn, a repeat from Harrington's *Games*, and his following her creates the expectation of rape, since Helen is presented as the more vulnerable person. Her room having been disturbed, and the broken glass, both appear to confirm this expectation, except that Hamilton disappears from the narrative. Harrington continues his horror movie conventions with an open window and wind, blood in the kitchen and on the stair rail, and a barking dog announcing Adelle's return. The rabbit hutch being covered is misleading, and it is only when Adelle uncovers it that we see the slaughter of Helen's rabbits, their throats cut. While it is possible that Hamilton has killed the rabbits, the severity is extreme, and even the sight of Helen with blood on her dress furthers the possibility of the rape scenario. However, Helen's confession turns the narrative when she reveals that she purposely pushed Matt into the plough blades and killed the rabbits to "release them" because no one else wanted them. By killing her love interest and admitting to her essential loneliness, the anticipation that Helen will want to "release" Adelle is created—and fulfilled.

The casting of Logan Ramsey as Sergeant West is unfortunate in his physical resemblance to Michael Mac Liammoir's Hamilton, since for a moment we think he *is* Hamilton. Rather, he is the bearer of news that would seemingly end the antagonistic threat to Helen, although it is too late for Adelle. That Helen has placed Adelle in the Academy's room for "our" recital is a reminder of Helen initially having started to decorate for the revue. Since we have never seen Helen as jealous of Adelle's romance with Linc, or possessive of Adelle, the final display of Adelle's corpse is more a sign of Helen's regression into the not-so-distant past, before Linc came into their lives. Helen playing "Goody Goody" to accompany the obviously dead and unable-to-dance Adelle is also an indication of her failure to accept reality. That Adelle's pose is an appropriation of the crucifixion is a nod to Helen's religion, though this time Adelle will not rise from the dead.

Harrington had offered the part of Adelle to Shirley MacLaine, who turned it down. He next approached Rita Hayworth, but claimed her mind was suffering the effects of the condition later diagnosed as Alzheimer's disease, though this did not stop her from being cast in other films at the time. Debbie Reynolds was his third choice. The film proved to be a change of pace for Reynolds, who had continued playing leading roles in romantic comedies and musicals in the 1960s after the end of the studio system. Her last leading role had been in *How Sweet It Is* (1968),

Poster for *What's the Matter with Helen?* (1971). The imagery is a spoiler for the film's ending.

before she tried her television series. Ironically, *What's the Matter with Helen?* would be her last leading role until *Mother* (1996). By contrast, Shelley Winters was 50 and had previously played leading roles in *Bloody Mama* (1970) and *Arthur! Arthur!* (1969) after her supporting role in *The Mad Room*.

Since Adelle is a less controlled character, Reynolds has the less dramatically interesting part, though her musical comedy background benefits Adelle's demonstrated performance ability. Reynolds was only 38 years old at the time of filming. She looks beautiful and is dressed flatteringly by Morton Haack, whose costumes were nominated for an Academy Award. However, Harrington does use low-key lighting on her for the Academy interiors—similar, though not as extreme, to that used by William Castle for Joan Crawford. Although the age lines on her neck are apparent, the subdued illumination provides shadow for the top of her head and under her chin, so that the main light is focused on the center of Reynolds's beautiful face.

Helen Hill (Shelley Winters) screams when she sees a mutilated cut-out of Adelle in *What's the Matter with Helen?* (1971).

During "Goody Goody" Harrington cuts away from Reynolds, limiting our appreciation of her skill. This may be a ruse to conceal the fact of Adelle as an incompetent dancer, which her mussed hair by the end of the dance also suggests. Adelle's tango with the Gigolo is filmed to show a better appreciation of her contribution, if one can accept the contrivance that such a finely detailed piece of choreography could be performed so perfectly by two seeming strangers. When Adelle helps Helen dispose of the body of the Man, her wet hair and running make-up is Reynolds's attempt to look disheveled, while Adelle's final marionette pose recalls the Baby Jane dolls of *What Ever Happened to Baby Jane?*

Although Helen's religious fanaticism doesn't provide much scope, her repressed anger does enable Winters to display funny and dangerous beginnings—before she catches and controls herself. Naturally, all this repression can only lead to an inevitable and uncontrollable outburst, which happens at the film's climax. Helen's look of revulsion at herself in the mirror after she's had a make-over is a sign of both the character's low self-esteem and the progressively dwindling attractiveness of Winters in her Grande Dame Guignol films. Winters' confrontation with Moorehead, finally seen after having been heard repeatedly on the radio, is a wonderful moment between two grande dames. Helen's last moment of laughing and crying as she plays the piano for Adelle's corpse is painful and disturbing and real.

Release

June 30, 1971, with the tagline, "So you met someone and now you know it feels. Goody, Goody" (a line from the song in the film). The poster imagery gave away Reynolds's character's fate, although one would need to see the film to realize that.

Reviews

"This movie is so perfunctory, it's likely to give misogyny a bad name.... The thing that's the matter with Helen is obvious so early in the movie that it never has much place to go.... Miss Reynolds looks like an ageless kewpie doll with platinum hair and Miss Winters wears the expression of a reproachful pudding most of the time."—Vincent Canby, *The New York Times*, July 1, 1971.

"An okay dual-bill exploitation shocker.... Harrington raises the interest and excitement level too early and lets the film coast to less-than-tense resolution.... For Miss Reynolds, the film is a change of pace.... Miss Winters's role is one she can do in her sleep."—*Variety*, June 2, 1971.

"Harrington bedecks the script with some brilliantly realized Hollywood memorabilia of the thirties.... It blows up, by way of some time-honored shocks, into a hugely entertaining and gory ending which remembers to pay homage not only to horror but to Hollywood."—Phil Hardy, *The Aurum Film Encyclopedia of Horror*.

Whoever Slew Auntie Roo? (1971)

(aka *Gingerbread House*; *Who Slew Auntie Roo?*)

American International Pictures/Hemdale

CREDITS: *Director:* Curtis Harrington; *Producers:* Samuel Z. Arkoff, James H. Nicholson, Jimmy Sangster; *Executive Producer:* Louis M. Heyward; *Associate Producer:* John Pellat; *Screenplay:* Robert Blees, Jimmy Sangster, based on a story by David D. Osborn; *Additional Dialogue:* Gavin Lambert; *Photography:* Desmond Dickinson; *Music:* Kenneth V. Jones; *Editor:* Tristam Cones; *Art Direction:* George Provis; *Make-up:* Eddie Knight, Sylvia Croft; *Hair:* Paul McDermott, Joyce James; *Production Manager:* Donald Toms; *Sound:* Richard Langford, Ken Ritchie; *Wardrobe:* Bridget Sellers. Color, 91 minutes. Filmed April to June 1971 in Shepperton Studios, England.

SONGS: "Thyme" (Traditional), sung by Shelley Winters; "Tit-Willow" (W. S. Gilbert, Arthur Sullivan), sung by Shelley Winters.

CAST: Shelley Winters (*Mrs. Forrest*); Mark Lester (*Christopher*); Ralph Richardson (*Mr. Benton*); Judy Cornwell (*Clarine*); Michael Gothard (*Albie*); Hugh Griffith (*the Pigman, aka Mr. Harrison*); Lionel Jeffries (*Inspector Willoughby*); Chloe Franks (*Katy*); Rosalie Crutchley (*Miss Henley*); Pat Heywood (*Dr. Mason*); Richard Beaumont (*Peter*); Jacqueline Cowper (*Angela*); Marianne Stone (*Miss Wilcox*); Charlotte Sayce (*Katharine*).

VHS/DVD: DVD: MGM (Video and DVD), released August 27, 2002.

Plot

Rosie Forrest, nee Miller, is a former American dancer and wealthy widow of a magician living in a gingerbread house called Forrest Grange in England. She has been traumatized by the death of her daughter, Katharine, who fell from the staircase banister as she attempted to slide down. Rosie, aka Aunt Roo, conducts séances to contact Katharine's spirit, with the aid of the medium Mr. Benton. She also keeps the mummified corpse of Katharine in her crib at night, placing it in a coffin during daytime. To compensate for her loneliness, Rosie hosts an annual Christmas party for ten children from the local orphanage. This year brother and sister Christopher and Katy Coombs are not invited, after they had previously run away and now refuse to speak. However, on the night of the trip they stow away in the trunk of the car that transports the children to Rosie's house. Caught by Rosie's servant, Albie, Christopher and Katy are brought to Rosie, who allows them to stay. Katy reminds Rosie of Katharine, although Christopher does not trust Rosie, equating her to the Witch from "Hansel and Gretel." That night Christopher is awakened by the latest séance. He sees Albie and the maid, Clarine, pretending to be the voice of Katharine; they are in league with Benton to take Rosie's money.

Rosie lends Katharine's teddy bear to Katy, who sees the secret compartment where Rosie keeps her jewelry. At Christmas Rosie gives Katy a new bear, but Katy rejects it, preferring Katharine's. Hearing Rosie singing, Christopher uses the house's dumb waiter to spy on Rosie in Katharine's room singing to Katharine's corpse. He determines that Katy must not be adopted by Rosie. When Katy cannot be found when it is time for the orphans to leave, Christopher knows Rosie is keeping her, but no one believes him and he is taken back to the orphanage. Aware that Rosie has Katy, Albie blackmails Rosie into paying him off so that he and Clarine can leave the house. He also admits their part in the Benton fraud. Christopher returns from the orphanage and finds Katy in Katharine's room, stealing Rosie's jewels and hiding them in the teddy bear Rosie has given her. Although Katy wants to stay with Rosie, Christopher convinces her to leave with him. However, Rosie catches them and locks them both away. When the police come to search for the children, they cannot find them, and Rosie feels sure that she can keep the children forever. When Rosie prepares a New Year's dinner that Christopher thinks will feature him and Katy on the menu, Christopher tricks Rosie and goes to get Katy. However, Rosie outwits them and locks them in the kitchen pantry. The children manage to lock Rosie in the pantry, and she burns to death when the house is set on fire. Having retrieved the teddy bear with the jewels, Christopher and Katy can now afford to leave the orphanage and still appear to be the victims of Rosie.

Christopher (Mark Lester) far left, holding the hand of Katy (Chloe Franks) at the orphanage in *Whoever Slew Auntie Roo?* (1971).

Notes

Starring Shelley Winters in her third Grande Dame Guignol, this appropriation of the Hansel and Gretel story provides a narrative limited by the scope of its origins. The idea of pitting a child against a grande dame recalls *The Nanny*, though here the outcome is unwarranted revenge. Although Curtis Harrington's fourth Grand Dame Guignol features some fine camerawork and production design that makes symbolic use of the color red, performances are uneven and the theatrical music score that begins so wonderfully soon deteriorates into standard horror movie convention.

Harrington had not made a film since *Games,* although he had directed the made-for-TV horror movie *How Awful About Allan* (1970), based on a teleplay by Henry Farrell. American International Productions had previously made the horror titles *Witchfinder General* (1968) and *The Oblong Box* (1969). *Whoever Slew Auntie Roo* was the first film made by Hemdale. Producer Samuel Z. Arkoff had previously made *Cry of the Banshee* and *Queen of Blood* with Harrington. Jimmy Sangster had previously produced *The Nanny.*

A pre-credit sequence establishes Rosie as delusional by not recognizing Katharine as dead, with the mummified remains recalling Mrs. Bates from *Psycho.* Katharine's bedroom being filled with dolls alludes to the attention Rosie lavished on her, as well as Rosie's wealth. It's a pity the flashback that introduces the child doesn't reveal any sense of her personality. Rather, she is a plot device used to display Rosie's vulnerability and mental deterioration. The red dress that Rosie wears as she sings to Katharine foreshadows the use of red in the narrative, as Rosie's wearing a tiara and necklace introduces her jewelry that will feature later. The wind, thunder and lightning under the credits are standard horror movie conventions, although the music promises an operatic level of drama that is not matched by the film itself. Harrington cuts from Rosie crying for Katharine during a séance to the sound of the orphans singing "Oranges and Lemons," Albie's decapitation of a dead turkey offers the film's first grande guignol touch.

The exposition indicating Rosie was a former dancer, one of the "Floradora Girls," includes the line, "She liked his tricks and he liked hers," referring to her marriage to Mr. Forrest. That Rosie has given up her career for love is an indication of her ability to sacrifice, and also an awareness of the financial reality of the union, considering her husband's wealth. That we don't know how he died is frustrating, with no suggestion made that he was as affected as Rosie by Katharine's death. However, Rosie's love has now transferred to the orphans, and soon Katy—even if it is maternal rather than sexual love. When Albie catches Christopher at the house he threatens to cut out his tongue, an amusing nod to the fact he and Katy refuse to speak. That Christopher and Katy have increased the number of children at Rosie's is a sign that they have created an imbalance that will resonate and eventually cost Rosie her life. Rosie uses the phrase "the other side of the mirror" to describe death, which is both a code for the children and a seeming reference to her husband's magic.

Harrington films the flashback death of Katharine in black and white. (Later, the sight of Katy on the banister recalls Katharine in the same position.) The blood trickling from Katharine's mouth after the fall is more grande guignol.

Christopher telling Katy the Hansel and Gretel tale seems an odd choice to help her sleep, though its children-triumphing-over-wicked-adult theme offers a form of empowerment. The tale will be further used by Harrington throughout the film in voice-over (with Christopher speaking it), as the narrative matches the succession of predicaments faced by both pairs of children. As a literary device, the use of the tale reads as somewhat obvious; it would have been preferable had the audience been allowed to make the connection rather than having it literally told to us.

Katy, overhearing a séance, becomes the Woman in Peril investigating a noise, which Harrington enhances by initially presenting Christopher following her as a shadow. The slowly opening door is another horror convention, and Harrington repeats it for Katy's entrance for obvious emphasis. The red motif is continued, with not only Albie's vest, but Christopher's sweater being red, while the rest of the orphans are dressed in whites or browns. The color draws attention to Rosie's red dresses and the children's resistance to her. When Albie confesses to Rosie about his culpability in the ruse to defraud her, he wears a red tie. The barn containing Mr. Forrest's mementoes from the past houses a magic cabinet with red doors, and when Albie scares the children he wears a fright wig with red hair. The guillotine which nearly decapitates Katy offers more grande guignol, and Harrington showing Albie's entrance to the barn via a shot of his legs is another horror movie convention.

The dumb waiter recalls the elevators of *Lady in a Cage*, *Games*, and *The Savage Intruder*, and the first time Christopher uses it, Harrington confronts the boy with a giant rat. One can link the rat to Rosie not only by its size, but also by the fact that the creature screams at Christopher but does not hurt him.

Katy's preference to stay with Rosie and lack of concern for Christopher is the mentality of a child and supposedly evidence of Rosie's manipulation, but it certainly confirms the idea that the children are more antagonist than protagonist. The song "Thyme" that Rosie sings to Katharine is a warning against men, which would seem to come from the disappearance of her husband, and a foreshadowing of Christopher's hostilities. Rosie's act of keeping Katy may be duplicitous, but she remains the protagonistic grande dame. Harrington holds the camera on the front door for a transition from night to day when Rosie catches the children trying to leave, with the Christmas wreath on the door eloquent in its silence. The narrative also shows Rosie wielding an axe to scare away a cat from the kitchen, recalling the axes of *Strait-Jacket*. A rocking-horse in Katharine's room recalls *Beast in the Cellar*.

Rosie's delusions about Katharine includes her belief that her daughter has "run away," and Rosie expresses the same concern about Christopher and Katy "abandoning" her. This victimized point of view receives a grande guignol jolt when the face of the mummified Katharine is accidentally crushed by Rosie, though such an occurrence would seem to cement Katy as the new Katharine in Rosie's mind.

The widowed Mrs. Forrest (Shelley Winters) handles the corpse of her dead daughter in lobby card for *Whoever Slew Auntie Roo?* (1971).

The New Year's dinner preparation sequence, in which Rosie gives Christopher an opportunity to leave under the guise of collecting wood, is dependent upon our knowledge that he won't "abandon" Katy. The cat-and-mouse behavior of Rosie and Christopher would seem to present an unfair match, which is exemplified by the sword fight Christopher has with her, as he holds a knife and she a block of wood. One may feel that Rosie is too easily fooled by the children, though her horrible death is perhaps one of the worst and unjustified suffered by a grande dame in Grande Dame Guignol. The smiles of the children at the end are therefore unbearably bitter, though hopefully their theft of Rosie's jewels to finance an escape from the orphanage will not be as readily accepted as their claims of "trying to help" Rosie.

Director Curtis Harrington and star Shelley Winters on the set of *Whoever Slew Auntie Roo?* (1971).

Shelley Winters was age 51 at the time of filming, and had previously made *What's the Matter with Helen?* with Harrington. He presents Rosie as beautiful in her own way, but also grotesque at times, filming Winters with double chins and in extreme close-ups that reveal the powder she uses. One shot of her in close-up sweating and eating an apple as she prepares the meal brings to mind images of a witch, specifically the witch from *Snow White* who traded in apples. To suggest Rosie's theatrical background, Rosie dresses in bold colors of red, maroon and purple, and wears a feathered negligee. The black-veiled mourning attire she wears to bury Katharine is over-scaled for dramatic effect, as are the white gloves that accompany her red dress and tiara for the opening scene by Katharine's crib.

Winters' performance is far more enjoyable than that of Michael Gothard's Albie, who cannot overcome the stereotype of a greedy servant, or the stilted acting of Chloe Franks as Katy. While Winters occasionally goes over the top (as in her transition from faux crying to laughing), she generally gives delicate line readings, and her singing of the opening lullaby reveals a serviceable voice. She provides the vulnerability and emotionalism that generates our sympathy for Rosie's madness, particularly with her tears at the first séance and her use of neurotic murmuring. The unfairness of her fate is underlined by the general unlikability of Katy and Christopher. The "Tit-Willow" performance shows that Rosie was never much of a dancer, or has now lost the ability, with Harrington exposing perhaps too much of Winters's legs (with red garters, of course).

Release

Released March 15, 1972, with the taglines, "She's taking A STAB at Motherhood!" "Have you ever held a skeleton in your arms?" and "The hand that rocks the cradle has no flesh on it!"

Reviews

"An Edwardian horror movie that opens up the full scope of Miss Winters's acting talent, which is insufficient reason for making a movie."—Roger Greenspun, *The New York Times*, March 16, 1972.

"...[S]cript is overly contrived, though Harrington's direction is sound.... Winters has the talent to establish this sort of character, and, at first, make it believable; later, it's anybody's guess what's in her mind."—*Variety*, December 10, 1971.

"Harrington tends to overdo the Grande Guignol sequences ... however, the relationship between Roo and the youngsters is handled well, her kindness to the somewhat sinisterly naive children being tinged with deeply neurotic overtones to prepare the ground for the changeover to the horrid ogre imagined by the little boy and lead to the gruesome climax."—Phil Hardy, *The Aurum Film Encyclopedia of Horror*.

"...[A]n entertaining but ultimately sick affair, with Winters giving yet another of her shrill and overwrought performances that have plagued her later career."—Gary A. Smith, *Uneasy Dreams: The Golden Age of British Horror Films, 1956–1976*.

Blood and Lace (1971)

American International Pictures/Contemporary Film-makers and Carlin Company.

CREDITS: *Director:* Philip S. Gilbert; *Producer:* Ed Carlin, Gil Lasky; *Associate Producer:* Chase Mishkin; *Screenplay:* Gil Lasky; *Photography:* Paul Hipp; *Music Editor:* John Rens; *Art Director:* Lee Fischer; *Make-up:* Dennis Marsh; *Sound:* Douglas Kennedy, James Maura; *Editor:* Dennis Film Services, Marcus Tobias. Color, 87 minutes.

CAST: Gloria Grahame (*Mrs. Dorothy Deere*); Milton Selzer (*Mr. Harold Mullins*); Len Lesser (*Tom Kredge*); Vic Tayback (*Calvin Carruthers*); Melody Patterson (*Ellie Masters*); Terri Messina (*Bunch*); Ronald Taft (*Walter*); Dennis Christopher (*Pete*); Peter Armstrong (*Ernest*); Maggie Corey (*Jennifer*); Mary Strawberry (*Nurse*); Louise Sherrill (*Edna Masters*); Joe Durkin (*Unidentified Man*).

VHS/DVD: Not available in either format.

Plot

Prostitute Edna Masters and her lover are attacked in bed by a person with a hammer, who then sets fire to the house. After surviving the fire, Edna's eighteen-year-old daughter Ellie is taken to a hospital where social worker Harold Mullins informs her that, not knowing her father's identity, she must be sent to an orphanage. When Ellie runs away, Detective Calvin Carruthers returns her to the hospital. Ellie divulges that she dreams the killer used a hammer, but claims she did not witness the murder. When Carruthers finds the hammer at the crime scene he becomes suspicious of Ellie, realizing that only she knew the wounds were caused by a hammer.

At the Deere Youth Home, a boy named Ernest tries to run away, and is chased by the handyman, Tom Kredge. In the forest, Tom chops off Ernest's hand and leaves him to bleed to death. The widow Dorothy Deere runs the Home on the government money she receives for each child, and forces her wards to work for their meals. She and Kredge have killed several children caught escaping and stored the bodies in the basement freezer. Harold brings Ellie to the orphanage, and Dorothy reveals that her late husband, Jamieson, had known Ellie's mother.

Ellie finds the dehydrated Jennifer tied up in the attic, but when she gets water for the girl, Tom threatens Ellie. When Ellie tells fellow orphan Walter, with whom she has been flirting, that she plans to run away and find out who her father is, he tries to dissuade her. Tom offers to help Ellie escape, and when she agrees to meet him in the cellar, he tries to rape her. Dorothy who learned of Ellie's plans from Walter, stops Tom and tries to fire him. However, Tom blackmails her to stay quiet about the murders. The increasingly insane Dorothy talks to the corpse of Jamieson, which she keeps frozen, about the pressures of running the home. A scar-faced intruder carrying a hammer frightens Ellie, and she becomes even more determined to escape when she discovers Walter having sex with another girl, Bunch. Dorothy locks Ellie in her room, and then Tom takes her to the freezer. Pete, who has witnessed this, tries to free her. He fails when he is caught by Tom and Mullins, who is back to inspect the Home.

When Mullins insists on looking inside the freezer, Tom kills him with a cleaver, as the scar-faced intruder reappears. They struggle, Tom is killed, and Ellie escapes. Dorothy drags Tom's body into the freezer, and the vengeful Jennifer locks her in. Ellie warns the other children to leave, but they do not, claiming they have nowhere else to go. Ellie runs into the forest and finds Ernest's body. The scar-faced intruder appears and chases her. Assuming him to be Edna's lover, disfigured by the burns he suffered in the fire, Ellie admits to killing Edna and setting the house on fire, begging for forgiveness. The intruder removes what is revealed to be a mask, and we see he is Detective Carruthers. He promises not to tell on Ellie if she will marry him. As Ellie considers this proposal, he also tells her that he was Edna's first lover and Ellie's father. Ellie bursts into maniacal laughter.

Notes

An obvious low budget saddles this Grande Dame Guignol starring Gloria Grahame with limitations. However, in the only film he has directed, Philip S. Gilbert does manage to provide some imaginative touches to a narrative concerning the conflict between a younger woman and an older grande dame. The grande dame here is another mentally unstable one because she talks to a dead husband whose corpse she has kept (shades of Norman Bates in *Psycho*). Even though the film offers plenty of grande guignol, the plot never reaches the gothic greatness of some other titles. It still, however, features some remarkable elements.

Producers Ed Carlin and Gil Lasky had previously made the horror title *The Night God Screamed* (1971), which presented the last leading film role for Jeanne Crain as a Woman in Peril and a potential grande dame. Lasky had also made *Spider Baby or the Maddest Story Ever Told* (1968). *Blood and Lace* was the first and only film to be made by associate producer Chase Mishkin, and the only film made under the Contemporary Film-Makers and Carlin Company names.

Theremin music plays under the opening credits of *Blood and Lace*, and will feature in the appearances of Dorothy to suggest her madness. Like the harp heard later in the music, this instrument adds exoticism and theatricality to the soundtrack.

The murder of Edna is shown with a subjective camera point of view, beginning with the killer approaching the house, and continuing with the camera roaming the interiors. A hammer is picked up and held in front of the camera, which gives the tool a strange sense of character, and also makes the audience identify with the killer. The sight of Edna and her lover in bed recalls the adulterous couple in *Strait-Jacket* seen by Joan Crawford, with the hammer to be used in the same way she used her axe. Gilbert intercuts between the killer in the house and Edna's room, with repeated shots of the doorknob telegraphing the notion it will turn for the killer's entrance. That Edna wears make-up in bed indicates that she is a prostitute, and her painted face recalls that of Debbie Reynolds in *What's the Matter with Helen?*

Gilbert uses jaunty music from a radio to offset the violence of the hammer killings, and while the quick edits may recall the shower sequence of *Psycho*, here there is more apparent gore. The lover being able to get out of the bed after the attack and during the fire sets up the possibility that he survived to become the scar-faced intruder who will appear at the Home. When Gilbert cuts to Ellie awakening from a nightmare, the conclusion is easily drawn that Ellie is the killer. This is because the dream is from her point of view and she is not seen in it, although we are told that she had been in the house and had escaped the fire.

Having a whore for a mother presents Ellie as a traumatized child, and also foreshadows Dorothy's treatment of her orphans. Ellie speaks of her mother with the disdainful line, "Every drifter, traveling salesman, and schoolboy over sixteen knew my mother." This attitude anticipates a mistrust of men, and we will see that all of the adult men in the narrative had known and presumably slept with Edna. Ellie is the film's protagonist, and Dorothy's appearance will not alter that status until the climactic revelation of Ellie having killed her mother, and perhaps not even then. Dorothy is to be considered an antagonist, though her speech about her lost youth and beauty clearly exists to create some ambiguity.

Gilbert employs the horror movie convention of having Ellie walk backwards before turning around to face the pursing Calvin when she runs away from hospital, though a train whistle is used to end the music that had also been following her. The clock that chimes twelve times for midnight is another convention, but the extreme close-up of the fleeing Ernest as our introduction to him is a shock. The axe that Tom will use to sever Ernest's hand recalls the weapon of *Strait-Jacket*, and the sequence generates a macabre chuckle from the sight of the thin Ernest hiding behind an even thinner tree. Gilbert produces a ghoulishly amusing payoff on Ernest's spilled suitcase having slowed the boy's escape progress when Tom throws the severed hand into it and repacks it to take back to the Home. The hand will produce another payoff when Ellie later takes the suitcase from the shed and discovers the disembodied member inside.

The introduction to the cellar freezer, which recalls the freezer of *Strait-Jacket*, includes this amusing dialogue exchange:

Poster for *Blood and Lace* (1971).

> TOM: It's freezing in here.
> DOROTHY: Well, that's the idea.

When bodies are moved from the freezer to the infirmary to thwart Harold's first inspection of the Home, melting blood seeps from a corpse. Coldness used to kill is something new in Grande Dame Guignol, though, ironically, Dorothy uses it to keep Jamieson "alive" for her. One can also consider the cold as a metaphor for Dorothy's emotional temperature, since she is harsh with the children and only mirrors Harold's sexual interest in her without considering him a real love interest. Like all great grande dames, Dorothy's real love is someone who is unavailable—in this case, dead. Dorothy will tell Ellie that Jamieson was "the only thing in my life that mattered; no children, no friends," and that he left her when she became "old." This neurotic, possessive kind of love finds the perfect afterlife in her preserving his corpse, which she hopes can be restored by future science. As to how Jamieson died or how she came by his corpse remains a mystery, and Dorothy's resentment of Edna as Jamieson's lover offers the (unlikely) possibility that Dorothy could be Edna's killer. The Home housing twelve orphans supplies a kind of mythic association, apart from the clear parallel one takes from the Oliver Twist–suffering of orphans.

The subplot in which Carruthers investigates Edna's murder is somewhat weakened by his casual clothes and unprofessional sexual interest in Ellie undermining his authority as a police detective. The age difference between Carruthers and Ellie—he is old enough to be her father—generates a payoff when it is revealed that he *is* her father, leading to the strange tone of the film's conclusion. The ending also caps Ellie's desire to find her father, who abandoned the family when she was a child, presumably in disapproval of Edna's lifestyle. The body shape of the scar-faced intruder makes it easy to identify him as Carruthers wearing a mask. The mask's clay-like texture supplies an additional resonant gruesomeness, even if it is obvious that it is a mask and not a disfigured human face.

Ellie's fear of a hammer that Tom asks her to hold recalls Joan Crawford's fear of an axe in *Strait-Jacket*, though the fear here is of discovery, since Ellie will be revealed as the killer. For suspense, Gilbert repeats the hammer-held-in-front-of-the-camera point of view when the intruder stalks Ellie, even though it is a red herring obfuscating the identity of the real killer.

The established antagonism between Ellie and Dorothy recalls the younger woman/older woman equation used in *Strait-Jacket*, *Lady in a Cage*, *Die! Die My Darling!*, *The Night Walker*, *I Saw What You Did*, *Games*, *Berserk!*, *Eye of the Cat*, and *Flesh Feast*. The battle between children and a grande dame is a scenario repeated from *The Nanny* and *Whoever Slew Auntie Roo?* The "lace" in the films title presumably refers to the seeming contradiction between violence and femininity, since the one scene showing Dorothy sewing does not feature lacework.

When the corpse of Jamieson, propped up in a wheelchair, is revealed, Gilbert uses jump zooms to emphasize the shock, with the wheelchair recalling those in *What Ever Happened to Baby Jane?*, *Whatever Happened to Aunt Alice?* and *The Savage Intruder*. The catfight between Ellie and Bunch over Walter (often seen semi-naked—Ronald Taft is beautiful but a limited actor) recalls the catfight in *Eye of the Cat*, and is preceded by this exchange:

> ELLIE: Walter was never interested in you, even before I got here.
> BUNCH: I'll make him interested.
> ELLIE: I'm sure you can make Walter. But you'll never interest him.

Ellie's conflict with Bunch is another calibrated older woman/younger woman scenario, even if they are only two years apart in age.

Gilbert inserts quick cuts of Ellie's memory of the intruder when she is locked in her room by Dorothy. The imprisonment recalls similar circumstances in *Strait-Jacket, Lady in a Cage, Die! Die My Darling!, The Night Walker, I Saw What You Did, Games, Berserk!, Eye of the Cat,* and *Whoever Slew Auntie Roo?* Images of an axe reappears when Dorothy uses a meat cleaver in the kitchen while cooking, and Tom stabs Harold in the back in the cellar. This is presumably what was used on all the orphan victims in the freezer, as it was to sever Ernest's hand. Dorothy's statement that the freezer "chills the blood to stop the bleeding" is both a practical analysis in line with her preservation hopes and a denial of the reality of the murders.

While Dorothy's imprisonment in the freezer is a deserved comeuppance, particularly since it is enacted by Jennifer, it also recalls the unwarranted death of Shelley Winters in *Whoever Slew Auntie Roo?* At the climax, when Ellie is caught by the intruder,

Alternative poster for *Blood and Lace* (1971).

her confession as Edna's killer is accompanied by flashbacks in which we see her using the hammer. The confession is instigated with her line "I didn't mean to hurt you," thinking that her pursuer is Edna's lover who has escaped the fire and now menaces her with a hammer. Her follow-up line, "I didn't even know that you were with her," is an obvious lie, since the flashback will reveal otherwise. Gilbert inserts extreme close-ups of Ellie smiling evilly when Carruthers removes the mask, which he calls "theatrical make-up," to tell her of his suspicion of her being Edna's killer.

The idea that he has "used her as bait" to make her run away from the Home by scaring her with her guilt, thus allowing an investigation into Dorothy's practices is a preposterous idea. But not as preposterous as the ensuing blackmail in which he agrees to keep Ellie's murderous secret if she marries him. His line about being "the first man that Edna slept with" recalls Ellie saying the same thing about her unknown father to Walter, identifying Carruthers as her father. While he still doesn't explain his absence, the implicit idea of his wanting to marry his own daughter is what instigates Ellie's hysterical laughter at film's end. This laughter can be interpreted as disbelief, shock at the idea of incest, and the cementing of Ellie's madness seemingly inherited from Carruthers.

Gloria Grahame was age 47 at the time of filming. She had worked on television in the 1960s and had last played a leading role in *Ride Out for Revenge* (1957). Grahame had won the Best Supporting Actress Academy Award for *The Bad and the Beautiful* (1952), and had experienced a personal scandal when she married her former stepson in 1960. A brunette, Grahame delivers an understated performance, with her Mae West-esque, tight-lipped intonation used to portray Dorothy's frustration and essential humorlessness. She is photographed with shiny facial skin (with only Walter shot in the same way at one point), which may indicate she is a woman who moisturizes badly. Her wardrobe is noteworthy for the dominatrix-style chain around her green skirt and the ironic use of symbolic white. When Dorothy flirts with Harold, she deliberately stands close to him, and Gilbert parodies this closeness later when Dorothy uses the same seductive voice when she intends that Harold be killed. Gilbert presents Grahame in shadowed profile for the first time Dorothy speaks to Jamieson, and the shadow of her head in close-up is also seen as she stands against a wall to tell Ellie about how she lost her husband. When Dorothy teases the dehydrated Jennifer with a glass of water by drinking it in front of her, Grahame makes the moment both nasty and funny.

Release

March 17, 1971, with the tagline, "SHOCK after SHOCK after SHOCK as DESIRE drives a bargain with MURDER!"

Reviews

"A low-grade exercise in shadows, screams, traumas and slayings that are largely more laughable than shocking.... The haggard Miss Grahame simply walks through her assignment."—Howard Thompson, *The New York Times*, March 18, 1971.

"Director Gilbert settles for fast pace to cover actors' inadequacies, [and] does manage to work up [a] nail-chewer climax.... Miss Grahame makes some brave stabs at cutting through the silliness, but eventually succumbs to the uneven style of acting supplied by the remaining cast members."—*Variety*, March 11, 1971.

"For its time remarkably graphic and unrelenting, an atmosphere of stark one-dimensional gloom prevails.... Amidst the welter of thoroughly unpalatable characters, Grahame is awesome in her matter-of-fact portrayal of human depravity."—Phil Hardy, *The Aurum Film Encyclopedia of Horror*.

The Baby (1973)

Quintet Films

CREDITS: *Director:* Ted Post; *Executive Producers:* Elliott Feinman, Ralph Hirsch; *Producers:* Milton Polsky, Abe Polsky; *Screenplay:* Abe Polsky; *Photography:* Michael Margulies; *Music:* Gerald Fried; *Editors:* Dick Wormell, Bob Crawford Sr.; *Wardrobe:* Diana Jewett; *Make-up:* Byrd Holland; *Production Manager/Assistant Director:* Jesse Corallo; *Sound:* Glen Glenn; *Sound Effects:* Richard Greer; *Set Director:* Michael Devine; *Nursery Paintings:* Stanley Dyrector. Color, 102 minutes.

CAST: Anjanette Comer (*Ann Gentry*); Ruth Roman (*Mrs. Wadsworth*); Marianna Hill (*Germaine Wadsworth*); Suzanne Zenor (*Alba Wadsworth*); Tod Andrews (*Doctor*); Michael Pataki (*Dennis*); Beatrice Manley Blau (*Judith*); Erin O'Reilly; Don Mallon; Joseph Bernard; Virginia Vincent; David Manzy (*Baby*).

VHS/DVD: DVD: Image Entertainment, released January 25, 2000.

Plot

Ann Gentry is a social worker for the Los Angeles County Department of Public Social Services, who has been assigned the case of the child of the Wadsworth family known as "Baby." Although he is a fully grown twenty-one-year-old man, Baby cannot walk or talk and is treated like a toddler, wearing diapers and sleeping in a crib. Ann comes to believe that Baby has been "buried alive"—imprisoned by sick love and deliberately discouraged from developing via negative reinforcement by his mother. Since Mrs. Wadsworth has been abandoned by the three successive fathers of her children, Ann thinks she is taking her revenge out on the only male member of her family. When Mrs. Wadsworth feels that Ann is getting too close to Baby and has her own agenda, she complains to Ann's supervisor, asking for a new worker. Ann responds by threatening to report Mrs. Wadsworth to the Public Guardian Office, who Ann believes would find her an unfit mother and take Baby away.

Mrs. Wadsworth invites Ann to Baby's birthday party, where she plans to dispose of her. After her drink is spiked, Ann is tied up and hidden in the house's basement, but Baby helps her escape. Ann takes Baby to the house she shares with Judith, her mother-in-law, and writes a letter to Mrs. Wadsworth to tell her that she will help Baby grow into the man he should be. Mrs. Wadsworth and her daughters come to Ann's house to get Baby back, but are entrapped. The girls are killed, and Mrs. Wadsworth is buried alive under the swimming pool that is under construction. It is revealed that

Ann has taken Baby to be the playmate of her husband Roger, an architect who has been brain-damaged in a sporting accident, and they all swim together in the pool.

Notes

A ridiculous yet disturbing horror movie about a retarded child and the perverted maternal instinct, the film suffers from occasional pacing lapses, but is lightened by the camp performance of Ruth Roman in the first of her three Grande Dame Guignols. The narrative also provides an almost exclusively femme environment, pitting a younger woman with an allied grande dame against another grande dame who is aligned with her own younger daughters. The music also adds to the gothic gruesomeness of the scenario, with the use of a music box and cello, in particular, and the rearrangement of the title theme for the party and for the Wadsworths' entry to the Gentry house. Director Ted Post had previously made *Beneath the Planet of the Apes* (1970). Producers Milton and Abe Polsky had previously made the action drama *Brute Corps* (1972). *The Baby* is the only film to be executive produced by Elliott Feinman and Ralph Hirsch.

Under the opening credits Ann looks at Baby's case file, and the photographs of him suggest a character's preoccupation with the past before we know the context. Ann will prove to be preoccupied with a trauma of her own past, and this establishes her as the film's protagonist, although her motives will be revealed to be as ambiguous and murky as those of the grande dame Mrs. Wadsworth. Ann's mother-in-law can also be viewed as a grande dame (who Post photographs with menacing camera angles), although she is a supporting player that barely exists in the narrative. The fact that the photographs show how Baby has aged physically but is still kept in a crib is the first suggestion that something is amiss in his universe, as something is equally amiss in Ann's.

Baby's lack of a name is evidence of the disassociation from his mother, although later she will express her gratitude that his condition means that he will never leave her (which will prove thankfully wrong). What makes him creepy is the pre-verbal murmurings and the squirming physicality that David Manzy supplies, which gets a remarkable payoff when Ann visits the Greenview School for Exceptional Children.

Mexican lobby card for *The Baby* (1973), with insert photo of Baby (David Manzy).

Our introduction to Mrs. Wadsworth suggests

she is a grande dame because of the largeness of Roman's performance, and the strangeness of her daughters, perhaps even emotionally stranger than Baby. Their social classification as white trash is established by their hair and wardrobe, and reliance upon welfare as income, with the size of the house they live in rationalized by the work the daughters do to make a contribution. Baby's father running off before the child was born is as much a comment on Mrs. Wadsworth as the man, since later we will be told that each of her children was fathered by a different man. Mrs. Wadsworth's behavior at Baby's birthday party, where she shows interest in what is apparently another woman's companion, attests to her flirtatiousness, which may extend to promiscuity.

Post gives Ann a long close-up of her reaction to Baby, both to show her realization of his retardation and a realization that she has found someone she has been seeking. Daughter Germaine's seeming romantic interest in Ann's private life can be read as a lesbian advance, since Germaine is not seen with any male romantic interest, even though she gets naked in bed with Baby. Ann's interest in Baby is soon commented on by her supervisor, Mr. Foley, who accuses her of "devoting herself exclusively to the case." In response, Ann says that Baby is the victim of "compromise, indifference, and criminal negligence" (the previous social worker had "disappeared"). The disappearance of the case worker should serve as a warning about the dangers of Mrs. Wadsworth, were it not that Ann shows herself to be equally dangerous. The slides of Ann and Roger that she watches at home suggest that Roger is dead, and though the exact details of the accident that affected him are never given, Ann blames herself.

When Baby's babysitter is caught feeding him her nipple, Mrs. Wadsworth delivers a funny line before she whips her with a belt: "You want kicks; well, I'll give you kicks." The whipping is preceded by Mrs. Wadsworth slapping the sitter, drawing blood—the first sign of grande guignol.

Mrs. Wadsworth's smirk in reaction to Ann's attempt to show her that Baby has potential and would benefit from a day clinic reads as Mrs. Wadsworth taking sick pleasure in her own child's limitation. Her line "Even a dog can do that" refers to Baby's seeming inability to retrieve a ball. What we can see—and what Ann doesn't—is that Baby is smart enough to know he isn't allowed to show Ann his potential, which is reinforced when his sister Alba prods him with an electric shock rod. Although Mrs. Wadsworth considers this excessive, and shocks Alba in retaliation, it becomes apparent that the regular punishment is being locked in a closet, an act that Ann will repeat for the film's climax.

Ann's visit to Greenview shows regular retarded children (the use of the word "exceptional" in the clinic's title is exceptional in itself), and the sad and touching vulnerability of them makes the contrivance of Baby all the more disturbing. Can such a narrative be viewed as exploiting the tragedy of retardation, given the exploitative nature of horror movies? Perhaps, but the decision to show us real victims of retardation confronts us with the possibility that Baby's condition may not be so unbelievable.

The swimming pool under construction in Ann's backyard will become important for the climax, and one should question the first sight of it, since both Ann and Judith would seem to be too depressed to want to go swimming. Mrs. Wadsworth's apology to Ann as an excuse to get her to come to the party is an obvious ruse, and one would think Ann too smart to fall for it, as she would seem too smart not to notice the switched drink.

The party, for Baby's birthday, is not for kids, as indicated by the presence of alcohol and marijuana. A funny exchange occurs when Ann is approached by Alba's boyfriend, Dennis:

> DENNIS: I'd like to pay you a sincere compliment. You've got beautiful skin.
> ANN: Don't tell me you're a dermatologist?
> DENNIS: No, just a skin freak.

Dennis's own skin will be tested when Alba agrees to have sex with him if he lets her burn his hand, to which he replies, "I'll do anything to get to paradise. But does it have to be in an ambulance?" The party scene is the first scene in which Post's pacing begins to lag, with the party going on far too long before any action relevant to the conflict takes place. Amusingly, Mrs. Wadsworth transitions from disdain for Ann to feigned niceness. The game of darts between Alba and Ann provides a sense of competition, with discussion about winners and losers clearly meant to apply to the battle over Baby. Baby himself gets a laugh when the Wadsworth women blow out the candles on his cake, and he looks displeased.

Post generates a moment of poignancy for Mrs. Wadsworth at the party when she gratefully observes that Baby will never leave her, suggesting that she doesn't mean to harm him, and with a single guitar playing on the soundtrack to add pathos. When Ann is taken to the basement cellar, this recalls the cellars of *Psycho*, *Die! Die! My Darling!*, *Eye of the Cat*, *Flesh Feast*, *The Beast in the Cellar*, and *Blood and Lace*. The antagonism between younger and older women recalls the same dynamics in *Strait-Jacket*, *Lady in a Cage*, *Die! Die My Darling!*, *The Night Walker*, *I Saw What You Did*, *Games*, *Berserk!*, *Eye of the Cat*, *Flesh Feast*, and *Blood and Lace*.

Baby finding Ann trussed up in the cellar thankfully does not lead into him becoming a hero by being able to untie her. Though we are amazed by Ann's dexterity in moving her hands that were originally tied *behind* her back to in front of her, we are also grateful that Baby's accidental smashing of a jar of preserves fails to alert the Wadsworths.

Post provides a payoff to Ann's abduction of Baby when Mrs. Wadsworth says, "She thinks of everything!" referring to Ann having slashed their car's tire to stop a pursuit. The high-backed cane chairs at Ann's house recall those in *Hush... Hush, Sweet Charlotte*, *Die! Die! My Darling!*, and *Games*. The trap that Ann lays for the Wadsworths, of course, relies upon coincidence and the unknowable, which is a movie convention, with Baby's teddy bear and doors left unlocked as bait. The narrative puts a spin on the Wadsworths as Women in Peril since here they are listening for sounds to locate Baby, while Ann uses Baby's crying to draw them in. Post

Mrs. Wadsworth (Ruth Roman) and Ann Gentry (Anjanette Comer) fight at the climax of *The Baby* (1973).

intercuts shots of Germaine and Alba searching the house with Mrs. Wadsworth waiting in the car, smoking. However, he spends too much time on the girls' search, thereby losing pace. The intercutting between the daughters and Mrs. Wadsworth reaches its climax when, after a shot of Alba with a look of shock on her face, Post cuts back to the car and stays on Mrs. Wadsworth. When she enters the house, suspense has been created as to the fate of her daughters, and her search culminates in a grande guignol drop of blood falling onto her face from above.

Mrs. Wadsworth's discovery of Germaine dead, her throat cut, is topped by Alba's deathly walk to her mother, with Suzanne Zenor's graceful fall making up for her otherwise uninspired performance. While we haven't seen Germaine or Alba attacked, the knife in Alba's back is a progression of gruesomeness that leads to Ann appearing with an axe, recalling *Strait-Jacket* and *Blood and Lace*. The fight between Ann and Mrs. Wadsworth offers a few surprises when Ann loses control of the axe, and Mrs. Wadsworth faces a dark room in which Ann hides. Mrs. Wadsworth running upstairs only to come face to face with Judith, carrying her *own* axe, offers another surprise when Ann stops Judith, from killing Mrs. Wadsworth, thinking it better to bury her alive under the pool. Additionally, Mrs. Wadsworth's concern for what will happen to Baby, more than for herself, again reveals that she is not a totally bad mother. The dragging of Mrs. Wadsworth and the disposal of the three bodies recalls the same activities in *What Ever Happened to Baby Jane?*, *Hush...Hush, Sweet Charlotte*, *Games*, *What Ever Happened to Aunt Alice?*, *The Mad Room*, *What's the Matter with Helen?*, and *The Savage Intruder*.

Post gives us a subjective camera point of view to show the dirt heaped over Mrs. Wadsworth's face, while the reveal of Roger, wearing a head bandage, exposes Ann's real agenda. One may question the type of brain damage that can be equated with a child's retardation, and also Ann's assumption that Roger and Baby will be compatible. We presume that Ann feels she can control the situation to make it work, which rather lessens the mad romanticism of her idea. However, one is reminded of the scene in which she had tried to show Mrs. Wadsworth Baby's potential, and Ann had admitted to her limited skills as a therapist. Post cuts from Ann throwing a beach ball in the playroom to the three of them in the now-completed pool. The end freeze-frame on Ann's happy face, rather than that of Baby or Roger, indicates that *her* happiness and success is the more important.

Ruth Roman had previously played a supporting role in *The Killing Kind*, and had last played a leading film role in *Bitter Victory* (1957), with most of her work in the 1960s being done on television. At the time of filming *The Baby* she was age 50. Looking blowsy in hair that is more like a series of fright wigs, and dressed mannishly in denim jeans or shapeless kaftans, Roman looks like a drag queen (match-

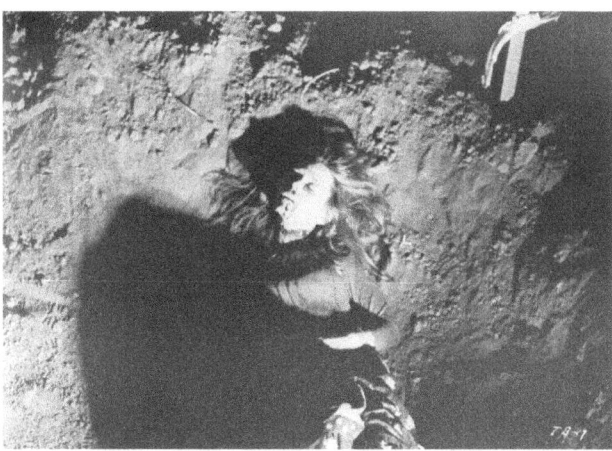

The murdered Germaine Wadsworth (Marianna Hill) is buried underneath a swimming pool in *The Baby* **(1973).**

ing her husky voice). Wearing make-up, false eyelashes and eyeliner, she gets laughs from the intensity of her reactions to Ann: an unblinking stare, grimaces, or a look of hatred that culminates in the tight-mouthed line "You damn bitch" when Ann threatens a custody dispute. Roman's face and wild black tendrils of hair recalls a gorgon and Greek tragedy. Additionally, Roman is good when reading Ann's letter, knowing to falter in reaction to words rather than reading out perfectly enunciated sentences. Anjanette Comer, who at times resembles Faye Dunaway, gives an earnest performance that works well in counterpoint to Roman's.

Release

March 1973, with the taglines, "Horror is his formula!" "Pray you don't learn the secret of ... The Baby," "Nothing in his nursery rhymes," "Three Four Close the Door!" and "There shall be mayhem wherever he goes."

Reviews

"Unpleasant low-budget shocker, with over-the-top performances and general grotesqueness."—David Gritten, *Halliwell's Film Guide*.

"Roman delivers a more than effective barnstormer of a performance, showing a real malicious flintiness as the matriarch of the show.... The film leaves you sitting there doing a double-take at the spectacular tackiness that the filmmakers throw at you ... a combination of lunatic dementia and the downright tawdry."—Richard Schleib, *The Science Fiction, Horror and Fantasy Movie Review*.

"...[T]he kind of queasy thriller that could only have been born in the psychosexually sick '70s ... an engaging sleaze flick that retains its power to disturb.... Roman is in rare form.... A truly unique entry into the horror canon."—Fred Beldin, *AllMovie.com*.

"Horror at its most bizarre ... one of the genre's most perverse pictures.... The ending is heralded as one of the most surprising in cinema history."—Christopher Null, *Filmcritic.com*.

The Killing Kind (1973)

Media Trend Productions

CREDITS: *Director:* Curtis Harrington; *Producer:* George Edwards; *Executive Producer:* Leon Mirell; *Associate Producer/Production Manager:* Sal Grasso; *Screenplay:* Tony Crechales, George Edwards, original story by Tony Crechales; *Photography:* Mario Tosi; *Music:* Andrew Belling; *Editor:* Bryon Crouch; *Set Decoration:* John Franco Jr.; *Wardrobe:* Tom Rasmussen; *Make-up:* Joe McKinney; *Hair:* Jinx Lambo; *Hair for Ann Sothern:* Carrie White; *Sound:* George Maly, Vic Williams. Color, 95 minutes.

CAST: Ann Sothern (*Thelma Lambert*); John Savage (*Terry Lambert*); Ruth Roman (*Rhea Benson*); Luana Anders (*Louise*); Cindy Williams (*Lori*); Sue Bernard (*Tina*); Marjorie Eaton (*Mrs. Orland*); Peter Brocco (*Father*); Helene Winston (*Flo*).

VHS/DVD: DVD: Dark Sky Films, released November 20, 2007.

Plot

21-year-old Terry Lambert returns to the Malibu boarding house of his photographer mother, Thelma, after spending two years in prison for his involvement in the gang rape of Tina Moore. Although the house usually accommodates elderly women, Thelma allows young model Lori Davis from Tucson to become a tenant. Terry shows a mixture of antagonism and interest in Lori, since his feelings about women have been affected by the trauma. Terry follows Tina and runs her off the road, killing her when her car explodes. He also plies his lawyer, Rhea Benson, with liquor and burns down her house—with her in it. When Lori attempts to seduce Terry, he strangles her. Thelma's suspicion of Terry's involvement in the deaths of Tina and Rhea is confirmed when she finds Terry in Lori's room, with Lori dead. Thelma and Terry dispose of the body by U-Hauling it to the dump. Back at home, Thelma poisons Terry's chocolate milk. He goes to sleep as Thelma hears the police arrive, called by their neighbor, Louise, who has been watching the house the whole time.

Notes

The fifth Grande Dame Guignol from director Curtis Harrington, and the second subgenre appearance by Ann Sothern, is a study in misogyny and murder with an unusual treatment of the grande dame. In a narrative full of grande dames in supporting roles, the Sothern character begins as an observer of the antagonist/protagonist serial killer, but then changes into an antagonist/protagonist herself at the end. With some interesting performances and judicious use of music, Harrington presents a character study with little blood but lots of grotesquery.

This was Harrington's first film after *What's the Matter with Helen?* Producer Edwards had made the horror title *Frogs* (1972) since *What's the Matter with Helen?* Executive producer Leon Mirell had made *That Cold Day in the Park*. Associate producer Sal Grasso had been assistant to the producer on *Frogs*.

A pre-credit sequence shows us the group rape that Terry was forced into, with his climactic yell interpreted either as sexual release or psychological humiliation. Harrington exposing Tina's breasts during the rape is acceptable for a sex scene, with the narrative adding the suggestion that the sex was consensual. Harrington will employ flashbacks to this trauma later in the film, and to the beach for a pivotal nightmare sequence. Terry's arrival at the house introduces us to the film's ambiguous stance on older women when a tenant looks at him suspiciously but then smiles at him. The cat next to her may be her pet or may be one of Terry's mother's, but either way the cat recalls those in *The Witches*, *Games*, and *Eye of the Cat*. Thelma's entrance is just as ambiguous, with her watching Terry from behind a glass door. Thelma's commenting on Terry's thinness is also a sly comment on the obesity of Thelma, with her condition eventually labeled "fat" by Terry.

The antipathy between Thelma and Lori begins with an exchange that occurs when Lori takes the room for rent, after Lori reveals that she wants to be a model:

> LORI: People tell me I have a very interesting face
> THELMA: Interesting, huh? Yeah, well, that's what they say when they don't say pretty.

Thelma's jealousy of Lori as a pivotal love interest for Terry is a warning that is borne out when Terry's interest in Lori ends with him killing her. Lori will continue to misread Terry's motives and pursue him, even after he aggressively pushes her under water in the swimming pool, and when she discovers that he has ripped her panties with a razor blade. Their climactic battle in her bathroom is full of misread signals, with her advances continuing until he finally overpowers her. However, their first dialogue exchange has some wit:

> LORI: How long have you been writing songs?
> TERRY: About seven years.
> LORI: My, my. You must be tired.

Terry's fondness for chocolate milk receives a payoff at film's end, though initially it represents his arrested development and Thelma's complicity. The milk being chocolate and not vanilla adds an extra juvenile touch. When Thelma asks Terry for a kiss and insists on being kissed on the mouth, it indicates her great need for love and the seeming inappropriateness of their boundaries. Although Terry wipes his mouth the first time we see this kind of kiss, his later kissing her on the neck and hugging her from behind are also inappropriate acts that approximate those of a sexual lover. Their laughing together at her story of a tenant who fell into the deep freeze at the market is an indication of their mutual insensitivity, with Thelma's throwing around the bacon strips in her hand as she laughs a sign of her carelessness with food.

The information that Terry set Thelma's house on fire is provided by a neighbor, referred to only as "Father," who calls Terry a "psychopath." Although setting a house on fire isn't necessarily the act of a psychopath, such a diagnosis for Terry is quite valid for other reasons. This becomes apparent when he strangles Thelma's favorite cat, Penny, to stop it making noise when Terry is spying on Lori in her underwear through her conveniently un-curtained window. The voyeurism is doubled when Harrington pans to show us that Louise, with binoculars, is watching Terry watching Lori.

The motif of Thelma taking photographs of Terry is repeated throughout the film, with Harrington using freeze-frames for the stills she has taken. The photography motif receives a payoff at the end when Thelma takes her final picture of Terry. Thelma also keeps a wall of photographs of Terry—a sign of overindulgence—as is her later attempt to photograph him naked in the shower. Photographs of a younger Thelma are featured in her

Poster for *The Killing Kind* (1973).

living room to show not a preoccupation with, but an awareness of, the loss of her beauty, with Lori's model portfolio seen in comparison. Terry masturbates to period photographs of bare-breasted women, as opposed to something contemporary, and Harrington intercuts the act with his memory of the rape.

Terry's claim that Tina lied about the rape is explored when he anonymously telephones her. When Terry refers to their sex under the pier, Tina names three men she thinks might be the caller. This sign of her promiscuity is enhanced by the fact that after the call she is revealed to be in bed with another man. Although a promiscuous woman can still be raped, the disinterested look on her face during the flashbacks certainly suggests that she did not want to have sex with Terry. Tina being regarded as promiscuous is paralleled with Thelma's past, when Terry reveals the number of "uncles" he had as a child (Thelma claims that his father left her before Terry was born).

Terry's complaint that Thelma is "suffocating him" leads him to call her a "whore." The narrative has Tina's lover call her "baby," and then Harrington cuts to Thelma calling Penny "baby," which further links Tina and Thelma. The idea of Terry as Thelma's "baby," apart from the fact of him being her son, will be included in the last line of the film.

When Terry pursues Tina she wears a leopard print jacket, presenting her as worldly. The leopard also makes the cat connection with Thelma, who keeps multiple felines in her house. Terry's tailgating of her car and bipping his horn at her creates suspense, with Harrington cross-cutting between the silence in Terry's car and the music in Tina's. When Terry's pursuit results in Tina's death, our sympathy for him lessens, particularly after his strangulation of Penny. However, if we believe that Tina lied about the rape and helped send Terry to prison for a crime that he didn't commit, then her death may be considered moral revenge. The same rationale can be applied to Terry's killing of Rhea; but it is his strangling of the guiltless Lori that makes such an argument untenable.

The caged myna bird that Terry buys for Thelma, as well as Mrs. Orland's bird, recalls the birds from *What Ever Happened to Baby Jane?*, *The Night Walker*, and *What's the Matter with Helen?* The myna bird not talking isn't given a narrative payoff, but it is an odd gift considering the number of cats that Thelma keeps. The rat in Mrs. Orland's room receives a payoff when she collapses at the same moment the rat's neck is snapped by the rat-trap. Terry coaxing the rat to take the cheese in the trap and die evinces more of his sadism and mental instability, though Mrs. Orland's collapse creates the false expectation of her own death. For this double-shock, composer Andrew Belling uses the tune of "Three Blind Mice" on the soundtrack.

Louise's drunken advances toward Terry begins with her opening, "It must be wonderful being raped," indicating that she is as psychologically disturbed as he (if her binoculars didn't already hint at that). Additionally, her fantasies of burning the books at the library where she works and putting glass in her father's food also show that she is just as dangerous, which will be borne out when she reports Terry and Thelma to the police. Louise as a repressed librarian is a stereotype, but, luckily, Luana Anders adds both eccentricity and humor to the role. It's just a shame that the narrative reduces the 35-year-old Louise to "the older woman" for Terry, with her "Too old" line capping her humiliation when he rejects her. What redeems this scene is the later payoff in which Louise challenges Terry about being a songwriter with, "That thing you hold so close to you, like a woman—you can't even play it."

Harrington photographs Ruth Roman's face in shadow when Terry visits Rhea, though she is presented as more feminine here than in *The Baby*. Rhea being a lawyer, a job usually associated with men, has her wearing a pink and tan pantsuit. Roman's trademark deep, almost masculine voice completes the picture. The narrative toys with our feelings about Rhea as someone who has failed Terry by not defending him successfully. Terry's limiting remark about the female judge applies equally to Rhea: "Women are supposed to be soft and cuddly. They smell so sweet and pretty." Terry cutting Rhea's face to convince her to drink the alcohol he forces on her is an attack on a woman's essential vanity, with the scene recalling the same action in *The Savage Intruder*. Terry's humming of the "Merry Widow Waltz" recalls the same music used in *Shadow of a Doubt*. Harrington uses a tilted camera for both Rhea's drunken perspective and Terry's unbalanced behavior. Rhea's attempt to lunge at Terry with the bottle becomes a dance macabre when he catches her, and Harrington spares us the sight of Rhea burning, as he had with Tina.

The scene in which Terry's massage of Thelma turns to strangulation recalls the same scene in *The Night Walker*, with Thelma only being saved by the opportune interruption of Lori. Terry's nightmare takes us back to the beach for two scenarios with him in a crib. Firstly, he is surrounded by doting older women, including Louise and Mrs. Orland, but not Thelma. Then Tina is in the crib with him as the women chant "Shame."

The scene of Lori's murder in the bathroom recalls the shower scene of *Psycho*. Harrington objectifies Lori by showing her legs as she sits on the toilet seat, from Terry's subjective point of view, and intercuts her talking with Terry's flashback to the rape. Lori's asking for a kiss is intercut with the same request from a grotesque Thelma, and the trouble begins when Terry kisses Lori too hard and Lori calls him "crazy." His slap produces the film's only human blood-letting, and the strangulation is performed without the need to use the running bathwater to also drown her. Terry's brutality and Lori's struggle recalls the struggle of Janet Leigh fighting off Mother, although it is clear that both women are in the weaker position, which cements their fate. Thelma finding Lori by pulling back the shower curtain is another *Psycho* reference, with the disposal of the body recalling the same activity in *What Ever Happened to Baby Jane?*, *Hush ... Hush, Sweet Charlotte*, *Games*, *What Ever Happened to Aunt Alice?*, *The Mad Room*, *What's the Matter with Helen?*, *The Savage Intruder*, and *The Baby*.

The narrative adds some gruesome black humor to the disposal of Lori's body by having Terry break the stiff corpse to make it fit into a trash can, culminating with the unbelievable sight of Lori's hand sticking out of the can when Terry and Thelma arrive at the dump. Suspense is created by the notion the attendant might see the hand that neither Terry nor Thelma have noticed. We get a laugh when he bends down just before he is able to see it, and also from Thelma's reaction when she sees the hand. The rat that crawls over Lori's corpse after the can has been pushed down a hill is more grotesquery, with the rat recalling the rat that Terry had killed earlier.

For emphasis Harrington occasionally uses zooms, slow motion, repeated shots and a freeze-frame (when Terry jumps into the pool clothed and assumes a Christ-like pose). He also utilizes the horror movie convention of a storm—thunder, lightning, and rain—when Thelma poisons Terry. The narrative teases us with the possibility that the plan will not work, since Harrington shows us Thelma tampering with Terry's glass of milk. The muteness that Terry has embraced after the death of Lori is another false expectation, since he speaks to Thelma to tell her that "The rain shuts everything out." Thelma's monologue about it having rained when he was born, and why he is so important to her, climaxes with her admission that a son meant "strength and protection" for her. That she is murdering him is in ironic accord to that idea, since we can foresee him killing her eventually if he is not stopped. Her act of antagonism, then, is also the province of a Woman in Peril. The tease continues when she stops him from drinking the milk so that she can have a kiss. His laying on her lap as she reflects on his childhood is his returning to a child-like state. Harrington has Thelma hold her face to Terry's for one last embrace before he ends in a freeze-frame of her in her darkroom.

Ann Sothern was age 63 at the time of filming. She had appeared in supporting roles in film since *Lady in a Cage*. Sothern's bloated appearance as Thelma is a continuation of the blowsy look she had in *Lady in a Cage*, and Harrington appears to protect her from double-chinned close-ups until they are absolutely necessary. With mountainous peroxide hair, wearing layered, draped clothing, make-up and false eyelashes, her Thelma suggests a tamer version of Mae West—with an additional maternal neediness. Her clothes even garner unintentional laughs when she wears all black for the disposal of Lori's body—and she still looks fat. While Sothern's performance is not bad, she doesn't match the quirkiness and surprise that some of the other actors bring to their roles.

Release

June 1973, with the taglines, "Terry loved soft, furry, little animals. He loved his mother. He loved pretty girls ... ALL DEAD!" and, "Did you ever want to strangle your Mother?"

Reviews

"Well shot, this crafty little item on murderous neurosis gets a bit predictable near the end.... There is a careful tautness in the direction that allays some surface characterizations.... Miss Sothern has the right blowsy air but also the underlying girlishness, raw charm and looks that made her a goodtime girl in her youth. Savage is competent."—*Variety*, June 12, 1973.

"A genuinely perverse horror film.... Quite a twisted little chiller, with several priceless bizarre moments.... Savage and Sothern are fabulous."—Robert Firsching, *Allmovie.com*.

"...[A] fresh and brutal portrait of dementia.... Sothern practically steals the show ... may be one of the best undiscovered classics from the 70s."—Rusty White, *Einsiders.com* (Video Risks review).

Night Watch (1973)

A Poll-George-Straus-Hutton Production

CREDITS: *Director:* Brian G. Hutton; *Producers:* Martin Poll, George W. George, Barnard Straus; *Associate Producer:* David White; *Screenplay:* Tony Williamson, based on the play by Lucille Fletcher; *Additional Dialogue:* Evan Jones; *Photography:* Billy Williams; *Music:* John Cameron; *Editor:* John Jympson; *Art Direction:* Peter Murton; *Set Decoration:* Peter James; *Make-up:* Eric Allwright, Ron Berkeley; *Hair:* Helene Bevan; *Hair for Miss Taylor:* Michaeljohn, Claudye Bozzacchi; *Wardrobe:* Yvonne Blake; *Wardrobe for Miss Taylor:* Valentino; *Production Managers:* Hugh Harlow, David Griffith; *Sound:* Cyril Swern, Bill Rowe. Color, 99/105 minutes. Filmed in London, England, at Elstree Studios.

SONG: "The Night Has Many Eyes" (George Barrie, Sammy Cahn).

CAST: Elizabeth Taylor (*Ellen Wheeler*); Laurence Harvey (*John Wheeler*); Billie Whitelaw (*Sarah Cooke*); Robert Lang (*Mr. Appleby*); Tony Britton (*Tony*); Bill Dean (*Inspector Walker*); Michael Danvers-Walker (*Sgt. Norris*); Rosario Serrano (*Dolores*); Pauline Jameson (*Secretary*); Linda Hayden (*Girl in Car*); Kevin Colson (*Carl*); Laon Maybanke (*Florist*); David Jackson (*Wilson*).

VHS/DVD: Not available on either format

Plot

Ellen Wheeler lives in a large London house with her investment adviser husband, John. Her childhood friend, school teacher Sarah Cooke, is currently staying with them. In her garden one day after buying new roses, Ellen sees her neighbor, Mr. Appleby, digging a trench. He tells her that as a child he lived in the house she now owns, although now he is reduced to living in her gardener's flat. He offers to plant her roses, and she accepts. That night Ellen is awakened by a nightmare about the death of her first husband, Carl. Looking out her window, she claims to see the body of a man with his throat cut sitting in a chair in the window of the house next door. The police are summoned but find no body, and are disturbed that Ellen's description of the man resembles Carl. Ellen believes that Mr. Appleby is involved, since the next day he has planted trees in the trench.

The next night, when both Ellen and Sarah see lights in the abandoned house, the police return to find Appleby in the room in question. His garden is dug up but no body is found, and the police close the case. However, Ellen calls them again when she claims to have seen a woman in the room this time. John encourages her to see their psychiatrist friend, Tony, who recommends that she leave the house and rest in a Switzerland clinic. Ellen agrees. However, the night before she is scheduled to leave, when John has her sign over power of attorney on their joint holdings, she discovers that John has purchased the house next door. She accuses John of being Sarah's married lover, and both of them of planning to drive her insane. Ellen is particularly insulted by the idea of adultery, since Carl had died after running off the road with his young lover, a fact Ellen had learned when she came to identify the body. Finding that John has a key to the house, Ellen dares him to accompany her to the room, and runs ahead. In the house John finds Ellen, but she attacks him and cuts his throat. She does the same to Sarah, who is lured by Ellen's scream. The next day, as she finishes her packing, Mr. Appleby confronts Ellen about her plan to kill John and Sarah. Ellen buys his silence by letting him stay in the house while she travels indefinitely.

Notes

Night Watch is the only Grande Dame Guignol to star Elizabeth Taylor. Although it offers some graphic grande guignol and a grande dame preoccupied with the past, Brian G. Hutton's direction is uninspired, and he over-uses a conventional horror music score. Hutton had not made a horror film before, but had previously worked with Taylor on the drama *X, Y and Zee* (1972). Producer Martin Poll had previously made the horror title *The Possession of Joel Delaney* (1972). *Night Watch* was the first and only film to date for producer Barnard Straus and associate producer David White.

The opening music includes a harpsichord, similar to that heard in *Dead Ringer, Hush ... Hush, Sweet Charlotte, Die! Die! My Darling!*, and *The Night Walker*. However, such novelty soon gives way to the sound of the wind and conventional horror movie music that is associated with the house containing the supposed corpses, and also with Ellen. Hutton uses an image of car headlights at night, foreshadowing Ellen's nightmare flashbacks, then cuts to flowers in the daytime that we see her buying. Her hobby of putting together jigsaw puzzles, and her fondness for mood music, identify her as lonely, the latter recalling the same behavior in *The Savage Intruder* and *What Ever Happened to Aunt Alice?* Ellen's flashbacks to the death of Carl, although she was not a witness to what she supposedly remembers, and her appearance at the morgue to identify him and his mistress are the traumatic events she is preoccupied with that define her as a grande dame.

Sarah's advice to Ellen—"Avoid your neighbors like the plague"—will prove to be good advice only for herself, since she is killed in a neighbors' house while Ellen is protected by Mr. Appleby. Hutton deliberately hides the face of Sarah's married lover, Barry, in his one scene with her to support Ellen's idea that it is really John. Sarah's line about Barry—"That he's not really the sort of man you could introduce to your friends"—continues this defensive stance, though the line can be interpreted in other ways which are just as unflattering to Sarah. Ellen's reaction to Sarah's hand on her shoulder as they look at her jigsaw puzzle is our first clue that Ellen is suspicious of her, as Ellen's repeated enquiries after Barry become a trap in which Sarah will be caught out in a lie. Whether or not Sarah is really having an affair with John is left open. Even if they are not having an affair, they are still bound together because of their feelings regarding Ellen's "illness."

Hutton introduces the first of Ellen's flashbacks as a nightmare. He uses cross-cutting, expressionist camera angles, and crying on the soundtrack as devices for heightening the drama, especially since it is presented from Ellen's psychological point of view. The quick edits don't allow us to take in much detail, but we understand enough that the car is driven off the road in an accident, presumably because Carl and his mistress were too busy having sex. Ellen will later comment, "There was more lipstick on his clothes than blood."

Although one might think a nightmare counts as sleep, Ellen calls herself an insomniac, a "watcher of the night, beset by memory and dreams." Since she has remarried, it appears that she has been able to move on from the trauma to some extent, though her anger over Carl's affair seems to have emerged as insomnia. This unresolved anger will explain the savagery of her murders at the film's climax and the ease

Poster for *Night Watch* (1973).

with which she believes John has betrayed her. The casting of Taylor as a wife of not only one but two adultering husbands tends to stretch believability, but the fact of Ellen's mental instability does allow for it. Who wouldn't need relief from such stress, no matter how beautiful the sufferer? The Wheeler marriage is also revealed to involve some resentment on John's part about Ellen's inherited wealth, and his desire to make a living so as not to "live off her."

Ellen's reported vision is introduced by the thunder and lightning of a storm, and the banging of a window shutter. The latter is not so obvious a cliché, since the house was first shown in daylight accompanied by the same banging. The shutter could not be closed because the owners are away, and we might be more concerned if it *didn't* bang, since that would tell us that someone unknown had fastened it. Hutton doesn't show us what Ellen sees, so that we only have her reaction to go by. What is interesting is that later we realize Ellen was lying, so that Hutton showing what she claims to have seen would not have been possible. The narrative thereby has it both ways, with the police's eventual non-response to Ellen's claims preventing the real bodies of John and Sarah being found.

Ellen gets a laugh from her nervousness at having to talk to the police, which will later take on another meaning, and is funny when being patronizing in the following exchange:

ELLEN: He was blonde and tall.
INSPECTOR WALKER: Tall? You said he was seated.
ELLEN: You can tell if a man is tall, even if he is seated.

When the police go into the neighboring house, Hutton uses darkness and dripping water for atmosphere, as well as the horror music. This darkness will also be used for the eight-minute climax, with the actors only seen via lightning. When the police return to Ellen, her emotionalism and anger is compared to their rational disbelief at not finding what she claims to have seen, resulting in another funny exchange between the Inspector and Ellen:

INSPECTOR WALKER: Could it possibly have been an optical illusion, caused by the storm?
ELLEN: It was a dead body, caused by a murderer.

A sleeping pill-induced sleep has the camera go out of focus for more flashback footage, with its earlier history confirmed by Ellen's shorter hairstyle and her somewhat frumpier appearance. Ellen's disappointment in John is exemplified by her manipulative comment to him, "If you love me, you would believe me." The appearance of Carl's cufflinks and lighter is used to create more suspicion of John and Sarah, although ultimately the items are red herrings. Hutton shoots Ellen in close-up, like a true horror movie queen, when she sees the shadowed reflection of John and Sarah talking.

That Appleby is found by the police in the room is a nice payoff, even if his rather lame excuse is accepted too easily. And his anger at how the police dig up his garden provides a reason for him not reporting Ellen in the end. The narrative might have been more interesting had he been in on the plan with Ellen from the beginning, though her playing him would not have appeared as clever.

Ellen pulling off petals from a flower is a sign of her frustration and unexpressed anger at the general disbelief over what she saw, which is also a tie-in to her buying roses in the first scene. The act recalls the "He loves me/He loves me not" game, which is appropriate, since she thinks John doesn't love her. While the police can dismiss Ellen after not finding the first body, it is Ellen's next sighting of a dead girl in the house window that makes John lose all faith in her. Hutton again does not show us the sight (and this time not even Ellen looking), but rather relies upon Ellen's scream and her telling John and Sarah. In hindsight, the latter seems risky on Ellen's part, but since it enables John to bring in Tony, it is successful. Hutton also uses the sound of the Carl/morgue flashback on the soundtrack to indicate Ellen's seemingly progressive madness.

John telling Ellen she has fired Dolores, something we have not seen occur (and doubt), cre-

Ellen Wheeler (Elizabeth Taylor) is comforted by Sarah Cooke (Billie Whitelaw) in *Night Watch* (1973).

ates more ambiguity. So does the revelation that John's company has bought the neighbor's house, and Sarah's lie about Scotland. Ellen's decision to confront John and Sarah about their supposed affair would seem to be more risk-taking, since this reveals Ellen's agenda, but neither John nor Sarah catch on in time to save themselves. They believe that everything Ellen says or does only reveals her to be an innocent victim, and this gullibility leads them to their deaths. Hutton uses the darkened rooms of the neighbor's house at the climax to conceal rather than reveal, so that there is more shock than suspense. This also conveniently leaves the sight of Ellen overpowering John to our imagination. We can assume Ellen has been in the room beforehand to assist in her plan—this must be the reason for the key she "finds"—so this gives her the advantage over a man who would be physically stronger than her.

Additionally, if we assume Ellen attacks John in the same way we see her attack Sarah—by catching him off-guard—then the outcome is believable. Sarah's murder is shown more graphically, or at least shown as much as the lightning permits, reflecting the convention horror movie that considers a female death more appealing. Hutton also changes Sarah, when she finds John's body, into Carl's lover—from Ellen's point of view—which fuels Ellen's rage. The stabbings recall the same murder method in *Lady in a Cage, Die! Die! My Darling!, I Saw What You Did, Berserk!, The Savage Intruder, The Mad Room*, and *What's the Matter with Helen?*

Ellen dressed in white the day after is a sly costume joke, as if her killings have returned her moral innocence. The last telephone call to Inspector Walker is used for a rather obvious comic effect, with the repeated appearance of the telephone recalling Lucille Fletcher's most famous play, *Sorry, Wrong Number*. The applause and entrance of Appleby reads like a stage contrivance—the screenplay is based on a play, after all—and perhaps Ellen's dismissal of him is too easy to be satisfying. The idea of John and Sarah's bodies never being found and decomposing in the neighbor's house is also perhaps too much of a romantic happy ending for Ellen, since one can assume that they will be missed by others. The more troubling question relates to Ellen's future. We assume that these have been her first killings, but will she feel justified in killing again if someone else disappoints her in love?

As one of the screen's great beauties, Elizabeth Taylor does not make a traditional grande dame whose looks have faded, in spite of the additional weight she carries (which Hutton endeavors to conceal with careful lighting). Taylor's down-to-earth persona also works against the idea of Ellen as being truly mad, and her enormous likeability makes it easy for us to empathize with her. As the film's protagonist, we believe her story, and this audience empathy doesn't falter, even after she kills as an act of antagonism. Ellen therefore continues

Ellen Wheeler (Elizabeth Taylor) sees a murder from her window in *Night Watch* (1973).

the subgenre's unique tradition of having the grande dame be both protagonist and antagonist.

Taylor had survived the end of the studio system by staying a leading lady in films during the 1960s and 1970s. She had made three pictures the year before *Night Watch*: *Hammersmith Is Out*, *Under Milkwood*, and *X, Y and Zee*. She had not made a horror film before, and was age 40 at the time of filming. Her dramatic range has always been limited, and while she gives Ellen the bored ennui of a wealthy matron and a sense of humor in the way she deals with her maid, she can only provide so much emotional depth to her trauma. She does play anger well, which works for the character (since her plan is based on anger), and makes her anger funny. Hutton doesn't reign in Taylor's theatrical mannerisms—the hand to the forehead to convey distress is perhaps her worst—but his focusing on her eyes reminds us that she can be as expressive with them as Davis and Crawford. Also, when Ellen gives her first report to the police, Taylor's voice acquires an interesting huskiness that it doesn't have at any other time in the film.

Release

August 9, 1973, with the taglines, "Once her nightmare begins ... the terror never ends!" and, "You'll be seeing this nightmare every night for the rest of your life."

Reviews

"A gorgeously brazen, logical swindle.... Seldom, at least recently, has a mystery carpet-yanking been so effective.... The deliciously cunning postscript may make you feel like a perfect fool. Once in a while it's fun.... Miss Taylor churns up a fine, understandable lather of nerves."—Howard Thompson, *The New York Times*, August 10, 1973.

"Hutton makes the most of the suggested violence in the film.... Taylor dominates the doings."—*Variety*, August 8, 1973.

"Hutton incorporates most of the clichés of the *Gaslight* tradition, including squeaking stairs, hysterical phone calls and many looks of lingering menace.... There is one thoroughly nasty and frightening sequence. But in order to get hooked by it, it is necessary to endure all the melodrama that goes before."—Jay Cocks, *Time*, September 17, 1973.

A Knife for the Ladies (1974)
(aka *A Knife in the Dark*; *Jack the Ripper Goes West*; *Silent Sentence*)

Bryanston Pictures

CREDITS: *Director:* Larry G. Spangler; *Producers:* Stan Jolley, Larry G. Spangler; *Executive Producer:* Lou Peraino; *Associate Producers:* Robert Shelton, Ron Janoff; *Screenplay:* George Arthur Bloom, Seton I. Miller, based on a story by Robert Shelton and Seton I. Miller; *Photography:* Irving Lippman; *Music Editors:* Dave Kahn, Jerry Cohen, Lettie Odney; *Editor:* Anthony Carras; *Production Design:* Stan Jolley; *Set Decorator:* William Calvert; *Sound:* Al Overton; *Make-up:* Monty Westmore; *Wardrobe:* Lambert Marks. Color, 51 minutes. Filmed on location in Tucson, Arizona.

SONG: "Evil Lady" (Bobby Hart, Danny Janssen, Dominic Frontiere), sung by Michael Stull.

CAST: Jack Elam (*Sheriff Jarrod Colcord*); Ruth Roman (*Elizabeth Mescal*); Jeff Cooper (*Edward R. Burns*); John Kellogg (*Simian Hollyfield*); Gene Evans (*Virgil Hooker*); Richard Schaal (*Walter Ainslie*); Diana Ewing (*Jenny*); Jon Spangler (*Seth McGee*); Derek Sanderson (*Luke Doolan*); Fred Biletnikoff (*Horace Doolan*); Peter Athas (*Travis*); Hank Kendrich (*Dr. Fairchild*); Pat Herrerra (*Nina*); Phillip Avenetti (*Ramon*); Brooke Tucker (*Myra Lynn*); Rob Lien (*J. B. Mullin*); Kit Kendrich (*Cora*); Al Hassan (*Riley*); Jean Wall (*Lattie*); Greg Little (*Amos*); Norm Tempas (*1st Rider*); Deen Pettinger (*2nd Rider*); Bud Stout (*Driver*).

VHS/DVD: Not available in either format.

Plot

The banker of the small Arizona desert town of Mescal, Simian Hollyfield, hires St. Louis private detective Edward R. Burns to investigate a series of throat-slashing murders of prostitutes. This irks the town's sheriff, Jarrod Colcord, who is also a drunkard. Another prostitute, Nina Torres is killed as Burns arrives. Burns finds the body of the man thought to be responsible—Mexican horse trader Ramon. Ramon was hanged by the Doolan brothers, Luke and Horace, on the orders of Virgil Hooker. When Luke and Horace attempt to leave town, they are shot by Virgil, who, in turn, is shot by the Sheriff. Unfortunately, the murders continue when Myra is found dead in Burns' room.

After a fistfight, the Sheriff and Burns decide to team up to solve the killings. They visit the widow of the town's founder, Elizabeth Mescal, who is in mourning over the loss of her son Travis. Burns discovers the large amount of medication she is taking and questions the apothecary, Dr. Fairchild. While he prescribes arsenic for Elizabeth, Fairchild suggests that in large amounts it could be used to treat syphilis. After the town's barber/undertaker is killed, Burns and the Sheriff open Travis's grave to discover that there is no body in his coffin. When Elizabeth tries to lure Jenny into the cage in which she hides the disfigured, syphilitic Travis, the girl's screams attract Burns and the Sheriff. Jenny escapes but is chased by a knife-wielding Elizabeth, who admits that she killed all the victims. Travis stops Elizabeth from stabbing Jenny, and Elizabeth turns on him. The Sheriff breaks into the Mescal house and shoots Elizabeth. Elizabeth and Travis fall from the staircase to their deaths, as Burns comforts the distraught Jenny.

Notes

The only Grande Dame Guignol western, this serial killer film offers some impressive grande guignol and Ruth Roman's third appearance in the subgenre. Though it sports a short running time and abrupt editing, and the material is ultimately unchallenging, director Larry G. Spangler does manage to add some stylistic touches. Paralleling *The Killing Kind*, the film features a grande dame who initially appears to be a mere supporting player, but who, as the killer ultimately assumes leading lady status. However, while Ann Sothern killed as a Woman in Peril in *The Killing Kind*, Ruth Roman here kills as an unbalanced antagonist. Spangler had previously made the western *The Soul of Nigger Charley* (1973). Producer Stan Jolley had been associate producer on the Robert Mitchum western *The Good Guys and the Bad Guys* (1969).

A pre-credit murder employs the horror movie conventions of wind, feet ascending a staircase, and a shadow passing by a door. The killer's feet descending the stairs after the act is welcome, and the black trousers and boots create a false expectation that they belong to Luke Doolan, since he is introduced while wearing the same. The throat of the victim being slit is the film's first moment of grande guignol, and the credits use the imagery of blood drops and a knife under the titles. Spangler utilizes screen wipes for transitions, and a subjective camera for the stabbing of Nina so that the knife comes at the cam-

Nina (Pat Herrerra) is about to have her throat slit in *A Knife for the Ladies* (1974).

era and blood smears over the screen. The victims of the killer all being prostitutes associates sex with death, with the knife as weapon becoming symbolically phallic.

Horace burping after eating baked beans appeals to a lowbrow sensibility, as does a spittoon scene and the fistfight between the Sheriff and Burns. The presence of the boy Seth creates an expectation that he will be important to the narrative, but he receives no specific payoff. Spangler delays the sight of the hanged Ramon by showing us Burn's reaction to finding it first, and repeats the subjective camera for Burns' arrival in town on the stagecoach. The blood on the undertaker's coat when he meets Burns is indicative of his profession and also foreshadows Ainslie's own murder.

Elizabeth Mescal is presented as a prim and wealthy widow who dresses in black, mourning for both her husband and her son, although later we make the connection to the killer's black trousers and boots. Her lines, "A great portion of my life is only memories now," and, "If I seem mired in self pity, I'm sorry; it's unavoidable for me," define her as a grande dame with a preoccupation with the past. The painting of her supposed dead son Travis in her living room is another indication of this. Elizabeth's psychological state is exposed by the fact she puts alcohol in her tea, and later we will be told she also takes medication for depression. Since the narrative does not reveal that she is the antagonist until the climax, the film generates no suspense, and Spangler relies upon shock as his horror device. This approach denies the audience sympathy for anyone as a protagonist. When Elizabeth's motive for killing is revealed, it does not change her into a protagonist, since she is clearly mad (as the end title song, "Evil Lady," confirms). However, the narrative does provide some sympathy for the caged Travis, who stops his mother from killing again but dies with her.

Spangler uses a bare-chested and trouser-less Jeff Cooper (as Burns) for beefcake, which probably explains his hair being longer than anyone else's in town. The harmonica music playing over the bonding scene between the Sheriff and Burns after their fight seems to be a western convention, since we don't see the player (although Mescal is conspicuously under-populated). Myra's bad blonde wig, her occupation in the unsubtly named Hooker Saloon, and the slap she receives from Virgil all foreshadow her killing. The vigilante killing of Roman, and the deaths of Luke, Horace and Virgil, are all red herrings. However, they do raise some interesting subplot questions, among them the issue of why the Sheriff didn't shoot to wound Virgil so that he could have been put on trial. The Sheriff being a drunk could explain his poor aim, though the idea of Virgil as a lawman-gone-bad is an intriguing one (which remains unexplored). Perhaps we are meant to accept the shooting as the primitive justice of the town, whereby the innocent Ramon must be avenged.

Since the killings continue after Luke is dead, clearly he is not the killer, and Burns and the Sheriff must continue looking. An argument could be made that either or both of them as a team are the film's protagonists (leaning more towards the Sheriff since he is the one to kill Elizabeth). However, since neither of them are threatened directly by Elizabeth in the scenario, this argument doesn't hold.

The information that Travis was a womanizer begins the inquiry into his death, though it is not clear what he supposedly died of. Spangler uses the thunder-and-lightning horror movie convention when Travis's grave is opened, as well as the shock device of a hand reaching into frame to grasp Burns' shoulder.

Ainslie slapping the dead Myra, and his cry, "You laughed at me," creates the expectation that he is the killer, with the act of slapping a corpse irrationally disturbing. The approaching black boots confirms that Ainslie is *not* the killer, as Spangler cross-cuts, however, between them and Ainslie. Ainslie conveniently walking into the knife presents a rather lame death, with the identity of the killer still shielded.

A bird heard singing at Ainslie's parallels the caged bird in Elizabeth's house, recalling the birds of *What Ever Happened to Baby Jane?*, *The Night Walker*, *What's the Matter with Helen?* and *The Killing Kind*. Travis will also be seen caged, recalling the prisoners of *What Ever Happened to Baby Jane?*, *Strait-Jacket*, *Lady in a Cage*, *Die! Die My Darling!*, *The Night Walker*, *I Saw What You Did*, *Games*, *Berserk!*, *Eye of the Cat*, *Whoever Slew Auntie Roo?* and *Blood and Lace*.

Elizabeth delivering Jenny to the disfigured Travis is an odd choice, since she later admits to having killed all the victims. Elizabeth faked Travis's death presumably out of shame for his condition, and the cage she keeps him in is both for punishment and their mutual protection. Spangler uses a subjective camera for Travis's attempted rape of Jenny—showing *both* their points of view—and adds the macabre touch of Elizabeth rocking in a chair, watching. Her insult to Jenny, "You're just like all the rest of them, you dirty little whore," is funny in light of Jenny's revulsion towards Travis.

When Elizabeth raises the knife to stab Jenny (and then Travis), the image recalls Norman Bates in the cellar of *Psycho*. The shot of Elizabeth and Travis on the floor, dead together with her arm over his, recalls the dead Olivia deHavilland and Joseph Cotten in *Hush ... Hush, Sweet Charlotte*. Spangler provides alternate angles for this image, ending with a high-angle shot reminiscent of Robert Aldrich's best. Travis stopping Elizabeth from killing Jenny demonstrates that the syphilis has not made him a total maniac, though her willingness to kill him for not appreciating what she has done for him is an unexpectedly quick transition.

Ruth Roman's previous leading role had been in *The Baby*, and she was age 51 at the time she starred in *A Knife for the Ladies*. Roman gives Elizabeth an amusing shyness and sensitivity, speaking softly in the initial interview with Burns. Her sudden yell of "Nonsense!" and the smile she uses to cover up her embarrassment indicates her repressed emotionalism, which will be released at the climax. Her high-collared black mourning dress will stand in opposition to the more glamorous, (yet still black) low-cut dress she wears in the scene with Jenny and Travis. We know from *The Baby* that Roman can easily play over-the-top, and she doesn't disappoint here when Elizabeth is revealed to be the serial killer.

Elizabeth Mescal (Ruth Roman) attacks Jenny (Diane Ewing) in *A Knife for the Ladies* (1974).

Release

May, 1974, with the tagline, "Nothing can stop the Killer with a Blood Lust for Ladies—Naked and Dead."

Reviews

"A rare genetic hybrid of 20th century serial killer pathology onto the codes of the West.... It is a genuine shame, considering its subversive potential, that the film is not better than the disappointing curio that it is."—Robert Cettl, *Serial Killer Cinema*.

"Not quite a Western, not quite a horror flick. Call it an oater-bloater ... a minor stab at best"—John Stanley, *Creature Features*.

"No cause for dancing in the streets.... Jack Elam and Ruth Roman are among the able actors picking up pocket change."—Hal Erickson, *Allmovie.com*.

Frightmare (1974)

(aka *Cover Up*; *Once Upon a Frightmare*)

Peter Walker (Heritage)

CREDITS: *Producer/Director:* Pete Walker; *Executive Producer:* Tony Tenser; *Screenplay:* David McGillivray, based on a story by Pete Walker; *Photography:* Peter Jessop; *Music:* Stanley Myers; *Editor:* Robert C. Dearberg; *Art Direction:* Chris Burke; *Make-up:* George Partleton; *Production Manager:* Robert Fennell; *Sound:* Peter O'Connor. Color, 88 minutes.

CAST: Rupert Davies (*Edmund Yates*); Sheila Keith (*Dorothy Yates*); Deborah Fairfax (*Jackie*); Paul Greenwood (*Graham Haller*); Kim Butcher (*Debbie*); Fiona Curzon (*Merle*); Jon Rule (*Robin*); Tricia Mortimer (*Lillian*); Pamela Fairbrother (*Delia*); Edward Kalinski (*Alec*); Victor Winding (*Detective Inspector*); Noel Johnson (*the Judge*); Michael Sharvell-Martin (*Barman*); Tommy Wright (*Nightclub Manager*); Andrew Sachs (*Barry Nichols*); Sue Sharper; Nicholas John (*Pete*); Leo Genn (*Dr. Lytell*); Gerald Flood (*Matthew Laurence*); Anthony Hennessey (*Detective Sergeant*); Jack Dagmar (*Old Man*); Uncredited: Bill Barnsley (*Patrolman*); L. W. Clarke (*Patrolman*); David McGillivray; Martin Taylor (*Guest*); Pete Walker (*Mr. Brunskill—voice*).

VHS/DVD: DVD: Image Entertainment, released February 20, 2001.

Plot

Dorothy Yates is convicted of the cannibal murders of six people and imprisoned in 1957 in the Lansdown Hospital mental institution, along with her husband Edmund, who is also found guilty by complicity. While in prison, Dorothy gives birth to a daughter, Debbie, who is sent to an orphanage. After fifteen years, the Yates are released, considered cured and no longer insane. They live on an isolated farm outside of London, with Edmund working as an aristocrat's driver. Edmund's daughter from his first marriage, Jackie, visits them once a week, always bringing a mysterious package for Dorothy. Jackie has taken in the adolescent Debbie to share her apartment, but has not told her of her parents' whereabouts. When Debbie instigates the gang murder of a barman at Flanagans, the local disco, she hides the body in a private garage. Feeling lonely, Dorothy places an ad in the newspaper under an assumed name to give tarot card readings, but murders her customers.

When Edmund finds one of Jackie's packages in the boot of his car, and Dorothy's tarot cards in the house, he fears that she has started killing again. A psychiatrist that Jackie meets at a dinner party, Graham, takes an interest in both Jackie and Debbie, and makes enquiries at the Lansdown Hospital about the Yates's history. Edmund catches Dorothy with a tarot victim, and she confesses, showing him the barn where she stores the corpses. Jackie informs the police about the body in Debbie's garage, but when they come for Debbie she has gone to the farm with her biker boyfriend, Alec. Debbie introduces herself to Edmund, revealing that she already knows Dorothy. When Alec discovers the barnyard burial site, Dorothy kills him with a pitchfork, as Debbie looks on passively. Edmund is disgusted by the killings, but both Dorothy and Debbie agree that one more is necessary—Jackie.

Jackie reveals to Graham that the packages she delivers contain butcher's brains—an effort to diminish Dorothy's killing instincts. Graham goes after Debbie, pretending that he is a new customer for Dorothy. While giving her reading, Dorothy realizes that Graham is not who he says he is, with his true identity confirmed by Debbie. Debbie telephones Jackie and urges her to come to the farm, which she does. Refusing to take heed of Edmund's warning, Jackie finds Graham's corpse. It seems she is to be the next victim, as Dorothy and Debbie advance on her.

Notes

As with *I Saw What You Did*, *Cry of the Banshee*, and *The Killing Kind*, this is another Grande Dame Guignol in which the grande dame appears in a supporting role but still makes an essential narrative impact. Here she is the antagonist to the protagonist leading lady, and the perpetrator of five of the six grande guignol murders seen in the film. While the narrative's many scattered subplots do eventually all come together, these distractions from the grande guignol does tend to make the film less effective as a horror movie. However, director Pete Walker does compensate by using a lot of gore and blood for the killings, and not relying too much on conventional techniques. Walker had previously directed the horror titles *Die Screaming, Marianne* (1971), *The Flesh and Blood Show* (1972), and *House of Whipcord* (1974). Since *The Beast in the Cellar*, executive producer Tony Tenser had previously made the horror titles *Blood on Satan's Claw* (1971), *Doomwatch* (1972), *Neither the Sea nor the Sand* (1972), and *The Creeping Flesh* (1973).

A black and white pre-credit sequence shows what is presumably Dorothy's trailer at a fairground, approached by a prospective customer. Dorothy remains unseen, as neither she nor Edmund will appear in the following trial sequence (though she is represented by a moving shadow on the wall). Walker uses a dripping tap as a horror movie convention, and films the sequence from Dorothy's point of view. The harpsichord music on the soundtrack recalls the use of same in *Dead Ringer*, *Hush ... Hush, Sweet Charlotte*, *Die! Die! My Darling!*, *The Night Walker*, and *Night Watch*. Once the victim enters the trailer, the camera roams the interior until it returns to him—sitting and dead, with what appear to be blood spots on the wall behind him. The door opens and closes, and this action makes the body fall so that we can see the blood on his skull.

The judge who speaks at the trial, where Dorothy and Edmund are represented by two hands holding each other, talks of the "depths of degradation" of Dorothy's crimes. The judge says that the death sentence has been avoided because medical evidence has deemed her insane. Under the credits, Walker shows a lit candle and tarot cards, recalling the same in *Games*.

The murder of the barman at Flanagans defines Debbie as a sociopath who lies in order to instigate the attack. She privately does her own torture, complete with eye-gouging and blood on the skull. The idea that she has inherited her mother's disorder will be suggested later in the narrative, with Debbie implicitly involved in the killing of Delia and Graham, and she being the one who advances first on Jackie at the end. As the daughter of Dorothy, Debbie also suggests what Dorothy was like in her youth.

It's a pity the narrative doesn't give us more backstory on Dorothy, since Debbie's promiscuity could be a result of a hatred of men. Graham diagnoses Debbie's problem as one of "identity," since she claims not to know about her parents. Her lie leads to an equally false conclusion, and is another example of her manipulation of men. She is as happy to betray Graham when he visits Dorothy as she does Alec when he finds the barn of corpses. Debbie's behavior labels her as an antagonist to Jackie, with Jackie established as the protagonist. The narrative subplot of a romance between Jackie and Graham, who meet at Merle's party, thankfully goes in a different direction when Graham offers to consult with Debbie. Jackie's preoccupation with her parents stops us from considering her a romantic figure, and she is even prepared to leave her first date with Graham in order to go to the farm (on Edmund's request).

Walker includes the horror movie convention of a hand grasping Jackie's shoulder at the farm, revealed to be Edmund in a chair, with his back to the camera. When Dorothy is finally seen, she presents as a strangely androgynous person. Her masculine energy later becomes aggressiveness towards Lillian, Delia, and Graham. Jackie's nightmare, which begins with her driving and ends with her waking up in bed, features Dorothy presenting her with one of the brown-wrapped parcels we later learn contains butcher's brains. Earlier, Dorothy had commented on how the parcel had left a "mark" on the table, which we later presume is blood. The nightmare shows blood dripping from the parcel, with Dorothy salivating. Dorothy is also seen to have red eyes and pale skin, as if this look is the result of a sole cannibalistic diet, although it could just as well present her as a standard nightmare figure. The black dress Dorothy wears initially suggests death, though we will later see that she wears the black dress often.

Jackie's unspecified job in the horror make-up field is a nice touch, with the artificial bruise on the eye of the person she works on later mirrored by the pitchfork attack on Alec's face, and the cut on the face of Edmund. Dorothy establishes that Lillian is a suitable victim by confirming during the tarot reading that she is alone, and that "no one will miss her"—as if this somehow justifies her death. Although Graham is told that Dorothy's use of the cards is a scam, since they are "marked," the suggestion is made that she does possess psychic insight, which is best demonstrated when she realizes Graham is "investigating." Although we are not shown Lillian's murder, we do see Dorothy's drilling into her brain, with the blood splattered on Dorothy face suggesting the gore. While the act of killing Lillian does not immediately affect the protagonist Jackie, it does confirm Dorothy as an antagonistic figure. Jackie is Dorothy's stepdaughter, and this lack of a blood tie will eventually make Jackie a disposable "enemy" to the family. Bringing Jackie and Dorothy together at the end of the narrative makes the antagonist/protagonist connection. Jackie, therefore, finally becomes the Woman in Peril to the grande dame.

Walker inserts mood music under the dialogues scenes set at the homes of both Merle and Jackie. He employs a howling wind, and Dorothy revealed only by her feet and holding a lantern as she treks to the barn, making her a horror movie monster. The opened parcel in the boot of Edmund's car is left unexplained, with Jackie's shock at the sight evidence that it is not the butcher's brains she has been supplying. The supposition that the package contains the murdered barman's brains placed there by Debbie, makes no sense, however, when later we learn that Debbie has been going to the barn regularly and might just as well have delivered them straight to Dorothy (and Dorothy has no reason to deposit any brains she has obtained in Edmund's car).

The murder of Delia is introduced with a subjective camera looking into the window at her and Dorothy, a point of view we later assume to be Debbie's. Dorothy's antagonism towards Delia begins even before Delia asks for her money back, with Dorothy withholding information and imitating her. This attitude can be explained, apart from Dorothy's madness, by Dorothy's growing confidence in her ability to overpower her victims, and by the arrogance of someone possessing clairvoyant insight. Dorothy's insults turn to mocking laughter, and the hot poker she uses to stab Delia produces blood from her mouth. The green curtain that Delia had opened when trying to escape the locked house presumably hides Debbie, though she is not seen, since Debbie will appear behind the same curtain later to meet Edmund. We know that someone is there, since before Edmund arrives to discover the act, Dorothy calls out for assistance. The blood on Dorothy's face, which Edmund sees before he spots Delia's body, suggests of the drilling/brain eating.

The Graham subplot reveals more information from the Hospital where the Yates were imprisoned. Dorothy's condition is described as "pathological cannibalism," and said to have originated from a childhood trauma. The eating of her pet rabbit is said to have changed her shock into pleasure. After a period of killing animals, (a standard phase in the development of a serial killer) whose brains held a special fascination for her, she progressed to a craving for people. No information is provided as to how Edmund met Dorothy or if he knew about her condition before he married her. There appears to be no power struggle in the marriage we see. In fact, Dorothy is fearful, when caught, of Edmund's "anger and disappointment." This implies that he is the partner in control, and his acceptance is more than implied by the fact he doesn't leave or report her. His surprise at Dorothy for hiding from him Debbie's relationship with her doesn't alter his acceptance, which will climax in his choosing his wife over his own daughter Jackie, whom he stops from escaping at the end.

The blood on Debbie's jacket being the barman's, and Jackie discovering this, is a plot convenience that leads Jackie to report the garage to the police. One wonders why Debbie didn't either wash or dispose of the bloodied jacket. She has been otherwise careful in killing the barman, hiding him in a secret garage, and also keeping her relationship with Dorothy secret from Jackie. Debbie's lie to the police about Alec having killed the barman with a bicycle chain foreshadows her later betrayal of him to Dorothy. Debbie's use of Alec to flee from the police, and her not taking him into the farmhouse, are further indications of her callousness. Although Alec is presented as being just as common as Debbie (both of them chew gum, for instance), he is not as amoral as her, since he had shown real concern for her after the gang attack on the barman. We don't condemn Alec's snooping in the barn as he waits for Debbie, with his stumbling across the corpses being an acceptable horror movie contrivance that sets him up as the next victim.

Dorothy's appearance with the pitchfork is a shock, but a worse one comes when Debbie refuses to react to Alec's cries for help when Dorothy attacks him. Walker makes this murder the most gruesome, with the camera lingering on the blood and Alec's anguish. Jackie's plan to alleviate Dorothy's appetite with the butcher's brains is judged by Graham to have been foolhardy, which suggests that the brains may have actually had the opposite effect and stimulated her cannibalism. Additionally, the fact that Dorothy had already progressed from animal to human brains would seem to have made Jackie's continued offerings unsatisfactory. Graham's pretence that he is "worried about his health" allows him entry to the farm, winning over Edmund's resistance, though the state of his health will, ironically, become more worrisome after Dorothy's reading. Walker cuts from Dorothy reading Graham's cards to Merle playing cards with Jackie, although Jackie seems remarkably passive about Graham going to see Dorothy.

When Debbie calls Jackie, Walker presents Debbie in shadow, which foreshadows her threat. Jackie entering the darkened farmhouse makes her the Woman in Peril. The cut on Edmund's face, which Walker saves to reveal to Jackie, brings with it an air of mystery, since it seems unlikely that Dorothy would have struck him. It is more believable that Debbie would have, though this remains unseen. If it is meant to entice Jackie to stay out of concern for him, it doesn't jibe with Edmund beseeching her to leave (although it does match up with his final betrayal). The sound of Dorothy's drill gives Jackie's Woman in Peril a conventional noise to investigate, and Walker only obliquely reveals Graham's bloodied drilled skull.

Debbie's advance with an axe recalls the weapons of *Strait-Jacket*, *Hush ... Hush, Sweet Charlotte*, *The Savage Intruder*, *Cry of the Banshee*, *Blood and Lace*, and *The Baby*. Walker lingers on Jackie's cornering, just as he had on Delia and Alec's, though Jackie's essential brittleness deprives her of the sympathy a protagonist should inspire. Walker cuts away from the advance on Jackie to end on Edmund in freeze-frame. The film concludes with a repetition of what the judge had said at the trial, as the image changes first into a negative x-ray, then dissolves to a red screen. The ending is interesting since the antagonistic grande dame is not defeated, which only makes the judge's line more ironic, and also lays the groundwork for a sequel involving more of Dorothy and Debbie's exploits:

> JUDGE: And let the members of the public be assured that you shall remain in this mental institution until there can be no doubt whatsoever that you are fit and able to take your place in society again.

Sheila Keith was 53 at the time of filming. She had played a supporting role in the Dick Emery comedy *Ooh. .. You Are Awful* (1972), and portrayed a whip-wielding warden in *House of Whipcord*. Keith's androgynous face and body language adds further dimension to Dorothy, since although she is a mother, she does not present as maternal (in spite of her old-lady shawls). She attempts to provide some pathos via Dorothy's suffering by imprisonment, the loss of her daughter and her apparent isolation on the farm. However, the savagery and perversion of her crimes makes it difficult to pity her. Keith smiles secretly in Dorothy's scene with Lillian to show her duplicity; and when she drills into Lillian's Keith transitions from wide-eyed horror to glee in licking her lips to frightening madness.

Release

UK: November 6, 1974; USA: July 1975, with the taglines: "Worse than your most shocking nightmare!" "Dare you see the film that shocked the critics?" "Far beyond a nightmare," and "What terrifying craving made her kill ... and kill ... and kill..."

Reviews

"A regressive body-in-pieces fantasy, with a flimsy narrative as simply an excuse to link numerous gory sequences.... The demented mother is forcibly played by Keith."—Phil Hardy, *The Aurum Film Encyclopedia of Horror.*

"This is the nastiest, most cynical and effective of the British horror films made by director Walker in the 1970s."—Robert Cettl, *Serial Killer Cinema.*

"Walker directs with no bare breasts in sight but gallons of Kensington gore on view. Keith is wonderful in her most deranged role ever."—Gary A. Smith, *Uneasy Dreams: The Golden Age of British Horror Films, 1956–1976.*

"Dark and gruesome little shocker, aided by some chilling performances."—David Gritten, *Halliwell's Film Guide.*

Persecution (1974)

(aka *Sheba*; *The Graveyard*; *The Terror of Sheba*)

Tyburn Film Productions

CREDITS: *Director:* Don Chaffey; *Producer:* Kevin Francis; *Associate Producer:* Hugh Attwooll; *Screenplay:* Robert B. Hutton, Rosemary Wootten; *Additional Scenes & Dialogue:* Frederick Warner; *Photography:* Kenneth Talbot; *Music:* Paul Ferris; *Editor:* Mike Campbell; *Art Direction:* Jack Shampan; *Make-up:* Jimmy Evans; *Make-up for Miss Turner:* Roy Ashton; *Hair:* Gordon Bond; *Hair for Miss Turner:* Joan Carpenter; *Wardrobe:* Rosemary Burrows; *Wardrobe for Miss Turner:* Anthony Mendelson, executed by Bermans of London; *Production Manager:* Robin Douet; *Sound:* Roy Baker. Color, 95 minutes. Filmed at Pinewood Studios, England.

SONG: "Good King Wenceslas" (John Mason Neale), sung by Chorus.

CAST: Lana Turner (*Carrie Masters*); Ralph Bates (*David Masters*); Olga Georges-Picot (*Monique Kalfon*); Suzan Farmer (*Janie Masters*); Patrick Allen (*Robert Masters*); Catherine Brandon (*Mrs. Deacon*); Shelagh Fraser (*Mrs. Banks*); Jennifer Guy (*Waitress*); Ronald Howard (*Dr. Ross*); Mark Weavers (*Young David*); Trevor Howard (*Paul Bellamy*); John Ryan (*Gardener*).

VHS/DVD: VHS: Electric Video (release date unknown).

Plot

Young David Masters drowns Sheba, the pet cat of his mother, Carrie, after it scratches him, claiming his mother loves it more than he. Carrie gives David a Christmas present of Sheba in a coffin and makes him bury it in the garden cemetery. She tells him that he will never leave her until she has told him everything. Headstones in the graveyard dated four years apart suggest that David continues to kill every new Sheba that Carrie acquires, as a sign of the ongoing battle between mother and son. As a grown man, David lives in the apartment over the garage of his mother's mansion, with Janie, his wife, and their newborn child, Paul. Carrie has her regular monthly meeting with the married Paul Bellamy, who is David's father, and whom she has been blackmailing for twenty-four years over the affair. Carrie tells Paul of their new grandson, though she hates him, just as she does Janie. Janie prepares a special dinner for David's birthday, but during the meal the latest Sheba goes to the baby's room and suffocates him.

Janie has a nervous breakdown, and Carrie hires a nurse for her, Monique. However, the nurse is actually a girl Carrie met at the Blue Grotto Club who she wants to seduce David away from Janie. The night Monique's seduction proves successful, Carrie informs Janie, who goes to see for herself. Upon seeing David and Monique in bed together, Janie trips over Sheba as she runs and falls down the staircase. Breaking her neck in the fall, Janie dies. David burns all of Janie's clothes, as well as the baby's crib, and blames his mother. He digs up all the Sheba graves and finds a human skeleton under the cat statue. The skeleton wears the ring of Carrie's husband, Robert. David accuses Carrie of murdering Robert, who he has been told had left her. Carrie confesses to him the identity of his real father. After David rips up the only photo Carrie has of Paul Bellamy, Carrie telephones him, begging him to come to the mansion to help her with David.

David presents the original Sheba's coffin to Carrie and has her bury it under the cat statue with Robert's skeleton. Carrie confesses that she stabbed Robert with a dagger, and then told the police that it was he who had crippled her. In fact, she now remembers that it was actually Paul and not Robert who had pushed her down the staircase when he learned of her pregnancy. To protect the baby in the fall, she had landed in a position which permanently broke her leg. Carrie discovers that David has killed Monique, who she had paid off and dismissed. Taking Sheba, David humiliates Carrie by making her meow and then drink from a bowl of milk like a cat. He drowns Carrie in the same way he had drowned the original Sheba, and buries something in the graveyard under a new Sheba gravestone.

Notes

This Grande Dame Guignol presents a grande dame, played by Lana Turner, who is initially an antagonist but becomes a Woman in Peril. The narrative offers a domestic set-up with perverse potential. However, the reliance of the director on post-modern film effects, such as point of view, soft focus, and quick edits, soon makes us aware of the thinness of the material. With competent but uninspired performances, and a generic music score, the film is ultimately slowly-paced and disappointing as a horror entry.

Director Don Chaffey had previously directed the fantasy adventure titles *Jason and the Argonauts* (1963), *One Million Years B.C.* (1966; starring Raquel Welch), and *The Creatures the World Forgot* (1971) for Hammer Film Productions. Tyburn Films had been formed by Kevin Francis, the son of Freddie Francis (the director of *Trog*), in an attempt to replicate the success of Hammer Films. *Persecution* was their first production.

The film begins with two white circles on a black screen, which suggest approaching car headlights and the eyes of an animal. Chaffey cuts to a door opening, where streaming light reveals a white cat in a kitchen. He employs the cat's point of view (one of the post-modern devices he will use repeatedly). The cat recalls the felines of *Eye of the Cat* and *The Killing Kind*. Blood is shown as the result of the cat's scratch (in a film in which there is otherwise little blood), and the screenplay gets a laugh from the Young David saying how he prefers dogs. Chaffey uses quick cuts for the drowning of the cat in the milk bowl, with David's "I hate you" on the soundtrack, and his "Mother, I've killed the cat" said to an unseen mother. This act presents David as both protagonist and antagonist, a dichotomy that will also apply to Carrie.

A slow zoom in to the Christmas tree under the credits, as a chorus sings "Good King Wenceslas," ends with the camera stopping on an angel at the top of the tree. Although the angel itself doesn't receive a payoff, we are presumably meant to equate it with David, although this is difficult given the brutal action we have just seen him perform. Carrie's cane recalls the disabled grande dames of *What Ever Happened to Baby Jane?*, *Lady in a Cage*, *Games*, *The Savage Intruder*, *What Ever Happened to Aunt Alice?* and *Eye of the Cat*. Her wealth is never explained, and presumably inherited, since Richard is said to have married her for it (and he is the only husband she is known to have had). Carrie giving David a coffin for Christmas alludes to her perversity, although it is not the only present, and her black dress presumably indicates her mourning. It is also hypocritical of her to punish David for killing a cat when we later learn that she has murdered Richard, and for no apparent reason. The long gold chains she wears will mirror the golden collar of the white sheath Carrie sports at the climax.

The first tombstone is dated 1954–1959, although no hair, wardrobe or set decoration detail identifies the period as 1959. The exchange between David and Carrie at the grave (his "I'm sorry" to her "You will be") presents her agenda as revenge. Chaffey uses a camera pan over the group of Sheba headstones, and an echoed voiceover for the passage of time to bring us to 1972, with each Sheba only living four years. The voiceover includes Carrie's claim that there is information she is withholding from David, which she is saving for the right time. Although David is twenty-four when the narrative comes to 1972, he has chosen to stay with his mother, so that his curiosity makes him complicit in his own impotence and entrapment. We aren't told when, where or how he met Janie. However, we presume that there was a period when he was away from home after his schooling, although he tells her that he has no skills to help him find employment.

Poster for *Persecution* (1974).

The battle between a grande dame and a child recalls *Strait-Jacket*, *I Saw What You Did*, *The Nanny*, *Berserk!*, *Whoever Slew Auntie Roo?*, *Blood and Lace*, and *The Killing Kind*. When Janie enters the garden to meet David, Chaffey intercuts between her and the baby carriage where she has left the baby, creating an initial expectation that the cat will attack. Janie abandoning the carriage suggests either that she is a neglectful mother or that she doesn't expect to be away long. The expectation of the cat as a threat to the baby, however, is thwarted when the cat pursues Janie instead. When she gets lost in the garden maze, Chaffey uses hand-held camerawork and high angles to illustrate her panic and disorientation, which is exacerbated by the screaming cat. We don't know why the cat is so antagonistic toward Janie, although Janie will comment that the cat and Carrie are the same (and it will eventually assist in Janie's death).

David's flashback nightmare about Sheba scratching him has him awaken to the cat in his room, with Chaffey including an extreme close-up of the cat's eyes. Wardrobe makes a witty contribution by giving Carrie a leopard-pattern negligee. Additionally, when she meets Paul at the zoo—at the cage of a lioness—her jacket has a fur trim. Carrie's attitude toward Paul presents her as coquettish and manipulative, with his anger justifiable considering the amount of time he has endured her blackmail. Her demand that he kiss her foreshadows her later demand that he come to her house, although the latter is not seen. Carrie's confession about her lack of feeling for their eight-week-old grandson—"I don't even touch it"—is a denial of David's adult life and her family heritage. It is interesting that her confession comes after Paul's demand of "Leave it alone," referring to the baby, presumably with his awareness of how Carrie has punished David. Carrie's lack of maternal feelings also defines her grande dame as abnormal compared to David's normal nuclear family.

Carrie attains grande dame status primarily via her wealth and the fetish relationship she has with her cats, highlighted by the scene in which she sits in The Blue Grotto Club with Sheba on a leash. Other grande dame elements include the painting of herself in the living room and the box of mementos she keeps, which include photographs of herself, David, Robert, and Paul. Her continued contact with Paul as David's father is another sign of her clinging to the past, even if the association is soured by her blackmailing him.

The initial idea that Robert has left her also defines Carrie as a grande dame—married for her money and abandoned when she was unfaithful. This lack of a romantic interest, with the additional rejection of Paul, is what accounts for her unnatural preoccupation with cats. Sheba being female alludes to Carrie's bisexual inclination, which her smiling at Monique at the Club also suggests, as does Monique's rolling around on Carrie's bed, caressing Sheba. The dagger that Carrie keeps in a box is later explained as the weapon she used to murder Robert, which is a bizarre item to keep as a memento. In the scene in which Carrie looks at the contents of her box, she tells Sheba, "I'm playing with him [David] the way you play with a mouse."

The occasion of David's birthday doesn't provide any presents, apart from the dinner Janie prepares, and at which Carrie hits a plate with a utensil in boredom. Ironically, David's birthday will be his son's death day, which can be viewed as Carrie's malignant gift to him. The cat following Janie to the baby's room again creates the expectation of menace, and this time the expectation is met. Chaffey intercuts between the dinner and cake, and the cat, using the feline's point of view for its approach to the crib.

Carrie's flashback to when she met Paul is shown from her point of view, so that a younger looking Turner is not required. Chaffey shoots this flashback in a sepia tone, which also incorporates what will later be revealed to be a phantom memory of how she was crippled. The death of the baby is not shown and we are also spared the sight of the dead body. Carrie's criticism of Janie's concern—"Can't she leave the child alone for five minutes?"—equates mothering with smothering, which is exactly what the cat does. Janie confirms the relationship between Carrie and Sheba as being intuitive by stating to David, "Your mother and Sheba are the same." Carrie later makes the comment that Sheba is "demanding and possessive," qualities that one can also attribute to Carrie.

Chaffey's superimposition of Carrie's head over the cat statue in the cemetery is mirrored at the climax when the statue's head is superimposed over Carrie's face. The narrative introduces Monique as an ambiguous figure, since it is conceivable that she really is a nurse hired to care for Janie. The scene in which Monique meets David, and she drops the medication, however, undermines her skill as a professional, with David's gloomy countenance additionally undermining the movie convention of instant attraction.

Monique's undressing in front of the window to attract David's attention, who conveniently stands watching her window, is more movie contrivance, and it cements our belief that Monique is playing him. David's hesitance in going to Monique is noticed by Carrie, and this creates the expectation that he will not go to her. His eventual sleeping with her, even though she is the sexual aggressor, is his complicity in being unfaithful. This complicity adds complexity to the idea of David as protagonist.

David burning his childhood toys recalls the line of soldiers seen in the post-credit Christmas scene, and allows for a flashback concerning the ashtray the schoolboy has made for his mother. The flashback shows Carrie being underwhelmed by the ashtray, although we don't know why. David having the ashtray in his possession confirms Carrie's rejection of it, although the adult David cannot bring himself to burn it.

When David comes to Monique's room, Chaffey has Sheba watching David's physical ascent (and moral descent). Carrie's approach to Janie's room is signaled by the horror movie convention of the thump of her cane as she walks. Chaffey provides three levels of chase, with Sheba, then Janie, then Carrie all going to Monique's room. The observing cat comes into play when Janie trips over it to her death, with her fall recalling Carrie's fall. However, after this point Sheba's presence will be a narrative red herring that Chaffey over-uses.

David's burning of Janie's clothes, and a photo of her and the baby crib, recalls his earlier burning of his toys. Chaffey adds Carrie's echoed "everything" to the burning, as a repeat from Carrie's "You'll never leave me, not until I've told you everything." David's claim that his mother has cost him everything is again a denial of his own complicity. David finding the skeleton of Richard under the cat statue is given a gruesome touch when

David Masters (Ralph Bates) burns the clothes and crib of his dead wife and baby in *Persecution* (1974; aka *Terror of Sheba*).

David holds the hands of the skeleton that wears Richard's ring. Carrie telling David that Robert didn't want Paul's "bastard" reads as shocking, although it is the correct description. However, since we learn that Carrie has re-imagined her past to conceal Paul's rejection, this indictment of Robert may be false.

David tearing up Carrie's photographs is a direct assault on the grande dame's mementoes of the past, and is met with an equally vicious act of Carrie hitting him with her cane. It is interesting that David's act of leaving Robert's ringed skeletal hand on Carrie's bed is what makes her telephone Paul at his home, something we assume from his response that she has never done before. Chaffey shows dirt on David's face from his digging up the graves to add to his antagonism, and the narrative mirrors the Young David carrying Sheba's coffin with David making Carrie do the same. Her seeming easy compliance with David's humiliation of her is an indication that she has lost her power over him, and she changes from antagonist to Woman in Peril.

A continuity error occurs when the gravestones we had earlier seen on the ground, presumably toppled by David, are now back standing upright. That is, unless we are supposed to believe that he has re-erected them. David having Carrie bury the original Sheba's coffin under the cat statue with the rest of Robert's skeleton may seem to be his forcing her to confront her murder, but it takes on further significance with the mirrored exchange:

> CARRIE: I'm sorry.
> DAVID: You will be.

Carrie's fight through the maze recalls that of Janie's, with Chaffey using extreme close-ups and expressionist angles to emphasizes Carrie's distress. The flashback that reveals Paul as the man who crippled Carrie has her claim that Robert was "crude and vulgar and cruel," although it is Paul that calls her a "dirty little whore." This stance from Paul is odd, given that he is complicit in the affair. Chaffey uses quick edits and a shot of hands reaching toward the subjective camera (Carrie's point of view) as she is pushed. The music that accompanies Carrie's admission of her corrected memory creates the expectation that she will be forgiven, although the music soon reverts to thriller/horror movie convention.

The slashed painting foreshadows the stabbing of Monique, and, along with the destruction of the photographs and the revelation about Robert, also the fall of the grande dame. Chaffey films Monique's exit as straight towards the camera, then out-of-focus, which can later be interpreted to mean that she was going to David, her killer. Chaffey adds to the degradation of Carrie being made to meow and drink milk from a bowl by shooting Turner in unflattering extreme close-ups. One wonders how David would have reacted had Carrie refused to meow and drink the milk, although his holding Sheba is an implied threat.

The last flashback of the young David employs sepia lighting, which is different from the earlier scene where he had drowned Sheba. Thankfully, Chaffey doesn't submit Turner to drowning in the milk bowl, but rather repeats David's line "Mother, I've killed the cat." The last shot of David burying something at the 1972 Sheba gravesite remains ambiguous as to whether the victim is Carrie or Sheba, although presumably we are meant to think it is Carrie. David's murder of his own mother, then, is the triumph of the antagonistic protagonist over the antagonistic protagonist grande dame.

Lana Turner was 52 at the time of filming and had not assayed a leading movie role since *The Big Cube* (1969). Her career had survived the end of the studio system in the 1950s, with a Best Actress Academy Award nomination for *Peyton Place* (1957), and her subsequent working relationship with producer Ross Hunter kept her in leading roles in the 1960s. Her career also survived the Johnny Stompanato murder scandal in 1958 wherein her daughter shot Turner's gangster boyfriend, something that Hunter deliberately referenced in his films with Turner.

Although known more as a beauty than an actress, Turner's dramatic limitations are aided by Carrie's disability, since she is seen either sitting or standing until the climax. Turner's casting also adds to Carrie's tacky cheapness, in spite of coming from money. In particular, Carrie having married her chauffeur recalls Turner's real-life multiple marriages, and her association with Stompanato.

Turner is first seen in long shot, as David opens his presents, with the only difference in the way she is lit between the 1959 scenes and the 1972 scenes being the yellow light on her in the flashback scene involving the ashtray. When she meets with Paul at the zoo, she wears a white scarf wrapped around her head to conceal the lines on her neck, although the heavy eye shadow she wears fails to conceal the lines under her eyes. Thankfully, the stiff hairdos she wears give way in the climactic scenes when Carrie trips in the garden and her hair becomes disheveled. Turner's tears in the scene indicate some skill, but Carrie's breathless anxiety when telephoning Paul, and her half scream for David, reveal her limited vocal ability.

Release

October 1975, with the taglines, "Warning: this film is NOT for the squeamish," "The horror of a twisted mind," and "Now it's David's turn to get even ... and he has a very special treat for his mother."

Reviews

"The old-fashioned meller is riddled with ho-hum and sometimes laughably trite scripting. Also, very tame in the shock horror department. Under the circumstances, Turner's performance has reasonable poise. There isn't much animation to Ralph Bates as the grown-up edition of the tormented son."—*Variety*, November 5, 1974.

"Although Turner's presence lifts the film and Talbot's cinematography is excellent, the script is so contrived that Chaffey appears to have given up hope of breathing life into the silly psychodrama."—Phil Hardy, *The Aurum Film Encyclopedia of Horror*.

"...[T]horoughly unpleasant film.... Turner gives a good performance far better than the film merits. Her star presence is the sole reason for watching."—Gary A. Smith, *Uneasy Dreams: The Golden Age of British Horror Films, 1956–1976*.

"Turner hams it up and she and Ralph Bates have fun playing games with one another.... Chaffey's pace is slow moving, despite occasionally inventive photography and some offbeat editing.... The story is confusing and the show stealer is seductive Olga Georges-Picot."—Richard Schleib, *The Science Fiction, Horror and Fantasy Movie Review*.

Homebodies (1974)

Cinema Entertainment

CREDITS: *Director:* Larry Yust; *Producer:* Marshal Backlar; *Executive Producer:* James R. Levitt; *Screenplay:* Larry Yust, Howard Kaminsky, Bennett Sims; *Photography:* Isidore Mankofsky; *Music:* Bernardo Segall; *Editor:* Peter Parasheles; *Art Direction:* John Retsek; *Set Decoration:* Raymond Molyneaux; *Wardrobe:* Lynn Bernay; *Make-up:* Louis Lane; *Sound:* Leroy Robbins; *Special Effects:* Donald Courtney; *Production Manager:* Carl Olsen. Color, 96 minutes. Filmed in Cincinnati, Ohio.

SONG: "Sassafras Sundays" (Bernardo Segall, Jeremy Kronsberg), sung by Billy Van.

CAST: Peter Brocco (*Mr. Blakely*); Frances Fuller (*Miss Emily Wilkins*); William Hansen (*Mr. Sandy*); Ruth McDevitt (*Mrs. Loomis*); Paula Trueman (*Mattie Spencer*); Ian Wolfe (*Mr. Loomis*); Linda Marsh (*Miss Pollack*); Douglas Fowley (*Mr. Crawford*); Kenneth Tobey (*Construction Boss*); Wesley Lau (*Foreman*); Norman Gottschalk (*Apartment Superintendent*); Irene Webster (*Woman in Floppy Hat*); Nicholas Lewis (*Construction Worker*); Michael Johnson (*Policeman*); Alma DuBus (*Apartment Superintendent's Wife*); John Craig (*Construction Worker*); Eldon Quick (*Insurance Inspector*); William Benedict (*Watchman*); Joe de Meo.

VHS/DVD: Not available in either format. A VHS tape was released on April 6, 1994, from Embassy Home Entertainment.

Plot

A new high-rise is being built on South 24th Street in Cincinnati as part of the Crawford Center. This development by Mr. Crawford includes demolishing the row of tenement houses nearby, which have been occupied by elderly people for over forty years. Although they have been advised of their eviction months ago, the six tenants of 522 refuse to leave their units. Since the city has returned their rent payments, the six are considered squatters. Miss Pollack, a girl from the city, advises that she will return with the police to force them out. One of the six, Maddie Spencer, likes to sit and watch the activity on the worksite. She witnesses a series of accidents that temporarily halts work. When the power, gas and water are cut off in the tenement, the group improvises to stay on. When Miss Pollack returns with the police, Maddie and her shut-in neighbor Emily Wilkins cannot be found, but the other four agree to leave without any trouble. They are taken to a large sterile condominium, where their furniture has been delivered.

Miss Pollack goes back to the tenement and is stabbed by Emily, who is hiding in her unit. Maddie drives Miss Pollacks's car away and abandons it when it runs out of gas, also disposing of the knife used by Emily. That night the four tenants return to the tenement, where Maddie and Emily show them Miss Pollack's body. A wheelchair is stolen from the condominium, and Miss Pollack is thrown from a bridge into the open freight car of a passing train. Maddie lures Mr. Crawford from the worksite back to the tenement, where he is tied up by the others. Since he refuses to stop the destruction of the building, they take him back to the site and drown him in a bath of cement. The next day the neighboring houses are destroyed by a wrecking ball, so Mrs. Loomis realizes that killing Crawford has achieved nothing. After the wrecking ball is tampered with, and an accident causes the death of another worker, Mrs. Loomis can no longer accept the situation. Her attempts to report what has happened are stopped by Maddie, who eventually drops an urn that contains the ashes of Emily's father onto Mrs. Loomis's head.

Emily wants to tell Mr. Loomis that it was Maddie who dropped the urn, but is chased out of the house by Maddie, who tries to push her off the high-rise. Maddie has also killed Mr. Sandy, who had tried to get Emily to reveal the secret to him. After Mrs. Loomis dies, Mr. Loomis, Mr. Blakely and Emily chase Maddie. They push her in front of traffic, then drown her in a park lake. When the wrecking ball comes for 522, the three survivors flee, with Mr. Loomis setting explosives in the basement. The explosives ignite when the wrecking balls strikes, and the building implodes. The three find a new condemned building. Just as they are about to move in, Maddie appears, alive and wanting to join them.

Notes

A little-known gem, this title by writer-director Larry Yust features grande guignol enacted by an ensemble of old people that includes two grande dames. Granted, Yust may overdo the post-modern use of expressionist camera angles, point-of-view and hand-held camerawork. However, he makes sparing use of music and brings a great deal of comedy to the grim narrative. Yust had only previously directed one feature, the action drama *Trick Baby* (1973), produced by Marshal Backlar and James R. Levitt.

Homebodies is the only film made to date by Cinema Entertainment, and the last film to be produced by James R. Levitt. Backlar had previously made the short *Skaterdater* (1965), directed by Noel Black, which won the Cannes Golden Palm Best Short Film Award and was nominated for the Academy Award. This led to Black directing the cult thriller *Pretty Poison* (1968), which Backlar also produced, and which centers on a female antagonist.

Homebodies' initial view of Mattie, with her squeaking shopping trolley and the horror movie music, changes when the song "Sassafras Sundays" plays under the credits, which makes her seemingly less of a threat and more of an eccentric character. We do not yet know that the purpose of her observing the high-rise worksite at the end of her street (as she eats from a box of prunes) is to see the result of her sabotage. Since she is the first seen of the six elderly people who are the film's protagonists, Mattie stands as the uber-protagonist. It is easy to draw parallels between Mattie and the younger workmen with the new building and the tenement the six live in.

Wood being hammered over windows, a "condemned" sign, and removal vans indicate the emptying of one of the tenements. The lack of concern of the removalists is indicated by the breaking of a vase of a departing tenant, witnessed by the tenants of 522 behind their curtained windows (and Mattie in the street). Emily leaving her window open so that the construction noise of the worksite can be heard indicates her passive resistance, with Mattie closing it indicating that Mattie is a more active opponent.

Mattie Spencer (Paula Trueman) disposes of the body of Miss Pollack (Linda Marsh) with the help of Mr. Loomis (Ian Wolfe) in this lobby card for *Homebodies* (1974).

Emily, as someone who hasn't left her unit in twenty years, is the more traditional grande dame. She wears period clothes, sports dyed-brown hair, and talks to her dead father whose ashes she keeps in a shrine. The second setting at her dinner table for "Papa" suggests a weak mind, making her killing of Miss Pollack that much more surprising.

Mattie's revelation of her own past indicates she has lived in the tenement for even longer than Emily—forty years—although we never get a good view of the interior of her unit. She delivers a short speech that sums up her predicament as a widow, and her place in the house:

> All the times we planned on moving out of here. Always looking forward to getting out. Now, all I wanna do is stay.

Later, Mattie will reveal that she has provided for Emily and indulged Emily's isolation (although when Emily tries to kill her, Emily will claim that Mattie hasn't allowed her to leave her unit). Mattie's repeated phrase of "It's me, Mattie" when she knocks on Emily's door will earn a payoff at the end of the film.

Writing-director Yust carefully delineates his elderly protagonists via both their actions and their personal environments. Mr. Loomis painting the house trim, for example, shows the former superintendent's resolve to stay, his need to be employed, and his fearlessness in working at heights. Mr. Sandy's piles of newspapers and books initially suggest he is a worse shut-in than Emily, although they are revealed to be material for the memoir he is writing of his fifty-five year marriage. He makes the valid point to Miss Pollack that it has taken him fifteen years to collect the material since his wife died, so it would take another fifteen years to unpack it all if he is to be relocated, and that he "doesn't have the time."

Mr. Blakely has a similar valid claim in response to relocation, as he is blind. Since he has lived in the house for thirty-eight years, he thinks he is "too old to learn over" any new streets and locations he must adapt to. However, the narrative adds an element of danger to Mr. Blakely as a disabled person when he plays his violin to distract the worksite's security guards so that Mattie and Mr. Loomis can enter and sabotage the electric elevator.

That Miss Pollack claims the tenants have known about the enforced move for weeks seems odd when she hands out notices on the day she arrives with the removalists. Although she may be "only doing her job," as Mrs. Loomis will later concede, Miss Pollack's failure to knock before entering some of the units indicates self-righteousness. Her behavior, then, is antagonistic towards the grande dames (and the other tenants), with her as a younger female recalling the dynamic of *Strait-Jacket*, *Lady in a Cage*, *Die! Die My Darling!*, *The Night Walker*, *I Saw What You Did*, *Games*, *Berserk!*, *Eye of the Cat*, *Flesh Feast*, *Blood and Lace*, and *The Baby*.

When she returns to find the front door is locked by the tenants, denying her access, Miss Pollack claims that they are "acting like children," and that she is "trying to help" them. The vision of the tenants behind the curtained front door makes them appear both vulnerable and threatening. The second accident at the worksite is prefaced by workmen carelessly tossing coffee on Mattie. Although Yust does not individualize the coffee thrower or the three men who are "fried like bacon" in the elevator, her burning (from the hot coffee) can be paralleled with theirs. The temporary work stoppage, like the later killing of Mr. Crawford, will not halt the threat to the tenants.

The return of Miss Pollack with police is met with no resistance, again creating a false expectation that the tenants have acquiesced (though Mattie's absence suggests that more resistance will be forthcoming). Mr. Blakely's claim that Mattie and Emily left in the night is rightly disbelieved by Miss Pollack, and this disbelief will bring her back to the house and her death.

The relocation condominium, with other tenants sitting silently in the foyer, resembles a nursing home. Mr. Blakely crashes into the furniture of his new unit as predicted, and Miss Pollack enters the unit without knocking, just as she had in the old tenement.

Her return to the tenement presents her as a Woman in Peril, with the sounds of her footsteps and a dripping tap in the basement used as thriller devices. Again Yust employs point of view, hand-held camerawork and horror movie music. When she gets upstairs, he uses no music, while a creaking door and other noises draws Miss Pollack to Emily's unit.

Miss Pollack dead on the floor with the knife sticking out of her is a horrible image, one enhanced by the camera being at floor level. We see blood when Mattie extracts the long-bladed knife, and its discovery is used for suspense *and* comic effect in the ensuing car sequence. Mattie's claim of not having driven a car in forty years prefaces her uncontrolled driving. The comical notion is enhanced by her hitting her head when she gets into the car, beeping the horn accidentally, setting off the windshield wipers, and starting in reverse.

Yust uses "Sassafras Sundays" to underline the comedy of Mattie driving on the footpath, blocking traffic, causing several near-misses, and eventually hitting another car. Mattie uses her old-lady smile to avoid a police inquiry, and the bloody knife being dropped into a garbage truck Mattie passes earns a laugh. The wheelchair that is stolen from the condominium recalls the wheelchairs used in *What Ever Happened to Baby Jane?*, *What Ever Happened to Aunt Alice*, *The Savage Intruder*, and *Blood and Lace*. Miss Pollack's body being moved in the daytime is a bold act, though perhaps one of time necessity, and her pale skin and stiff body highlights the ghoulishness. Both a traffic cop assisting her crossing the street, and the interest of the Woman in the Floppy Hat, adds to the comedy, with Mattie's dismissive abuse topping it all.

Miss Pollack's car being towed away just as the group arrives to deposit her body is more comedy (and bad timing), and the image of her corpse being thrown into the freight car offers more ghoulishness. Mattie riding back in the wheelchair previously occupied by the corpse gives a reason for them to have it (as well as providing her a rest), and it will be later used to transport Mr. Crawford.

Mrs. Loomis's disapproval of the killing of Miss Pollack makes Mattie perceive her as an antagonist. Yust shows Mattie approaching Mrs. Loomis in a telephone booth as an out-of-focus figure. Mrs. Loomis being seen by a boy throwing a ball at the house further makes her an unintentional antagonist, since this gives away the presence of the group in the house.

Mr. Crawford lured by Mattie to the house is preceded by him being alone on the site, with his arms raised in triumph at his own success. Yust uses horror music and the squeak of Mattie's shopping cart to create suspense. Crawford agreeing to go with Mattie, urged on by her repeated "It's important" line, is only believable because he has forgotten seeing her on the site the day the men were killed in the elevator. His arms hanging down beside him while he hangs upside down in the trap mirrors his raised arms on the site, with Yust using Crawford's point of view and the squeak of the swinging rope to generate menace.

Yust creates pathos for Crawford when he transitions from anger to murmuring incoherence, presumably from the shock. The expectation of the gagged and tied Crawford in the wheelchair being led to the edge of a floor of the worksite so that he can be pushed off to his death is not met. His fate is far more grande guignol. Yust cuts to the security guards to allow time for the cement to fill the container in which Crawford has been placed, with Mrs. Loomis patting the sweat from his forehead being a comic and sensitive touch. This act, and her looking away in horror, further defines her character is being more humane than the others.

The air bubbles that signal Crawford's last breath is another comically horrifying aspect, as is the axing of his foot poking outside the bottom of the container. The axe recalls *Strait-Jacket*, *Hush ... Hush, Sweet Charlotte*, *The Savage Intruder*, *Cry of the Banshee*, *Blood and Lace*, *The Baby*, and *Frightmare*. The blood from the decapitated foot is, along with the blood from the knife in Miss Pol-

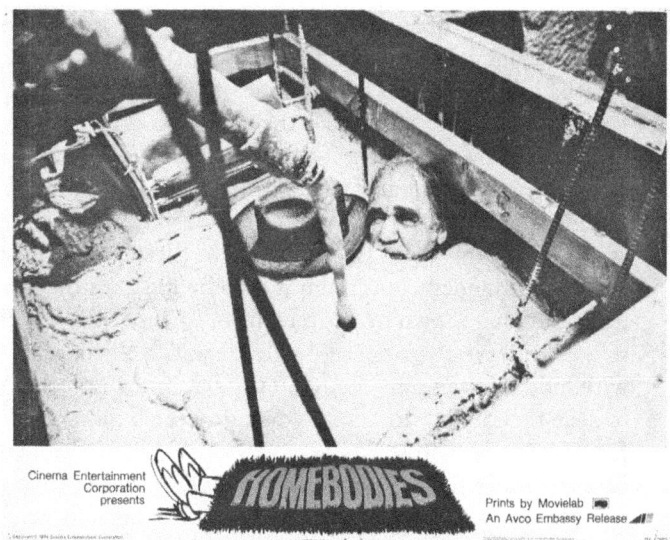

Mr. Crawford (Douglas Fowley) is buried alive in wet cement in this lobby card for *Homebodies* (1974).

lack's back, the only moment of blood shed in the film. The foot, discarded in a river the group passes as they return to the house, is disposed of as casually as Mattie had disposed of the knife. Crawford being killed without the security guards' awareness is an indication of how clever the group of killers are.

Mattie's fear of betrayal by Mrs. Loomis leads her to follow Mrs. Loomis to a church confessional, then stopping her from talking to a policeman, who is on the telephone. Mattie's confession that all the worksite accidents were caused by her, Mr. Blakely and Mr. Loomis is meant to silence Mrs. Loomis, since her husband is involved, but it only makes her more determined to confess. Yust gets a laugh from the next act of sabotage on the worksite when the wrecking ball falls onto a Port-a-Loo, and this foreshadows Mattie dropping the urn on Mrs. Loomis.

The dropping of the urn creates a secret bond between Mattie and Emily, although it's one of control since Mattie stole the urn from Emily and threatens Emily into keeping quiet. Mattie's aggression extends to letting Emily take the blame for her action, and it is this act that finally makes Emily leave her unit and the house, perhaps out of a greater fear of Mattie. This aggression turns to paranoia when Mattie kills Mr. Sandy when he attempts to speak to Emily about the death of Mrs. Loomis. Since Emily had called out to Mr. Loomis after the urn incident, her inquiry seems more than just regret, which is something only Mr. Sandy (and Mattie) seems to realize. Yust shows Mattie lifting the weapon to strike Mr. Sandy but not the impact.

Although Mrs. Loomis's "I don't want to leave you" may be considered a standard last wish of the dying, it is delivered more as an apology to Mr. Loomis, after her previous determination to leave. This makes it all the more touching when she dies. Yust adds a comical and sad touch when Emily flees from the house, pursued by Mattie, and her dress catches on something and rips as she runs. Mattie trying to push Emily off a high floor at the worksite lacks any comedy, and is notable for the one time the security guards come to someone's assistance. However, the turnaround is full of comedy when Emily, Mr. Loomis and Mr. Blakely pursue Mattie. This includes Mattie, sitting at a cafe table with three young women, smiling at their flight; and the chase on the lake. Mattie being pushed in front of traffic isn't funny, but the chase itself is pure farce, with foot-paddle boats used as the mode of transport, their slowness matching the age of the participants. Mattie allowing the others to catch her is a surprise (although it can be rationalized by her tiredness), and the horror of her drowning is enhanced by the use of an underwater camera. Yust adds a family of ducks swimming past the murder sight as a comic payoff.

When Emily, Mr. Loomis and Mr. Blakely arrive at the new condemned tenement, the Superintendent tells them it is to be replaced by "apartments for rich people." The determination shown by the tenants of 522 is echoed by the Superintendent's wife, who refuses to leave their house, so that Emily's response of "Maybe we can help" is laden with hidden meaning. Though it can be argued that the remaining tenants of 522 failed to keep their units, the act of blowing up the building (not to mention murdering Crawford) has to be admired. Like the Jewish ghetto dwellers in Warsaw who resisted the Nazi relocation to concentration camps, which the narrative deliberately reflects, the tenants display a dogged determination to pursue what is ultimately a hopeless cause.

Paula Trueman was primarily known as a stage actress, though she did take the occasional supporting film role, and was 73 at the time of filming. Frances Fuller had played the lead in *Elmer and Elsie* (1934), and was 66. Trueman infuses Mattie with an old-lady cuteness that conceals the hardness of a gangster. Her layered clothing suggests that Mattie has little money and cares little about clothes. This likeability fosters our sympathy for her as a grande dame, even when she murders Mr. Sandy and attempts to murder Emily. If Trueman's portrayal lacks the eccentricity of a Ruth Gordon performance, it is because the narrative fails to give her the requisite witticisms. Frances Fuller's deep voice and mechanical body language supplies the pathos for Emily's shut-in, even if she is not as likable as Mattie.

Release

September 1974,, with the tagline, "A Murder a Day Keeps the Landlord Away!"

Reviews

"Low-budget suspense has sleeper potential ... finely crafted ... meticulously portrayed by talented performers. To single out one would be unfair."—*Variety*, September 4, 1974.

"...[A]n odd little item indeed ... plotted out and done up with competence, so it does not look like the usual sleazy horror flick.... All the actors muster up a dignity that is touching under the circumstances."— Jay Cocks, *Time Magazine*, April 7, 1975.

"[T]opnotch production values, an inventive script which manages to combine grisly black humor, gripping suspense and genuine pathos, crisp direction and superb character performances all round.... Mankofsky's cinematography is wonderfully atmospheric."—Phil Hardy, *The Aurum Film Encyclopedia of Horror.*

"Classy and creative.... Tightly directed from a clever script, portraying its geriatric killers with wit and empathy but never shying away from shocking scenes of violence."—Cavett Binion, *All Movie Guide.*

Poster for *Homebodies* (1974).

Ruby (1977)
(aka *Blood Ruby*)

Dimension Pictures

CREDITS: *Director:* Curtis Harrington/Allan Smithee (television version); *Producer:* George Edwards; *Executive Producer:* Steve Krantz; *Screenplay:* George Edwards, Barry Schneider, from a story by Steve Krantz; *Photography:* William Mendenhall; *Music:* Don Ellis; *Editor:* Bill Magee; *Art Direction & Wardrobe:* Tom Rasmussen; *Set Decoration:* Charles D. Tomlinson; *Make-up & Hair:* Jeffrey B. Angell, Cid Urrutia; *Executive in Charge of Production:* Brice Mack; *Production Manager:* Penny L. Vaughn; *Sound:* Glen Glenn Sound; *Sound Effects:* Loraine Mitchell, Fred Brown. Color, 85 minutes. Filmed at Franklin Canyon and the Old Hollywood Studio Club.

SONGS: "Ruby" (Don Ellis, Don Dunn), sung by Don Dunn, "Love's So Easy" (Don Ellis, Sally Stevens), sung by Piper Laurie.

CAST: Piper Laurie (*Ruby Claire*); Stuart Whitman (*Vince Kemper*); Roger Davis (*Dr. Paul Keller*); Janit Baldwin (*Leslie Claire*); Sal Vecchio (*Nicky Rocco*); Paul Kent (*Louie*); Len Lesser (*Barney*); Crystin Sinclaire (*Lila June*); Jack Perkins (*Avery*); Edward Donno (*Jess*); Fred Kohler (*Jake Miller*); Rory Stevens (*Donny*); Raymond Kark (*1st Man*); Jan Burrell (*1st Woman*); Kip Gillespie (*Herbie*); Tamar Cooper (*Woman "A"*); Patricia Allison (*Pickup Man's Wife*); Stu Olson (*Man "A"*); Mary Robinson (*Maybelline, Sheriff's Wife*); Michael Alldredge (*Sheriff's Wife's Date*); *Uncredited:* Allison Hayes (*Attack of the 50 Foot Woman*) (archive footage); Roy Gordon (*Dr. Isaac Cushing*—*Attack of the 50 Foot Woman* archive footage).

VHS/DVD: DVD: Vci Video, released June 26, 2001.

Plot

In a Florida swamp in 1935, handsome mobster Nicky Rocco is gunned down by the other members of the Dade County gang. As he dies, Nicky swears revenge on all the members, including his pregnant girlfriend, singer and movie star Ruby Claire. Sixteen years later Ruby runs Ruby's Drive-In, near the same swamp, and employs all the gang members who have served prison time. At the roadhouse where she used to entertain she cares for her mute 16-year-old daughter Leslie (child of Nicky), and the blind and wheelchair-bound former gang leader Jake Miller. She is romantically involved with the drive-in's ticket salesman, Vince Kemper. When the former gang members begin dying, killed by an unseen force, Vince brings in parapsychologist Dr. Paul Keller, who believes that Nicky is responsible for the murders. Ruby believes this too, having had several sightings of Nicky herself, although these could be explained by her excessive alcohol consumption. Dr. Keller theorizes that Leslie has invoked Nicky's presence because of Ruby wanting to move her to an institution.

In the house's attic, Leslie speaks in Nicky's voice and tries to strangle Ruby. When Dr. Keller hypnotizes Leslie, it becomes clear that she has been possessed by Nicky, who performs feats of levitation and telekinesis. Ruby realizes that it is she that Nicky wants, since he falsely believed she had betrayed him to the mob. She goes to the swamp to surrender herself just as Vince is to be killed. Dr. Keller prevents Vince from rescuing Ruby, who is taken by Nicky and drowned.

Notes

This low-budget tale of a poltergeist serial killer and a woman in peril protagonist is a disappointing exercise in horror, redeemed somewhat by some imaginative grande guignol murders and violence. It is also noteworthy as the first leading role for Piper Laurie in 15 years. Although the still beautiful Laurie may not appear to be a traditional fading hag, her preoccupation with her past, alcoholism, and mental deterioration still classifies her as a grande dame. The film is also the sixth Grande Dame Guignol by director Curtis Harrington—but one he considers butchered, since it was re-edited for television by the executive producer to provide a newly shot and different ending. Since making *The Killing Kind* four years earlier, Harrington had not directed another film and had only worked in television. Producer George Edwards's previous film was also *The Killing Kind*. Executive producer Steve Krantz had previously made the comedies *Fritz the Cat* (1972), *Heavy Traffic* (1973), *The Nine Lives of Fritz the Cat* (1974), and *Cooley High* (1975).

The film begins with a prologue to establish the nature of the trauma that will preoccupy the grande dame. This kind of prologue is a device also used in *What Ever Happened to Baby Jane?*, *Strait-Jacket*, *Hush ... Hush, Sweet Charlotte*, *The Witches*, *What's the Matter with Helen?*, *The Killing Kind*, *Frightmare*, and *Persecution*. For the prologue Harrington employs hand-held camerawork, smoke, and soft-focus on Ruby to present her as young (and also to romanticize the past).

Harrington pans across the faces of the five shooters in the swamp to identify them for the later killings, Harrington uses expressionist camera angles for the violence, with Ruby's anguish transitioning to the beginning of her labor. The gunshots to Nicky's face are a deliberate attack on his beauty, since we are later told that he has cuckolded Ruby's lover, Jake Miller. Harrington doesn't show Jake at the murder, which is a pity, since it would have allowed us to compare his looks to Nicky. However, Jake's absence allows for Nicky to believe that Ruby, and not Jake, has betrayed him and therefore rationalizes his vengeance upon her.

The song "Love's So Easy," which plays over the opening credits, suggests Ruby's easiness (i.e., her promiscuity), which she will later admit to Dr. Keller. It is also used for irony, since Ruby's affair with Nicky is anything but easy. On the DVD audio commentary track Piper Laurie admits to recording her vocal as that of someone who could not sing well. The red titles in the credits presage a red motif in the film. Red can be found in Ruby's name, her ruby ring, her red hair and wardrobe, red cars at the drive-in, red curtains in her bedroom, the ruby red jacket of Dr. Keller, and the redness of blood.

Ruby uses a telescope to watch the drive-in, adding a touch of voyeurism to her character and also showing her controlling nature, which is evident from her decision to dispose of Leslie. While Nicky's murders establish him as the narrative's antagonist, Ruby's attitude toward Leslie makes her an enabler of the antagonism so that she shares the shifting antagonist/protagonist mix of other grande dames in Grande Dame Guignol. Harrington uses Ruby's telescopic point of view to see the drive-in in black and white, matching the black and white film being screened, *Attack of the 50 Foot Woman*. Ruby living at the roadhouse by the swamp, near the site of Nicky's murder, and her owning the drive-in only a short distance away, indicates her attachment to the past and how her life has deteriorated since the incident. Since she employs all the former gang members, it is apparent that she doesn't blame them for Nicky's murder, while her blaming Jake is indicated by the fact that she has blinded him.

The choice drive-in movie, wherein a woman seeks revenge upon a man, presents a violent female antagonist. *Ruby*'s screenplay draws attention to the Fifty-Foot Woman's sexuality with the following exchange (in which the woman speaker is desexualized by wearing hair-curlers at night and in public):

> MAN: It's about a 50-foot woman.
> WIFE: With a 25-foot bosom, I suppose.

Nicky's first killing (of Jess the projectionist) is introduced with a moaning noise. Harrington uses simple effects to show Nicky's attack, with objects falling, a film reel rolling across the floor, and film stock dropping onto Jess. Harrington cuts from the killing to *Attack of the 50 Foot Woman*, so that our view of Jess's corpse is delayed until Ruby discovers the body. The screening abruptly stopping indicates Jess's death and attracts Ruby. Harrington's use of a swinging overhead light to reveal Jess hanged by film loops recalls the cellar scene in *Psycho*.

When Vince comes to see Ruby at the roadhouse, he is shown entering her bedroom via reflection in her mirror. Ruby will be

Spanish poster for *Ruby* (1977).

seen repeatedly looking at herself in mirrors as a way to show her preoccupation with her appearance, culminating in her dressing for Nicky and asking him, "Have I lost my looks?" The mirrors that are later smashed in front of Dr. Keller suggest Nicky's reaction to Ruby's vanity. The interior of Ruby's house offers shadows for plenty of atmosphere, while the Flamingo Room features a giant portrait of Ruby in her youth, and a stage where she used to perform. Ruby is a drinker, like Jess, with her alcoholism used to rationalize her delusions of seeing Nicky's ghost. It also allows her to wallow in the pain of her past.

Jess (Edward Donno) is hanged in the projection room of Ruby's Drive-In in this lobby card for *Ruby* (1977).

The anger she feels toward Leslie comes from jealousy over who Nicky loves more (although Nicky never knew Leslie, since he was killed before she was born), and frustration over Leslie's mutism and seeming mental retardation. That Leslie is mute creates more irony since Ruby is a former singer, while Leslie said to have Nicky's eyes can be read that Nicky is watching, and allows for the idea that Leslie invokes Nicky's presence. The antagonism between mother and daughter, and older and younger woman, is a motif repeated from *Strait-Jacket, Lady in a Cage, Die! Die! My Darling, The Night Walker, I Saw What You Did, Games, Berserk!, Eye of the Cat, The Mad Room, Blood and Lace, The Baby, The Killing Kind,* and *Frightmare.*

That Jake is in a wheelchair recalls the wheelchairs of *What Ever Happened to Baby Jane?, Die! Die! My Darling, The Savage Intruder, What Ever Happened to Aunt Alice, Eye of the Cat,* and *Homebodies.* While his need for being in the chair is less obvious, apart from being blind, the shaking of his hands attests to the savagery of Ruby's attack when she blinded him. The character of Lila-June as a girl who is "easy" by being with a different man every night at the drive-in parallels Ruby herself. Lila-June's attempts to find happiness with whatever man she can recalls Ruby's "small-time" success, and what she sacrificed to become a gangster's moll. Nick's next attack, on Louie, is prefaced by Louie's attempted rape of Lila-June, for whom he has stolen a necklace of Ruby's.

Harrington intercuts this scene with that of Ruby's drunken delusion of a crowd and music in the Flamingo Room, which receives a payoff when Nick slaps Ruby in the same manner that he punches Louie. Again Harrington uses the moaning noise to suggest Nicky's presence. Since this attack is more violent, it would seem that Nicky is growing stronger, as he is able to throw Louie high enough to impale him on a tree. The blood that drips down Louie's leg is the film's first moment of gore (no blood was shown when Nicky was shot in the face during the prologue).

The scene of Ruby's nightmare in her darkened bedroom allows for the ghostly visage of the now-bloodied face of Nicky, which disappears once Ruby turns on a light. Nicky's appearance is preceded by Harrington's flash-cuts back to the prologue as Ruby calls out in her sleep. Leslie, as the innocent discovering Louie's body, fails to deliver the expected clichéd reaction (even though she is mute and can't scream). Harrington pans up to Louie, with the buzzing flies a reminder of the hot locale. A red-masked child at the drive-in provides a red herring, as does the Lila-June subplot.

Dr. Keller's appearance in the narrative drags it down to a pedestrian level, since his character being a parapsychologist (who Vince has met in prison) is a contrivance to begin with. Harrington substantiates Keller's claim that he can communicate with spirits by giving him a vision of Nicky at the swamp. What redeems Keller somewhat is his curiosity about Ruby and his questioning of her, which reveals more of her history. The screenplay provides a laugh when Leslie bites Keller upon meeting him, though whether this is Leslie being herself or Nicky is unknown. Leslie's psychic relationship with Nicky will soon be demonstrated by Ruby's vision of Nicky's bloody face replacing Leslie's, though again it comes when Ruby is drinking.

Harrington utilizes a soft-drink machine as a plot point, but delays the double-payoff it ultimately provides. This helps draw attention away from Keller's rationale that something has "upset the balance" (since Nicky has been angered by Ruby's intention toward Leslie). The double pay-off finds Barney stuffed *inside* the machine (though we don't know how Nicky got him in there), with the second payoff being his blood dispensed into a cup that a fat woman drinks.

The killing of Avery at the drive-in begins with Ruby wandering alone at night and hearing her name called by Nicky through the car speakers, accompanied by the moaning noise associated with the previous murders. Avery's death—impaled by a speaker stand—is the most spectacular of the killings, although Harrington uses it for shock rather than suspense, as we don't see how Avery got up there.

Ruby's fondling of a wrapped memento allows for a flashback to her blinding Jake, though Harrington delays the shock by first showing only blood stains on a satin bed sheet and bloodied scissors. The later revelation that Ruby keeps the eyes in a glass jar comes when Jake is stabbed, presumably killed by Nicky. Ruby's declaration of the proof of her love for Nicky, though clearly a horrific act, is the work of a deranged mind, since only the most perverse could consider it a romantic gesture. Even the notion that Jake wanted to get rid of Leslie after Nicky had been killed cannot rationalize such a vengeful and sadistic attack.

The scene between Ruby and Leslie in the attic, where Ruby keeps more mementos of her past, begins with Ruby wearing an orange and crème negligee. Leslie wears a short night dress, adding a sexual frisson to the dance, which turns into a strangling fight after Leslie invokes Nicky's voice. While Harrington adds the standard horror movie rainstorm, complete with thunder and lightning, the remarkable thing about the scene is Ruby's acceptance of Leslie as Nicky. Ruby hitting Leslie with a conveniently discarded hammer to stop her/him from strangling her is a disappointingly obvious thriller device, but the blow receives a payoff when Dr. Keller reports that Leslie is now in a "somnambulistic trance state." This comment is also rather comical, since Leslie's behavior indicates she had previously been close to such a state anyway.

Keller hypnotizing Leslie to free her from the somnambulism allows her to say "Happy Birthday" in her own voice (recalling a memory of being five), while the memory of an earlier trauma that frightens her is meant to be the memory of Nicky being shot. This trauma recollection seems to exist more for Ruby's reaction, since only she sees the stigmata-ish gunshot wounds of Nicky's face. Ruby's line, "Stop it, you're killing her," gets a laugh from its clichéd nature, as does Ruby's hyper-emotional reaction to Leslie's screaming.

Harrington intercuts between Ruby telling Keller of her past with Leslie's possessed gyrations in her bed. (Although the hysterical body arching that Leslie performs predates the same effect done for, and cut from, the original version of *The Exorcist* (1973), its impact is lessened by Leslie's previous gymnastic poses.) Ruby's backstory is an intriguing one. Born Ruby Kresky, she was fourteen and fat while in the chorus of *The Scandals*, then became a Wampas Baby star with a movie contract. Her film career "went up in smoke" when she was spotted at the scene of a gangland killing, and Jake pimped her to other gangsters so that he could take over their territory. Jake bought Ruby the roadhouse to compensate for her lost movie career. Nicky joined the gang and tried to take over leadership and ownership of Ruby when Jake was sent away for a year on a tax rap.

Ruby's tale of degradation allows for Nicky's presence when Jake's corpse enters the room in the wheelchair. We see the knife in Jake's chest before the chair makes a turn, and his fallen body allows us to see the empty eye sockets.

Nicky's attack on Vince at the drive-in is again introduced by the moaning noise and Vince having a vision of Nicky. The wind this time is of near-hurricane force, centralized in Vince's ticket-booth and then spreading to the outside when Vince flees (accompanied by a B-grade flash of lightning). The cords of the speaker stands move in the wind like snakes, with the speakers striking Vince, and then the glass windows and windshield of his car. Nicky appears on the film screen, while an overdone music score whips up the turmoil. Harrington cuts to Leslie's bed, where she knocks out Dr. Keller when he senses Nicky's active presence. After crashing his car, Vince appropriates someone else's, only to leap from it after a few shots of him driving (in what look like primitive studio inserts of a stationary car being buffeted by stagehands). The car inexplicably bursting into flames causes the wind and the noise to stop. Vince is the only one of the gang members to survive Nicky's attack, presumably because Ruby's self-sacrifice has saved him and exorcised Nicky from Leslie.

The climactic scene at the swamp features the title song and the illusion of Nicky being joined by Ruby. This romantic ending, in which Keller stops Vince with, "It's what she wants," is negated by the re-edit in which Nicky says "She's mine now," while Ruby is heard screaming. Continuity is compromised by the sudden lighting and the length of Ruby's hair, since Laurie had refused to participate in the additional

Ruby Claire (Piper Laurie) goes to meet her dead lover in this lobby card for *Ruby* (1977).

filming. Ruby, with her back to the camera, is dragged underwater and strangled by an inanimate prop skeleton. A freeze-frame dissolves to Laurie in close-up as the Ruby of the prologue. The punishment of the grande dame in the re-edited version is a more appropriate narrative conclusion for a horror film, as opposed to the more romantic one that Harrington originally filmed. Ruby's status as a romantic figure is lessened by the mixed messages she has given Nicky and Jake, declaring each to be her true love. And her antagonism towards Leslie, and the disfiguring of Jake requires some moral retribution after all. (Obviously, Harrington's original ending was more romantic and less horror-minded.)

Former Universal contract player Piper Laurie had not assayed a leading role in film since *The Hustler* (1961), for which she had been nominated for the Best Supporting Actress Academy Award. After having left the industry to be a housewife and mother, she returned for *Carrie* (1976), for which she received another Best Supporting Actress nomination. Laurie was age 44 when she made *Ruby*.

Ruby's wardrobe includes a feather boa, furs, and a turban, adding to her glamour and her presentation as a grande dame. She sports smeared make-up when drunk or crying. Laurie uses her deep masculine, voice to supply emotion to her performance, and any accusation of androgyny is silence by the low-cut red gown she wears to meet Nicky at the film's climax. Ruby's maintained beauty, in spite of her alcoholism, works against Vince's comment that she "used to be a knockout."

Harrington objectifies Ruby when she arrives at the drive-in to find Jess, by showing her shapely legs getting out of the car, then panning up her body to her face. He also gives Laurie a wonderful zoom-in close-up during her recollection of the shooting at the swamp when Ruby and Vince come to dispose of the bodies of Jess and Louie. Harrington gives Ruby a grande dame moment that recalls both *What Ever Happened to Baby Jane?* and *Die! Die My Darling!* when Ruby drunkenly reapplies lipstick (but here its shown in her car's rearview mirror).

Release

June 23, 1977, with the taglines, "A love affair with the supernatural," "Christened in BLOOD, raised in SIN, she's sweet sixteen, let the party begin!" and "PIPER LAURIE-Frightening in 'Carrie.' Now ... Terrifying as 'RUBY.'" The version released on videotape removes 6 minutes of footage wherein Dr. Keller's narration is wrapped up as he records the story on a tape recorder.

Reviews

"In the cookbook school of filmmaking, *Ruby* is strictly left-overs.... Performances are generally poor; technical credits fair; storyline confusing."—*Variety*, May 18, 1977.

"...[I]nteresting, though idiosyncratic film from one of the most inventive horror practitioners.... The plotting may be awkward at times, but the film is still a powerful example of Harrington's neo-gothic fascination with make believe private worlds and with ringing the changes on show business stereotypes.... Laurie turns in an expert performance."—Phil Hardy, *The Aurum Film Encyclopedia of Horror*.

"While never entirely leaving the film's quickie exploitation nature behind, Harrington crafts it with a series of often striking set pieces that lifts *Ruby* well above most *Exorcist* copycats.... Laurie gives another of her deep-throated, fierily passionate powerhouse performances that she does so well."—Richard Scheib, *The Science Fiction, Horror and Fantasy Film Review*.

"A few moments, comic and horrific, stand out in generally uneven supernatural thriller."—Leonard Maltin, *2009 Movie Guide*.

Windows (1980)

Mike Lobell Productions

CREDITS: *Director/Photography:* Gordon Willis; *Producer:* Mike Lobell; *Associate Producer/Unit Production Manager:* John Nicolella; *Screenplay:* Barry Siegel; *Music:* Ennio Morricone; *Editor:* Barry Malkin; *Production Designer:* Mel Bourne; *Art Direction:* Richard Fuhrman; *Set Decoration:* Les Bloom; *Wardrobe:* Clifford Capone; *Make-up:* Irving Buchman; *Hair:* Robert Grimaldi; *Sound:* Christopher Newman. Color, 96 minutes. Filmed in New York City.

CAST: Talia Shire (*Emily Hollander*); Joseph Cortese (*Bob Luffrono*); Elizabeth Ashley (*Andrea Glassen*); Kay Medford (*Ida Marx*); Russell Horton (*Steven Hollander*); Michael Lipton (*Dr. Marin*); Ron Ryan (*Detective Swid*); Linda Gillen (*Police Woman*); Rick Petrucelli (*Lawrence Obecny*); Michael Gorrin (*Sam Marx*); Tony Di Benedetto (*Nick*); Bryce Bond (*Voice-Over*); Ken Chapin (*Renting Agent*); Marty Greene (*Ira*); Bill Handy (*Desk Officer*); Robert Hodge (*Desk Sergeant*); Kyle Scott Jackson (*Detective*); Pat McNamara (*Doorman*); Gerry Vichi (*Ben*); Oliver (*Jennifer the Cat*).

VHS/DVD: Not available in either format.

Plot

Brooklyn Children's Museum worker Emily Hollander is assaulted by taxi driver Lawrence Obecny while returning from work one night to her Brooklyn apartment. Unbeknownst to Emily, the assault has been organized by lesbian poetess Andrea Glassen. Andrea has a crush on Emily and has paid Obecny to record the sounds of the assault. Detective Bob Luffrono investigates Emily's case and begins a romance with her. Andrea becomes aware of it as she uses a telescope to observe Emily in her new Bridge Tower Apartment. When Emily happens to flag the taxi that Obecyn drives, she recognizes him and manages to have him drive to the police station, where Bob arrests him. Obecyn tells the police that he performed the assault but will only give the name of the person who hired him if he is not charged.

When Andrea witnesses Bob and Emily embrace on a date, she telephones and threatens Bob, which makes him realize that Emily is being watched. After Emily's neighbor Sam Marx disappears while investigating noises in Emily's apartment, his body is found in the building's basement. When Andrea's psychiatrist, Dr. Marin, becomes concerned about her mental state, he arranges to have her committed to a hospital, but she kills him before he can take her there. Andrea observes Emily's reaction to finding her missing cat Jennifer in her refrigerator freezer, and invites Emily to come to her neighboring loft. After Emily leaves with Andrea, Bob arrives at her apartment. He waits for information about who has recently purchased a telescope and where a taxi would have taken Emily. In Andrea's loft, Emily finds the telescope, and Andrea admits her love for her. Frightened by Andrea, Emily spends the night with her, and Andrea confesses that it was she who hired Obecyn. When Andrea repeats the noises Emily and Obecyn had made on the tape, Emily slaps Andrea to stop her. Andrea regresses to the state of a frightened child, and Bob and the police come for her after making the connection between Andrea and the telescope.

Notes

This film is noteworthy as being the only movie to date to be directed by the celebrated director of photography Gordon Willis, *and* for the overwhelmingly negative reviews it received upon release. Although it only offers minimal grande guignol (one blood stain and one unseen knife murder), *Windows*' lesbian grande dame antagonist is so extraordinary that it had to be included in this collection. Visually striking, and making excellent use of silence and shadow, the film is fascinating. It builds to the climactic confrontation between antagonist and protagonist in an extended sequence that hovers between comedy and horror.

Known in the industry as "the Prince of Darkness" because of his shadowy lighting technique, Willis worked with directors Alan J. Pakula, Francis Ford Coppola and Woody Allen on such memorable films as *Klute* (1971), *The Godfather* (1972), *The Godfather, Part II* (1974), *All the President's Men* (1976), *Annie Hall* (1977), and *Manhattan* (1979). Later nominated for the Best Cinematography Academy Award for *Zelig* (1984) and *The Godfather, Part III* (1990), he would be nominated for the Worst Director Razzie Award for *Windows*. *Windows*' is also the only film to date made by producer Mike Lobell.

The opening image at the Brooklyn Children's Museum shows a multi-colored, neon-lit tunnel from which the protagonist emerges. Emily is presented as a mousey frump. Her failed wardrobe attempts to conceal her overweight body make the idea of her being someone desirable rather unbelievable. She begins the narrative by announcing that she is divorcing her co-worker Steven. While she asks him to help her move, we don't know anything else about their marriage or why it failed. Emily suffering from stuttering adds an additional layer of vulnerability (even disability) to her character. The stuttering earns a payoff during the assault, since she is made to speak, and at the climax when Andrea mimics her. Emily owning a cat brands her as something of a spinster. The cat being orange recalls the similarly-colored antagonist feline from *Eye of the Cat*, and the other cats in *Die! Die! My Darling!*, *The Night Walker*, *The Witches*, *Games*, *What's the Matter with Helen?*, *The Killing Kind*, and *Persecution*.

The assault implies rape, though later we learn that only a knife was inserted into her mouth as her cries were recorded on the tape machine Andrea will listen to. Emily's cries of fear can be interpreted as sexual excitement, which is the way Andrea chooses to hear it, denying the context from which they were obtained. Willis spares us the image of the knife in Emily's mouth, and also protects Emily from nudity when Obecyn wants to see her breasts. Andrea is first seen jogging on the way to Emily's apartment. Andrea's heavy breathing as she runs mirrors her heavy breathing upon hearing the tape, though at this point we don't know that she is responsible. However, in retrospect her visit is like a criminal returning to the scene of the crime to witness the aftermath, particularly the anguish of her victim.

Willis shoots Andrea's face half in shadow at Emily's apartment when the police are present, and her mirrored reflection when she exits symbolizes her duplicity. Andrea's claim that "He's never going to catch who did it" is a dismissal of Bob Luffruno's competence, a statement of confidence in her getting away with it, and a comment that shows surprising insensitivity towards Emily. It is little wonder that Emily asks Andrea to leave. Andrea is wrong about Luffruno, since he eventually catches her.

Emily sneaking her cat into a new apartment, in opposition to the lease agreement, shows the rebellion that will ultimately save her from Andrea. It also marks her as being selfish and therefore morally questionable. As a new tenant using her neighbor's telephone, her being watched is both a funny and sad indictment of the untrusting and invasive nature of modern society. The speech pathology exercises she plays are counterbalanced with the tape recording of the assault, and her failure to install drapes over her window allows herself to be spied upon by Andrea's telescope (a visual feature repeated from *Ruby*).

Andrea smokes as she listens to the tape, with the language suggesting oral sex. Her repeated use of Obecyn as a driver seems reckless, particularly when she has her own car. Obecyn's re-visit to Emily's apartment remains a mystery as to whether Andrea requested it, since she is also in attendance and violently crushes his arm and hand with Emily's door to get it closed. Although the situation allows Andrea to give Emily a hug after "rescuing" her, it's hard to believe that any amount of money she would have paid Obecyn is worth the potential damage she inflicts upon him.

We assume that as a result of Andrea's rescue, Emily has allowed her to move her furniture to the new apartment. This action also reveals to Andrea the location of Emily's new apartment, while the red roses Andrea leaves is a gesture that is clearly romantic. The roses being red prefigures the red pajamas Andrea will wear at the climax, and the red pinewood interior of her loft. Our view of Andrea's apartment, complete with paintings, antiques and statues, confirms her as a wealthy grande dame. Her wealth allows her to afford the apartment and the loft close to Emily's new apartment. Similarly, she wears stylish, expensive-looking clothes that suggest a sensual sexuality.

When Emily finds Luffruno waiting at her new apartment, she asks how he located her, to which he replies, "Trade secret." It seems odd that Emily would not tell the police

Andrea Glassen (Elizabeth Ashley), the grande dame of *Windows* (1980).

of her new address since she's involved in an ongoing investigation into finding her assailant. The fact that she doesn't implies that she has come to believe that the man will not be caught, or perhaps she is just careless. However, Luffruno's pursuit of her allows for his romantic, unprofessional demeanor.

Although it is assumed that Emily has been seeing Dr. Marin about her stuttering, or the reason behind her divorce, we aren't told why Andrea is forced to see him. Emily leaving his office and taking Obecyn's taxi that has delivered Andrea is an acceptable coincidence. Emily failing to get out once she realizes the driver is her attacker and him failing to recognize her, stretches one's suspension of disbelief to the breaking point—though the topper is her getting back into the taxi once she has alerted the police. Willis doesn't show us her conversation, and has Obecyn's attention distracted by his own memories just as the taxi conveniently gets to the station house.

Andrea's heavy breathing as she watches Emily alone in the apartment confirms her desire, even if it is an obvious choice to present Andrea as a controlling and exploitive pervert. Dr. Marin's analysis of Andrea differentiates between her fantasy and reality, implying that what she has told him may not be true. The imagination she needs as a poet is then paralleled with her personal life, where the distinction between fiction and truth is how Dr. Marin determines her mental health. Although Andrea doesn't reveal her feelings about Emily, her hesitancy to act could be due to instability or a realization that Emily will not return her feelings, with the subtext that homosexual love is even more fraught with trauma than heterosexual politics.

Andrea telephoning Emily when she sees her and Luffruno embrace allows him to take the call. This then gives Andrea the opportunity to say to Luffruno, "You son of a bitch, don't touch her," thereby revealing herself and her voyeurism (how else would she know what they were doing?). It is the embrace between Luffruno and Emily that presumably makes Andrea drink so much that she's hungover when next she sees Marin (and vomits during her session).

The deaths of Sam Marx and Jennifer the cat can be attributed to Andrea if we are to believe that Sam interrupted her in Emily's apartment when she went there to kill the cat. However, Ida Marx' illness reads as a red herring, since there is no seeming connection with Andrea and no narrative payoff. Emily looking in Ida's refrigerator for ice is matched with her looking in her own refrigerator and finding Jennifer; and it is the cat's death that finally makes Emily hang curtains, sheer though they may be. Jennifer falling out of the freezer even gets an unintentional laugh due to its frozen stiffness, but Andrea's observation of the horrific discovery allows her to invite Emily to her loft.

Dr. Marin makes the arrangements for Andrea to be hospitalized for "her own piece of mind," though he says it will only be temporary. However, this underestimating of Andrea leads him to his own death, thinking it safe to be in her apartment. Although Andrea's knife attack is not shown, we see her taking it out of a drawer, and she leaves a blood stain on the door as she exits to go to her loft and witness Emily's discovery of Jennifer. Emily's visit to Andrea's loft begins with steam from Andrea's shower, which will serve as a red herring. This, along with a matching red color scheme, establishes her location as hell. The only apparent furniture is a bed, and Willis delays Andrea's entrance so that Emily can discover the telescope, which Andrea has left still focused on Emily's apartment (where Luffruno waits).

Willis photographs Andrea's face in full shadow, presenting her as a vampire. The kittenish way she lounges on the bed makes her both sexual and animalistic waiting to pounce on her prey while giving the false impression of disinterest. Willis cuts between this long scene and Luffruno (as he waits to learn of Andrea's connection, with the plot point of the missing page from Emily's telephone directory expressed visually rather than verbally). After bolting the door, Andrea encourages Emily to look into the telescope; and Andrea dismantling, then breaking, the telescope demonstrates her violent impulses. Andrea's response to Emily's fleeing—"You could never love me"—is reverse psychology, so that Emily's "I could" reads as an obvious device to appease the antagonist. Andrea touching Emily's face, then, attaches a threat to what is otherwise an act of loving intimacy, with Andrea's repeated "I'm not going to hurt you" carrying the same ambiguity.

The passage of time that transpires, during which Andrea and Emily "spend the night together," is only indicated by Andrea's line, "I could have hurt you, but I didn't," which is a variation on "I'm not going to hurt you." Whether the women had sex is left ambiguous (though one's feeling is no), so the concept here of spending the night is simply being in the same room at the same time. Clearly Emily is there under duress, something which Andrea, in her delusion, prefers to ignore. Andrea's admission of ordering Obecyn's assault—"I told him exactly what to do"—receives a bizarre coda with the suggestion that Andrea's instruction involved both kindness and restraint. This kindness soon gives way to Andrea's perverted frustration when Andrea uses a switchblade to approximate Obecyn's treatment of Emily. Perhaps it's even the same knife that he used.

After pointing the knife at Emily's chin, Andrea goes over the line by putting it in Emily's mouth. Her demand that Emily show her what she showed Obecyn clearly demonstrates that Andrea is a deranged and obsessed maniac. While he occasionally cuts back to Luffruno in Emily's apartment, Willis's extended close-up of Andrea as she mimics Emily's cries on the tape are almost unbearable to watch, so that viewers seek relief in laughter from a situation whose con-

Poster for *Windows* (1980).

text does not warrant it. This reaction is also due to the performance of Ashley, with Andrea's use of the switchblade no doubt why the gay community was so offended by Andrea's character.

Thankfully, Emily stops Andrea with the slap, which also spares the audience any more of Ashley's impression. Andrea's slow reaction to the slap provides a moment of unknowingness, so that the child-like, regressive vulnerability of her repeated "Don't hurt me" somehow inspires audience sympathy for Andrea's underlying trauma. This empathy, however, does not extend to making Andrea a protagonist as well as an antagonist, as in other Grande Dame Guignol entries. Willis superimposes a red police car light over Ashley's close-up to indicate the arrival of the police—the final splash of red being turned against the person for whom that color had been a chromatic talisman.

Emily Hollander (Talia Shire) learns that Andrea Glassen (Elizabeth Ashley) is obsessed with her at the climax of *Windows* (1980).

Known more for playing roles on the stage than in films, the grand exotic and outgoing Elizabeth Ashley had played occasional leading roles in films like *The Third Day* (1965), *Paperback Hero* (1973), *Golden Needles* (1974), and *Rancho Deluxe* (1975). She had won the 1962 Best Supporting Actress Tony Award for *Take Her, She's Mine*, but was passed over for the leading roles in the film versions of her Broadway hits *Barefoot in the Park* and *Agnes of God*.

Ashley's mannered acting style gives Andrea a certain weirdness, which makes Andrea's madness believable. Andrea staring at Emily telegraphs her feelings, though Emily seems unaware of it, and Ashley's natural husky voice fits perfectly with Andrea's habit of smoking. When Ashley mimics Emily's taped cries, the extended close-up she receives is ripe for embarrassment, with Ashley's choices seemingly indulged by Willis. However, Ashley's braveness in allowing herself to be so *nearly* embarrassed by Andrea's excesses has to be acknowledged.

Release

January 8, 1980, with the tagline, "Somebody loves Emily ... too much." The UK cinema and video versions were cut by two minutes, editing the opening rape scene.

Reviews

"Willis makes the movie look good but fails to make it about things we come to care about.... Its lesbian villainy is such a shameful compilation of every two-bit cliché on the subject that we're distracted from the movie's possible thrills and scares by plain embarrassment for the filmmakers."—Roger Ebert, *Chicago Sun-Times*, January 18, 1980.

"A moody piece of urban female victimization which fails to synthesize the parallel psychological and thriller elements with which it grapples. Public will find tale too muted and far-fetched to swallow.... Ashley does well what she's asked, but what that is is another matter."—*Variety*, January 15, 1980.

"Bomb. Reactionary, offensive thriller whose only element of mystery is why it was ever filmed."—Leonard Maltin, *2009 Movie Guide*.

The Fan (1981)

Paramount Pictures

CREDITS: *Director:* Edward Bianchi; *Producer:* Robert Stigwood; *Executive Producer:* Kevin McCormick; *Associate Producers:* Bill Oakes, John Nicolella; *Screenplay:* Priscilla Chapman, John Hartwell, based on the novel by Bob Randall; *Photography:* Dick Bush; *Collaborating Director of Photography:* Leon Perer; *Music:* Pino Donaggio, conducted by Natale Massara; *Additional Show Songs:* Louis St. Louis; *Musical Staging and Choreography:* Arlene Phillips; *Editor:* Alan Heim; *Production Design:* Santo Loquasto; *Art Direction:* Paul Eads; *Set Decoration:* Leslie Bloom; *Production Manager:* Joan Bradshaw; *Wardrobe for Lauren Bacall:* Halston; *Associate Wardrobe Design:* Jeffrey Kurland, Tom McKinley; *Make-up:* Joseph Cuervo; *Ms. Bacall's Make-up:* Margaret Sunshine; *Hair:* Masarone; *Sound:* Arthur Bloom. Color, 94 minutes. Filmed in New York City.

SONGS: "Hearts, Not Diamonds" (Marvin Hamlisch, Tim Rice), sung by Lauren Bacall; "A Remarkable Woman" (Marvin Hamlisch, Tim Rice), sung by Lauren Bacall.

CAST: Lauren Bacall (*Sally Ross*); James Garner (*Jake Berman*); Maureen Stapleton (*Belle Goldman*); Hector Elizondo (*Police Inspector Raphael Andrews*); Michael Biehn (*Douglas Breen*); Anna Marie Horsford (*Emily Stolz*); Kurt Johnson (*David Branum*); Feiga Martinez (*Elsa*); Reed Jones (*Choreographer*); Kaiulani Lee (*Miriam*); Charles Blackwell (*John Velta*); Dwight Schultz (*Director*), Dana Delany (*Linda*); Terence Marinan (*Young Man in Bar*); Lesley Rogers (*Heidi*); Parker McCormick (*Hilda*); Robert Weil (*Pop*); Ed Crowley (*Caretaker*); Gail Benedict (*Assistant Choreographer*); D. David Lewis (*Pianist*); Griffin Dunne (*Production Assistant*); Themi Sapountzakis (*Markham*); Jean De Baer (*Stage Manager*); Liz Smith (*Herself*); Haru Aki, Robin Albert, Rene Ceballos, Clif de Raita, Edyie Fleming, Linda Haberman, Sergio Lopez-Cal, Jamie Patterson, Justin Ross, Stephanie Williams, Jim Wolfe (*the Dancers*); Thomas Saccio (*Prop Man*); Victoria Vanderkloot (*Pen Thief*); James Ogden (*Drummer*); Terri Duhaime (*Nurse*); Donna Mitchell (*Party Hostess*); Hector Osorio (*Donut Vendor*); Lionel Pina (*Record Store Customer*); Miriam Phillips (*Woman on Steps*); Jack R. Marks, George Peters (*Doormen*); Esther Benson, Eric Van Valkenburg, Ann Pearl Gary, Madeline Moroff, Leo Schaff (*Fans*); James Bryson, J, Nesbit Clark, Tim Elliott, Paul Hummel, Jacob Laufer (*Stagehands*).

VHS/DVD: DVD: Paramount, released September 24, 2002.

Plot

Record store clerk Douglas Breen is the greatest fan of Broadway star Sally Ross. Sally finishes the show *It's Called Tomorrow* and is next set to appear in her first musical, *Never Say Never*. Douglas writes fan letters to Sally and is offended when he only receives replies from Sally's secretary of seven years, Belle Goldman. When Belle finds an inappropriate letter from Douglas in which Douglas states that soon he and Sally will become lovers, she writes back to advise that she will no longer answer his correspondence. When Belle tells Sally of Douglas's letters, Sally suggests they just ignore him. Douglas takes a new letter to the dance studio where Sally is rehearsing and sees it given to Belle. After he buys a razor, Douglas follows Belle into the subway and slashes her face. Since Douglas has stopped supplying his address and last name in the letters, and Sally doesn't keep old fan mail, the police are unable to identify him, and neither can Belle.

Sally reads Douglas's next letter, in which he admits to assaulting Belle, and the police realize that she is in danger from someone they consider a "psychotic." Inspector Raphael Andrews assigns policewoman Emily Stolz to accompany Sally at all times. Sally is also emotionally vulnerable at this time because her ex-husband, Jake Berman, is now engaged to Heidi, the woman he had been cheating with during their marriage. Douglas stops working at the record store and spends his time at a cafe across the road from the dance studio, hoping to see Sally. When he spies Sally with dancer David Branum, Douglas follows Branum to the YMCA pool and attacks him with the razor. Douglas also kills Sally's maid, Elsa, and trashes Sally's apartment. Sally drugs Emily and flees the city, hiding out at her isolated beachside property. However, Jake follows her there, and they reconcile and spend some romantic time together.

Douglas goes to a gay bar and murders a patron to give the impression that he has committed suicide. This allows the police to locate his apartment, which contains evidence of his obsession with Sally. Sally goes back to the show, and on opening night Jake tells her that he has ended his engagement to Heidi so that he can try it again with Sally.

Poster for *The Fan* (1981).

Douglas appears at Sally's show and waits for her to be alone after everyone else has gone to the opening night party. He confronts her, after killing her maid, Hilda, and the theatre's doorman, Pop. A fight ensues, and Sally scars Douglas's face; in an embrace, she manages to cut his throat with his own razor.

Notes

An effective slasher pic with the grande dame as a celebrity Woman in Peril, this film is clearly a reaction to the murder of singer John Lennon, who was gunned down by a fan in 1980 in New York. Additionally, as with *Windows*, the film was lambasted in *The Celluloid Closet* documentary for its seeming homophobia (as portrayed by the despicable murder of a gay man). However, what makes the treatment intriguing is the appropriation of Lauren Bacall's own biography to inform the stalker, and the playing with assumptions of sexual preference. As a first-time horror movie director, Edward Bianchi uses cross-cutting, elegant pacing, and an Hitchcockian music score to achieve his grisly effects. He shows a pleasing restraint in blood-letting and isn't afraid to let the camera stay on an image longer than expected, generating some surprising results.

Producer Robert Stigwood had previously made the musicals *Tommy* (1975), *Saturday Night Fever* (1977), *Grease* (1978), and *Times Square* (1980). He had also produced the notorious bombs *Sgt. Peppers Lonely Hearts Club Band* (1978) and *Moment by Moment* (1978). Apart from working previously with Stigwood, associate producer John Nicolella had also made the Hitchcockian thriller *Last Embrace* (1979), which centers on a female antagonist.

The film opens with music resembling that of Bernard Herrmann's score for *Psycho*, and the sound of a typewriter. The camera reveals a framed photograph of the young and glamorous Lauren Bacall, then a pile of *Playbill*'s, with the one on top autographed by "Sally Ross" next to a closed switchblade knife. The switchblade recalls the one used in *Windows*. The weapon's proximity to Sally Ross artifacts links her to violence and prefigures the slasher attacks in the film. Douglas's voiceover lets us hear the content of his letters, although the first letter we hear is not his first letter to Sally. We can tell this by the content, and because his first letter will be used at the end of the film. That he identifies himself as "your greatest fan" is evidence of his hyperbole, and his "I want nothing from you" we will learn to be untrue.

Bianchi pans the camera in extreme close-up over items on Douglas's table, and a toy doll with a vibrating skull head seems especially creepy. A knife on a plate of food continues the blade motif, as do the keys of the typewriter slashing like knives, and the movement of the typewriter's head towards the camera. The extreme close-up of Douglas's eyes presents him as a grotesque, though his hooded eyelids match Sally's, and his full lips are like those of a woman. Bianchi will use the question of Douglas's sexuality to add a layer of irony and horror to the treatment. This is aided by the look of Michael Biehn, which can be both prettiness and the self-conscious twisted face of adolescence. Bianchi's casting of Bacall as the object of desire mixes homosexual and heterosexual appeal, with the former confirmed when a picture of her is featured at the gay bar.

Our introduction to Sally is from her point of view as she exits the theatre and is confronted by fans, who Bianchi presents as just as grotesque and demanding as Douglas. One fan's pen runs out, so Sally produces her own, only to have it stolen. This action ends in a delicious payoff when Douglas steals the pen from the first pen thief—an example of the perverse law of the jungle in fandom. Bianchi continues this theme of Sally as an object by placing her alone in a lift with her image multiplied around her. When she looks at her reflection we can see that she is as lonely as Douglas; the intercutting between them both alone in their apartments, both parallels and connects them. The shadows in their domiciles are evidence of both of them needing to conceal—he his obsession and she her age.

What makes Sally different from most grande dames in Grande Dame Guignol is that she has no apparent preoccupation with the past—apart from her failed marriage and maintained beauty. Bianchi withholds the sight of Sally's mementoes in her apartment for when Douglas breaks in and smashes a self-portrait and framed photographs of her with other celebrities. However, the implicit preoccupation is that of an aging star, since the images Douglas treasures are those of the younger Sally. Sally's age comes to the fore by the fact of Jake having cheated and then left her for a younger woman, with James Garner's casting suggesting that Jake is younger than Sally (although Garner is only four years younger than Bacall). Finally, Sally's age is highlighted by the lack of an alternative and new romantic interest, and because her main companion is her employee, Belle, another older and sexless woman.

Sally's maintained romantic interest in Jake is represented by the photograph of them she keeps in her bedroom, though her frustration about the limitations of their present relationship is expressed in the following exchange:

> JAKE: If you had called I would have come over.
> SALLY: Sure you would have. You'd comfort me. Hold me. Make me laugh. Make me think I could take it. Make me think I could take anything. Then you'd look at your watch and go meet Heidi for dinner. That's not a relationship. That's the Red Cross.

The knife that Douglas uses at the record store to open a shipment box prefigures his use of other knives, while his disinterest in Linda as a romantic interest his own age both questions his heterosexuality and confirms his love for Sally. The visit from his sister, Miriam, allows us to learn how he has rejected his family (something a gay man might do because his activities are not accepted). Since Miriam arrives while he is having an imaginary dinner with Sally, Miriam's urging him to "face the world" and stop pretending as he did when he was a child establishes Douglas's history of delusion. Bianchi pays off Miriam's concern for Douglas by having him slam the door in her face, with his delusion blocking out her loud banging on the door.

Douglas Breen (Michael Bien) and his wall of obsession feature in this Mexican lobby card scene from *The Fan* (1981).

Douglas spying on Sally with binoculars establishes that he knows where she lives. Bianchi cuts between Sally rehearsing and Douglas's letter-writing to continue their connection, climaxing in the slow pan to what is revealed to be Douglas's shower curtain. The curtain gives an obvious nod to the shower scene in *Psycho*, with Douglas sexualized (as he is naked). The foam of his shampoo matches his "pornographic" voice-over talk of how he and Sally will become lovers.

Sally ignores Belle's warning about Douglas's letters, demonstrating Sally's "star" attitude and self-absorption, as well as her disinterest in her fans and a disbelief in the importance Belle places on the issue. By failing to convince Sally of her concerns, and advising Douglas that she will no longer forward his letters to her (without Sally's permission), Belle sets herself up for punishment.

Douglas's growing unbalance is perfectly demonstrated in his own rehearsal—an appropriation of the "You Talkin' to Me?" scene from *Taxi Driver*—wherein he practices confronting his boss about Linda. His subsequent attempt is destroyed when the boss criticizes Douglas before asking what it is Douglas wants to tell him; and Douglas' impotence is portrayed by a long shot of him sitting in Central Park among a sea of empty chairs. This metaphorical disarming of Douglas will be repeated in the climactic confrontation with Sally when he cannot bring himself to use the knife on her.

Belle's hard-line stance ironically forces Douglas to try to get to Sally directly, and Bianchi uses Douglas's entry to the dance studio to deliver a letter to deliciously position him and Belle in the elevator together. Each is unaware of the other's identity, and the situation allows Douglas to identify Belle when he witnesses his letter being passed to her. Bianchi shows Douglas looking at the window display in a knife shop, without needing to show him making a purchase, and Douglas's threat is enhanced by more cross-cutting.

Sally argues with Belle over the Douglas situation, as she has now read the new letter, while Douglas walks around the block of Sally's apartment. The argument provides a telling exchange between the women, and shows Maureen Stapleton's ability to shift from anger to comedy:

> BELLE: Did it ever occur to you that my job isn't exactly heaven?
> SALLY: Neither is mine. Whoever told you that life is meant to be uninterrupted bliss?
> BELLE (Angrily): What is this Bliss shit? I'm a secret service escort, a butler, nurse, letter-writing machine, floor mop. I got a phone growing out of one ear and a big fake smile on my face—eight, ten, twelve hours a day. [The telephone rings and Belle answers it in a sweet voice] Hello?

That Sally cannot see Douglas's threat—"Ignore him. He's harmless"—is an error in judgment which leads to Belle becoming Douglas's first victim. Presumably this is the first time Sally has had a fan behave inappropriately, and the first for Belle, so their poor choice in not contacting the police sooner can be rationalized. However, by not reacting appropriately they enable Douglas's rage to build and therefore become his antagonists. Since Sally is his object of desire and Belle's employer, that makes her the greater antagonist, and his love quickly turns sour. As in other Grande Dame Guignol films, the grande dame is both protagonist *and* antagonist.

Sally running into Jake and Heidi at a party, and Heidi refusing to shake Sally's offered hand, adds to Sally's humiliation, though a social snub will pale next to what happens to Belle. Bianchi films Belle as a victim even before she is attacked by showing her feet as she walks, then moving up to her face for a subjective point of view of

Douglas following her. Douglas calling her name, and his not wearing any disguise, would seem to be unwise, though Belle will not be able to identify her attacker to the police. The blood on her face resulting from the razor cut is the film's first gore, and we are not spared Belle's suffering.

Douglas's letter that Sally reads provides irony in that he has finally got her attention, and also because he admits to attacking Belle (although he cannot be traced). That the police consider him a psychotic is another reference to *Psycho*, and his attack on David in the pool, with its attendant use of water, harkens back to *Psycho*'s shower scene. Douglas's stalking David and following him into the YMCA offers a gay subtext, with the knife attack a phallic metaphor and the blood-letting a metaphorical rape. The blood in the water is another potent image, with Bianchi employing Hitchockian suspense for the attack, since we know Douglas has a knife and has followed David.

Douglas stalking Sally at the dance studio by waiting at the cafe across the street implies that he has abandoned his job, is independently wealthy, or perhaps has been fired. Sally walking out on rehearsal when criticized is presumably a result of her stress, although it could also be the ego of a star. Although by the time of the preview Sally has fled the city, her withdrawal could be seen as more star acting-out. Douglas's attack on Elsa is troubling, since he has gained access by a means that is not shown. Douglas appears to slash Elsa across her breasts, which, like his attacking Belle's face, is a man's revenge upon the body parts women prize.

The issue of Douglas not wearing gloves and being unafraid of incriminating fingerprints can be accepted if he has no existing police record, and Bianchi holds the camera on Douglas in the hallway longer than expected, before he finds Sally's painting. Douglas's rage is calibrated via the terms of endearment of his letters, going from "Dear Miss Ross" to "Dear Sally" to "Darling" to "Dear Bitch." The fact of Douglas phoning her at home, knowing the number (which presumably is unlisted), can also be accepted if his break-in helped him find it.

Sally's house on the beach is presented by Bianchi as a horror house, sitting isolated on a hill while a thunder and lightning storm rages. The ranger who checks on the house is used as a red herring, although her closing shades and turning off the house lights seems a lame redundancy. The gay bar where Douglas waits offers more gay subtext, with the song "How Sweet It Is (to Be Loved by You)" used for irony, considering his agenda. The silent cruising objectifies the "Young Man

Sally Ross (Lauren Bacall) watches her secretary, Belle Goldman (Maureen Stapleon), open a fan letter in this Mexican lobby card for *The Fan* (1981).

in Bar" victim, unnamed and therefore disposable. The off-screen fellatio of Douglas only gives Douglas a better attack position, since presumably the Young Man's throat is cut. Douglas taking pleasure from the murder can also be interpreted as pleasure at being serviced. It is the burning of the Young Man's body that reads as overkill by the gay community, although it works as a plot point for Douglas's faked suicide. However, the idea that Douglas would suicide seems unbelievable to the audience, even if the police accept it.

Belle returns to Sally without scars, and David will survive his attack, though Elsa is not so lucky. Bianchi cross-cuts between Sally's opening night performance and Douglas getting ready to attend. The fact that he is late during Sally's "Hearts, Not Diamonds" number creates the expectation that she will notice him, but she does not. The fact that Douglas is late also tells us that he has more on his mind that just seeing Sally, and that her performance has become irrelevant, in spite of the hardy applause he provides at the end of her song. If only Bacall's rendition deserved it—her vocalizing is frankly terrible, matched by the awful choreography of the production. Douglas leaving during the applause makes us wonder momentarily where he is going, though it isn't a surprise when both Hilda and Pop are dispensed with. Pop's murder comes with a nice close-up of blood on the knife.

The blood on his tuxedo shirt reveals Douglas' identity to Sally without resorting to words, and if the resultant chase is disappointing, her hitting him and leaving a scar on his face redeems it. So does his making Sally crawl on the floor while he whips her, humiliations which match those dished out to Joan Fontaine in *The Witches*, and Miriam Hopkins in *The Savage Intruder*. Douglas pulling Sally's hair is the final insult, a caveman attack on perhaps Bacall's greatest feature. Douglas's seductive advance for a kiss gets a laugh from Sally's defiant "You're pathetic." Here Bacall shows you Sally's bravado and fear, even if her speech becomes didactic in the following exchange:

> DOUGLAS: I gave you everything.
> SALLY: Took. You took like the animal you are. [She sees his knife.] C'mon Douglas, here's your chance to be one of those hoodlums that kill their victims for nothing. The thief who murders little old ladies for a quarter. Goddamn terrorist who slaughters innocent people. That's what you really are. Well, I've had it. It's not just me. We're all sick of this reign of terror. I will not be a victim.

When Douglas regresses to a childlike state with "I love you, please love me," he becomes vulnerable, and this makes Sally being able to stab him with his own knife unsurprising. However, Sally presumably seating the dead Douglas in the audience is an amusing touch, returning him to where he belongs, since killing her would have given him his own twisted form of infamy. Sally leaving the theatre with her face in shadow, as Douglas's first letter is heard in voice-over, suggests that she is responsible for creating the monster. While we know that Sally would not have read this inaugural fan letter, it reminds us of the initially innocent intention of the writer.

Lauren Bacall had last played a leading role in *The Shootist* (1976), and had only assayed two leading roles in the 1960s in the grande guignol drama *Shock Treatment* (1964) and *Harper* (1966). She lived in the Dakota apartment building when John Lennon was murdered, adding a resonance to the parallel *The Fan* makes with Lennon's stalking. (In its theatrical release, the film's distributors cannily evoked the Lennon case by noting in the credits that the movie was based on a 1977 novel, and had finished production before the murder.) Sally doing her first musical mirrors Bacall doing the Broadway musical *Applause* in 1970 (for which she won the Best Actress Tony Award), and we even see that Sally has autographed one portrait to Douglas with "Here's looking at me." This play on the famous "Here's looking at you" line from *Casablanca* is a deliberate reference to the fact that Humphrey Bogart, as the speaker of the line, was married to Bacall.

Although still beautiful, wonderfully attired by costumer Halston, and occasionally photographed in soft-focus, Bacall isn't spared by Bianchi's lighting, which sometimes reveals her age lines. Although Sally is meant to be 49, Bacalls's real age of 57 has her playing younger than herself, and this adds to the disparity between her and Biehn, who is 25. The antagonism between an older and younger person recalls *Strait-Jacket, Lady in a Cage, Die! Die! My Darling, The Night Walker, I Saw What You Did, Games, Berserk!, Eye of the Cat, The Mad Room, Blood and Lace, The Baby, The Killing Kind, Frightmare*, and *Ruby*.

Bianchi often uses Bacall's questioning or disturbed face to present her as an ugly gargoyle, such as when she reads Douglas's letter and takes his telephone call. Bacall's lined eyes are exposed in a merciless extreme close-up at the climax, and Sally's smoking and drinking are known to be counter-productive habits to maintaining one's beauty. Bacall's casting also adds an androgyny to Sally, with her deep voice and thin-lipped, masculine directness. This androgyny is further reflected in the costumes Sally wears in *Never Say Never*, which are men's suits, so that she looks like a drag queen. While her sheer white nightgown may restore some femininity, the shimmery black pant suit she wears in *Hearts, not Diamonds*, and the gold gown she wears at the climax, is more drag.

Release

May 15, 1981, with the taglines, "The final act is murder," and "This is the story of a great star and a fan who went too far."

Reviews

"Bacall transforms an essentially creaky lady-in-distress into something approaching a cinematic event.... Binachi's fondness for close-ups displays an infuriating lack of confidence in himself and the audience."—Vincent Canby, *The New York Times*, May 22, 1981.

"...[A] pretty fair thriller.... Bacall makes the film work with a solid performance."—*Variety*, May 15, 1981.

"...[N]ot exactly high art, it is a well-made, quite intelligent piece of popular entertainment, containing a sensibly moral examination of how obsession with a celebrity can lead to mayhem.... Bacall is brave, flashy and riveting.... Biehn combines a sort of mad innocence with creepiness very effectively."—Richard Schickel, *Time Magazine*, June 22, 1981.

"A so-so slasher film.... Bacall is rather awful—she seems to be only barely resisting the desire to give an arch reading.... Bianchi is a sometimes stylish director with an eye for cold pictorial glitter. Best of all is Pino Donaggio's stunning score."—Richard Scheib, *The Science Fiction, Horror and Fantasy Film Review*.

The Hunger (1983)

MGM/A Richard Shepherd Company Production

CREDITS: *Director:* Tony Scott; *Producer:* Richard A. Shepherd; *Screenplay:* Ivan Davis, Michael Thomas, based on a novel by Whitley Strieber; *Photography:* Stephen Goldblatt; *Photography, New York:* Tom Mangravite; *Additional Photography:* Hugh Johnson; *Music:* Michel Rubini, Denny Jaeger; *Editor:* Pamela Power; *Production Design:* Brian Morris; *Art Direction:* Clinton Cavers; *Set Decoration:* Ann Mollo; *Wardrobe:* Milena Canonero: *Make-up Illusions:* Dick Smith, Carl Fullerton; *Special Make-up:* Antony Clavet; *Monkey Effects:* Dave Allen, Roger Dicken; *Sound:* Clive Winter; *Executive in Charge of Production:* Terence A. Clegg. Color, 97 minutes. Filmed in London at Shepperton Studios, and in New York City.

SONG: "Bella Lugosi Is Dead" (Daniel Ash, Kevin Haskins, David J, David Lawson, Peter Murphy), performed by Bauhaus; "Trio in E Flat, Opus 10 (Franz Schubert); "Le Gibet" (Maurice Ravel); Duetto "Viens Mallika.... Dôme épais le jasmin," from the Opera *Lakme* (Leo Delibes).

CAST: Catherine Deneuve (*Miriam Blaylock*); David Bowie (*John Blaylock*); Susan Sarandon (*Dr. Sarah Roberts*); Cliff De Young (*Dr. Tom Haver*); Dan Hedaya (*Lt. Allegrezza*); Beth Ehlers (*Alice Cavender*); Rufus Collins (*Charlie Humphries*); Suzanne Bertish (*Phyllis*); James Aubrey (*Ron, the Prostitute*); Ann Magnuson (*Young Woman from Disco*); John Stephen Hill (*Young Man from Disco*); Shane Rimmer (*Arthur Jelinek*); Bauhaus (*Disco Group*); Douglas Lambert (*TV Host*); Bessie Love (*Lillybelle*); John Pankow (*1st Phone Booth Youth*); Willem Dafoe (*2nd Phone Booth Youth*); Sophie Ward (*Girl in London House*); Philip Sayer (*Boy in London House*); Lise Hilboldt (*Waiting Room Nurse*); Michael Howe (*1st Intern*); Edward Wiley (*2nd Intern*); Richard Robles (*Skater*); George Camiller (*Eumenes*); Oke Wambu (*Egyptian Slave*); Kent Miller, Fred Yockers, Susan Hunter, James Wassenich, Allan Richards, Hilary Six, Carole-Ann Scott (*Cadavers*).

VHS/DVD: DVD: Warner Home Video, released October 5, 2004.

Plot

In a New York nightclub, Miriam and John Blaylock pick up another couple and take them to their sumptuous townhouse. A session of sex turns to murder as both Blaylocks use Egyptian ankh pendants which conceal knives to slash the throats of the couple and drink their blood. Unable to sleep the morning after, John recalls the offer Miriam, a 4,000-year-old Egyptian vampire, had made him 300 years previously for a life of immortality. A bite from her allows some of her blood to enter a human being, and in exchange for love, she teaches the lover how to "feed" to satisfy his hunger. Miriam recognizes John's insomnia and aging features as a sign that his time with her is dwindling, as the time of her previous lovers had been just as finite. Seeing Dr. Sarah Roberts being interviewed on television about her book *Sleep and Longevity*, and intrigued by her claims about reversing the aging process, Miriam buys the book at a shop where Sarah is signing copies.

Miriam goes to the Park West Research Clinic where Sarah works, but intuits that they will not be able to help John. John himself goes to the clinic, but Sarah thinks him a "nut" and leaves him to wait in the patients' lounge. As John waits, the aging process accelerates, and he leaves after two hours. Sarah sees him leaving and is shocked by his progressively aged appearance, but he refuses to consult with her. Driven by his bloodlust, John had tried to attack a man in the clinic's bathroom but had failed. He attacks a skater in a darkened street, but the skater escapes. However, John succeeds with Alice, although her blood does nothing to help him.

Miriam finds a Polaroid that had been taken by Alice's camera during her struggle with John, and realizes that he has killed the child. During an argument, John falls down a flight of stairs, his legs no longer able to support his own weight. Miriam carries John's withering body up to the attic and puts him in a casket—next to the caskets containing her eight earlier lovers.

When Sarah comes to Miriam's townhouse looking for John, Miriam sees in the doctor a replacement for John in her life. However, with her intuition warning of the approach of Lieutenant Allegrezza, Miriam postpones her seduction. Sarah has left her telephone number with Miriam, which Miriam uses to protect her from being killed in traffic by an oncoming truck. Miriam uses her psychic powers to entrance Sarah, drawing her back to the townhouse. Miriam gives Sarah sherry, which Sarah spills on her t-shirt. Sarah confronts Miriam about making a pass at her, and they make love, with Miriam biting Sarah and infecting her with her blood.

At dinner with her boyfriend Tom, Sarah wears an ankh that Miriam has given her, and is preoccupied with women swimming in a pool that is attached to the restaurant. At the clinic Sarah has her blood analyzed and learns that she has been infected with alien blood, and that the two strains in her are fighting for dominance. Sarah confronts Miriam about what happened between them and Miriam explains what she has done. Her lifestyle dictates that she sleep six in twenty-four hours, and feed one day out of seven. They fight, and Sarah leaves, but Miriam predicts that she will be back to learn how to feed her hunger. Sarah returns, and Miriam picks up Ron, a male street prostitute, who Miriam kills for Sarah.

Tom arrives at the townhouse looking for Sarah, and Miriam takes him to her. Miriam and Sarah kiss, but Sarah attempts suicide by cutting her own throat with Miriam's ankh as they kiss. Sarah's blood pours into Miriam's throat, and then Sarah collapses. Miriam is horrified at what Sarah has done, but she dutifully carries Sarah's limp body into the attic to place among her other lovers. This time, however, she finds the cadavers out of their coffins, waiting for her. They surround her, and as she tries to flee, she falls from the balcony. When she lands, she ages as her lovers crumble into dust. Lt. Allegrezza returns to question Miriam, only to find that the townhouse is now mysteriously empty and up for sale. All of the luxurious furnishings in the home are gone and the money funneled to the sleep clinic where Sarah, presumably missing, used to work. Sarah now lives in a high-rise luxury apartment, while Miriam is imprisoned in a coffin, just as her own former lovers had been. As Sarah kisses her new lover, we hear Miriam screaming for her release.

Notes

While Tony Scott's direction is stylish but shallow, the treatment featuring a female vampire as a grande dame is redolent with grande guignol horror. Scott indulges in postmodern technique—quick cutting, slow motion, displaced dialogue, extreme close-ups, billowing curtains, and classical music—to swamp the production in arty touches. Thankfully, the grande dame's trauma is touchingly performed by Catherine Deneuve, even if we have to wait until the climax to see her revealed as a hag. While the screenplay has some clunkiness, Scott succeeds in presenting horror in parallel stories. These stories are the fate of some research monkeys and the real-life medical condition of progeria, a blood disease in children which causes premature aging. Additionally, like *Eye of the Cat* and *Ruby*, the narrative was altered to compromise the original intention, which lessens the film's effectiveness.

MGM had offered the directing job to Alan Parker, who had made a success of their *Fame* (1980), but he declined. Parker, ironically, had come from the same film-school background as Scott, who is the brother of Ridley Scott. *The Hunger* is Tony Scott's feature film debut as a director, after having made music videos, television commercials, and two short films. Producer Richard Shepherd had previously made such high-profile titles as *The Hanging Tree* (1959), *The Fugitive Kind* (1960), and *Breakfast at Tiffany's* (1961).

During the opening credits of *The Hunger* Peter Murphy sings "Bela Lugosi Is Dead," performing for the camera as the point of view of Miriam and John in a smoky nightclub. In his DVD audio commentary, Scott says had wanted to use Murphy for his vampirish look, prefiguring the agenda of Miriam and John. Scott will continue to intercut between the singer and the killing of a monkey at Sarah's research laboratory. Wearing sunglasses at night in the club creates the false impression that the vampires are traditional vampires (we later learn that neither of them are scared of daylight). The style of this sequence demonstrates Scott's emphasis on post-modern technique, with quick jump cuts, freeze frames, slow motion, extreme close-ups, and portentous music. The art direction for the townhouse also presents a stylized and theatrical canvas, where the doomed Young Woman dances against a white-lit screen. That all four of them smoke is a sign of their supposed sophistication, though the heterosexual pairing off is disappointingly conventional. Miriam smoking is juxtaposed with Sarah smoking in her laboratory, alluding to their later connection via Miriam's psychic powers.

Both the Young Woman and the Young Man throw their heads back in pleasure simultaneously, which exposes their throats to attack. Scott shows the blood from slashed skin, with the knives recalling those used in *Lady in a Cage, Die! Die! My Darling!, The Night Walker, I Saw What You Did, The Witches, Berserk!, The Savage Intruder, What's The Matter With Helen?, Night Watch, Knife for the Ladies, Homebodies, Windows*, and *The Fan*. The murderous monkey is used to parallel the vampires in both its sexuality and violence, since the monkey unpredictably attacks its female companion. Scott also juxtaposes the blood of the human victims with the half-eaten carcass of the monkey victim, since the male monkey had killed her and then eaten her flesh in its own "hunger." Bloody water and drops of blood begin a blood motif seen throughout the film, along with the use of the color red. Red permeates the picture, including the hair of the Young Woman, the interiors of the townhouse, the wood of Alice's violin, the interior of the townhouse elevator, Sarah's hair, light in the attic, and the Roman sky at the end.

"Schubert's Trio in E Flat" introduces the love scene between Miriam and John, removing the association sex has had with violence during the murder of the couple. The couple's leather clothes are burned in a furnace, presumably along with their bodies, and the music continues during John's recollection of being with Miriam in an earlier century. While Scott initially presents the memory in long shot, so that we can't identify Miriam and John, he will provide subsequent close-ups to confirm their identities. Miriam watching Sarah being interviewed on television (the extreme close-up of the observer mirroring the extreme close-up of the interviewee) piques Miriam's interest in the doctor's research—and person.

Miriam can be defined as a grande dame because of her designer clothes, her accent (although the Egyptian Miriam is played by a Frenchwoman), her grand townhouse furnishings and antiques, and her piano playing. Her smoking could also be seen as a sign of her grandness, except that Sarah and John—and even the doctors at the Clinic—all smoke as well. Miriam's preoccupation with the past is aligned to the curse of the vampire, who is doomed to live forever but yearns for a mate to share it with. The ankh pendant she kills with stands ironically as a symbol of everlasting life. Her repeating trauma arises from the tragic fact that none of her chosen lovers survive, and their corpses become mere mementoes of her past stored in her attic. Miriam also matches other grande dames in Grande Dame Guignol by being both antagonist and protagonist. Even Miriam's romantic stance is hypocritical, since she is aware of the limited time her lovers have, yet still promises them eternal life. This makes the climactic revenge upon her, and her own final entombment, a deserved and horrific retribution.

French movie card for *The Hunger* (1983).

The trio of Miriam on piano, John on cello, and neighbor Alice on violin seem to indulge John's interest as a period musician. Scott uses a black and white video image to show Alice at the townhouse's intercom (just as he will later show Sarah and Tom), and drained color for video footage of the dying monkey. The scene in the bookstore where Miriam gets Sarah's attention by psychic means receives a payoff in the character of Lillybelle, a grande dame with a wire hat and yellow teeth. Lillybelle's decay is contrasted with the beauty of Sarah and Miriam. John watching cartoons after he reads Sarah's book suggests his immaturity, which would have initially attracted Miriam but also mocks his premature aging.

Miriam entering the research clinic is photographed in shadow, like the horror threat she is. When John enters the clinic he appears as a blurred image in Sarah's compact mirror—another horror movie threat. However, this is misleading in relation to the conventional vampire whose reflection cannot be seen in a mirror, since both vampires look at themselves in mirrors at one time or another.

The sequence in which John visibly ages years in just two hours in the patients' lounge is paralleled with the far more gruesome imagery of a dead monkey decomposing on video. The rotting monkey prefigures the destructive release of Miriam's lovers at the climax. Sarah's indifference and callousness to John's request to see her is rationalized by her claim that he is another "nut" (she demonstrates little empathy for a 30-year-old man who shows her liver spots). This indifference prefigures her murder of Tom, her lover, so that she can pursue a life with Miriam. Sarah's fear of telling John that she will not see him, and choosing to let him wait until he leaves out of frustration, is also an indication of moral cowardice. This moral cowardice prefigures her suicide attempt, while the moral ambiguity makes her both protagonist and antagonist. Susan Sarandon underlines Sarah's character by using the repeated gesture of running her hand through her hair and smoking.

The screenplay features a clumsily constructed speech by Sarah that includes the lines, "Ok, I don't understand exactly how it works, but I'm going to find out if it kills me. We are talking about the secret of life and death here." While Sarah's experience will lead to her death and rebirth as a vampire, Miriam's assessment of Sarah is correct in that she cannot help John because she is professionally incompetent.

Scott uses obvious heartbeat sounds for the bathroom scene in which John considers attacking a half-naked man. Since it is a male bathroom, there is a gay subtext to John's interest in the younger man, whose flesh is compared to John's aged skin. The breathing sounds Scott employs in the following elevator scene is another obvious device to signal John's deterioration, as is the line by a taxi driver—"Stupid old fuck"—yelled at John for nearly being hit as he crosses a street. However, the screenplay gets a small laugh from John's response to Sarah as he leaves the clinic, when he tells *her* to wait in the patients' lounge. Slow motion is used to present the skater in shadows when John next attacks, although this second potential victim survives a cut to the throat. The two failed attacks create the expectation that a third will succeed, and Alice's visit to the townhouse meets that expectation.

Why Alice doesn't recognize the aged John's voice is a mystery, although she recognizes his eyes and asks if he is John's father. Scott sadistically lingers on Alice's assault, utilizing slow motion and focusing on Alice's screaming, and the time he takes to exploit this violence prefigures the time he will use to linger on Miriam's writhing at the climax. The ugliness of Alice's murder is increased by the fact her blood does not help John, making it pointless. Miriam's anger at John's killing of Alice is fleeting, and gives way to one of the strongest images of the film—her kissing the aged John on the lips.

This sight is both romantically tender and grotesque, more the latter because we know that John has deteriorated into such an old man. It's a pity that Scott needs to add an unnecessary flashback to the young John and Miriam kissing to drive the difference home.

Scott presents Miriam's attic romantically, with red billowing curtains, doves, and an angelic choir. As she takes John there, she explains their predicament, seemingly for herself, since it can hardly be a comfort to John:

> Humankind die one way. We another. Their end is final. Ours is not. In the earth, in the rotting wood ... in the eternal darkness ... we will see and hear and feel.

Scott cross-cuts between Lt. Allegrezza interviewing Miriam and Sarah walking in slow motion in the street. The truck stopping before it hits Sarah can be put down either to the driver's alertness or Miriam's powers. These powers recall the seductive hypnosis of the alien queen in *Queen of Blood*. Miriam as a horror movie reflection is seen in Sarah's bathroom mirror, and their connection is presented through mutual tears when Miriam plays Ravel's "Le Gibet" on the piano while Sarah sleeps. Miriam's tears can be interpreted as tears for John, since she wears a black veil, as much as tears of sadness and love for Sarah. Scott introduces the love scene between the women by having Sarah playing the song from Lakme on the piano, a love song between a princess and her slave, and continues with the Delibes duet in an orchestral arrangement.

Miriam is not a traditional lesbian, but rather a bisexual creature, although the documentary *The Celluloid Closet* includes the film as a treatment of gay love. The device of Sarah spilling sherry on herself allows Sarah to remove her t-shirt and expose her breasts, which Miriam touches, then kisses, before they go to bed. Sarah being open to the "pass" suggests that she, too, is bisexual, or at least curious and flattered. Scott uses curtains to partially conceal the actresses' nudity, and slow motion for the love scene, with portentous music leading to Miriam's bite and the resultant two drops of blood. He also intercuts the bite with a blood slide to prefigure Sarah's blood test at the laboratory.

The screenplay gets a stronger laugh when Sarah cuts into a raw steak at a restaurant after the love scene and its blood drops. Sarah lying to Tom about having sex with Miriam is further evidence of her moral ambiguity. Scott illustrates Sarah's distraction by intercutting her talking to Tom with shots of a pair of women swimming in a pool, which the restaurant overlooks. The two women swimmers are naked, but this is revealed to be Sarah's idealized per-

Miriam Blaylock (Catherine Deneuve, standing) seems indifferent to Dr. Sarah Roberts (Susan Sarandon) in *The Hunger* (1983).

ception after her lovemaking, since eventually they are shown to be suited. The scene gets another small laugh from the exchange that presents Tom either as a concerned boyfriend or a jealous lover:

> TOM: I think you should see a doctor.
> SARAH: I am a doctor.

Sarah's vomiting can be interpreted as a reaction to her heavy drinking—as much as to Miriam's infection. The two strains of blood in Sarah that are fighting for dominance recalls the battle in Norman Bates's mind in *Psycho* (a battle which his "mother" won). Mirroring their love scene, Scott shows the fight between Sarah and Miriam in slow motion. What it reveals is Miriam's unnatural strength, though perhaps she is only stronger in relation to Sarah's weakened state, while the confrontation allows Miriam to supply the following exposition:

> You belong to me. We belong to each other.... I made an incision. I drew your blood and then you took mine.

"You belong to me" implies that Miriam is the one in control. She chooses the life for Sarah, even though Sarah's participation in their lovemaking implies consent. The scratch that appears on Miriam's face after the fight is perhaps the beginning of Miriam's descent, since she licks the blood. Scott repeats Sarah having a vision of Miriam at a telephone booth, and has Sarah mistake a man's necklace for an ankh, to show Miriam drawing Sarah back to her. (Although Miriam claims to be confident that Sarah will return independently, a little reminder never hurts). Scott presents Miriam from Sarah's point of view, with a tilted camera and walking in slow motion, as an advancing threat, with Miriam in shadow as she kisses Sarah on the mouth. That Sarah is ill, and curled into a fetal position, reinforces the idea of her rebirth.

That Miriam seeks out a male prostitute is a momentary surprise considering Miriam's new lesbian preference, but, again, Miriam as a vampire cannot be so easily defined. Scott cross-cuts between Miriam's seduction of the prostitute and Sarah's illness to associate the feeding with sickness. The throat slashing, like the previous ones, is shown in close-up. Miriam's call to Sarah is given an echo, a theatrical enhancement to show the physical and psychological distance between them.

Whether Sarah feeds off Ron the prostitute is unclear, since she is not seen to, although her condition improves enough for her to get out of bed. We see her with blood running from her mouth and down her neck, and the timing indicates that Tom's arrival interrupts Sarah's opportunity. This narrative ambiguity extends to Tom's fate, since we don't see Sarah kill him. She does draw her ankh as if to attack him, and the thumping on the floor that Miriam hears as the chandeliers shake suggests a struggle. Perhaps we have to believe that Sarah kills Tom to rationalize her suicide attempt as a rejection of the life Miriam has given her. A parallel can also be made between Sarah's killing of Tom and Miriam's memory of herself as the Egyptian feeding off her slave, though the slave was male and not the one associated with the Delibes duet.

Sarah's attempted suicide is open to interpretation because of the issue of the film's ending having been changed. Whatever the consequence, the decision to suicide comes from Sarah's rejection of the life Miriam offers her. On the DVD commentary Scott calls it a "backfired" suicide, claiming that she actually kills Miriam, although this argument is flawed. Sarandon however, rationalizes Sarah's suicide by stating that Sarah doesn't want to live forever as an addict, something which the new ending violates in the studio's naive hope for a sequel. As is, the film doesn't make sense for Sarah to suicide and not die, in spite of the idea that Sarah cannot kill herself now that she is a vampire, since all of Miriam's lovers are still alive and only physically weak. Sarandon says that this altered ending changes the film from an "interesting failure" to a "derivative compromise."

Like her licking her own blood from the scratch received during the fight, it appears that Miriam drinking Sarah's blood during the suicide attempt is another factor that weakens Miriam's powers and explains why her lovers revolt at the climax—in spite of them supposedly being physically unable to stand. However, another argument could be made that it is Sarah's youth and blood that sets off the other lovers. Interestingly, the cadavers do not attack the bloody body of Sarah, while Miriam has Sarah's blood all over her. Scott goes all out for the climax, adding quick cuts, slow motion, zooms, a rocking floor, and an angled camera to the existing billowing curtains, shadows, and doves. The doves and their flapping wings provide additional aggression towards Miriam.

Miriam's repeated screaming and writhing as she withers is intercut with the deterioration of the cadavers, accompanied by a sound that could be either wind or a howl. Miriam's metamorphosis into a cadaver lacks the horror of the murder of Alice, since Miriam is a more antagonistic character. However, Scott once again parallels the dying monkey video footage with a character's demise (even if, like John in the patients lounge, Miriam does not die). John is not seen to be destroyed with the other cadavers, although we assume that he is, since Miriam is the only one left in Sarah's new apartment.

The sale of the house appears to be an act initiated by Sarah, and hence something added for the epilogue, since Miriam had not mentioned a sale to Sarah before the suicide. That the profits should go to the clinic can be interpreted as irony—and either generosity or greed on Sarah's part. Scott uses the same Schubert music heard after the first murder to present Sarah in her new life, with matching billowing curtains and a younger female lover. Miriam now trapped in a basement coffin signals a defeat and punishment for the grande dame, with Sarah estab-

Poster for *The Hunger* (1983). The Egyptian ankh is featured as the vampires weapon of choice.

lished as the new grande dame living in luxury in Rome via Miriam's wealth. Miriam's call to Sarah repeats the call she had made for Sarah when Ron had been killed for her, and also recalls the wind/howl accompanying Miriam's physical death throes.

Catherine Deneuve had played leading roles in French films from her breakout title *The Umbrellas of Cherboug* (1964) up to the time of *The Hunger*, but her Hollywood movie roles were infrequent. She had appeared in *Mayerling* (1968), *The April Fools* (1969), *Hustle* (1975) and *March or Die* (1977). *Repulsion* (1965), made in England for director Roman Polanski, had been Deneuve's only previous horror film.

Although the 39-year-old Deneuve's beauty doesn't present her as a traditional grande dame whose looks are fading, the narrative gives Miriam a grand guignol pay-off at the climax when she ages to an old crone and her lovers turn on her. Denueve has the advantage over David Bowie in regards to screen presence, so that when John is removed from the narrative the film improves via its tighter focus. Deneuve's ice-maiden presence and limited range also fit Miriam, since she is not playing a human. However, her tears when she kisses the aged John, when she wears a sheer black veil and cries simultaneously with Sarah, and the convincing horror of her entrapment at the film's climax all provide empathy for Miriam. Scott is more protective of Deneuve's nudity than Sarandon's in their love scene, and it appears that a body double could have been used for Deneuve in Miriam's love scene in the shower with John.

Release

April 29, 1983, with the tagline, "Nothing human loves forever." A spin-off anthology series would be made for television from 1997 to 2000, in which David Bowie appeared and for which Tony Scott served as executive producer (and director of two episodes).

Reviews

"The movie reeks with chic, but never takes itself too seriously, nor does it ever slop over into camp.... The screenplay, direction, performances, photography and the production design are all of a piece.... It is not strictly a horror film. Rather it is a film of visual sensations."—Vincent Canby, *The New York Times*, April 29, 1983.

"Like so many other films from British commercials directors, *The Hunger* is all visual and aural flash, and is so bizarre that it possesses a certain perverse appeal.... Tony Scott, brother of Ridley, exhibits the same penchant for elaborate art direction, minimal, humorless dialog and shooting in smoky rooms."—*Variety*, April 29, 1983.

"A determinedly upmarket vampire movie, full of modish trappings and haute couture.... High production values and insistent visual elaboration are not organic to the film, but seem merely like glossy top-dressing to a fairly pedestrian narrative.... Bowie is effective but Deneuve is required to be little more than a clothes-horse."—Phil Hardy, *The Aurum Film Encyclopedia of Horror*.

"[A]n agonizingly bad vampire movie, circling around an exquisitely effective sex scene.... A movie that has been so ruthlessly overproduced that it's all flash and style and no story."—Roger Ebert, *Chicago Sun-Times*, May 3, 1983.

Night Warning (1983)
(aka *Butcher, Baker, Nightmare Maker*; *Momma's Boy*; *Mrs. Lynch*; *Nightmare Maker*; *The Evil Protege*; *Thrilled to Death*)

S2D Associates/David D Hennessy and Richard Carrothers Presentation/Stephen Breimer Production

CREDITS: *Director:* William Asher; *Producer:* Stephen F. Breimer; *Co-Producer/Production Manager:* Eugene Mazzola; *Executive Producers:* Dennis Hennessy, Richard Carrothers; *Screenplay:* Stephen F. Breimer, Alan Jay Glueckman, Boon Collins, based on a story by Alan Jay Glueckman & Boon Collins; *Music:* Bruce Langhorne; *Photography:* Robbie Greenberg; *Editor:* Ted Nicolaou; *Hair:* Maria Wikke; *Make-up:* Erica Ueland; *Special Make-up Effects:* Al Apone; *Wardrobe:* Linda Bass; *Sound:* Val Kuklowsky. Color, 96 minutes.

SONG: "Little Boy Bill" (Joyce Bulifant), sung by Susan Tyrrell.

CAST: Jimmy McNichol (*Billy Lynch*); Susan Tyrrell (*Cheryl Roberts*); Bo Svenson (*Detective Joe Carlson*); Marcia Lewis (*Margie*); Julia Duffy (*Julia Lindon*); Steve Eastin (*Coach Tom Landers*); Caskey Swaim (*Phil Brody*); Britt Leach (*Sgt. Cook*); Cooper Neal (*Frank*); William Paxton (*Eddie*); Kay Kimler (*Anna Lynch*); Gary Baxley (*Bill Lynch, Sr.*); Vickie Oleson (*Lady Police Officer*); Clemente Anchondo (*Jail Arrestee*); Alex Baker (*Police Officer Westcott*); Randy Norton (*Student Tony*); Kelly Kopp (*Student*); Steve DeFrance (*Lab Man*); Bill Keene (*Radio Announcer*); Chuck Strang (*Riley Morgan*).

VHS/DVD: No release in either format.

Plot

Bill and Anna Lynch leave their three-year-old son Billy with Aunt Cheryl to baby-sit as they drive to visit their own parents. On the road, Bill discovers that his brakes have been tampered with and the car crashes into a logging truck. Bill is beheaded by a log that smashes into the windshield, and Anna is killed when the car falls over a cliff and explodes as it lands in a river. Fourteen years later, Billy is a high school basketball star who wants to study at the University of Denver under an athletic scholarship. However, his Aunt Cheryl does not want him to leave her since she devotes her time to caring for Billy and preserving fruit in bottles. When Phil Brody comes to fix their television on Billy's seventeenth birthday, Cheryl propositions him out of sexual frustration. When Phil rejects her, she stabs him. Billy comes home and finds Phil's body. Cheryl tells the police that Phil had tried to rape her and she had acted in self-defense.

When Cheryl tells Billy that she plans to clean out the attic for a new bedroom for him, he discovers photographs of Chuck Strang, who, Cheryl tells him, was his mother's high school boyfriend. In his investigation into Phil's death, Detective Carlson finds a ring Phil wore with an inscription from Billy's basketball coach, Tom Landers. It appears that Phil and Tom were gay lovers, which discounts Cheryl's claim of attempted raped. Carlson believes that Billy murdered Phil after a lovers' quarrel, although Billy has a girlfriend, Julie Lindon. To ensure Billy is not chosen by a talent scout that is coming to the next school basketball game, Cheryl drugs his milk. Billy misses a key shot and collapses at the game, becoming housebound. When Cheryl offers Billy some of his mother's jewelry, he refuses it but becomes curious about what else is kept in the jewelry box. Enlisting Julie to distract Cheryl, Billy finds his birth certificate, which shows that Cheryl is his real mother.

Cheryl tells Billy that Chuck was *her* boyfriend and not Anna's, and that he is Billy's father. Anna and Bill had adopted Billy to spare Cheryl from any scandal. When Chuck wanted to abandon Cheryl, she stopped him from leaving. Cheryl's neighbor Margie overhears Cheryl's confession, but she is caught in the woods behind the house by Cheryl and killed. When Julie escapes from the basement, where Cheryl had put her after knocking her unconscious, Cheryl chases her. Julie discovers the body of Chuck, with his head preserved in a bottle in the same way as Cheryl's fruit. Sgt. Cook, who has been monitoring the house, comes across Cheryl and Julie, but Cheryl kills the policeman before he can rescue Julie. Cheryl and Julie fight in the river, and Cheryl hits Julie with a rock, leaving her for dead. A drugged Billy staggers to the telephone to call for help but is caught by Cheryl. They fight, and he kills her with a fire poker, then calls Tom for help. Detective Carlson arrives and thinks that Tom has killed Cook and Cheryl, in spite of the eyewitness testimony of the recovered Julie. When Carlson threatens to shoot Tom, Billy gets the gun and shoots Carlson. End titles tell us that Billy is acquitted of Carlson's murder by reason of temporary insanity.

Notes

This feature by director William Asher has plenty of grande guignol murders and explores homophobia in a way that makes it far more interesting than *Windows*, *The Fan*, and *The Hunger*. It also features an eccentric performance by Susan Tyrrell as a grande dame whose preoccupation with a sacrifice in her past leads her to kill. Asher uses music in a predictable horror movie fashion, overuses slow motion, and indulges in too many climaxes. However, the film still satisfies as Grande Dame Guignol since the grande dame's sacrifice of motherhood establishes moral ambiguity and presents her as both antagonist and protagonist.

Asher was previously known as the director of beach party movies and television comedies like *Our Miss Brooks*, *Make Room for Daddy*, *I Love Lucy*, *Gidget*, *Bewitched*, and *Alice*. He replaced Michael Miller as director of *Night Warning*. Miller had previously directed the Chuck Norris martial arts/horror title *Silent Rage* (1982). *Night Warn-*

ing is the first and only film to be produced by Stephen F. Breimer. It was the first made by executive producers Dennis Hennessy and Richard Carrothers.

Although the opening scene operates as a kind of prologue, it doesn't serve as a narrative device similar to those in *What Ever Happened to Baby Jane?*, *Strait-Jacket*, *Hush ... Hush, Sweet Charlotte*, *The Night Walker*, and *Ruby* because the grande dame's trauma in the past occurred even earlier. Therefore her antagonistic action is a result of the prior trauma and not an immediate result of anything that happens in the opening scene. Asher uses a freeze-frame for the image of Cheryl holding Billy when Bill and Anna leave, with portentous music and Cheryl smirking indicating something is amiss (we later learn that she has fixed the car's breaks). The beheading of Bill is pure grande guignol, and Asher repeats shots of the oncoming log and the couple's horrified reaction for effect. He spares us the gore of the impact, but the death of Anna gets an unintentional laugh in its excess, from the car going down a hill, to falling over a cliff, to landing in the river, to exploding. The photograph of Billy that they had been admiring in the car receives a payoff when it floats away from the car in the river before the vehicle explodes.

Asher dissolves from the photograph to one of the older Billy and Cheryl to show the passage of time, which we also get from her change of hairstyle. Cheryl as a grande dame is represented by the religious icons in her house and her large collection of framed photographs in her bedroom, which are later rationalized by the revelation that she is Billy's real mother. The preserves she keeps stored in the basement adds an eccentricity to her character and will receive a gruesome payoff from the discovery of Chuck's preserved head. The candles in the basement, which we will learn are for a shrine to Chuck, and Cheryl talking to herself are signs of her madness. The house itself, one that she has lived in her whole life, is Cheryl's domain, so it's a pity that we don't know whether Bill and Anna had also lived there. Since the narrative withholds the fact of Cheryl's motherhood, her behavior appears to have a sexual and inappropriate context for an aunt, which Asher adds to by objectifying Billy's body. Her purring to awaken Billy

Poster for *Night Warning* (1983) under one of its many alternative titles, *Butcher, Baker, Nightmare Maker*.

is one example of this strange behavior, although it will come full circle when she uses it in her pursuit of Margie.

Asher cuts from Billy throwing a basketball into a basket at home to the same activity on the school basketball court, and uses freeze frames again for the photographs of him that Julie takes. Eddie's homophobia receives a payoff when Tom is revealed to be gay, but Asher provides subtext by showing the players semi-naked and wearing short shorts. Asher uses horror music for Billy alone in the locker room, culminating with Julie scaring him by taking another photograph. Cheryl slapping Billy when he doesn't accept her refusing his entry to University shows of her capacity for violence, which will erupt in her attack on Phil.

Cheryl's obsession with Billy is revealed when she tells Margie that she is not interested in dating, although she describes herself as Billy's date for his birthday party and refuses to let Julie attend. The narrative presents Margie as Cheryl's only friend, and makes her a funny egg (as evidenced by her reaction to Frank repeatedly beeping his car horn at her). She even has the chance to leave the house at the climax, warned by Cheryl, but does not. That Cheryl propositions Phil before Billy gets home for the party shows how impetuous and sexually frustrated she is.

Cheryl's attack on Phil is interesting in retrospect, after the revelation of him being gay, since his initial rejection of her is replaced by his asking for a blowjob when she tells him, "I'll let you do anything you want." As to why Cheryl slaps him when he asks is odd, as if she perceives her providing one as somehow degrading. When Cook later learns that Phil used to be married, this counteracts Carlson's theory that Phil being gay refutes Cheryl's claim of rape. Asher presents Cheryl's attack in slow motion, and the red of Phil's blood follows a red motif for the scene. She has red flowers in her hair, and red balloons for the party, "Happy Birthday Billy" is written in red on a banner, and the pickled tomatoes in a jar are red. Cheryl seen by Billy with her breasts exposed and blood on her face and neck is a classic horror movie image, recalling Sissy Spacek covered in blood in *Carrie*.

Her bloody handprints on Margie's white dress is more effective gruesomeness, and the narrative gets a laugh from a balloon bursting, and Cheryl and Margie screaming when Detective Carlson calls for Cheryl from the next room. Asher uses horror music when Billy goes to the attic, where a rat scares him enough to enable his fall down the stairs. The boarded up attic would appear to be where Cheryl had kept the body and head of Chuck, although this makes the basement a second "shrine." Moving Chuck into the basement so that Billy can live in the attic cleans up the narrative in terms of Cheryl's demented base of operations. Along with the candles, the attic shrine receives another gothic touch in the use of dripping water, though we don't see the source.

Cook entering the house when no one answers the door creates an expectation of an attack, which is not met, in spite of the horror movie music (although he will not be so lucky the second time). Although the schoolyard fight between Billy and Eddie over homophobia doesn't receive a payoff, Billy pouring milk over Eddie's head does have a symbolic resonance, with milk being what's produced by heterosexual mothers. Asher presents enactments of Carlson's theory that Billy and Phil had a lovers' quarrel, leading to the murder, again using slow motion for the attack; and Carlson gets a laugh from his basketball tip to Billy to keep a limp wrist. Although the joke is obvious, it works because of Jimmy McNichol's slow burn at the repeated accusations of Billy being gay.

Carlson rationalizes his idea that Billy is gay by the fact that Billy has grown up without a father, though he is unaware of the psychiatric influence of a woman like Cheryl as a mother, which may actually support such a theory. This issue of Billy's possible homosexuality continues, with Carlson asking Julie if she and Billy are "making it." Her refusal to answer him is followed by her lame retort: "He's more of a man than you'll ever be." The idea of Carlson being homophobic because he is a closet case presents itself through his office featuring giant phallic bull horns, and the tightness of his trousers (which matches the tightness of Tom's).

The sex scene between Billy and Julie is imbued with ambiguity due to Billy's initial passivity, so that we are unsure whether this is foreplay, post-coital behavior, or simply Billy's disinterest. Asher uses a subjective camera, which is just as ambiguous in the identity of the observer. When Cheryl bursts into the room we could interpret her as being the observer, but perhaps the exterior observer is also the stalking Cook, who is seen outside.

Asher uses Hitchcockian suspense for the basketball game, since we are aware that Billy has been drugged beforehand and we wait for the results. Cheryl sitting in the audience to witness the success of her scheme adds an element of sadism and another layer of voyeurism to the event. Billy's altered point of view is shown by an out-of-focus shot of the basket, and the narrative adds more ambiguity when he collapses after running into a wall. Billy as a prisoner in the attic recalls the prisoners in *What Happened to Baby Jane?*, *Lady in a Cage*, *Die! Die! My Darling!*, and *Trog*.

Horror music is heard during Billy's search of Cheryl's room, with the rustle of a tree's leaves becoming an audio red herring. Cheryl dropping the plate of food that she carries when she discovers Billy is a typical over-reaction and indication of her skewed mental state. Cook telling Carlson that he has learned that it was Cheryl and not Anna who dated Chuck in high school reveals Cheryl's lie, and creates the expectation that Billy will find out. Additionally, the disappearance of Chuck connects Chuck to Cheryl, although she has gotten away with his murder. The parallel is made between Cheryl's love for Chuck and that for Billy, and Cheryl's mental imbalance creates the possibility that Billy has inherited some of it. Asher cross-cuts between Billy's search of Cheryl's room and Cheryl with Julie, with the meat tenderizer used by Cheryl on meat a rather obvious weapon that she will ultimately use on Julie. By having Julie open the refrigerator door to block her face, Asher spares us the sight of Julie being hit.

The long climax begins with a generic horror movie storm, featuring thunder and lightning but no rain. In a moment of expressionism, Asher gives us Billy's point of view of Cheryl and Margie looking over him after he collapses. Cheryl's suggestion that Margie take an umbrella from the broom closet, where Cheryl has left Julie's camera and handbag, reveals Cheryl's preoccupation (since she would not want Margie to find these items otherwise). Margie pretending to leave the house because she is suspicious is an interesting narrative choice for a character that had not previously displayed such mistrust, but it also prefigures Margie's doomed fate.

Cheryl's attack on Cook in the basement features a swinging light bulb that recalls the same in *Psycho*, though the idea of Julie throwing rope on Cheryl to make her drop the sword she had used on Cook is laughable. However, Julie taking the sword after Cheryl drops it allows Cheryl to use an axe, which recalls the axes of *Strait-Jacket*, *Hush ... Hush, Sweet Charlotte*, *The Savage Intruder*, *Cry of the Banshee*, *Whoever Slew Auntie Roo?*, *Blood and Lace*, *The Baby*, *Frightmare*, and *Homebodies*. The narrative scores another laugh when Cheryl's axe gets caught in the dead Margie when Cheryl lunges for Julie.

The fight in the river between Cheryl and Julie is another presentation of the battle between an older and younger woman, a dynamic that appears in *Strait-Jacket*, *Lady in a Cage*, *Die! Die! My Darling*, *The Night Walker*, *I Saw What You Did*, *Games*, *Berserk!*, *Eye of the Cat*, *The Mad Room*, *Blood and Lace*, *The Baby*, *The Killing Kind*, *Frightmare*, *Ruby*, and *The Hunger*. Julie's momentary victory when she holds Cheryl underwater is soon displaced by the greater strength of Cheryl, while the expectation of Julie's murder being false prefigures the murder of Cheryl by Billy. Asher repeats Billy's drugged point of view when he crawls down the stairs, and his attempt to use the telephone receives two payoffs when Cheryl strangles him with the cord and Billy telephones Tom, putting him in danger.

The idea of Cheryl coming back to life is a horror movie shock cliché, the earliest use of it probably being *Carrie*. The final killing of Cheryl by having her impaled on a fire poker pays off her earlier scene in which she burned her papers from the attic. The death is also appropriately grande guignol, and, for once, Asher doesn't cheapen the effect with slow motion. Death by impalement is a device also used in *Berserk!* and *Trog*. If the appearance of Carlson and his efforts to kill Tom seem redundant, Billy's somewhat premature shooting of Carlson is another suggestion that Billy has inherited a little of his mother's madness. This makes the ruling of temporary insanity apt, although it is also reasonable that his behavior would be extraordinary given his drugged state and the multiple ordeals he endures at the climax.

Susan Tyrrell had previously played leading roles in *Been Down so Long It Looks Like Up to Me* (1971), *The Killer Inside Me* (1976), *September 30, 1955* (1977), and *Forbidden Zone* (1980). She had been nominated for the Best Supporting Actress Academy Award for *Fat City* (1972), and tended to be cast as whores, harridans and grotesques after she became known on Broadway for playing an array of dysfunctional characters. Tragedy entered her private life in 2000 when she contracted a rare blood disease that required both of her legs be amputated.

At the age of 37, Tyrrell's performance is a clever balancing act between weirdness and bad acting, but which is acceptable as a character choice for a woman who has been traumatized and is somewhat mad. Her wardrobe helps, particularly the headbands she wears that match the design of her dresses, as does the way Tyrrell shows Cheryl eating with childish pleasure. Initially seen with blonde short hair, she returns to the same look but with darker hair when we see her cut off her shoulder-length locks as a sign of her mental deterioration. Tyrrell's bizarre choices include Cheryl licking spilt milk on Billy's neck even

Publicity portrait of Susan Tyrrell, the grande dame of *Night Warning* (1983).

though she knows it to be drugged, kissing him before she dies for the first time, and hissing when she comes back to life.

Release

February 1983, with the taglines, "They didn't go looking for trouble. They were just too curious. Now they know too much to live," and "She was lonely. He was all she had. No-one would take him from her—and live..."

Reviews

"...[A] fine psychological horror film.... Tyrrell gives a tour-de-force performance."—*Variety*, February 1983.

"Explosive tour-de-force acting by Tyrrell distinguishes this formula horror film." Leonard Maltin, *2009 Movie Guide*

"Fascinating.... Tyrrell lets all stops out and gives a leery, totally demented performance."—Richard Scheib, *The Science Fiction, Horror and Fantasy Film Review*.

"A unique entry into the slasher film cycle ... a bit too bizarre for general audiences, its one-of-a-kind blend of kitsch and shocks make it fun for horror fans with a sense of humor.... Tyrrell is one of the most memorable screen psychos of the 1980s."—Donald Guarisco, *All Movie Guide*.

Epitaph (1987)

(aka *Mommy's Epitaph*)

City Lights

CREDITS: *Director/Producer/Screenplay:* Joseph Merhi; *Producer/Photography/Editor:* Richard Pepin; *Executive Producer:* Ronald L. Gilchrist; *Associate Producer:* Richard W. Munchkin; *Music:* John Gonzalez; *Production Manager:* Michele Pepin; *Sound:* Mike Hall; *Special Effects:* Gary Bentley; *Special Visual Effects:* Constance J. Damron, Aaron Sims, Judy Yonemoto, Jim Crouch. Color, 94 minutes.

CAST: Natasha Pavlova (*Amy Fulton*); Delores Nascar (*Martha Fulton*); Jim Williams (Forrest Fulton); Flint Keller (*Wayne Hollander*); Linda Tucker-Smith (*Dr. Shirley Lewis*); Liz Kane (*Virginia,* aka *Grandma*); R. W. Munchkin (*Warren*); Paula Jamison (*Melanie*); Mike Mendoza (*Restaurant Customer*); Ed Reynolds (*David, the Painter*).

VHS/DVD: DVD: Bci/Eclipse release of *Toxie's Triple Terror*, Volume 7, released March 22, 2005.

Plot

The Fulton family, comprised of father Forrest, mother Martha, daughter Amy and Grandmother Virginia, move into a secluded new house in Los Angeles. Martha is clearly unhappy in her marriage, since she has a drinking problem and is not interested in sleeping with Forrest. Martha stabs David, who has been hired to paint one of the rooms, when he rejects her sexual advances, and Forrest buries the body on the grounds. Although she claims that David attempted to rape her, Forrest is disbelieving and consults a psychiatrist, Dr. Shirley Lewis. Since Forrest knows that Martha will never agree to see Shirley, they concoct a plan in which Shirley can visit under the pretext of being a neighbor welcoming them to the neighborhood. Forrest is killed with a pick axe by David, who has escaped, still alive, from his burial, but Martha shoots David to finish him off.

Shirley's visit extends to a two week stay, although a friend of Shirley's that they meet at the mall lets it slip that she is a doctor. Martha becomes jealous of the friendship developing between Shirley and Amy and asks Shirley to leave. She confesses her real agenda to Amy, who she visits at school. Amy is interested in a boy she has met at school, Wayne, but knows that her mother has forbidden her to date. When Shirley goes to visit Martha, Martha knocks her unconscious. She then ties Shirley up and attaches a starved rat to her stomach so that the rat eats through her to escape. When Amy tries to leave the house, Martha locks her in the room where David had been stabbed. Virginia tries to help Amy, but Martha kills her with an electric kitchen knife.

Wayne comes looking for Amy, and Martha tells him that she has gone away. When Wayne returns, Martha attempts to seduce him, but he rejects her. She douses him in gasoline and tries to burn him, but he knocks her unconscious. Rescuing Amy, Wayne is caught by Martha, who burns him alive. When Amy buries the body, she hits her mother with a shovel. The next day we see that Amy has packed all the family belongings and drives away with the bloodied corpse of Martha in the front seat next to her.

Notes

This is another scenario in which the supporting grande dame drives the narrative, and gets to perform various acts of grande guignol. If the pedestrian treatment makes her one of the least interesting of the grande dames in Grande Dame Guignol, and director Joseph Merhi battles a generic horror movie music score, he does manage to demonstrate a compensatory strong visual sense. The biggest disappointment is that this grande dame does not have the protagonist/antagonist ambiguity of others in Grande Dame Guignol, thereby reducing her to a one-dimensional horror antagonist. The problem isn't just in the screenplay. It's also in the tiresome performance of Delores Nascar, who provides no empathy for a character who is supposedly suffering.

British-born Merhi's previous horror films were *Mayhem* (1986), *Fresh Kill* (1987), and *The Newlydeads* (1987), which featured the novel idea of a reincarnated and murderous transvestite who kills honeymooning couples. These titles were also produced by Richard Pepin and Ronald L. Gilchrist. *Epitaph* was the first film produced by associate producer Richard W. Munchkin.

Merhi opens with flames under the credits, an image that prefigures the killing of Wayne and the blowtorch used in Shirley's murder. One can assume that Martha has killed using fire before, although it is only one of the murderous choices she makes in the film. Generic horror music, which includes an angelic choir, accompanies the image of the exterior of the house into which the Fulton's will move. Merhi's repeated shots of the house imply that the house itself has some sort of power over Martha, since it is a former church, though this is a red herring. These shots often feature Amy, as the narrative's protagonist, looking out her window, prefiguring the idea that she inherits her mother's madness. Merhi plays with this idea when he uses a subjective camera for her approach to Virginia after Forrest speaks of Martha to Shirley. Amy as a prisoner is also represented by the bars on her windows, recalling the bars of Blanche's room in *What Ever Happened to Baby Jane?*, as well as those in *Die! Die! My Darling!*, and *Trog*.

Our first sight of Martha presents her as an alcoholic, but wearing full make-up and dressed in designer clothes. Although she is not really an aged hag, her long black hair, extra poundage, and smoking (using a dragon-design cigarette holder) do make her a grande dame. The trauma of her past is eventually revealed to be the fact that she became pregnant with Amy and had to give up a career as a ballerina, with the additional burden of having to live with Forrest's mother. The idea of Martha as a ballerina is laughably unbelievable, since nothing in the performance of Nascar suggests she is a former dancer (apart from an obviously played arrogance). Martha's prudishness in regards to sixteen-year-old Amy dating, and an insistence that she wears her hair in pigtails and dresses as a virginal child, is violated by Martha's attempted seductions of David and Wayne, Amy's own boyfriend. The ban on make-up also gets a laugh because Martha wears so much of it. While this behavior could be seen as the expression of an unbalanced mind, they read rather as the hypocrisy of a pampered, self-indulgent woman.

The act of moving into the house provides an exchange which is the only form of humor in the entire film, with the rat getting a later payoff:

> AMY: That filthy kitchen. I saw a rat in there.
> VIRGINIA: I know. We met.

The scene of Martha coming on to David recalls the same scenario in *Night Warning*, although here David responds by calling Martha a "horny old bag." Martha's line, "I can walk down the street and men still whistle at me," is juxtaposed with her disinterest in sex with Forrest. The red paint on the wall of the room where David works begins a red motif that continues through the film, and Merhi shows David's blood dripping into the white paint he uses when Martha stabs him. Merhi cuts from David's rejection to Virginia in the garden, delaying Martha's retribution. Forrest burying the presumed dead David recalls the husband assisting the female killer in *Frightmare*, but here adding a sexual component, since it is this act that motivates Martha to provide Forrest with (unseen) fellatio.

Martha's defensive claim that David attempted to rape her also recalls *Night Warning*, and in his meeting with Shirley Forrest will attest that this is Martha's standard response, because "She thinks men want to rape her." Although Martha never has been raped her claims imply the erroneous assumption rape is due to overwhelming physical desirability. Since Martha always presents herself made up and never in her natural state, this expectation is reinforced by her supposed need for strangers to see her in "nightgowns" (i.e. underwear slips). Martha's murderous behavior also implies the reason for their frequent moving house, without Martha admitting that she has a problem. It's just a pity that Nascar doesn't suggest this level of psychological turmoil. Later Martha will tell Shirley that she had a disinterested stepfather, so that her fantasy of wanting to be a Las Vegas showgirl (as opposed to a ballerina) suggests teenage rebellion stemming from neglect.

The issue of Amy's emerging sexuality is raised with her having the book *A Teenage Guide to Sexuality* on her bed, and her interest in Wayne. Martha's warning about boys at school "only wanting one thing" is the obvious stance of a prude, but Merhi adds a wicked menstrual touch when the resurrected David leaves a blood stain on the virginal Amy's shoulder. The pick-axe murder of Forrest recalls the axes used in *Strait-Jacket, Hush ... Hush, Sweet Charlotte, The Savage Intruder, That Cold Day in the Park, Cry of the Banshee, Whoever Slew Auntie Roo?, Blood and Lace, The Baby, Frightmare, Homebodies,* and *Night Warning*. The re-killing of David is cleverly presented by having David as a shadow when Martha shoots him, with his subsequent fall out the window shown in slow motion.

An image of Martha, Virginia and Amy in black crying together at the kitchen table has a wonderful resonance. Their crying over the corpse of Forrest, all wearing black, is like something out of Ingmar Bergman. Merhi excels with a montage showing the three women's separate reactions, and his later montages of Martha and Shirley shopping will attest to the same proficiency.

The red silk scarf that Shirley gives Amy extends the red motif, like Martha's Bloody Marys, Wayne's shirt and car, Virginia's dress, and, of course, the blood. That Shirley visits for two weeks before Martha questions her motives seems excessive, but the screenplay has trouble with time allocation anyway. Scenes where Amy and Wayne play tennis, and Wayne and another school boy play soccer, drag on needlessly and read as mere padding.

Martha making Amy wear pigtails and a white dress prefigures the end of the film, where presumably Amy has lost her mind and is more accepting of her dead mother's demands. Shirley returning to the house at night presents her as a Woman in Peril. In fact, because of her pretence, Shirley is a more morally ambiguous character than Martha, and ultimately even Amy. The entrance of a dog is used as a red herring shock before Martha strikes Shirley with a fire poker, recalling the same impromptu weapon from *Night Warning*. The attack is accompanied by the same string shrieks used for the shower sequence of *Psycho*. However, Martha's torture of Shirley has no such references, with the starved rat that burrows through her stomach to escape the blowtorch standing triumphantly as pure grande guignol. We can even forgive the simplistic effect of the blood coming out of the bucket which holds the rat because of the gruesomeness of the shot of the rat emerging from the flesh of Shirley's back. Although the fact that the rat doesn't attack Martha as she dangles it is a surprise, considering that she claims it hasn't eaten for three weeks, it is also a payoff to the earlier rat reference. And while Merhi sadistically lingers on Shirley's suffering and screams, the emergence shot redeems him.

When Amy is locked in the room where David was stabbed, Virginia comes to her aid. Merhi showing us Martha returning at the same time provides the Hitchcockian suspense. However, Martha's attack from behind Virginia is as much a surprise as the electric knife Martha uses on her (perhaps overdue revenge on being saddled with a live-in mother-in-law). While the gasoline that we see Martha collect creates the expectation (ultimately met) of it being thrown on Wayne, his punching of her is another surprise. Her not being where he left her unconscious is *not* surprising, though, and neither is her appearance in his car to finally burn him. Like David's fall out the window, Mehri uses slow motion for Wayne's fiery death, reminding us of the flames under the credits.

Martha drinking as she watches Amy bury Wayne aids Amy in her vengeful attack, although Mehri uses a freeze frame to conceal the moment in which Martha is struck by Amy's shovel. Amy alone at the kitchen table is the progressive result of the family violence, and the fact that she wears the pigtails and white dress she so disliked earlier tells us that something is wrong with her. This is confirmed when we see Amy talking to the bloodied corpse of Martha in the front seat of the car next to her as Amy drives away. Although the pigtails and the dress psychologically aligns her with Martha, Amy's reaction can also be attributed to the loss of Forrest, Virginia and Wayne. Amy's defeat of Martha can also be referenced with the battles between the older and younger women of *Strait-Jacket*, *Lady in a Cage*, *Die! Die! My Darling*, *The Night Walker*, *I Saw What You Did*, *Games*, *Berserk!*, *Eye of the Cat*, *The Mad Room*, *Blood and Lace*, *The Baby*, *The Killing Kind*, *Frightmare*, *Ruby*, *The Hunger*, and *Night Warning*.

Epitaph was the film debut of Delores Nascar, who would subsequently be seen in supporting film roles. Her age is unknown. The back cover blurb of the DVD claims that Nascar's "heart-stopping" performance rivals that of Oscar-nominated Faye Dunaway in *Mommie Dearest* (here spelt *"Mommy" Dearest*). The problem with this claim, apart from its over-reaching hyperbole, is that Dunaway was *not* Oscar-nominated for *Mommie Dearest* (1981). In actuality, Dunaway did win the Worst Actress Razzie Award for her work in that film, and it reduced her to supporting roles for many years, which is the same effect *Epitaph* seems to have had on Nascar's career.

Release

Film release date unknown. Video release in 1987 from City Lights with the tagline "Yes Mother. I've done my homework, cleaned my room, and buried Daddy." The DVD release tagline is "The Family that slays together stays together."

Reviews

"A twisted but uninteresting psycho movie.... A hectoring picture with overstated performances and padded dialogue between extensive if ordinary murder moments."—Phil Hardy, *The Aurum Film Encyclopedia of Horror.*

"Passably engaging but far from being a great film ... not completely formulaic—for better or worse—the slashing often takes a backseat to the abundant melodrama. The gore is standard."—Scott Aaron Stone, *The Gorehound's Guide to Splatter Films of the 1980s.*

Misery (1990)

Castle Rock Entertainment/Nelson Entertainment

CREDITS: *Producer/Director:* Rob Reiner; *Producer:* Andrew Scheinman; *Co-Producers:* Jeffrey Stott, Steve Nicolaides; *Screenplay:* William Goldman, based on the novel by Stephen King; *Photography:* Barry Sonnenfeld; *Music:* Marc Shaiman; *Editor:* Robert Leighton; *Production Design:* Norman Garwood; *Art Direction:* Mark Mansbridge; *Set Designer:* Stan Tropp; *Set Decoration:* Garrett Lewis; *Wardrobe:* Gloria Gresham; *Make-up:* John Elliott, Margaret Elliott; *Hair:* Judith Cory; *Production Manager:* Steve Nicolaides; *Sound:* Mark "Frito" Long; *Special Effects:* Hans Metz, Ray Svedin; *Book Cover Illustrator:* Rob Rupple. Color, 107 minutes. Filmed on location in northern California and Nevada, and at Hollywood Center Studios.

SONGS: "Shotgun" (Autry DeWalt), sung by Junior Walker & the Allstars; "Tchaikovsky Piano Concerto #1," "Moonlight Sonata," and "I'll Be Seeing You" (Irving Kahal, Sammy Fain), performed by Liberace.

CAST: James Caan (*Paul Sheldon*); Kathy Bates (*Annie Wilkes*); Frances Sternhagen (*Virginia*); Richard Farnsworth (*Buster*); Lauren Bacall (*Marcia Sindell*); Graham Jarvis (*Libby*); Jerry Potter (*Pete*); Tom Brunelle (*Anchorman*); June Christopher (*Anchorwoman*); Julie Payne (*Reporter #1*); Archie Hahn III (*Reporter #2*); Gregory Snegoff (*Reporter #3*); Wendy Bowers (*Waitress*); Misery the Pig (*Herself*). Uncredited: Rob Reiner (*Helicopter Pilot*); J.T. Walsh (*State Trooper Sherman Douglas*).

VHS/DVD: DVD: released December 22, 1998, through Polygram Video. Collector's Edition DVD released October 2, 2007, by MGM (Video & DVD).

Plot

Paul Sheldon has finished writing his new untitled novel, and is driving from the Colorado Silver Creek Lodge back to New York when his car swerves off the road during a blizzard. He is rescued and taken back to the home of Annie Wilkes, who sets his fractured legs in splints and relocates his dislocated shoulder. Annie confesses that she had been following Paul fortuitously, since she is his number one fan. She asks to read Paul's novel, a departure from the Misery Chastaine romance series he is famous for, but she is offended by his use of profanity. Annie brings home a copy of the latest Misery book but is angered when she learns that Paul has killed off Misery. She informs him that she hasn't told anyone that he is alive, and that he is dependent upon her. Annie persuades him to burn Paul's new novel in her charcoal lighter and write a new book in which Misery comes back to life.

A hairpin on the floor gives the now wheelchair-bound Paul the idea of using it to unlock his door, and he asks Annie to buy some different paper for him because the paper she has supplied smudges. Although he cannot get out of the house, he takes more sedatives from her medicine closet. In the study Paul accidentally knocks a small ceramic penguin off the table and puts it back the wrong way. He also realizes that Annie's phone is a fake one, canceling his chances of contacting the outside world. When his chair gets stuck in a doorway, Paul crawls to the back door of the house, but retreats when he hears Annie returning. He gets back to his room in time and collects the sedatives powder he's gathered.

Annie rejects Paul's first chapter because she thinks he has cheated—the way the chapter plays she saw as a child did. Meanwhile, the State Trooper finds Paul's car, and though it is apparent that he got out of the wreck, it is assumed that he died in the snow. Annie approves of Paul's changes, and he suggests that they have dinner together to celebrate Misery's return, seeking an opportunity to use the collected sedative. Before making a toast, he asks if Annie has any candles, and while she is getting them he drugs her wine. However, when she returns she spills her glass, ruining Paul's plan. When Annie goes out at night because she is depressed, he reads her scrapbook, which includes newspaper clippings of her being imprisoned for infanticide. Paul takes a knife from the kitchen and hides it under his bed. However, when Annie returns she does not come into his room, and he falls asleep. He awakens to Annie sedating him. In the morning she ties him to the bed and reveals that she knows that he has been out of his room. Then she "hobbles" him (puts a block of wood between his feet and hits them with a sledgehammer) to break his ankles and stop him from ever walking again.

Buster, the local sheriff, has been investigating Paul's case. Buster believes Paul may be alive, since he saw that the car door had been opened from the outside, meaning that someone had rescued him. He reads the *Misery* books and makes note of a phrase the character uses when she is on trial. When he overhears Annie swearing at another driver in town, Buster researches Annie's notorious past and learns that Annie used that same *Misery* quote at her own trial for murder. Learning that Annie has purchased a typewriter and paper, and is a *Misery* fan, he links her to Paul's disappearance. Annie sees Buster's approach and hides Paul in the basement. Looking over the house and unable to find any clues, Buster is about to leave when he hears the noise of Paul knocking over the charcoal lighter to attract attention. Buster finds Paul but is shot by Annie, who then wants to kill Paul, then herself. Paul talks her out of it by requesting that he be allowed to finish the book first; she agrees because she knows it is nearly done.

At the celebration for the book's completion, Paul requests his standard—a cigarette, matches, and Dom Perignon champagne. When Annie goes to get a second glass for their toast, Paul pours flammable liquid onto the manuscript. On her return he lights the match and burns the new novel, then hits her with the typewriter. Annie shoots him with the gun, but he kills her in the ensuing struggle with an iron pig doorstop. Eighteen months later, Paul walks with a cane. In a restaurant with his agent, Marcia, they celebrate the publication of his new novel, *The Higher Education of J. Philip Stone*. Although she encourages him to write about what happened with Annie, he refuses.

When the waitress appears with the desert cart, Paul has a vision that she is Annie holding a knife, as she repeats Annie's signature line: "I'm your number one fan."

Notes

Considered more thriller than horror movie, this film features only one murder, but its grande guignol hobbling and the entrapping grande dame more than make up for it. Director Rob Reiner ill-advisedly employs a bombastic music score, expressionist angles and unnecessary extreme close-ups, but compensates with a red color motif and inspired performances. He is aided by a tight screenplay which hinges on the cleverness of a writer challenged by a cat-and-mouse scenario. The narrative includes the horror movie cliché of the nighttime storm, but presents most of the action in daylight giving the false expectation of relief from antagonism. Even though the grande dame here has a preoccupation with her past, her violent imperative is in reaction to the protagonist's actions.

In spite of being the heroine of her own perverted love story, Annie never crosses over into being a protagonist herself, in spite of a potential vulnerability via her "blues" and mood swings (identifying her as suffering from mental illness). Her lack of moral ambiguity is due to the overwhelming empathy given to the grande dame's object of obsession, who possesses his own moral ambiguity. *Misery* was a change of pace for director Reiner, who had previously made *This Is Spinal Tap* (1984), *The Sure Thing* (1985), *Stand by Me* (1986; also based on a Stephen King novel), *The Princess Bride* (1987), and *When Harry Met Sally...* (1989). Producer Andrew Scheinman had previously made the horror title *The Awakening* (1980).

The red titles begin the red color motif, with the red contrasting with the white of the snow. The loud music that Paul plays in his car prefigures the accident, which Reiner shoots in slow motion from Paul's point of view. The flashback plays with the idea of Paul dying in his car, and his rebirth as a writer by killing off Misery. It is this new novel that nearly kills him, and his forced return to Misery that will save him. Paul's bloody face in the car wreck is one of the few gore shots in the film, and it prefigures Annie's bloody face at the climactic fight.

Reiner withholds our sight of Annie's face as the rescuer providing mouth to mouth resuscitation as a lover's kiss which breathes life into him. She is shown as bulky and strong enough to carry Paul from the wreck, and the figure is assumed to be male until her voice is heard. Paul hears the voice distorted, and Annie is first shown from an unflattering angle as Paul looks up at her and the image comes into focus. The red painkillers continue the red color motif, as will the sweater and pants Paul wears, the soup, Annie's car and nightgown, the Memory Lane scrapbook, Virginia's hat, the walls of the study, and the dinner wine. When Annie unleashes her tirade about the new novel, her spilling soup suggests blood.

Kathy Bates's fat, rather than her age, helps make Annie a grande dame, although other grande dames have been fat (e.g., Ann Sothern in *The Killing Kind*). While she isn't preoccupied with her youth, her comment that she is "Not the movie star type" is an admission of her unattractiveness compared to Paul's handsomeness. Her calling Michelangelo a "Diego" is more small-town prejudice than stupidity, and her use of words like "oogy" and "cockadoodie" add character quirkiness. The crucifix necklace she wears underscores her religious faith, which is apparent when she tells Paul that he was delivered to her from God "to show him the way." Although she has appropriated lines from one of the *Misery* books in her trial defense—"There is a justice higher than that of man; I will be judged by Him"—it is also an expression of her faith in God. Whilst Buster uses this line to catch Annie harboring Paul, she is not punished by the law (she outsmarts Buster). Additionally, her faith is self-serving since eventually she claims that God has told her to kill herself and Paul so that they can be together forever. Annie identifying herself as Paul's greatest fan recalls the same declaration of *The Fan*, with both scenarios exploring the ultimate frustration of unrequited adoration.

Annie's backstory is presented in the scrapbook, in which she was accused of infant deaths. Amusingly, one headline calls her a "Dragon Lady." Presumably found guilty, we get no sense of how long she was incarcerated. She tells Paul that her husband left her, but again the scrapbook does not mention him. The house interior recalls the interior of the Bates house in *Psycho*, as a twisted version of domesticity. Even the dysfunctional telephone recalls the pretense of Mrs. Bates' clothes and corpse. Annie's middlebrow romantic yearnings, represented by her Liberace records, suggest a stifled sexuality that is now fed by food and the adolescent obsession with silly romance novels. That her loneliness has led her to *Misery* is not a compliment to Paul, in spite of her claims that he is a great writer. This loneliness has made her an overweight matronly frump with graying hair, who dresses in shapeless pinafores and aprons, living in an isolated rural area.

A pan down Paul's legs shows the gruesome bruises of the damage, although the later hobbling will top that. The fact of Annie following Paul in the first place (leading to her "fortuitous" rescue of him) should be a warning of her inappropriate behavior, information which becomes doubly threatening in its foreshadowing since Annie is shaving him with a razorblade when she reveals it. We can forgive Annie's snooping to find the new novel, though her dislike of it is not a surprise given that we know of Paul's desire to break away from the *Misery* series that Annie loves so much. Paul not warning Annie about Misery's death in the book she buys makes him complicit in his fate, as much as he is a victim of his own success. Her first declaration of love for Paul is rationalized with, "Your mind, your creativity, that's all I meant." Virginia's sexual interest in Buster, wearing a red hat no less, is paralleled with Annie's unrequited love for Paul.

Misery the pig introduces humor into the narrative, thanks to Paul's distaste in reaction to her, and receives a payoff when Annie snorts at the pig. Reiner introduces Misery the pig via a horror movie cliché of a slowly opening door for the pig's entry, defying the viewer's expectation. That Misery is a sow is no surprise since the fictional Misery is female, but it is interesting that Annie's only companion is female. Her repeated use of "Mister Man" when she is annoyed by Paul expresses her justifiable distrust of men. More humor is supplied by the urine container that Annie throws around as she gesticulates, recalling the spilt soup. This action will be repeated with the lighter fluid she sprays onto Paul, adding more ambiguity to her intention.

Reiner shows it to be a full moon the night of Annie's reaction to Misery's death. We hear her enter Paul's room, but don't see her. She is finally revealed half in shadow as she says, "You Dirty Bird." This is Annie as a horror movie monster, one who causes Paul pain by shaking the bed and breaking a wooden stool against the wall after threatening him with it. Her locking Paul into his room recalls other Grande Dame Guignol about imprisonment: *What Ever Happened to Baby Jane?*, *Lady in a Cage*, *Die! Die! My*

Darling!, *The Savage Intruder*, *Trog*, *The Beast in the Cellar*, *Night Warning*, and *Epitaph*. Annie admitting to having lied to Paul about telling anyone about him is a sign of her duplicity and untrustworthiness, which will ultimately earn her the fate she deserves.

Annie's request for Paul to burn his new novel, to "rid the world of filth," is an interesting stand-off wherein she uses her knowledge of Paul's writing habits to trap him. Here is where she throws the lighter fluid onto Paul, which would seem to be counter-productive to him lighting the match. The implication may be that she will burn him (and the novel) if he doesn't, and her making him do it is a demonstration that she has the power to control him. Annie's manipulation continues with her rationalization that he must write a new Misery, "in her honor," because she has saved his life. The ideas of burning the only copy of a writer's work and then forcing him to revisit something that he has moved beyond carries artistic horrors, even if Paul's creativity is considered an elitist quality. His bravery and willingness to sacrifice continues with his hiding the painkillers and depriving himself for a long-term goal.

Paul in the wheelchair recalls the wheelchairs of *What Ever Happened to Baby Jane?*, *Die! Die! My Darling*, *The Savage Intruder*, *What Ever Happened to Aunt Alice*, *Eye of the Cat*, *Homebodies*, and *Ruby*. Paul's rejection of the smudging paper is both truthful and a plot device to get Annie out of the house, with the ceramic penguin he knocks over becoming the device for a later payoff. In the DVD audio commentary, Reiner admits to having studied Hitchcock movies to learn the film grammar of thrillers. In this scene he uses cross-cutting to establish Hitchcockian suspense between Annie's return, Paul's chair being unable to fit through the doorway, and his return to his room. Reiner has said that this is the scene he is most proud of because of the orchestrated and accumulated tension. Annie's key in the lock is juxtaposed with the hairpin that Paul uses, but which can't help him get out of the house. Annie's lumbering in the snow presents her as a Frankenstein-like, ungraceful monster, although Paul's sweating from his exertion is equally unflattering. The sweating is rationalized by his claim that she has not given him enough medication, which is also truthful because of his self-denial.

Director Rob Reiner and James Caan on the set of *Misery* (1990).

The typewriter Annie obtains missing its "n" is indicative of Annie's missing something, but also of her quirkiness. The screenplay gets a laugh from her "You fooler" response to his telling her that "n" is two of the letters in the name of his favorite nurse. Annie's awareness of her anger problem, believing it has made her unpopular, is more humor and irony, considering that she is Paul's antagonist. We see Paul shot through the bars of his bedstead, as if he is in prison, as he empties the painkillers into the paper sachet he has made.

Reiner uses Liberace's "I'll Be Seeing You" to add comic romance to the dinner scene, and potential irony to Paul's attempt to sedate Annie. Reiner also uses a montage to show the passage of time, set to Tchaikovsky's "Piano Concerto #1," while Paul exercises his arm by lifting the typewriter as a weight, and including a succession of images of Paul's changing shirts. The expectation of a storm as a horror movie cliché setting for an attack by Annie is not fully met when she presents as having "the blues" and appearing appropriately disheveled. The "blues" shows Annie at her most unattractive, but it is in this mood that she declares her love for Paul, with the knowledge that it is unrequited and therefore doomed.

The knife that Paul gets from the kitchen recalls all the other Grande Dame Guignol entries in which knives are used, including *Lady in a Cage, Die! Die! My Darling!, The Night Walker, I Saw What You Did, The Witches, Berserk!, The Savage Intruder, What's The Matter With Helen?, Night Watch, Knife for the Ladies, Homebodies, Windows, The Fan,* and *The Hunger.* The threat of Annie's shadowed feet in front of Paul's door is another expectation of violence initially not met, until a lightning close-up reveals Annie from Paul's point of view when she drugs him. The narrative uses Paul's sedation as a passage-of-time sequence before presenting the film's most famous sequence as a classic horror attack shot in daylight—the hobbling.

Reiner deliciously underscores the scene with Liberace's "Moonlight Sonata," and the narrative reveals Annie's motivations for the act: the discovery of the turned ceramic penguin, the knife, and the hairpin. In Stephen King's novel, Annie cuts off Paul's feet, but the screenplay was altered so that only his ankles are broken. The site of the ankles after Annie's strike shows the turned feet, with the real horror coming from James Caan's screamed reaction. This act of permanently crippling the man she loves in order to keep him with her is like a lesson learned from the husband who had abandoned her, as much as a punishment for Paul's duplicity. Reiner sadistically prolongs the anticipation with Paul's begging, again using Hitchcockian suspense. The hobbling is also a perceived emasculation and, even though Paul survives it, probably the reason the part was notoriously hard to cast.

On the DVD commentary, William Goldman lists the actors who turned down the part of Paul. They include Warren Beatty, Robert De Niro, Michael Douglas, Richard Dreyfuss, Harrison Ford, Gene Hackman, Dustin Hoffman, William Hurt, Kevin Kline, Jack Nicholson, Al Pacino, and Robert Redford. Goldman suggests that the problem was that Paul was perceived as being subordinate to Annie, and the hobbling emasculation is aligned to the romance novel *Misery* series as more emasculation. Ironically, Richard Dreyfuss initially accepted the role without reading the script, after having regretted turning down *When Harry Met Sally.* Then he changed his mind after reading the screenplay.

The narrative's subplot involving Buster's investigation and his suspicion of Annie creates another expectation: that Buster will rescue Paul. Annie's swearing "Cockadoodie," helping Buster link her to Paul, is a rather contrived plot point, but the way his inspection of her house is carried out compensates. There is more humor and irony in

Annie's comment to Paul as she hides him in the basement after drugging him again: "You continue to fight me. When are we going to develop a sense of trust?" The basement recalls the basement of *Psycho*, and Paul's knocking over the charcoal lighter to get assistance recalls Joan Crawford with the same intention in *What Ever Happened to Baby Jane?*

Annie's claim to Buster that God told her to replace Paul as the writer of *Misery*, thus rationalizing the writing studio, is an interesting psychological stance. What is more interesting is that she admits to being a failure as the new Paul, even asking Buster to read what she has written. She is lucky that he does not accept her offer, because she is unaware that Buster has been reading Paul's books. Annie's willingness to let Buster explore her bedroom prefigures the way he will re-enter the house upon hearing Paul's noise, with no sign of Annie. Reiner creates the expectation of an attack with the camera point-of-view approach to Buster's back, which is not met when Annie simply offers cocoa. Whether it, too, is drugged is not revealed, since Buster doesn't accept it. The gunshot hole in Buster is a shock, although Annie's absence creates the expectation of her attack, with the hole itself being gruesome without revealing any blood.

Paul uses his novelist's reasoning to outsmart Annie's attempt at murder/suicide in the basement, and his resourcefulness includes taking the lighter fluid to be used as a weapon at the climax. He is smart enough not to correct her mispronunciation of "Dom Perignon," and shows his contempt for the new work by his willingness to burn it. The climactic fight incorporates a host of weaponry, with his using the typewriter as his writer's revenge and shoving the ashes of the burned papers into her mouth. It is no

Annie Wilkes (Kathy Bates), the grande dame of *Misery* (1990).

coincidence that Annie's face is the focus of Paul's attack—an attack on her physical unattractiveness—with her bleeding eyes recalling the blinding of Oedipus. His tripping of her, causing her to fall onto the typewriter, is the use of injured legs against the person that has inflicted that injury.

Annie's return to life for a second attack recalls *Night Warning*, and the iron pig doorstop used as the final weapon is the ultimate statement on her ugliness. The doorstop also recalls Misery the sow as one of Annie's beloved, who was named for Paul, while her dead body landing on top of him is like a post-coital embrace. Regrettably, Reiner doesn't hold long enough on Bates's disappointed look at Paul just before she dies, which is indicative of his occasional mistrust of the actress. The narrative epilogue, in which Paul imagines seeing Annie alive and threatening him with a knife, recalls the similar epilogue from *Carrie*. Although Paul has refused to write about his experience, it still haunts him. The grande dame is not totally defeated.

In his commentary, Goldman tells that he wrote the screenplay for the 41-year-old Bates and recommended her to Reiner. Bates had only played supporting parts in films up to this time. She was better known as a Broadway star, having been nominated for the 1983 Best Actress Tony Award for *Night Mother*—and not being cast in the film version of the play. Bates would also be overlooked for the film *Frankie and Johnny* (1991), in a leading role that she had originated on stage in 1987. Considered unphotogenic and unattractive by Hollywood standards, she was usurped by film stars who were younger, prettier and more established. Ironically, both Sissy Spacek and Michelle Pfeiffer made themselves look less attractive for the roles they took from Bates.

As Reiner makes Annie look necessarily unflattering, he overdoes the emphasis on her outbursts by using zooms which violate the integrity of Kathy Bates's performance. While her madness occasionally tips over into cartoon excess, Bates also provides a likable aspect to Annie. A good example is her twirling in happiness at the rebirth of Misery, and the sweetness she brings to the dinner scene. Although dressed more flatteringly in a lace-collared pilgrim dress, Bates is still lit with half her face in shadow. Annie's repeated question "Did I do good?" is that of a child seeking approval, which Bates delivers with childish innocence and pleasure.

Release

November 30, 1990, with the taglines, "This Christmas there will be ... Misery," "The Tide Has Come," and "Paul Sheldon used to write for a living. Now, he's writing to stay alive." Kathy Bates won the Best Actress Academy Award for her portrayal of Annie Wilkes. She is the only actress to win the Oscar playing a grand dame in any Grande Dame Guignol title.

Reviews

"...[A] very obvious and very commercial gothic thriller.... Bates has a field day with her role, creating a quirky, memorable object of hate."—*Variety*, 1990.

"...[A] blunt instrument that fractures the kneecaps more often than it tickles the funnybone.... It seems to want to be a Hitchcockian kind of cat-and-mouse suspense melodrama, which demands a lot more ingenuity than Reiner or Goldman can muster.... Bates gives a genuinely funny performance."—Vincent Canby, *The New York Times*, November 30, 1990.

"One of the best modern horror movies.... Popular moviemaking—elegantly economical, artlesstly artful—doesn't get much better than this.... Bates's performance is simply spectacular.... Caan partners her with edgy smarts."—Richard Schickel, *Time Magazine*, December 10, 1990.

"Bates is a convincing and affecting monster.... Regrettably, it somewhat smudges the power of its superbly staged climax with another re-use of the last minute return from the dead, although it takes care not to turn its female monster into a misogynist's fantasy hate figure."—Phil Hardy, *The Aurum Film Encyclopedia of Horror*.

Bad Blood (1993)

(aka *A Woman Obsessed*; *A Woman's Obsession*)

Platinum Pictures

CREDITS: *Director:* Chuck Vincent; *Screenplay:* Craig Horrall; *Photography:* Larry Revene; *Music:* Joey Mennona; *Editor:* James Davalos; *Wardrobe:* Jeffrey Wallach. Color, 104 minutes. Filmed in Toronto, Canada.

CAST: Ruth Raymond (*Arlene Bellings*); Gregory Patrick (*Ted Barnes*); Troy Donohue (*Jack Barnes*); Carolyn Van Bellinghen (*Wanda Barnes*); Linda Blair (*Evie Barnes*); Wanda-Gayle Logan (*Miss Greenfield*); Marion Backman (*Older Woman*); Haskell Phillips (*Older Man*); Frank Stewart (*Bobby*); Miriam Zucker (*Betty*); Christina Veronica (*Crystal*); Harvey Siegel (*Jasper Stevenson*); Scott Baker (*Henry the Tailor*); Jane Hamilton (*Crystal's Mother*); Tony Gigante (*Crystal's Father*); Stan Schwartz (*Doctor Hughes*); Dan Chapman (*Sheriff Stevens*); Richard Guide (*Parking Boy*); Robinette L. Lloyd (*Flower Girl*); Ken Marchinko (*Minister*).

VHS/DVD: Released on video through Academy Home Entertainment on August 25, 1993.

Plot

While jogging on his lunch hour one day, New York attorney Ted Barnes is confronted by Bobby, who takes him to a local art gallery to see a painting by Arlene Bellings that resembles Ted. Attending the opening night with his wife Evie, Ted meets Arlene, who confesses that the painting is of her late husband, Joe Jenkins, who had taken their son. When Ted learns that Arlene's son has the same birth date as himself, he questions his mother, who tells him that he is not her natural child. Ted was given to Wanda in exchange for sexual favors by a man Wanda met during a low point in her marriage to Jack, and Ted comes to believe that Arlene is his real mother. Invited to her Long Island estate, Ted and Evie stay on when Evie falls ill with stomach cramps. Ted also learns that Joe had been murdered by Arlene's father, and is disturbed to see Arlene talking to both headstones in her private graveyard one night. Clearly the loss of Arlene's son has caused her some mental problems.

Arlene kills Crystal, her maid, when she witnesses Crystal making a pass at Ted. Evie warns Ted about what she sees as Arlene's growing possessiveness of him, and their plan to return to Manhattan is ruined when Ted drives over Crystal's corpse as they leave the grounds. While Evie becomes bedridden, Arlene dances romantically with Ted, confusing him with Joe. Evie realizes that Arlene has been poisoning her food when Twinky the cat dies after eating food Arlene has prepared for her. Evie staggers downstairs to find Ted but Arlene kills Evie with a knife. Arlene now holds Ted prisoner in the attic and breaks the toes of one foot when he tries to escape. The deluded Arlene arranges for a new wedding with Ted, thinking him Joe, and rapes him. Jack and Wanda come to the estate looking for Evie and Ted, but are unable to gain entry. On the wedding day they return, and Wanda finds Arlene with Ted. Wanda and Arlene fight, and Jack shoots Arlene, who dies as she tells the minister to begin the ceremony. In an epilogue, Ted plays volleyball, only to be grabbed by a buried Arlene as he retrieves the ball. We then see that this is only his nightmare.

Notes

This tale of deluded incest, murder and imprisonment went straight to video, which is not surprising given its barely-competent performances, generic score, and tedious pacing. Director Chuck Vincent makes admirable use of slow motion for one scene, however, and the grande guignol is represented primarily via knife slashing (though the broken toes recall the hobbling in *Misery*). Most importantly, *Bad Blood*'s grande dame has the moral ambiguity and audience empathy that was absent from *Misery*, making the treatment more representative of the better Grande Dame Guignol. Vincent was an adult film producer, writer, director and editor turned feature director, who died of AIDS in 1991 before the film was released. His previous horror titles include *Voices of Desire* (1972) and *Deranged* (1987).

With Toronto as a faux New York City, we open with portentous music and an objectification of Ted as he changes into track pants. Vincent will continue to use Gregory Patrick as beefcake, later showing him shirtless and, by implication naked. The camp behavior of Frank Stewart as Bobby prefigures the excesses of Christina Veronica as Crystal and Ruth Raymond as Arlene, even if these performances remain uninspired and lacking in emotion.

Arlene's drunkenness at the gallery's opening signals what is presumed to be an alcohol problem. Vincent has the camera track forward when Arlene sees Ted, but he also includes clichéd breathing on the soundtrack. The narrative provides three alternative fates for Joe, with none of them believably cementing Ted's acceptance of his being Arlene's son. We are simply asked to take it for granted following Wanda's confession. However, the idea that baby Ted was stolen from Arlene provides both audience empathy and a degree of rationalization for her madness. It also adds moral ambiguity to Wanda's character (and Jack's by association), which will be important when considering the climactic fight with Arlene.

Vincent uses a cheesy arrangement of "Pachelbel's Canon in D" to underscore Wanda's seven-minute confession monologue, which is a marginal improvement on the horror movie music used elsewhere. The crying baby sound effect we hear on the soundtrack during her speech is unnecessary, and prefigures another sound effect during Arlene's monologue. The museum-like, isolated estate of Arlene, complete with indoor fountain, chamber orchestra, and servants, adds to her stature as a grande dame. Twinky, the marmalade cat, recalls the feline from *Eye of the Cat*, as well as other cats in grande

Dame Guignol entries, such as *Die! Die! My Darling!*, *The Night Walker*, *The Witches*, *Games*, *What's the Matter with Helen?*, *The Killing Kind*, *Persecution*, and *Windows*.

Christina Veronica's Crystal, with her Marilyn Monroe-ish voice, is so tiresome that one welcomes her removal from the narrative. Arlene gets her own confession monologue—four minutes worth—which is upstaged by the score, a gunshot sound effect, and the sound of Raymond's heels striking the floor. This speech, with Ted and Evie sitting listening, makes the treatment seem static and theatrical, as Vincent delays the horror to come. Vincent supplies the genre's requisite mist at the graveyard, with the headstones recalling those in *Hush ... Hush, Sweet Charlotte* and *Persecution*. Arlene spitting on her father's grave remains ambiguous, although the version of events she has told Ted and Evie claims her father killed Joe. This act of sacrilege is all the more pointless because she is, in effect, addressing a dead person.

That Arlene is watched by Ted in the graveyard receives a payoff when Arlene is seen watching Crystal's attempted seduction of Ted. Crystal exposing her breasts to Ted is an indication of Vincent's perceived audience, but it also prefigures Raymond's later exposure in the sex/rape scene. Crystal eating a carrot as she comes on to Ted, and offering him a bite (which he takes), is unsubtle sexual innuendo; but, interestingly, it makes Ted the passive character. The plot points revealing that Arlene was an only child raised by her father, and that she gives Ted Joe's purple heart, have only a minor impact, and the film reads as if it suffered from heavy cuts before release. Much is made of Arlene attending a black-tie benefit with Ted, but the event is only included for a few seconds.

Vincent presents the murder of Crystal aurally, as something Evie overhears, which makes its veracity highly questionable, given her illness. Ted vomiting at the sight of Crystal's run-over body is unnecessary, with Crystal's bloodied corpse being the first gore of the film. The dancing scene with Arlene and Ted is the film's greatest achievement, even if it lacks the grande guignol element seen at the climax. Vincent uses slow motion, and slows down the music soundtrack to match the dance, so that Evie's murder is presented in stop-motion. Arlene's ball gown recalls that worn by Miriam Hopkins in *The Savage Intruder*. Vincent cross-cuts between Ted's dizzy point of view of the ceiling, the dance, and Evie in her bed. Evie's hysteria at the death of Twinky, and her realization of Arlene's attempted murder, matches Arlene's delirium in the dance, which is like a perverted version of Jennifer Jones's dance in Vincente Minnelli's *Madame Bovary* (1948).

The dance climaxes with Ted's collapse—a narrative weakness—and Evie witnessing Arlene kissing Ted on the mouth. The framing of these two actions together is masterful, and the slowed soundtrack continues for Arlene's attack on Evie and Ted's yelling for it to stop. Arlene slashing, and the final throat cutting, are perhaps more effective because of the slow motion, with Evie's dying collapse almost poetic in its balletic beauty. Ted, then, as Arlene's prisoner recalls the prisoner scenarios of *What Ever Happened to Baby Jane?*, *Lady in a Cage*, *Die! Die! My Darling!*, *The Savage Intruder*, *Trog*, *The Beast in the Cellar*, *Night Warning*, *Epitaph*, and *Misery*.

The thirty minutes devoted to Ted as a prisoner naturally slows down the film's pace, although Vincent breaks it up with the sounds of Evie being buried by Arlene (described as "planting"), and the Sheriff's visit. Ted spitting food back at Arlene, him being gagged and tied to the bed, his wetting the bed, and the rape are all examples of the power struggle between the two. The fact that Ted's antagonist in his own mother adds an element of perversion, (although her delusion causes her to think him Joe). Ted exists as a victim, entrapped by the physical similarity to his father, and Arlene's resistance to Ted as Joe indicates the violence of her marriage.

Vincent uses the horror movie convention of the storm, and presents Arlene in shadow as a movie monster. The Sheriff's visit and the cross-cuts to Ted's attempt to get his attention recalls similar scenes in *What Ever Happened to Baby Jane?* and *Misery*. The approach is practically the same as in *What Ever Happened to Baby Jane?* since Arlene becomes aware of Ted's effort but the Sheriff does not. Arlene in the attic looking out or Ted's window is an iconic horror movie image, and leads to the toe breaking incident. Arlene is photographed in golden light, looking beautiful as she recites "This Little Piggy," with a music-box tune as underscoring. Ted's yelling makes the scene excessively unbearable and nearly unwatchable. While some horror *should* be unwatchable, it is a cause for concern when the filmmaker forces us to look away.

The repetitious visits by Jack and Wanda indicates narrative weakness, while the jump cuts used while Arlene tells Ted of her wedding plans suggests more post-production editing. Ted repeats the making-a-noise scenario for one of Jack and Wanda's visits, but this repetition is forgivable in light of the consequence of Arlene wrecking the room in anger. Her confession that it was she who killed Joe, rather than her father, comes before the rape scene. Arlene's shimmery red dress is stripped off to reveal a floor-length white slip, which she wears as she mounts Ted. The sight of her exposed breasts is a follow-up from Arlene fondling her breasts earlier. Her sexuality is in counterpoint to Ted's moaning, which expresses both psychological revulsion and physical pleasure.

Interestingly, it is only after the rape that Ted is able to escape the ropes that bind him, and Arlene's crying is an expression of her perceived betrayal. His stabbing her with a shard of glass begins the series of improbable weapon wielding at the climax, although Ted's inability to walk adds realism to the otherwise cartoonish action. For the second return of Jack and Wanda, Vincent uses a split-screen effect to simultaneously show them trying to gain access to the house as they circumnavigate the exterior and Arlene's interior actions to keep them out. The expectation of Jack's arm reaching in a window, seen from both sides, being attacked by Arlene is not met.

The third return comes on the wedding day, where we see Arlene shaving Ted, the razor blade later to be used as a weapon. The wedding planners provide a jarring note of realism, although their presence will receive a startling payoff. Vincent uses a Hitchcockian alternating point of view for Wanda's advance into the house, and her ten-minute fight with Arlene is aided by a lull in which Ted is dragged by Arlene by his neck, tied like an animal. If Wanda being faux-drowned and Jack falling down the stairs in slow motion are standard genre devices, Arlene's wedding veil being caught in the rotating blades of a window fan is a redeeming Isadora Duncan moment. Arlene's multiple resurrections recall those from *Night Warning* and *Misery*, and they can be forgiven as they confirm her monstrousness. We can even forgive Arlene's ability to beat Wanda and Ted to the exit because of how Ted slows Wanda down. The narrative adds more humor in Arlene's "You missed" after the expectation of a gunshot, followed by her shocked reaction, and the epilogue recalls the epilogue of *Misery* and *Carrie,* although the loss of Evie precludes a completely happy ending.

Ruth Raymond starred in adult films under the pseudonym Georgina Spelvin, which is to actors what Alan Smithee is to directors (i.e. a pseudonym for those who wish to remain anonymous). She achieved notoriety as the leading lady of *The Devil in Miss Jones* (1973), for which even the mainstream critic Roger Ebert in *The Chicago Sun-*

Times praised her performance. After retiring from adult films at the age of 47, she made cameo appearances as a hooker in the comedies *Police Academy* (1984) and *Police Academy 3* (1986), and played a supporting role in the action film *Return to Justice* (1989). Since the date of production of *Bad Blood* is unknown, we can only guess at Raymond's age in the film. However, since she was born in 1936, a reasonable guess would indicate that she was in her 50s.

Arlene as a grande dame is evident both from her wealth and Raymond's comically broad performance (for which she seems to channel Miriam Hopkins from *The Savage Intruder*). Her thick brown hair and gold warrior necklace, which recalls the one worn by Joan Crawford in *I Saw What You Did*, add to her allure. Although the lighting is not as obvious as the illumination given to Joan Crawford in *Berserk!*, it still protects Raymond's aging neck. The shimmery pant suit she wears is typical of the concern allotted her wardrobe, which also includes a red pant suit, a white negligee, white ball gown, and white wedding gown. Raymond's cackle in the graveyard, her girlish romantic pleasure in reaction to Ted pretending he is Joe and flattering her, and the gusto with which she wrecks the attic when angry are a testament to her commitment. It's just a pity that she isn't quite good enough an actress to make Arlene a tragic figure as she staggers down the aisle, dying, even though Raymond uses an effective demonic screaming for her climactic fight.

Release

Straight to video on August 25, 1993, with the tagline, "Love is the most dangerous obsession of all."

Reviews

"...[D]erivative of *Misery* ... there's some nifty use of split-screen.... Still, fairly lame overall"—Brian J. Wright, *The Cavalcade of Schlock*.

Mommy (1995)

M.A.C. Film Productions

CREDITS: *Executive Producer/Director:* Max Allan Collins; *Producer:* James K. Hoffman; *Co-Producer:* Phillip W. Dingeldein; *Associate Producer:* J. Douglas Miller; *Screenplay:* Max Allan Collins; *Photography/Editor:* Phillip W. Dingeldein; *Lighting Design:* Steven Henke; *Music:* Richard Lowry; *Wardrobe:* Lynne Allison; *Patty McCormack's Wardrobe:* Fashion Boutique; *Make-up:* Lisa McDougall, Michelle Vanderpool; *Production Manager:* Barbara Collins; *Set Design:* Marie Lindsay; *Sound:* Jim Wheeler. Color, 89 minutes. Filmed on location in Muscatine, Iowa in 1994.

SONG: "Mommy, Mommy" (Max Allan Collins), sung by Children's Choir.

CAST: Patty McCormack (*Mommy*); Jason Miller (*Lt. March*); Brinke Stevens (*Beth*); Michael Cornelison (*Mark Jeffries*); Majel Barrett (*Mrs. Withers*); Mickey Spillane (*Attorney Neal Ekhardt*); Sarah Jane Miller (*Miss Jones*); Rachel Lemieux (*Jessica Ann*); Marian Wald (*Principal*); Mark Spellman (*Detective*); Janelle Vanerstrom (*Substitute Teacher*); Judith Meyers (*Hallway Teacher*); Nathan Collins (*Gleeful Kid*); Tom Castillo (*Ambulance Attendant #1*); Tom Summit (*Ambulance Attendant #2*); George Michael (*Mr. Sterling*); Dwayne Hopkins (*Daddy*); Cruisin' (*Band at Charity Ball*); Debi Hahn (*Mrs. March*); Gary Coderoni (*Plainclothes Cop*); Jason Shepley (*District Attorney's Office Representative*); Greg Meyers (*Little Boy*); Gary Meyers (*Little Boy's Father*); Lucie Nelson (*Little Girl*); Barb Trainor (*Little Girl's Mother*); Dick Lafrenz (*Little Girl's Father*); Elly Lloyd (*Bus Driver*); Max, Alex (*Junkyard Dogs*); Don Phelps (*Deputy Sheriff*); Jeffrey Benson (*Highway Patrol Officer*); Brian Hammer, Howard Hughes, Tom Tovar (*Detectives*); Jerry Ewers, Kevin MCarthy (*Fire Department Rescuers*); A. P. Anderson, Al Dobert, Phil Sargent, Rob Yant (*Police Officers*); Tami Allyson, Michelle Levenhagen, Paula Lofgren, John Maw, Patti Meyer, Melanie Poock, Kerry Powell, Stephanie Quade, Jim Renkes, Allison Sohr, Kathy Sternberg (*Teachers*); Patricio Cadena, Renee Dunakey, Shannon Lael, Elisabeth Maurus, Lindsay Trumbull, Robyn Vedvik (*Jessica Ann's Classmates*).

VHS/DVD: DVD: released October 26, 1999, from ROAN.

Plot

Judith Helen Sterling, aka Mommy, comes to the Muscatine McKinley School where her daughter Jessica Ann attends to confront Jessica Ann's teacher, Miss Withers. Although a past winner, Jessica Ann has been overlooked for this year's Outstanding Student of the Year award in favor of a Mexican boy. After arguing with Mommy, Miss Withers falls from a ladder and is strangled by Mommy. After Jessica Ann is taunted by the school janitor, Miss Jones, Mommy comes back to the school and electrocutes Miss Jones in the boiler room. Jessica comes to believe in Mommy's guilt when she finds the award plaque in Mommy's bedroom. Mommy's boyfriend, Mark, is revealed to be an undercover insurance investigator, since the death of Mommy's second husband is thought to be suspicious. Police Lt. March also suspects Mommy of the murder of Miss Withers and call upon Mark to help trap Mommy.

When Mommy overhears Mark confessing his agenda to Jessica Ann, she shoots him dead. She justifies the killing by telling Jessica Ann that Mark had done bad things to her in her bedroom and was afraid he would do the same to Jessica Ann. Mommy is again questioned by Lt. March, but is released. She packs her clothes and leaves town with Jessica Ann. They stop overnight at a motel where Mommy decides to kill her daughter. Jessica Ann runs away, and just as she is caught by Mommy in a junkyard, a dog attacks Mommy. Mommy fights off the dog and attempts to strangle Jessica Ann, but is shot by Lt. March. Mommy is taken away by the police.

Notes

Shot on film but giving the appearance of video, this title features a spectacular performance by Patty McCormack as the grande dame who is a Midwest serial killer in a narrative that deliberately references McCormack's childhood success as the murderous ten-year-old Rhoda Penmark in *The Bad Seed* (1956). Max Allan Collins presents some well-directed action scenes and employs a Bernard Herrmann-ish score, even if his screenplay's focus on the protagonistic child of the grande dame is disappointing. The film has two grand guignol set pieces (an electrocution and a dog attack), as well as a shooting to provide the blood necessary for the horror genre. Collins had previously written the screenplay for the action film *The Expert* (1995) and is known as a novelist. *Mommy* is his directorial debut, and the only film to be produced by James K. Hoffman. The film is also the first to be made by co-producer Phillip W. Dingeldein, and associate producer J. Douglas Miller.

The children's choir singing the song "Mommy, Mommy" establishes Jessica Ann as the film's protagonist, which her narration will confirm. The song also accompanies romanticized views of parents as they meet their children after school, an ideal that is shattered by the horror movie reveal of Mommy behind a departing school bus, complete with horror movie music. Her dark glasses and silent reaction to Jessica Ann convey the emotional coldness she will be accused of, and her angry intention to confront Miss Withers.

Mommy's arrogance comes from a natural assumption of her superiority to others, much the same as McCormack's Rhoda. This association, and the murder of her two previous husbands as the traumas of the past that she must overcome, establish Mommy as a twice-widowed grande dame. (She is referred to only as "Mommy" or "Mrs. Sterling," and never by her Christian name, which adds to her status as grande dame.) Mommy using her attitude to justify murder is evidence that she is mentally ill, something that Mark acknowledges to Jessica Ann. Since she is perceived as "sick," she is only partially responsible for her behavior. This attitude colors the narrative's conclusion, since we assume that Mommy will be sent to an asylum rather than prison.

The killing of Miss Withers is not seen, but rather suggested by a shot of Mommy's outstretched hands. This gesture is repeated for her attack on Jessica Ann at the climax. In the face of Jessica Ann as protagonist, Mommy as the serial killer is an antagonist, as eventually she will be even to Jessica Ann, the Woman in Peril. However, Mommy is also a protagonist by the nature of Mark's exploitation of their relationship, and the sympathy that McCormack's performance inspires. Therefore, the grande dame here comes replete with the moral ambiguity so necessary for Grande Dame Guignol. Jessica Ann receiving more screen time than Mommy is disappointing, since she is a reactive and far less interesting character (as evidenced by the extended dialogue scenes she shares with Beth and Mark). The relationship between Mommy and Jessica Ann is tinged with obsession by Mommy's repeated questioning, "Who's your best friend? Who loves you more than anything on God's green earth?" Mommy deciding that Jessica Ann is dispensable reveals the same exploitive opportunism she has shown to her husbands.

The screenplay features a lot of humor to give the film camp appeal. An exchange between Mommy and Jessica Ann reveals the tension between the two after Miss Wither's murder, and perhaps Jessica Ann's instinctive feeling that Mommy is the killer:

> MOMMY: People die, dear. It's natural.
> JESSICA ANN: What's so natural about falling off a ladder?
> MOMMY: Is that a smarty tone?!

Collins uses a subjective zoom for Lt. March's approach to Mommy, and she is shown with her face half in shadow while being interrogated. The car bumper sticker "I'm the mommy, that's why" gets another laugh, as does Mommy's "A little unpleasantness is not going to stand in the way of good nutrition." Beth makes the humorlessly understated comment, "Your mother is a special person," an ambiguous, patronizing compliment. Beth's talk with Jessica Ann delineates Mommy's lack of emotionalism—"She doesn't always feel things like she should"—as well as revealing that Mommy was the eldest of four daughters. The idea of Mommy as a "pampered" child gives way to the more believable notion that being the eldest made her an Amazonian leader (if Beth's passive blandness is any example).

Even though Mark is a decoy, the fact that Mommy has a love interest and has been married twice previously attests to her sexual allure, which can be seen in the black shimmery dress she wears to the dance. Collins uses a moment in which Mommy opens a jar that Mark cannot to recall the strangling, within the scene also offering an amusing exchange that prefigures her killing him:

> MARK: Remind me not to cross you.
> MOMMY: Don't cross me.

Lt. March's interview has Jessica Ann flashing back to the jar opening scene when March tells her of Miss Wither's strangled and broken neck. The lighting in this sequence favors Jessica Ann, with March always seen in shadow, perhaps establishing him as Mommy's determined antagonist.

The murder of Miss Jones is perhaps the film's best horror sequence, even if the dog attack in the junkyard offers more grand guignol. We see close-ups of Mommy's hands on her car's steering wheel, and her high-heeled feet standing outside the school gate. Mommy is presented as a horror movie monster in shadow, wearing pearls in the darkened corridor. Her close-up is lit with the red light of dusk, and the expectation of her attack is not immediately met. We hear footsteps walk away, and she is not where she was when Miss Jones turns around. We next see Mommy sitting on a swing, then no longer there, after Collins cross-cuts to Miss Jones.

Mommy turning off the lights darkens the corridor further, the blackness broken by the red emergency light and Miss Jones' flashlight. Collins defies more expectation with a red herring scare when the Hallway Teacher turns a corner and runs into Miss Jones. The use of *The Bad Seed*'s "Au Clair de la Lune" music on the soundtrack signals Mommy is around. Miss Jones is the Woman in Peril, even when she has acted as antagonist to Mommy, and Collins uses a burst of steam in the boiler room as another shock red herring. Miss Jones turning the power back on raises the expectation that the terror is gone, but water thrown on her, and then a bucket, are shock effects that lead to her electrocution at the electricity junction box. The flashlight

Poster for *The Bad Seed* (1956), which *Mommy* (1995) deliberately references.

comes into play when Miss Jones's face falls into the light of its beam, with a close-up of her dead eye recalling Janet Leigh's dead eye in *Psycho*. A close-up of Mommy's high heels is the only sign that Mommy is the killer.

Collins inter-cuts between the murder scene and Jessica Ann searching in Mommy's bedroom. This creates the expectation that she will be caught, despite the fact that we know Mommy is at the school. Jessica Ann dropping the plaque that she finds, and leaving it on the floor, further the expectation that she will be found out, which is later thwarted when she puts the plaque back. Mommy's return employs a shock effect for her sudden entry into Jessica Ann's room, something that is repeated when she enters to find Jessica Ann and Mark.

Lt. March supplies humor when he says to Mark at the hotel urinal, "Don't be surprised to see me here; this is where all the dicks hang out." Again March is lit darkly, presumably because his surveillance of Mommy is even more threatening than Mark's. Collins transitions music from the dance for a pan and slow zoom over Mark and Mommy in bed to show the growing unease that will lead him to confess to Jessica Ann. The shooting of Mark receives a payoff from the blood spatter on Jessica Ann's face and when Mommy leaves the gun under Jessica Ann's photograph of her Daddy.

Mark's hand falling out of the body bag is a shock effect that recalls *The Killing Kind*, and Collins scores another laugh from an exchange between Lt. March and Beth:

BETH: Of course I believe her. She's my sister.
MARCH: And Jeffrey Dahmer was somebody's brother.

Collins dissolves from a shot of Mommy in a chair to Jessica Ann in the same chair, wearing the same outfit at the police station. Mommy smoking is another monstrous sight, with her long white fingernails looking like claws. Collins wipes from Mommy closing her suitcase to Jessica Ann opening hers, and Jessica Ann's nightmare of Mark is suffused with green light. He repeats the lines that we presume Mommy overheard—"She is a sick person. She has to be stopped and helped,"—which portray Mommy as an ambiguous figure, since sick people deserve our sympathy.

The long scene in the motel room recalls the scene of the attempted murder of Rhoda by her mother in *The Bad Seed*. Mommy talking to herself while Jessica Ann sleeps is the only time in the narrative she does this, and her reflection is as sinister as her past murders. Her rationalization that "If they take Mommy away, who will look after you?" is pseudo-maternal, since we know Jessica Ann to have relied upon Beth earlier. The narrative adds ambiguity to Mommy's chase of Jessica Ann, since Mommy could be acting from concern over a runaway child. Collins withholds Mommy's intention until a close-up shows her as a monster again, also revealing the full moon as the classic horror movie time of strife. Mommy breaking through the bathroom door recalls Jack Nicholson acting similarly in *The Shining* (1980*)*, and the subsequent chase reflects that film's subsequent chase.

Jessica Ann momentarily hiding in a car recalls Libby hiding in the car in *I Saw What You Did*. Interestingly, Mommy pushes her out of the way to save her from the attacking junkyard dog, which gets laughs because of the obvious use of the car to conceal the mechanics of the dog's attack. The scene becomes camp because of the obvious effects used: the sound of the dog growling, Mommy screaming and her smearing blood on the car window. The dead dog and the disappearing Mommy are more horror movie contrivance, saved by her laugh line, "Now do you see why I'd never let you have a dog?" Her "This hurts me more than it hurts you" is a less amusing line accompanying her attempt to strangle Jessica Ann, and justifies Jessica Ann's strike with the metallic pipe.

Although it is unclear whether Lt. March's gunshot hits Mommy, and the dark lighting obscures her strangling of Jessica Ann, Mommy's attack on her daughter is the attack of the elder grande dame on her younger female rival, a scenario repeated from *Strait-Jacket, Lady in a Cage, Die! Die! My Darling, The Night Walker, I Saw What You Did, Games, Berserk!, Eye of the Cat, The Mad Room, Blood and Lace, The Baby, The Killing Kind, Frightmare, Ruby, The Hunger, Night Warning*, and *Epitaph*.

McCormack gets a beautiful reaction close-up to the sound of the gunshot, and Jessica Ann stopping March from shooting Mommy allows McCormack to deliver perhaps Mommy's most touching line. Asked why she hesitated, Mommy replies, "For a moment, in the moonlight, she looked like me." Although Collins errs in ending the film on March watching Mommy being driven away, the repeat of the opening song and a close-up of Mommy in the police car (a preferred closing shot) almost redeems him.

After having been nominated for the Best Supporting Actress Academy Award for *The Bad Seed*, Patty McCormack played leading roles in *Kathy O* (1958), *The Explosive Generation* (1961), *Jacktown* (1962), and *The Young Animals* (1968). *Mommy* was her first leading role in 27 years, with her last film role being a supporting one in the comedy *Saturday the 14th Strikes Back* (1988).

McCormack's manner and clothes are both period and contemporary, with her creepy white fingernail polish matching her peroxided dirty-blonde hair. Mommy's clothes are glamorous—she gets to wear a shimmery black dress for the hotel dance—but she dresses down when she leaves town. At the age of 49, McCormack presents both as an aged hag (with the exposed lines of her neck), and a well-preserved woman with a dazzling smile. McCormack's performance makes Mommy's anger funny, with the hint of her Brooklyn accent adding flavor to her dialogue. She has a great moment of faux hysteria when reporting Mark's death, and also supplies vulnerability when she must convince Jessica Ann of her rationalization for killing Mark. McCormack brings surprising subtlety and dramatic force to Mommy, as well as pathos when she sits pensively in the motel room considering her future and whether she has to kill Jessica Ann.

Publicity portrait of the ten-year-old Patty McCormack in *The Bad Seed* (1956). McCormack's *Mommy* (1995) is Rhoda Penmark of *The Bad Seed* as a murderous adult.

Release

Straight to video on January 1, 1995, by Eagle Entertainment, with the taglines, "Never let her tuck you in," and "June Cleaver with a cleaver."

Reviews

"Pretty good little thriller.... McCormack is chillingly good, and the film seldom betrays it's low-budget status."—Leonard Maltin, *2009 Movie Guide*.

"McCormack steals the movie with her chilling, disturbing performance.... Collins avoids most of the clichés of this genre.... If the film suffers it is from slow pacing and lousy lighting"—John Stanley, *Creature Features*.

Mother (1996)

(aka *The Haunted Heart*)

Kings Road Entertainment/Osmosis Productions

CREDITS: *Director:* Frank LaLoggia; *Producer/Production Manager:* Patrick Peach; *Co-Producer:* Diane Ladd; *Executive Producers:* Stephen Friedman, Sydney Kimmel; *Screenplay:* Michael Angelella; *Photography:* Gerry Lively; *Music:* Peter Bernstein; *Editor:* Bette Jane Cohen; *Production Design:* Jonathan Carlson; *Art Direction:* Jeremy Cassells; *Set Decoration:* Susan Degas; *Wardrobe:* Sister A. Daniels; *Wardrobe for Olympia Dukakis:* Sigrid Insull; *Hair:* Kaye Pownall; *Make-up:* Francis Kolar; *Make-up/Hair for Olympia Dukakis:* Tom Brumberger; *Production Coordinator:* Jean Costello; *Production Supervisor:* Betsy Pollock; *Sound:* Itzhak "Ike" Magal; *Special Effects:* Bruce Mattox, Wesley Mattox, Stephen DeLollis. Color, 96 minutes.

SONGS: "It's Easy to Remember"(Lorenz Hart, Richard Rodgers), sung by Bing Crosby; "Two Sleepy People" (Frank Loesser, Hoagy Carmichael), sung by Bing Crosby.

CAST: Diane Ladd (*Olivia Hendrix*); Olympia Dukakis (*Mrs. Natalie Jay*); Morgan Weisser (*Tom Hendrix*); Ele Keats (*Audrey Simms*); Matt Clark (*Ben Wilson*); Scott Wilson (*Dr. William Chase*); Lucy Lee Flippin (*Chloe Birch*); Steven Anderson (*Dr. Baeden*); Phyllis Applegate (*Nurse*); Andy Garrison (*Gravedigger #1*); Jason Adams (*Gravedigger #2*); Jana Robbins (*Flower Lady*); Rick Grove (*Bartender*); Jake Schmittler (*Little Cowboy*); Noelle McGrath (*Receptionist*); Mel Wells (*Mr. Brimley*); Jack Andreozzi (*Sgt. Nick Ross*); Bette Rae (*Mrs. Stallings*); Sean Patrick McNamara (*TV Newscaster*); Flo Di Re (*Shop Owner*); Russ Fega (*Photographer*).

VHS/DVD: Not available in either format.

Plot

In Rochester, New York, Olivia Hendrix lives in a house behind the From the Heart card shop with her nineteen-year-old son Tom, who designs card covers. After giving his mother a rose and a handmade card for her birthday, Tom visits the doctor for nausea and headaches. He sees Audrey Simms, the receptionist, crying over the death of her father and designs a special card for her. When Tom returns for his test results, which are inconclusive, Audrey gives him her telephone number. Tom believes his own father has died, and he writes to him in a journal about his loneliness. Madly possessive, Olivia hides the registered letters that Tom receives from William Carry University, where he has applied to study creative writing.

Detective Ben Wilson, Tom's father, is alive and visits the grave of Tom's younger brother who died at the age of four. When a graveyard attendant tells Ben that a woman in black visits the grave, Ben confronts her. She tells him that she is hired to leave flowers every year, and Ben learns that her payment comes from a Rochester address.

When Olivia learns about Tom dating Audrey, she embarrasses Tom by making a scene, warning Audrey to stay away from him. When the William Carry admissions officer, Chloe Birch, comes to offer Tom a scholarship, Olivia scalds her with hot water. When Olivia burns Tom's journal, he tries to leave home but is stopped when she stands in front of his car. Olivia is admitted to the St. Dominic's Psychiatric Hospital after a suicide attempt, and her friend Natalie attempts to seduce Tom. He rejects her advances, and we see that Natalie has cancer. While Olivia is away, Tom and Audrey repaint the shop. Medicated on her release, Olivia seems better. However, she kills Dr. Chase, her therapist, when he tries to take her back to the hospital. As a witness to Olivia's killing of Chase, Natalie becomes an accomplice to the murder. She blackmails Olivia by demanding half the shop's worth. Together they plan to kill Audrey, which Olivia does by dropping a radio into her bath. Tom finds Audrey's body, and meets Ben, who has tracked him down and followed him to the steel works where Tom has gone to cry. Olivia kills Natalie when she learns of her attempted seduction of Tom, and Olivia is shot by Tom in a struggle at the house. The weakened fire escape railing crushes her when she falls.

Notes

Admirable production values, some good writing, and a narrative featuring two grande dames are all featured in this film by director Frank LaLoggia. However, it is weakened by a limited lead performance, a generic music score, and LaLoggia's occasional indulgence in postmodern film style. The tale of a possessive mother is not new to Grande Dame Guignol, though here a difference is established by having her mental illness provide a hesitancy to her murderous behavior. Although the grand guignol included is fairly standard, the horror is given psychological resonance. LaLoggia had previously written the screenplays and music for, and produced and directed, the horror films *Fear No Evil* (1981) and *Lady in White* (1988). *Mother* is the first screenplay by writer Michael Angelella, and the only film to be produced by Diane Ladd. Kings Road Entertainment had previously made the horror title *My Best Friend Is a Vampire* (1988), and *Mother* is the only horror title made to date by Osmosis Productions.

We hear period music from an oldies radio station under the opening credits, as the postman goes to the card shop, watched by Natalie (as a horror movie monster) from behind a curtain. This suggests Natalie's predatory and antagonistic character from the beginning, in the face of her guise as Olivia's only friend. It also presents Olivia as a Woman in Peril and an equal antagonist in her possessiveness of Tom. The narrative is unique for having two grande dames with equal moral ambiguity, although Olivia is clearly the leading role and Natalie a supporting one. Olivia's mental illness and duplicity is demonstrated in the multiple reflections we see in our first view of her as she sits in front of a mirror.

Olivia's grande dame traits come to the fore in the handmade clothes she wears, the hint of a southern accent in her speech, her long blonde hair, and her whispery soft-spokeness. Progressively revealing flashbacks will show the trauma of her past as the death of her eldest son, which has made her abandon her husband and caused a nervous breakdown. The period music she prefers to play on the radio in her shop, and her box of mementoes (which include the deputy sheriff's badge worn by her dead son), are expressions of her preoccupation with the past. The treatment's empathetic attitude towards Olivia's mental illness underscores her moral ambiguity.

Natalie is a grande dame by dint of her vampish cigarette holder, Chinese wrap, and Louise Brooks-style wig. Her sexual frustration is exemplified by the romance novels she reads, and her designs upon Tom. Olivia, in comparison, has sublimated her sexuality to be a mother, since she has no other romantic interest.

Olivia's repressed sexuality is also expressed in her jealous prudishness in reaction to Tom's emerging sexuality, with his smoking—and her anger against it—being both teenage rebellion and sexual metaphor. Although one cat becomes a plot point, little is made of Olivia's habit of taking in stray cats, as opposed to the feline portrayals in other films like *Eye of the Cat* and *Games*. The cat also recalls the other cats of *Die! Die! My Darling!*, *The Night Walker*, *The Witches*, *What's the Matter with Helen?*, *The Killing Kind*, *Persecution*, and *Windows*.

The rose that Tom gives Olivia for her birthday recalls the rose in the flashback sequence, whose petals shatter like glass when it falls. Natalie's line, "I see she has you on your knees again," is both sexual innuendo and acknowledgment of Tom's servile reaction to Olivia. Olivia feeding Tom a biscuit reads as a maternal and romantic gesture, with the food being associated with Tom's illness, a plot point that is not resolved. The smoky interior of the shop adds to the old-world ambience, but also works to underscore the duplicity of the grande dames. LaLoggia's use of a tilted camera and expressionist angles for shots of the two women adds to this effect, though the technique is unnecessarily obvious. The age of the grande dames is highlighted by Olivia's invitation to play bridge, which Natalie rejects with a disdain for aging women who only have time to kill. Their habit of tea drinking would seem to be as benign as playing bridge, although the tea receives a payoff in the scalding of Chloe Birch.

Tom's introversion with Audrey is ironic given his Anthony Perkins–type beauty, with their deceased-father connection providing an emotional bond (even if Tom's is misinformed). Olivia is given a great line during her interruption of Tom and Audrey's date: "The morning has gold in its mouth, but a young man can't find it if his eyes are filled with sleep." It is interesting that Tom yells in anger at Olivia yet still retreats from the date, guilty for having behaved this way towards his mother. Olivia also gets a horror movie monster close-up when she comes right up to Audrey's face and hisses, "You leave him alone." Olivia's antagonism towards Audrey is again the older woman versus younger woman scenario seen in *Strait-Jacket*, *Lady in a Cage*, *Die! Die! My Darling*, *The Night Walker*, *I Saw What You Did*, *Games*, *Berserk!*, *Eye of the Cat*, *The Mad Room*, *Blood and Lace*, *The Baby*, *The Killing Kind*, *Frightmare*, *Ruby*, *The Hunger*, *Night Warning*, *Epitaph*, and *Mommy*. LaLoggia redeems the otherwise disappointing music score with the languid underscoring in this scene, which matches both the date and the drama of the confrontation.

Olivia locking Tom into his room recalls the imprisonments of *That Cold Day in the Park*, *What Ever Happened to Baby Jane?*, *Lady in a Cage*, *Die! Die! My Darling!*, *The*

Savage Intruder, *Trog*, *The Beast in the Cellar*, *Night Warning*, *Epitaph*, *Misery*, and *Bad Blood*. The extreme close-up of Natalie eavesdropping on Olivia talking to Chloe as she reads one of her romance novels is more of LaLoggia's postmodern technique. However, the scream of the kettle to express Olivia's reaction to Chloe is witty, even if the cat's cry is narratively ambiguous as to whether it was burned or trod on by Chloe.

The storm as Olivia burns Tom's registered letters is horror movie convention, although the fire does prefigure her burning Tom's journal. Olivia's hand on Tom's shoulder as he writes is more horror movie shock. The fact that he lets her read his journal is surprising, given that we know of its description of his trouble with her, which makes her burning it *un*surprising in spite of her claim that she does it to rid him of the delusion of a dead father he can communicate with. There is irony in that he *will* be able to communicate with his father, since he is not dead. Olivia standing in front of Tom's oncoming car in the rain shows her as a horror movie monster, which receives a payoff in his later fantasy of hitting her with the car.

The idea of Olivia's suicide attempt with vitamin C tablets is a plot hole, since presumably she is found unconscious. Although her pretence is later revealed, and we know that she should be institutionalized, it is another narrative weakness. Natalie gets a funny line at the hospital in reaction to a nurse's concern about her weakness: "I find your sincerity deplorably nauseating." Her cancer receives the payoff of the removal of her wig after Tom's rejection, and the irony of her murder by Olivia as ending her suffering.

Natalie's attempted seduction of Tom presents her as a vampire in black, and in this scene Olympia Dukakis demonstrates a performance range that outshines anything Diane Ladd does as Olivia. Natalie's mirrored self-reflection recalls Tallulah Bankhead's meltdown in *Die! Die! My Darling!*, with Dukakis's expression of humiliation and pain something out of Greek tragedy (as well as succeeding on another level as camp). LaLoggia teases us with the seduction into thinking that Tom will acquiesce to Natalie, which is probably an example of his instinct to obey a mother figure. Natalie breaking the glass frame of the photo of Olivia and Tom, and smearing her blood onto her face before she reveals her cancer-ravaged hair, is horror movie perversity.

The swinging metallic balls in the office of the policeman who questions Ben is more of LaLoggia's upstaging technique, since it reduces the dialogue to blather. Ben as a dying man is a nice plot conceit, although we have to consider him a poor detective when it has taken him nineteen years to find a good lead. Tom and Audrey seen behind the bars of the fire escape is a representation of their mutual entrapment, with a prefiguring of the fire escape used at the end. Olivia wearing her hair up when she is released from the hospital is a sign of her controlled and medicated new state, so that when we see her with it down again we know that she has relapsed. Natalie telling her that Audrey slept over at the house, resulting in Olivia's relapse, is a sign of Natalie's agenda.

Dr. Chase's fate is sealed when he tells Olivia that he checked up on her claim that Ben is dead and found it to be false. Her pushing him leads him to the horror movie basement. LaLoggia uses sunlight, much as *Misery* did, to seemingly lessen the horror threat, and the murder of Chase is helped by this lighting. The Chase killing also offers a comic element in his refusal to be killed easily and Olivia's frustration, with Diane Ladd presented with an unattractively sweaty face from her exertion. LaLoggia cuts to the cat meowing, and ball bearings scattering over the floor and dropping into the grate where Chase will be buried. Olivia's axing is seen in shadow, with the use of the axe recalling *Strait-Jacket, Hush ... Hush, Sweet Charlotte, The Savage Intruder, That Cold Day in the Park, Cry of the Banshee, Whoever Slew Auntie Roo?, Blood and Lace, The Baby, Frightmare, Homebodies, Night Warning,* and *Epitaph*.

The television broadcast of the missing person report on Chase is observed by Olivia, Natalie, Ben, Tom and Audrey simultaneously in a narrative contrivance, and the cat's attempt to retrieve Chase's spectacles from under the grate is pleasingly unsuccessful and unseen by anyone else. This last helps confirm that this is where Olivia has stored the body. We wonder why she doesn't take his body to Chase's car (which she leaves at a hangout for the homeless), but perhaps this would involve a greater chance of it being found.

LaLoggia has Olivia enter Audrey's building like a horror movie murderer—only showing her feet. Audrey having left her front door open can be forgiven since she is expecting the return of Tom, and LaLoggia has the door creak to indicate menace. He also uses the source music of her radio to underscore Audrey as a Woman in Peril investigating a noise. The period music tells us that Olivia is there, although Audrey is not aware of Olivia's preference. Audrey acquiesces to Olivia's order in the face of her gun, and LaLoggia cross-cuts between Audrey's apartment and Tom and Ben at the house. This triple narrative pursuit adds to the suspense of Audrey's predicament, and her telling Olivia about Natalie's advances towards Tom creates the false expectation that Audrey will survive.

LaLoggia makes the music louder before the radio is used to kill Audrey, and uses the lonely sound of the wind for Olivia's walk back to the house. The shower curtain that Tom pulls back to discover Audrey's body recalls the shower scene in *Psycho*, and LaLoggia uses quick cutting between traffic lights and Tom's fantasy version of Olivia crashing through his car's windscreen to visualize Tom's reaction to Audrey's death. The red traffic light that seems to rain blood is too much, however, and we have to accept another narrative contrivance of Tom running to the steelworks rather than driving there or going back to the house.

Ben appears out the darkness at the steelworks as if a ghost, and he finishes the flashback to explain that Tom has been renamed after his dead brother. The flashback shows a Western playing on television, although why the deputy sheriff's badge is pinned to a curtain and not worn, and why the boy goes to the ledge, are more contrivances. LaLoggia uses slow motion for Tommy's fall, and Olivia is seen wearing her hair in a peroxide-colored wave, as opposed to the straight golden blonde style she now sports. There is an implied shared guilt between Ben and Olivia, since he left Tommy unsupervised, and she did not get to him in time to save him.

Olivia's murder of Natalie is presented as partly an accident, with Natalie falling onto the knife after Olivia slashes her face. LaLoggia spares us the face slashing, although we see the result when Natalie is later found in the pantry. The song "It's Easy to Remember" is used as irony, since Olivia's mind has deteriorated into confusion, perhaps in reaction to the medication as much as the murders of Audrey and Natalie. She has the delusion of the younger Ben and Tommy that turns into the real Ben and Tom, with the bloody bucket that Tom finds evidence of the bloody murders of Natalie and Chase. If the discovery of Natalie's body is a simple shock effect, her death gasp redeems it somehow.

The end of the film has too many climaxes, with the dissipation of Olivia's threat making her death unnecessary. Olivia able to escape from handcuffs is forgiven when it is Ben's attempt to stop Tom from shooting her that sets off the gun after Tom has decided not to fire. Her fall over the fire escape ledge, her hanging from it when the handcuffs catch, and her final fall and crushing by the fire escape railing all present possibilities for her survival, even if they still read as extended contrivances. However, the last shot of her holding the deputy sheriff's badge is a nice touch as she cradles her last mementoes of the past.

Diane Ladd had been nominated for the Best Supporting Actress Academy Award three times, for *Alice Doesn't Live Here Anymore* (1974), *Wild at Heart* (1990), and *Rambling Rose* (1991). She had played leading roles in *The Wild Angels* (1966), *The Rebel Rousers* (1970), *Sweetwater* (1983), *The Cemetery Club* (1993, in which she co-starred with Olympia Dukakis), *Carnosaur* (1993), and *Mrs. Munck* (1995, which she also directed and wrote). She is also known as the mother of Laura Dern, her daughter by actor Bruce Dern, and the cousin of playwright Tennessee Williams.

Publicity portriat of Diane Ladd, the grande dame of *Mother* (1996).

Since she co-produced *Mother*, it clearly had meaning for Ladd, although the role also gives her a leading lady opportunity at the age of 63. She plays Olivia as a tentative killer, with her madness seemingly providing more confusion for her than a clear agenda. Ladd never goes over the top, preferring to give Olivia a small emotional range and some physical quirkiness in the murder of Dr. Chase. In the scene with Chase at the hospital, she uses playful line readings to deliver Olivia's backstory (though it is later revealed to be lies). Ladd looks beautiful in close-up, with madness in her eyes, as she recalls more of the flashback death of her son.

Release

January 1996, with the tagline, "She'll love you to death."

Reviews

No reviews available.

Mommy's Day (1996)
(aka *Mommy 2*)

M.A.C. Philms/Eagle Entertainment/The Television Syndication Company/The Roan Group

CREDITS: *Executive Producer/Director:* Max Allan Collins; *Producer:* James K. Hoffman; *Co-Producer:* Steven Henke; *Associate Producers:* Michael Dominic, Richard Marcus, Cary M. Roan, Robert and Cassie Yde; *Co-Executive Producer:* Patty McCormack; *Screenplay:* Max Allan Collins; *Photography/Editor/Co-Producer:* Phillip W. Dingeldein; *Lighting Design:* Steven Henke, Robert Hurst; *Music:* Richard Lowry; *Production Design:* Paul Steffensen; *Sound:* Greg Ballard; *Production Manager:* Barbara Collins; *Art Director:* Mary Alice Sessler; *Hair/Make-up:* Lisa McDougall; *Wardrobe:* Lynne Allison. Color, 88 minutes. Filmed on location in Muscatine and the Wild Cat Den State Park, Iowa, in August 1996.

SONG: "Mommy's Day" (Max Allan Collins), performed by Children's Choir; "Little Ice Princess" (Max Allan Collins), performed by Paul Petersen; "If Life Was Fair" (Paul Thomas), performed by Patty McCormack.

CAST: Patty McCormack (*Mommy*); Paul Petersen (*Paul Conway*); Gary Sandy (*Sgt. Anderson*); Brinke Stevens (*Beth*); Mickey Spillane (*Attorney Neal Ekhardt*); Arlen Dean Snyder (*Lt. March*); Michael Cornelison (*Dr. Price*); Rachel Lemieux (*Jessica Ann*); Sarah Jane Miller (*Jolene Jones, Action Double for Pamela Cecil*); Todd Eastland (*Jerry*); Paula Sands (*Herself*); Del Close (*Warden*); Laurence Coven (*Dr. Stern*); Pamela Cecil (*Glenna Cole*); Mark Cockrell (*Skating Instructor*); Tom Castillo (*Dr. Black*); Carol Gorman (*Lethal Injection Guard*); Marian Wald (*Mrs. Evans*); Jason Michael (*Chris*); Steve Moris (*Brad*); Max A. Collins Sr. (*Choir Director*); Scott Casber (*Janitor*); Kimber Medcalf (*Jessica Ann's Classmate*); Judy Mull (*Library Teacher*); Nate Allan (*Gleeful Bully*); Joel De Somber (*Gleeful's Pal 1*); Greg Meyers (*Gleeful's Pal 2*); Tania Mishler (*Audience Dope 1*); Dena Cox (*Audience Dope 2*); Danny Mackey (*Audience Dope 3*); Gary Meyers (*Check-in Guard*); Wayne Dundee (*Burly Guard*); Lynn Meyers (*Warden's Guard*); Gary Coderoni (*Shotgun Guard*); John Mull (*Prison Guard*); Ken McFarland (*Control Room Director*); Sara Strunk (*Control Room Assistant*); Kelsey Harrison (*Papergirl*); A.P. Anderson (*Police Officer*); Barbara Collins (*Ms. Cecil's Double*); Chad Yokum (*Mr. Eastland's Double*); Elena Cockrell (*Olga*).

VHS/DVD: DVD: released October 26, 1999, from ROAN.

Plot

Following her arrest in *Mommy*, Mommy is scheduled to die by lethal injection for the murder of Mark Jeffries. Jessica Ann visits her in prison with her guardian Beth and Paul Conway, the author of Mommy's biography, "The Mommy Murders," who is also Beth's husband. When the doctor comes to administer the fatal dosage, the strapped-down Mommy asks for her hands to be released so she can pray. Her hands released, Mommy kills the police guard and holds the doctor hostage in an attempt to escape. Mommy is shot by Lt. March, who suffers a stroke as he fires. One year later, Mommy's sentence has been suspended as she participates in a social experiment in which an implanted silicon rod that releases anti-psychotic medication is meant to short circuit her aggressive impulses.

Mommy lives in a prisoner's halfway house, and Beth has a restraining order against her seeing Jessica Ann. However, Mommy defies the order to watch Jessica Ann practice ice-skating. She is seen by the skating instructor, who warns her to keep away. That night the instructor is murdered, and Sgt. Anderson suspects Mommy, who proclaims her innocence. Mommy visits Jessica Ann at her school, and they are seen together by a teacher. Mommy goes on the *Paula Sands Live* television show to plead her case. She is ambushed by hostile questions from the audience and the guest appearance of Jolene Jones—whose sister Mommy had killed in *Mommy*. Mommy expresses her anger at the show's producer, Jerry, who is later murdered after hours in the studio.

Jolene visits Paul and offers to collaborate on a new book about Mommy, but he rejects her idea. Jolene is then murdered in her shower. Jessica Ann is kidnapped, and Mommy overhears a telephone conversation that confirms that the kidnapper is Paul's accomplice, Glenna Cole. Glenna has been committing the new murders as a Mommy copycat killer. Mommy removes her implant and kills Paul after confronting him. She finds where Glenna is to meet Paul and rescues Jessica Ann, killing Glenna. There is, however, some doubt as to whether Glenna killed Jolene, or if it really was Mommy. At Jessica Ann's ice-skating competition she wins first prize, and Mommy ominously comments to Beth that "They're lucky they did the right thing."

Notes

The only Grande Dame Guignol sequel, this follow-up to Max Allan Collins's *Mommy* has the wit to use self-reference and an awareness of the usual disappointment of sequels. Featuring more grand guignol and a copycat killer, the film is again aided by the remarkable performance of Patty McCormack, who co-produces and even sings on the soundtrack. If the narrative shows when it moves away from her, Collins redeems himself somewhat with some funny lines and directorial touches. Collins had not made a film since *Mommy*. *Mommy's Day* is the only film to be produced by Steven Hanke and Patty McCormack. Associate producer Richard Marcus had previously made the horror title *Parasite* (1982).

The opening song "Mother's Day" seems an odd choice of a song to be sung in church, and the only significance of the day is that it is the day of Mommy's planned execution. Unlike in the first film, here Collins uses expressionist angles in the camerawork, and more shadowing than is necessary. The narrative's plot reminders are standard for a sequel, and the dark shadows under Patty McCormack's eyes suggest her trauma. The film's sequel status allows the events of the last film to stand as her grande dame trauma and it is these events and the ambiguity that Collins infuses into the presentation of the killings that continue to cast Mommy as an antagonist. Interestingly, she is the film's protagonist because of McCormack's empathetic performance, and also a Woman in Peril as the ambushed victim of Paul and Glenna.

Collins peppers the narrative with self-references, with Mommy's comment to Paul—"Looks like a short sequel,"—relating both to his follow-up book and the film itself if she is killed so early. The screenplay's humor is intermittently successful, with the following exchange that occurs when Paul tells Jessica Ann about Mommy's injection being one of the lesser attempts.

> PAUL: Do you know what a drip is?
> JESSICA ANN: Yeah, him [referring to Lt. March].

Jessica Ann's response is a weak joke, but worse is the fact that while she may harbor resentment over Mommy's arrest, she helped convict her. Collins slowly zooms in on McCormack when she is strapped down to a gurney, and dissolves to an evocative back-lit long shot of the doctor and the guard walking toward the camera to herald their fateful arrival. The use of a heartbeat on the soundtrack is disappointing, but is redeemed by a funny incident. Lt. March makes the sign of the cross over Mommy, to which she replies, "I'm a Baptist, but thanks," with the Warden clearing his throat in self-consciousness before reading the sentence decree. Collins cuts from the darkness of the door March closes to the black medical bag placed on the table.

Collins shoots McCormack from unflattering angles as she lays on the gurney, but Mommy's ploy to get her hands untied in order to fold them in prayer becomes almost comical in her use of different strategies. Her fake sincerity is particularly amusing, and Collins dissolves from the guard's sympathetic look to her bloodied corpse. Although we don't see what Mommy used to kill the guard, the murderous act links Mommy to her behavior in the previous film. She delivers a funny line while holding the lethal injection to the doctor's neck—"The boys at med school are going to have a familiar cadaver." While her easy capture is a letdown, March's stroke is a convenient narrative device to transfer the police interest to Sgt. Anderson, who is stopped from shooting Mommy dead. The blood smeared on the wall behind her when she is shot continues the gore of the guard's death, and also establishes Mommy's vulnerability for the manipulation ahead.

Although the romance with Dr. Price is soon abandoned, it is initially noteworthy for two reasons: for again showing this grande dame having a romantic and sexual life, and for the casting of Michael Cornelison, who had played her doomed lover in *Mommy*. Collins shoots McCormack in a golden glow as Price explains the silicon implant, and she has a funny line in "No man's ever thought I needed implants before."

Paula Sands Live features news file footage of Mommy's arrest, which is different from that seen in *Mommy*, and a pan over the photographs we saw in *Mommy* of her, Jessica Ann and Mr. Sterling. Collins has *The Mommy Murders* book feature a foreword by himself as more self-reference. Sarah Jane Miller, as Jolene, being the twin sister of Miss Jones, is perhaps the film's wittiest recasting. Bleeps are provided for Jolene's swearing as evidence of the seven-second delay, and her swearing aligns Jolene with her sister as trailer trash.

Jessica Ann's "I Love My Daddy" framed photograph from *Mommy* gets a partner here with a framed photograph of Mommy—complete with a similar hand-made "I

Love My Mommy." Presumably Jessica Ann had made the photograph after Mommy was arrested and before she saw her on the day of execution. The recasting of Marian Wald as Mrs. Evans gets a laugh from her line to Mommy at the halfway house: "I know, dear, you're innocent—like O.J."

Mommy watches Jessica Ann skating while standing under the bleachers, with the horizontal line of the seat across her face covering her nose and mouth, so that we focus solely on her eyes. McCormack displays her acting range when Mommy rejects Dr. Price, going from girlish pensiveness to sarcasm. Collins shows Jessica Ann's reflection in the Plexiglas wall of the skating rink when she talks to Mommy. The echo added to Mommy's "She's my daughter" allows for her presence to be noticed by others, as well as adding a horror reverberation which is misleading in the narrative (since Jessica Ann is a Woman in Peril only at the end).

The murder of the skating instructor begins with a beautiful image of yellow spotlights on the blue-lit rink, while a Mommy's presence is indicated—just as it was for the murders in *Mommy*—high heels shown in close-up. The ice shavings the instructor sprays on her as he approaches is a nice antagonistic touch, and the murderer's use of an ice skate blade as a weapon recalls the use of knives and axes from other Grande Dame Guignol films. The slashing recalls the slashing in the shower scene from *Psycho*, with the killer seen from a high angle as she repeatedly strikes. The blood spreading on the white ice makes a nice horror effect. While this murder doesn't project the kinkiness of the high-heeled killing of Jerry, it is perhaps the most horrific in its excess. Although Glenna's confession does not specify that she killed the instructor, Jerry and Jolene, we presume she did, with Collins's concealing the face of the killer establishing deliberate mystery. McCormack's believability and empathy sells the idea that Mommy is innocent of the murders—except that of Glenna at the film's climax.

Sgt. Anderson gets a clever though not particularly funny, line when confronting Mommy after the instructor's murder—"When it comes to shopping for murder, you're something of an impulse buyer"—while the ice skating competition itself recalls the competition scenario surrounding Jessica Ann in *Mommy*. Collins gets bogged down in a pedestrian and expository dialogue exchange between Dr. Price and Anderson, and returns with an exchange between Jessica Ann and Mommy. When Mommy describes the killing of the instructor as an accident, Jessica Ann replies, "It wasn't an accident; you don't accidentally get stabbed 100 times" (although he was only stabbed 37 times). The teacher, finding Mommy and Jessica Ann together, becomes involved in an amusing dialogue exchange stemming from Jessica Ann's belief that it was Mommy who killed the instructor:

> TEACHER: You're not supposed to be seeing your daughter.
> JESSICA ANN (to Teacher): I wouldn't do that if I were you.

Mommy's appearance on *Paula Sands Live* allows for an ambush reminiscent of *The Jerry Springer Show*. An Audience Dope provides another funny exchange, which acknowledges Mommy's presumed guilt, *and* her pretensions:

> AUDIENCE DOPE 3: People like you don't deserve to live. Lethal injection is too damn good for you. They oughta hang your snooty ass.
> PAULA SANDS: That really isn't a question.

Jerry's murder scene offers another self-reference in that one of the film posters seen behind him is for one of McCormack's films—*The Explosive Generation* (1961). Again

Collins introduces the killer by a close-up shot of her heels, and the expectation of a light that is dropped on him killing him goes unfulfilled. The killer's comment "You're a heel," and her driving a spiked heel into his face parallels Mommy calling Jerry a heel as she leaves Paula Sand's set. Collins again presents the strike in shadow, but the killer removing the heel and wiping off the blood so she can wear the shoe again generates a black-comic laugh, albeit a gruesome one. Mommy's comment to Anderson that if she had killed Jerry she would have made it look like an accident (by using the falling light), so as not to incriminate herself with the heel after her television behavior, is valid and believable.

Jolene's collection of wigs creates the Suspicion that she is the copycat killer. The use of a painted clown motif in her house confirms her tackiness, while McCormack singing "If Life Was Fair" on the soundtrack is more self-reference. Of course, life has not been fair to Jolene, or Mommy, for that matter, a fact reinforced by McCormack's awful singing. The electrocution murder of Jolene in the shower recalls the similar bath murder in *Mother*, with Collins deliberately copying the frame composition and editing from *Psycho*.

Mommy using her crucifix to dig out the implant is a payoff to her having worn it as a necklace. The blood as she pulls back the skin on her arm is more gore—after Jolene's death has deprived us of blood—as is Paul's stabbing. Collins gives Mommy an amusingly self-referential line before she pushes Paul's head into the computer terminal (an apt fate for a writer): "Don't you know that the sequel is never as good as the original?" Additionally, Paul having written down "the Old Mill" as the meeting place for Glenna is a plot contrivance to allow Mommy to find her.

The climactic confrontation between Mommy and her copycat is lessened somewhat because of the ease in which Jessica Ann is rescued, and the arbitrary character of Glenna. We are told that Paul had met her when writing a previous book on contract killers, but her lack of connection to Mommy deprives her of any resonance. Jolene would have been a far more logical choice for the copycat killer, even if that would have meant depriving us of her shower murder sequence. However, the setup does allow Collins to give Mommy perhaps her best line: "Imitation is the sincerest form of plagiarism." Collins uses unusual (for him) extreme close-ups of Mommy and Glenna during the showdown, and shots of Glenna seen through Mommy's legs. Glenna's backwards fall out the window doesn't really provide a satisfactory payoff, and it is odd that the knife stuck in Mommy is not removed.

The repeat of "Who's your best friend?" works because Collins hasn't used it so much this time, and because here it is asked of Mommy by Jessica Ann. The epilogue brings us back to the skating competition, and we learn from her last line that Mommy retains her violent impulses (in spite of us being told she has a new implant). This ending is not only funny, it paves the way for another sequel, yet to be made.

Patty McCormack had not made any films between *Mommy* and *Mommy's Day*, and was 51 at the time of filming. To date, she has not played another leading role.

Release

Straight to video on May 5, 1998, from United Home, with the tagline, "You can't escape a mother's love."

Reviews

"...[T]he kitschy murders are predictable, and a last-minute twist makes little sense. *Mommy 2* probably sounded funny on paper, but something's missing in the executions."— William Stevenson, *Entertainment Weekly*, March 21 1997.

"The whole film is shot like some poor local government video, almost as though the director ran to Goodwill to pick up a Super8 camcorder.... The acting is laughable bad, and the dialogue makes it fun to watch.... [T]he plot is beyond stupid, which is always a plus."— Dad's Sticky Axe, *Stupid Scary Movie Society*.

The Landlady (1997)

Image Organization

CREDITS: *Director:* Robert Malenfant; *Producer:* Pierre David; *Co-Producers:* Clark Peterson, Noel A. Zanitsch, Ken Sanders; *Associate Producers:* Talia Shire, Frank Rehwaldt; *Screenplay:* George Saunders and Frank Rehwaldt, from a story by Brent Thompson and George Saunders; *Photography:* Darko Suvak; *Music:* Erik Lundmark; *Editor:* Julian Semilian; *Production Design:* Aaron Osborne; *Set Decoration:* Christopher H. Davis; *Art Director:* Erin Cochran; *Production Manager:* Ashley R. Friedman; *Sound:* Alan Samuels; *Make-up:* Cynthia Bornia; *Hair:* Genelle Lee Baumgardner; *Wardrobe:* Nanette Acosta. Color, 98 minutes. Filmed in San Diego, California.

CAST: Talia Shire (*Melanie Dade Leroy*); Jack Coleman (*Patrick Forman*); Melissa Behr (*Liz Reese*); Susie Singer (*Venice Dorian*); Bette Ford (*Justine Welch*); Nathan LeGrande (*Ralston Leroy*); Dee Freeman (*Jenny Hagen*); Courtney Gains (*Tyson Johns*); Clement von Franckenstein (*Laurence Gerard*); David Parker (*Detective Troyer*); Bruce Weitz (*Pepper McAllen*); Luisa Leschin (*Mrs. Inez*); Laura A. Pursell (*Louanne*); Christopher Kriesa (*Ralphie*).

VHS/DVD: DVD released November 10, 1998, by Lions Gate.

Plot

Nevada housewife Melanie Leroy learns that her husband Ralston is cheating on her, and she poisons him by serving him crabmeat (to which he is allergic). Having inherited an apartment building from her recently deceased Aunt Lydia in Los Angeles, she decides to move there and take over as manager. Melanie becomes infatuated with her tenant, social worker Patrick Forman, but clashes with the building's existing manager, Justine Welch. While snooping, Justine finds a newspaper article that describes Ralston having died "under strange circumstances," and she confronts Melanie, who kills her. Melanie buries Justine's body in the basement and is able to offer Justine's apartment to Patrick. Melanie installs a video camera and a two-way mirror so that she is able to spy on Patrick in the apartment. She erases a telephone message that Patrick's girlfriend, Liz, leaves on his machine, and sets off the fire alarm to stop them kissing.

Melanie follows Liz to her home, makes her complete a questionnaire about Patrick at gunpoint and then forces her to eat sleeping pills. Melanie is unable to cater a planned post-game party for Patrick's Little League when she becomes trapped in a closet at tenant Venice's apartment while Venice has sex with a client. Apologizing to Patrick, Melanie offers him a make-up dinner, and he agrees. Melanie tries to evict Venice for being a prostitute, but Venice sees Patrick in Melanie's mirror and blackmails Melanie into silence. Melanie then kills Venice and sets up Venice's boyfriend, Tyson, as the killer. At the dinner, Melanie confesses her love to Patrick, but he is not interested because he wants Liz. Melanie knocks him unconscious and ties him to her bed. Performing a wedding ceremony, she believes them now to be man and wife.

Melanie tells Patrick how she has killed Liz, and then murders the building's handyman, Pepper, who finds Patrick in Melanie's apartment after she asks him to fix her freezer. She asks another tenant, Mr. Gerard, to help her carry the trunk containing Pepper's body to the basement, then kills Gerard. A client of Patrick's, Jenny Hagen, comes to the building looking for him, and Melanie tries to kill her. Patrick frees himself with a pair of scissors that fell from Pepper's utility belt and saves Jenny. Melanie's gun goes off in a struggle between her and Patrick, and Melanie dies.

Notes

This narrative of romantic obsession and murder doesn't cover any new ground, but good production values, some effective grand guignol, and a quirky performance by Talia Shire makes it mildly interesting. Shire's second turn in Grande Dame Guignol cinema takes her mousy virginal Woman in Peril from *Windows* one step further by turning her into an antagonist, although a morally ambiguous one. Some clever plot twists and pay-offs help matters, and director Robert Malenfant can be commended for not drawing attention to his technique.

The film was produced by Canadian Pierre David, the executive producer of the early David Cronenberg films *The Brood* (1979), *Scanners* (1981) and *Videodrome* (1983). In the 1990s David began making psycho-thrillers, often featuring a female antagonist. Some of these films are *Dolly Dearest* (1992), *Twin Sisters* (1992), *Daddy's Girl* (1996), *The Nurse* (1996), and *The Night Caller* (1998). Malenfant was Pierre David's former assistant director, who graduated to directing with *The Nurse,* and *The Night Caller.*

The Landlady begins with a prologue, much like *What Ever Happened to Baby Jane?*, *Strait-Jacket*, *Hush ... Hush, Sweet Charlotte*, *The Night Walker*, *Ruby*, and *Night Warning*. This prologue presents the traumatic marriage of the grande dame, who kills to escape it, but by killing learns how successful violent behavior is in dealing with conflict. There is the suggestion in Melanie's childlike, sexless clothes, and in her religious fanaticism (represented by the iconography in the house), that the dissatisfaction of Ralston is the catalyst to her acting out and that this acting out, is a form of liberation from a life of repression and servitude.

Melanie riding a bicycle for her shopping, rather than driving a car, is more of her regressive childishness, while her seeing Ralston's infidelity through a window recalls Joan Crawford doing the same in *Strait-Jacket*. Her failing to confront Ralston directly but rather fleeing the scene creates the expectation that she is a victim, something that the crabmeat poisoning counters. Her comment, "I have to make dinner," may read as denial to what she has witnessed, since Malenfant portrays Melanie spotting the crab meat as discovery rather than deliberate purpose. However, his use of the echoed laughter she hears cements her humiliation. Melanie, then, is the narrative protagonist, and, in spite of her murder of Ralston, she won't change into a real antagonist until the murder of Liz.

The narrative uses the device of Melanie talking to herself as a sign of her madness, occasionally giving her funny lines to accompany her actions. Malenfant also pays off this device at times by having Melanie converse with Ralston's urn. Malenfant will later repeat the echoed voices of Ralston's scene sex with Louanne in relation to Melanie's exposure to Venice's sexual behavior. Ralston at dinner is shown to be verbally abusive, but the scene reveals how Melanie was a nursing home attendant before she was married. This former career ambition will match her future ambition to be the apartment building manager. The Leroy interior, presumably decorated by Melanie, has red walls, which prefigures the same color she will paint Patrick's new apartment.

Complementing Ralston's piggishness (as evidenced by his burping and sweating), he justifies his infidelity to Melanie with, "She [Louanne] knows how to treat her man." The implication is that Melanie is bad or neglectful in bed, and that her marriage is sexless and loveless (with him calling her "butt ugly"). Melanie confronts Raltston only *after* she knows him to be poisoned, but, as she will later show, she is brave and assertive enough to stage a confrontation when necessary. Malenfant uses a drum roll on the soundtrack to augment the Hitchcockian suspense, since we know of the crabmeat before Ralston does.

Melanie is also presented as forward thinking by hiding Ralston's medication and the telephone, and removing the bullets from his gun—all to insure that he dies. Her using a photograph of the two of them as a defensive weapon is amusing, and Malenfant doesn't overdo Ralston's gasping for breath before he dies (and as she prays for a new love and family). Melanie's later crashing into Patrick would be a romantic comedy meet-cute moment if we weren't aware of her instability, which brings the added horror element of being witnessed by Justine with her face half in shadow. It's a pity that Justine doesn't remain longer in the narrative, since she has the potential to become another grande dame, with her long, thick, dyed hair, stylish clothes and smoking.

Melanie's threat to fire Pepper if he takes the Lord's name in vain ("goddamn") again shows Melanie's fanaticism and strength of purpose. Narratively, it is Pepper fixing Patrick's shower that leads Melanie into his apartment, with the spilling of what is presumably coffee on Patrick's baseball sweater as foreshadowing. Melanie gives the sweater a payoff when she joyfully dances with it, deciding that Patrick "is the one." Patrick's disapproving search through Liz's handbag would seem to be an unattractive quality, even if Liz is established as having a drug problem; but Melanie being a witness to it allows for her line of irony and foreboding: "You need something different—honesty, stability, a future with someone."

The adjoining door that Justine had installed between her apartment and that of Lydia's (to care for her) now allows Justine to watch Melanie, as Melanie will use it to watch Patrick. Malenfant cross-cuts between Justine looking into Melanie's apartment and Melanie returning after her makeover, and the idea of Justine using the adjoining door to escape being detected is repeated with Melanie. Melanie presumably has taken her new clothes from Lydia's trunk, and her haircut earns an amusing exchange between Melanie and Justine.

> MELANIE: I'm not very happy [referring to the fact that Justine does not pay rent].
> JUSTINE: It's a son of a bitch getting a bad haircut.

Justine's confrontation with Melanie seems both brave and foolish of Justine, since it leads to her death and shows a fatal underestimation of Melanie's threat. Melanie using the freezer door to hit Justine recalls the same action in *Night Warning*, and Justine's blood is the film's first moment of grand guignol (since Ralston's murder was bloodless). Pepper's supposed romance with Justine is only mentioned after her murder—while questioning Melanie—although it is interesting and not surprising that Justine would have had a love life. Melanie moving Justine's body recalls the body disposal of *What Ever Happened to Baby Jane?*, *Hush ... Hush, Sweet Charlotte*, *The Savage Intruder*, *The Mad Room*, *The Baby*, and *The Killing Kind*. The narrative provides an amusing interruption in the form of Venice, who places a high-heeled foot on the "laundry." This interlude allows Melanie to learn of Venice's occupation, which will have further narrative use. Venice's brazen sexuality (and hooker underwear) contrasts vividly with Melanie's made-over dowdiness and sexual repression.

Justine buried in the building's basement recalls the many basements of other Grande Dame Guignol films. The video camera that Melanie has installed in Patrick's apartment also records sound, which will let her hear the message Liz leaves on the telephone answering machine. At one point Patrick preens in front of his mirror while Melanie watches him, eating popcorn. The expectation that she will touch the mirror, as if she is touching him, is met, though her line somewhat redeems the cliché: "One day soon there'll be nothing between us." The line's double meaning makes it funny.

Melanfant's repeated use of establishing exterior shots of the apartment building for time transition becomes tiresome, though occasionally it is needed (e.g., for the plot point of Melanie leaving Justine's cane chair on the street, which will be used by Venice and Pepper). Melanie pulling the fire alarm to stop Patrick and Liz kissing is let down by its own rapidity, and then by Patrick telling Liz that he has a Spanish class to attend anyway. Melanie's "Patrick questionnaire" earns a laugh from it asking his favorite "desert"—rather than "dessert"—although Liz's sarcasm about it probably doesn't help her position. The gun that Melanie uses is presumably Ralston's gun, and it's a nice touch that it will be the cause of her own death.

Melanie's murder of Liz makes Melanie an antagonist in a real sense for the first time, since our empathy lay with Liz (in spite of Melissa Behr's ordinary performance). This scene also shows Melanie blatantly declaring her love for Patrick as an example of her bravery and madness. She is also capable of wit. When Patrick tells her that "You deserve a gold medal" for getting him a new apartment, she replies under her breath, "A gold medal. I deserve a gold ring. And I'll get it too." Melanie's half-finished look when she goes to Venice's apartment on the night of the Little League party is made funnier by Venice's sex marathon and Melanie's frustration at being trapped in the closet. Malenfant uses close-ups of Melanie behind the closet door slats both to show her unhappiness and to present Melanie as a horror movie monster.

Melanie uses the flimsy pretext of the couch Venice has blackmailed Melanie into buying for her to enter Venice's apartment to kill her, even though Melanie's strike with a candlestick comes as a surprise. The candlestick as weapon echoes the candles Venice uses (for ambience) for her dates. Melanie utilizes the seemingly forgotten remark by Pepper about Venice's boyfriend Tyson—a minor character we only see once and who is not a tenant—to set him up and free herself from suspicion for Venice's murder. The double murder generates two funny lines. After killing Venice, Melanie says, "Good girls can only be pushed so far." After shooting Tyson, which Malenfant shows in slow motion, she says, "I love to get rid of garbage."

Unlike her earlier watching of Patrick, Melanie is now shown with her face in eerie full shadow as she says, "Soon, my love." Her dinner with Patrick references Liz's questionnaire, since Melanie uses music, food, perfume, and a gift to cover all his favorite things. Melanie holding a Mardi Gras mask over her face for a moment longer than expected as she looks at him creates a bizarre image, one almost matching in creepiness her face in full shadow. Patrick's remark that Mardi Gras links him to Liz because he met her in New Orleans, and his rejection of Melanie because of his feelings for Liz, brings Liz back into the narrative. Melanie suddenly hitting Patrick to make him stay with her is as surprising as Melanie's hitting of Venice. Jack Coleman's playing of Patrick makes his character's rejection of Melanie rather surprising, and it feels narratively pleasing.

A shirtless Patrick kept a prisoner and tied to Melanie's bed recalls the same entrapment of *Epitaph*, as will Melanie's later appearance in the wedding gown she found in Lydia's trunk. Although the narrative does not repeat the rape of *Epitaph* (since Melanie is a more sexually repressed character), she does kiss Patrick's chest. Her wedding vows garner laughs when she employs Ralston's urn as a witness, and her voicing a mute Patrick's agreement. That his mouth is taped provides a convenient excuse for him not to answer, although we know that he would not agree if he could speak. The scene's nuttiness is enhanced by Shire's playing and the sheer beauty of her dress and veil. A marvelous touch comes when Melanie uses the dress as a sheet to cover her and Patrick for their sexless wedding night. It's a pity that the wedding cake isn't referenced further in any way (since the water she gave to Patrick had been drugged), although Melanie's use of the mouth tape earns a laugh when she cuts off Patrick mid-sentence.

The newspaper article that Justine finds makes its way from her to Venice to Pepper by being hidden under the cushion of the cane chair, with the detective that Peppers calls (and who had asked Melanie about Justine) returning for the climax. The detective's appearance coincides with Pepper fixing Melanie's freezer (making a double threat to Patrick being discovered); and this is where Melanie's earlier reaction to Pepper's "goddamn" comes full circle when *Melanie* says it to Pepper. That she should take the Lord's name in vain shows her slipping fanaticism (understandable, given her possession of Patrick and presumed deteriorated mental state). The knife in Pepper's back gets a laugh from the timing, since he is about to remove Patrick's mouth tape with the warning, "This might hurt a little." Patrick seeing Melanie approach the oblivious Pepper recalls a similar moment before the murder of Elvira in *What Ever Happened to Baby Jane?*

Melanie's earlier rejection of Gerard as a romantic interest earns a payoff when he admits his advance was based on his need for a green card marriage. This also sours the only romantic prospect offered to Melanie, a woman who must suffer from unrequited love. Gerard helping Melanie with the trunk, and his subsequent murder, is visually juxtaposed with Patrick's attempt to cut himself free from his ropes. The blood leaking out of the trunk, as seen on Gerard's hand, prompts not only his startled reaction but an amusing exchange as well:

> GERARD: Bloody Hell!
> MELANIE: Which is exactly where I'm sending you.

Jenny attacked in Patrick's bedroom allows the attack to be seen by Patrick through the double mirror, and Jenny's extended struggle suggests that she will be saved. Her attack is also the film's most savage bit of antagonism, even if it features no grand guignol blood. The somewhat messy climax involving Melanie stabbing Patrick's leg, and their subsequent struggle for the gun, is redeemed by her "I wanted to be a family" before she dies, and the exchange between Patrick and Jenny:

> JENNY: Who the fuck was that?!
> PATRICK: That's someone who had no chance.
> JENNY: Somebody out of their fuckin' mind!

Patrick using the word chance recalls his hope for Liz when confronted by Melanie's declaration of love, where he had told Melanie that he still had a chance with her. The screenplay does not provide a narrative prologue, which is pleasing, and Malenfant's return to the image of the dead Melanie works as both evidence of triumph over the horror movie monster and defeat of the grande dame.

Publicity portrait of Talia Shire, the grande dame of *The Landlady* (1997).

Talia Shire had last played a leading role in the romantic comedy *Bed and Breakfast* (1991), but since then had appeared in supporting parts in film or on television. After *Windows*, she repeated her leading role of Adrian in the *Rocky III*, *IV*, and *V* sequels. At the time of *The Landlady* she was 52. As an associate producer of *The Landlady*, the property meant something to her, although she had produced two earlier films. These were the science fiction title *Hyper Sapien: People from Another Star* (1986, in which she also had a supporting role) and the adventure drama *Lionheart* (1987, in which she did not appear).

Although Shire's makeover makes her look somewhat more attractive, her Melanie is generally presented unflatteringly. The lines on her face are apparent, though shapeless pinafores and hastily-tied long hair give way to tighter clothes and a styled bob. Shire's face can look both attractive and ugly at the same time, adding to her ambiguity. Shire has Melanie react with child-like pleasure to the slightest attention from Patrick. In spite of the horror of Liz's murder, Shire adds a feminine fragility to Melanie's menace, though the negligee she wears under the wedding dress is the only attempt to present Melanie as sexually desirable. The scarf Melanie wears, and her khaki top when she deals with Pepper in the trunk, make her look like a safari adventurer, and Malenfant's long last look at Melanie makes her finally, touchingly beautiful.

Release

October 11, 1998, on video, with the tagline, "Evil doesn't knock. It has the key."

Reviews

"One enters expecting nothing more than another of Pierre David's formulaic and predictable thrillers. The surprise about it is contrarily what a good film *The Landlady* actually is.... Shire quite surprises by giving the absolute performance of a lifetime.... Malenfant racks up some superb tension, particularly at the climax."—Richard Scheib, *The Science Fiction, Horror and Fantasy Movie Review Site*, September 9, 2008.

"This movie is touted as a horror flick but is better suited in the 'horrible' genre.... Shire is not showing her best this time out.... While the premise offers fertile ground for a good story, many potentially interesting twists are ignored in favor of a boring straight line to a merciful ending."—Mike DeWolfe, *Apollo Movie Guide*.

Inside (2007)

La Fabrique de Films/BR Films

CREDITS: *Directors:* Julien Maury, Alexandre Bustillo; *Producers:* Verane Frediani, Franck Ribiere; *Associate Producers:* Rodolphe Guglielmi, Teddy Percherancier, Frederic Ovcaric; *Screenplay:* Alexandre Bustillo; *Photography:* Laurent Bares; *Editor:* Baxter; *Art Director:* Marc Thiebault; *Music:* Francois-Eudes Chanfrault; *Sound:* Jacques Sans, Sebastien Savine, Cedric Lionnet; *Wardrobe:* Martine Rapin; *Make-up:* Sabine Fevre; *Visual Effects:* BR Films, Rodolphe Guglielmi. Color, 83 minutes, French language. Filmed in Paris, France, in 2006.

CAST: Beatrice Dalle (*the Woman*); Alysson Paradis (*Sarah Scarangelo*); Nicolas Duvuchelle *(BAC Policeman 3)*; Francois-Regis Marchasson (*Jean-Pierre Montevant*); Nathalie Roussel (*Louise*); Aymen Said (*Abdel Hanusian*); Jean-Baptiste Tabourin (*Matthieu*); Claude Lule (*the Doctor*); Dominique Frot (*the Nurse*); Hyam Zaytoun (*Policewoman*); Tahar Rahim (*Policeman 1*); Emmanuel Guez (*Policeman 2*); Ludovic Berthillot (*BAC Policeman1*); Emmanuel Lanzi (*BAC Policeman 2*).

VHS/DVD: DVD released April 15, 2008, by Genius Products (TVN).

Plot

Photographer Sarah Scarangelo and her husband Matthieu are involved in a car crash in which he is killed and the Woman in the other car miscarries. Four months later, on Christmas Eve, Sarah is due to go into labor. She declines the offer of her mother, Louise, to join her for dinner, and arranges to have her editor, Jean-Pierre, accompany her to the hospital for the birth. That night the Woman comes to Sarah's house, under the pretext of wanting to use her telephone, but Sarah refuses her entry. Sarah takes photographs of the Woman, who she sees through her window, but they do not capture a clear image. She telephones Jean-Pierre, asking him to help her enhance the photographs, and calls the police. The police are unable to find the Woman around the house, so Sarah goes to sleep. She is awakened by the Woman in the house, attacking her with scissors. Sarah hides in the bathroom as Jean-Pierre arrives to check up on her.

Jean-Pierre assumes the Woman to be Sarah's mother, but is suspicious when he finds one of Sarah's photographs. When Louise arrives, she goes to Sarah, but Sarah kills her, assuming she is the Woman. The Woman kills Jean-Pierre and manages to pin Sarah's arm to the wall with her scissors. The police return and, seeing that the Woman is not pregnant, try to arrest her. However, she outmaneuvers them and kills the three policemen (along with Abdel, a riot suspect who is handcuffed to one of the officers). The Woman tells Sarah that she was the passenger in the other car at the accident, which stops Sarah from killing her. When Sarah goes into labor and believes that the baby is stuck, the Woman cuts it out of Sarah's belly. We then see the Woman nursing the born newborn in a rocking chair, as Sarah lies motionless and apparently dead.

Notes

After a 10-year absence, Grande Dame Guignol returned with this supremely effective shocker. So gruesome that is it almost unwatchable at times, the film offers an impressive body count and bloodletting, but also moments of quiet lyricism. In what is essentially a two-hander, the narrative features a cat-and-mouse struggle for survival between an antagonistic grande dame and a younger, pregnant Woman in Peril. Like the best Grande Dame Guignol entries, the treatment offers moral ambiguity (along with superb work by first time co-directors Julian Maury and Alexandre Bustillo). This is the first feature for BR Films, and the second for La Fabrique de Films, who had previously made the drama *One to Another* (2006). Producer Franck Ribiere had previously made the French horror titles *Maléfique* (2002), *Bloody Mallory* (2002), *Requiem* (2001), and *Children's Play* (2001).

The film uses a prologue to establish the trauma of the grande dame, although she is not shown in it until a later flashback. The prologue recalls the openings of *What Ever Happened to Baby Jane?*, *Strait-Jacket*, *Hush ... Hush, Sweet Charlotte*, *The Night Walker*, *Ruby*, *Night Warning* , and *The Landlady*. The later flashback will repeat the opening lines of the film as we see a baby floating in amniotic fluid, although we do not know whether the baby is that of the Woman or Sarah:

> THE WOMAN: Finally inside me. No one will take him from me. No one can hurt him now. No one.

These lines telegraph the Woman's singlemindedness and the film's ending. The crash is indicated by the baby's reaction, a device repeatedly used in the film. The redness of Sarah's blood is heightened by the contrast to the monochrome colors of the cars, with the rain continued for the credit sequence. Under the credits, where the titles bleed, we see blood washed away, body organs and more baby imagery.

The narrative being set at Christmas aligns the birth of Christ with the birth of Sarah's baby, as well as the rebirth of the Woman's baby. The slow closing of doors at the hospital introduces the Nurse—a funny and strange performance by Dominique Frot—which sets the tone for the Woman's character. In fact, our first view of the Woman lighting a cigarette suggests that she is the Nurse (aided by the fact that the Nurse's baby was born dead, and her smoking). Sarah's scarred face suggests the physical trauma of the crash, as much as her morose manner, which will come full circle when she remembers Matthieu, and in the Woman's justifiable claim that Sarah does not want the baby.

The black cat in Sarah's house recalls the cats from *Die! Die! My Darling!*, *The Night Walker*, *The Witches*, *What's the Matter with Helen?*, *The Killing Kind*, *Persecution*, *Windows*, and *Mother*. Sarah's annoyance at the cat will receive a shocking payoff when the Woman initially caresses, then kills it, with the cat being black suggesting Sarah's dark fate. Sarah's walled display of photographs of herself with Matthieu is her memento of the past, and also allows us to see her smiling in happiness. Her fantasy of a naked Matthieu holding her is stopped by the abrupt image of his head smashing through the car's windshield, although it is an angle that Sarah could not have seen.

Her nightmare of the baby coming out of her mouth begins with Sarah vomiting and then rolling in her vomit, with an extreme close-up of the cat before the baby appears. The cat shot creates the horror expectation that it will jump into Sarah's gaping mouth, an expectation not met, and also falsely presents the cat as a threat. After the crash, where blood drips from Sarah's cut, the excess vomiting foreshadows more gore to come.

The Woman's face is first seen in shadow, like a vampire, and the sight of Sarah answering the door, shot between the bars of the staircase, presents her as a prisoner. Ominous horror movie music is heard on a soundtrack which otherwise remains understated. The rain returning for the Woman's arrival suggests the typical horror movie storm, although there is thankfully no thunder and lightning. The Woman seen at Sarah's window in long shot, still in shadow, is more of her as vampire. After lighting a cigarette, the Woman is seen in extreme close-up, revealing her mad eyes. The window pane that cracks from her strike shows the result of her violence, with the slowly cracking glass a resonant horror image.

Sarah's idea that the Woman can be seen in the photograph she has taken in the park, even though it is darker than the one she takes of the Woman at the window, remains dubious. However, it makes sense that the Woman would be stalking Sarah, since we don't know how else the Woman has found her house. (The police will point out that Sarah's name being on the letter box explains how the Woman knows her name). The blue flashing light of the police car reflected in the house is a subtle way to present their arrival, and also adds to the lighting ambience.

The subplot of the immigrant riots in the suburbs of Paris is paid off with the appearance of Abdel, but is only relevant to the Woman's attack if you consider her an immigrant intruder. The Woman's sudden appearance in Sarah's bedroom is one of the film's best shocks, since it is never explained how she gained entry, and the expectation of her attack is delayed. The Woman's antipathy towards Sarah echoes the older-versus-younger-woman scenario from *Strait-Jacket*, *Lady in a Cage*, *Die! Die! My Darling*, *The Night Walker*, *I Saw What You Did*, *Games*, *Berserk!*, *Eye of the Cat*, *The Mad Room*, *Blood and Lace*, *The Baby*, *The Killing Kind*, *Frightmare*, *Ruby*, *The Hunger*, *Night Warning*, *Epitaph*, *Mommy*, and *Mother*.

It is interesting that scissors are the Woman's choice of weapon, although she uses others, and her stabbing of Sarah's belly button repeats our view of the baby's trauma. Sarah battling on after the stabbing (which was obviously not deep enough to disable) shows her strength, with the climactic cutting into her belly presenting how difficult such a thing is to do with scissors. The Woman's slashing of Sarah's face is also an attack on Sarah's youthful beauty by an older woman. It is Sarah's quick thinking that allows her to lock herself in the bathroom; and it's fortuitous that just when she does so, her water breaks. The narrative then doubles the anguish of Sarah's condition—the physical pain of labor *and* the emotional horror of being terrorized by a maniac. The Woman assisting in the delivery of the baby at the climax is a representation of the Woman's female compassion, even if it is tainted by her own agenda. The Woman's yelling in frustration reads more as funny than sympathetic, since we want Sarah to be safe. Although

Sarah carries her own moral ambiguity by virtue of her character's surliness, she is also held partly responsible for the crash, though she was not driving.

The Woman stopping Jean-Pierre from leaving before he becomes suspicious, and before Louise arrives, is an unexpected plot twist. He points out that the mother will become a grandmother, which ages the Woman further than the mother role she desires. Her dialogue here is laced with irony: "She [referring to Sarah] went through hell after the accident. Of course, so did I. These last few months have been awful, but I know the birth will save us."

The Woman rejecting Jean-Pierre's hand of comfort arouses his suspicions, and the convenience of his finding Sarah's developed photograph of the Woman in the sofa is an acceptable contrivance. What is pleasing is that Jean-Pierre doesn't recognize the Woman from the photograph, even after Louise arrives, although he is a little dim not to. The Woman having to cope with three crises at once (if you also count Sarah in the bathroom) is saved by the narrative decision to have Sarah kill Louise, thinking her to be the Woman. This is a sublime undercutting of the clichéd cavalry arrival, and more irony in light of Sarah's previous dismissal of her mother.

Publicity portrait of Alyson Paradis and Beatrice Dalle, the stars of *Inside* (2007). The embrace is ironic, given their antipathy in the film.

Louise's blood that spurts from her neck is more excess and creates the expectation that Jean-Pierre will be dealt with in a similarly grisly fashion. His unseen attack from behind, with the discovery of Louise dead distracting him, is slight restraint before the excess of his murder. The Woman stabbing the scissors into his groin is pure misanthropy, as her slashing of his face is a nastiness that she has already demonstrated on Sarah. Sarah's retreating to the bathroom rather than helping Jean-Pierre can be seen both as self-preservation and moral weakness. Jean-Pierre's resurrection, and need to be killed more effectively, is the conventional horror device seen in *Night Warning*, *Misery*, and *Epitaph*. The Woman's use of a pillow creates an expectation of a softer weapon, but the scissors again defy the expectation.

The Woman pulling out some of Sarah's hair as Sarah retreats to the bathroom showcases more female warfare, like the Woman slashing Sarah's face. The narrative again plays with timing to allow Sarah another momentary escape, with the Woman's smoking more expression of her frustration. Jump cuts are used to reveal more of the Woman's madness, the first of only two times in the film such postmodern devices are employed. The following exchange provides the Woman with a teasing rationale (as well as some humor for Sarah):

> SARAH: Why me?
> THE WOMAN: I want one.
> SARAH: What kind of man would fuck a maniac like you?!

The Woman locking Sarah into the bathroom with a cupboard to stop the door handle from turning is a reverse of Sarah's self-imposed entrapment, while the expectation of the fire poker that the Woman takes to deal with the returning police officers is not met. Sarah's hand pinned to the wall with the scissors is a classic horror scenario, even if the expectation is obvious. The fact that the Woman leaves the hand like that shows some momentary restraint from her, allows her to observe rather than act, and gives relief to the narrative before the oncoming police onslaught. The Woman being able to defeat three men—police officers trained to deal with violence—shows her cunning and creates the expectation that she will ultimately triumph.

The poker coming into play is only delayed, and its insertion into an eye is more excessive gore. The shooting of the second police officer continues the idea of the Woman's kamikaze attack, in the same fashion as the attack on Jean-Pierre. Again the narrative establishes the expectation of Sarah's rescue when her hand is freed, only to be undercut by the second best shock of the film—a policeman's face exploding. The treatment mixes Hitchcockian suspense with shock horror. We know the Woman is a present threat, but we also know she can strike in surprise. Three-way cross-cutting between the first officer with the Woman, the second officer and Sarah, and the third officer in the police car generates suspense.

Cruel perversity arrives with the entry of the third officer, with Abdel imprisoned by handcuffs, and black humor from his nausea at the sight of the gore from the Woman's attacks. The lights being turned off adds the horror movie convention of fear of the dark, with the idea of the Woman as vampire having a nighttime advantage. Suspense is teased out by the narrative decisions to delay Sarah's rescue by the third officer, and by him deciding to fix the lights rather than leave the house. The third officer's shooting is heard by Sarah but not seen by us, although Adbel's murder gets the full grand guignol scissors-in-the-head treatment. The Woman attacking him while he's handcuffed makes her seem especially heartless, as does her smoking as she watches him die.

The jump cuts used for when the Woman crawls over Sarah in bed—like an animal sniffing its prey—receive a marvelous payoff in Sarah's biting the Woman's lips, given Beatrice Dalle's big lower lip, as an erotic fetish. (In France, Dalle is known as "Le Grande Bouche," which means the Big Mouth.) This is really the first narrative suggestion that Sarah can triumph over the Woman—a notion strengthened when she later burns her. The burning comes from Sarah's surprise use of an aerosol can when the Woman lights another cigarette after brutally bashing Sarah with a toaster. The burning is also Sarah's attack upon the Woman's female beauty, creating the deformed gargoyle that will provide comfort to the baby at film's end.

Sarah cutting into her own throat to assist her breathing and then covering the cut with masking tape highlights her determination and ingenuity, and furthers the expectation that she will triumph. Sarah is presented as a warrior after she improvises a spear-like weapon and uses her camera flash for light, the latter a rediscovery of her power in the same way taking the photograph was earlier. A comment by the Woman when Sarah finds her stops Sarah from striking when the Woman is disempowered by the burn, which will prove to be a fatal error in judgment. The exchange also introduces the flashback to the crash, where the Woman is seen to be driving the other car: "You can kill me again, Sarah; you already did once."

The Woman considers the crash her death, which suggests the extent of the psychological trauma, the importance of the baby to her, and her madness. However, if she considers herself dead, we have to ask if the Woman's imperative to take Sarah's baby is the Woman's own rebirth. The opening dialogue is elaborated on in voice-over when we see the Woman in the car, with "My child, my baby" preceding "No one will take him from me," providing context. Sarah taking more photographs of the Woman is another odd character choice, but the return of the lights to the house quickly changes the tone.

The lights having been fixed by the third police officer is strange, and signals another resurrection, with his attack on Sarah being ironic given that he was not shot by her. The Woman's attack upon him—using Sarah's spear—can be seen as a defense, although the Woman is also defending the baby and herself. The officer's murder presents more excess, with his impaled body suggesting sexual penetration. The river of blood down the staircase from Sarah's scissor-cut belly matches the blood being rinsed away during the opening credits and adds to the grotesquery of the cutting.

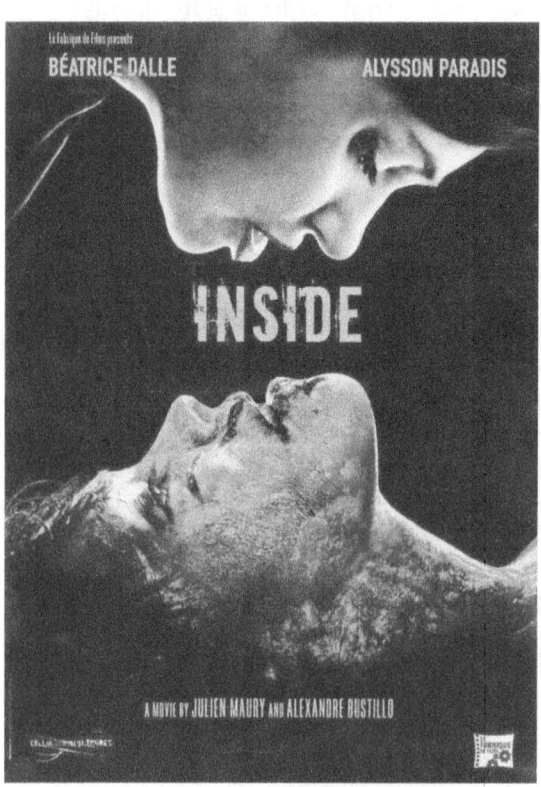

Poster for *Inside* (2007).

The dissolve from Sarah's screaming to silence gives pause, and adds a bizarre delicacy to the charred Woman nursing the baby. There is ambiguity in Sarah left on the staircase, since she may not be dead, although we would image the Woman would want her to be. The sound of the baby crying is ironic as it indicates it is alive, but perhaps also that is it terrified by the Woman's appearance; and the final poignant and disturbing image of her in the rocking chair with the baby signals the triumph of the grande dame.

Beatrice Dalle was age 42 at the time of filming, as opposed to Alysson's Paradis's 24. Although Dalle had assayed some supporting roles, she had last played the lead in *Tete d'or* (2006). She had been discovered at the age of 22 for the title role in Jean-Jacques Beineix' *Betty Blue* (1986), and has had a controversial private life. In 1991 Dalle received a suspended sentence and was fined for repeated shoplifting. In 1999 she was arrested and fined for attacking a meter maid in Paris. In 2005 she married a prison inmate. She had been arrested for alleged cocaine possession in Miami while making *The Blackout*, which resulted in her being declared an "Undesirable Immigrant" and denied a work permit to act in *The Sixth Sense*.

As the Woman, Dalle is dressed in black, in a stylized draping floor-length dress with wide sleeve cuffs, and gloves. Shadows on her face suggest the car crash, and her smoking alludes to her sensuality and addictive tendencies. The ponytail she initially wears gives way to her long brown hair being loose, although we aren't show the Woman releasing it. Dalle gives the Woman odd pauses before she moves, which adds to the idea of her instability but also implies that she was mad before the loss of her baby. That she would be so determined about the baby, as evidenced by the dialogue in the opening scene and flashback, also implies that the pregnancy did not come easily for her. The ring she wears implies a husband, but we aren't given any other details of the Woman's life.

Although we feel sorry for the Woman's loss, her violent behavior as retribution denies her the empathy we have with Sarah, which dilutes the grande dame's moral ambiguity. Her seizing upon Sarah as a depressed pregnant woman makes the Woman seem all the more opportunistic, in spite of her perception of Sarah's guilt. Ultimately, however, the Woman is a conventional horror movie monster because she lacks the dimension that extra empathy would provide. Dalle sells her mounting pain from Sarah's attacks, especially from her face and hair being burned, but this is considered deserved in light of the Woman's far greater savagery.

Release

June 13, 2007, in France, and October 17, 2007, at the ScreamFest Film Festival.

Reviews

"...[P]ic restarts the French gore genre with an over-the-top sadism sure to please fans of schlock horror.... Fright level is average, with laughs dependent on whether skewers in eyes tickle the funny bone. Soundscape, like Dalle's crazed character, is unrelenting."—Jay Weissberg, *Variety*, May 28, 2007.

"...[G]ut-splattering delirium to come.... Genuinely disturbing, poetic and precise, every cut, frame, shock, and thought fine-tuned to freak you out, *Inside* is a neo-horror near-masterpiece."—Nathan Lee, *The Village Voice*, February 5, 2008.

"...Claustrophobic shocker.... The filmmakers pile on the gore in relentless fashion.... It would all be laughable if it wasn't also so damn effective, with the expert photography and editing providing a nonstop barrage of visceral shocks. Strictly for those who like their horror on the extreme side."—Frank Scheck, *The Hollywood Reporter*, February 27, 2008.

Bibliography

Bacall, Lauren. *By Myself and Then Some*. London: Headline Book Publishing, 2005.

Bogdanovich, Peter. *Who the Devil Made It?; Conversations with Robert Aldrich et al.* New York: Alfred A. Knopf, 1997.

Brode, Douglas. *The Films of the Sixites*. New Jersey: Citadel Press, 1980.

Brown, Peter Harry, and Pamela Ann Brown. *The MGM Girls: Behind the Velvet Curtain*. New York: St. Martins Press, 1983.

Busch, Charles, and John Epperson. *What Ever Happened to Baby Jane?* DVD audio commentary. Warner Home Video, 2006.

Busch, Charles, and Boze Hadleigh. *Dead Ringer* DVD audio commentary. Warner Home Video, 2005.

Cettl, Robert. *Serial Killer Cinema*. Jefferson, NC: McFarland, 2003.

Chandler, Charlotte. *The Girl Who Walked Home Alone: Bette Davis, a Personal Biography*. New York: Simon & Schuster, 2006.

Considine, Shaun. *Bette & Joan: The Divine Feud*. New York: E.P. Dutton, 1989.

Da, Lottie, and Jan Alexander. *Bad Girls of the Silver Screen*. New York: Carroll & Graf, 1989.

Dixon, Wheeler Winston. *The Films of Freddie Francis (Filmmakers, No. 24)*. London: Scarecrow Press, 1991.

Edwards, Phil. *Shocking Cinema*. Beaconsfield, NSW: Mentmore Press, 1987.

Epstein, Rob, and Jeffery Friedman. *The Celluloid Closet DVD*. Sony Pictures, 1995.

Erickson, Glenn. *Hush... Hush, Sweet Charlotte* DVD audio commentary. Warner Home Video, 2005.

Fischer, Dennis. *Horror Film Directors, 1931–1990*. Jefferson, NC: McFarland, 1991.

Fontaine, Joan. *No Bed of Roses*. London: W.H. Allen, 1978.

Goldman, William. *Misery* DVD audio commentary. MGM/UA, 2003.

Grant, Barry Keith. *The Dread of Difference: Gender and the Horror Film*. Austin: University of Texas Press, 1996.

Gritten, David. *Halliwell's Film Guide 2008*. London: HarperCollins, 2007.

Hamilton, John. *Beasts in the Cellar: The Exploitation Film Career of Tony Tenser*. London: Fab Press, 2005.

Hanke, Ken. "Attack of the Horror Hags," *Scarlet Street*, No. 49, 2003: 32–73.

_____. "Attack of the Horror Hags, Part Two," *Scarlet Street*, No. 50, 2004: 32–67.

Hardy, Phil. *The Aurum Film Encyclopedia of Horror*. London: Aurum Press, 1993.

Harrington, Curtis. *Ruby* DVD interview by David Del Valle. Vci Video, 2001.

Harrington, Curtis, and Piper Laurie. *Ruby* DVD Audio commentary. Vci Video, 2001.

Haskell, Molly. *From Reverance to Rape: The Treatment of Women in the Movies*. New York: Holt, Rineheart and Winston, 1974.

Heyman, David C. *Liz: An Intimate Biography of Elizabeth Taylor*. New York: Birch Lane, 1995.

Higham, Charles. *Olivia and Joan: A Biography of Olivia deHavilland and Joan Fontaine*. Sevenoaks, Kent: New English Library, 1984.

Humphries, Reynold. *The American Horror Film: An Introduction*. Edinburgh: Edinburgh University Press, 2002.

Iaccino, James F. *Psychological Reflections on Cinematic Terror: Jungian Archetypes in Horror Films*. Westport: Praeger, 1994.

Kael, Pauline. *5001 Nights at the Movies*. New York: Holt, Rineheart and Winston, 1984.

Kinnard, Roy. *Horror in Silent Films: A Filmography, 1896–1929*. Jefferson, NC: McFarland, 1995.

Ladd, Diane. *Spiraling Through the School of Life*. Carlsbad, CA: Hay House, 2006.

Lanier Wright, Bruce. *Nightwalkers: Gothic Horror Movies, the Modern Era*. Dallas: Taylor Publishing, 1995.

Maxford, Howard. *The A–Z of Horror Films*. Bloomington and Indianapolis: Indiana University Press, 1997.

Maltin, Leonard. *2009 Movie Guide*. New York: Plume, 2008.

McCarty, John. *Movie Psychos and Madmen*. New York: Citadel, 1993.

McCormack, Patty, with Max Allan Collins. "A Conversation." *Mommy* DVD. Roan Group Entertainment, 1995.

_____. *Mommy* DVD audio commentary. Roan Group Entertainment, 1995.

Newman, Kim. *The BFI Companion to Horror*. London: Cassell, 1996.

Quirk, Lawrence J. *The Films of Joan Crawford*. New York: Citadel Press, 1968.

_____. *Fasten Your Seat Belts: The Passionate Life of Bette Davis*. New York: William Morrow, 1990.

Rebello, Stephen. *Alfred Hitchcock and the Making of Psycho*. London: Mandarin, 1990.

Reiner, Rob. *Misery* DVD audio commentary. MGM/UA, 2003.

Sangster, Jimmy. *Do You Want It Good or on Tuesday? From Hammer Films to Hollywood! A Life in the Movies*. Baltimore: Midnight Marquee Press, 1997.

Sarandon, Susan. *The Hunger* DVD audio commentary. Warner Home Video, 2004.

Schow, David, and Jeffrey Frentzen. *The Outer Limits: The Official Companion*. New York: Ace Science Fiction Books, 1986.

Scott, Tony. *The Hunger* DVD audio commentary. Warner Home Video, 2004.

Signoret, Simone. *Nostalgia Isn't What It Used to Be*. London: Weidenfeld and Nicolson, 1978.

Smith, Gary A. *Uneasy Dreams: The Golden Age of British Horror Films, 1956–1976*. Jefferson, NC: McFarland, 2000.

Stanley, John. *Creature Features: The Science Fiction, Fantasy, and Horror Movie Guide*. New York: Boulevard Books, 1997.

Stine, Scott Aaron. *The Gorehound's Guide to Splatter Films of the 1980s*. Jefferson, NC: McFarland, 2003.

Thomas, Bob. *Joan Crawford: A Biography*. New York: Simon & Schuster, 1978.

Tudor, Andrew. *Monsters and Mad Scientists: A Cultural History of the Horror Movie*. Oxford and Cambridge: Basil Blackwell, 1989.

Winters, Shelley. *Shelley*. London: Granada, 1980.

Index

Aldrich, Robert 14, 16, 19, 22, 23, 24, 26, 27, 28, 29, 30, 31, 42, 57, 58, 59, 60, 61, 62, 63, 64, 65, 79, 100, 124, 157
Altman, Robert 144, 145, 146, 147, 148, 149, 214
Arsenic and Old Lace 9
Asher, William 269, 270, 271, 272, 273
Ashley, Elizabeth 1, 249, 250
Astor, Mary 59, 60, 63, 65
Autumn Leaves 14–16, 19, 22, 24, 25, 28, 30, 43, 114

The Baby 124, 193–198, 202, 203, 214, 220, 232, 233, 239, 258, 272, 273, 277, 278, 298, 302, 304, 315, 321
Bacall, Lauren 1, 253, 254, 257, 258
Bad Blood 289–293, 303
The Bad Seed 113, 295, 297, 298
Bankhead, Tallulah 1, 67, 68, 70, 71, 72, 303
Bates, Kathy 1, 287, 288
The Beast in the Cellar 161–166, 184, 196, 217, 284, 291, 303
Bergner, Elisabeth 1, 3, 171, 172
Berserk! 16, 105, 109–114, 131, 140, 145, 151, 158, 163, 176, 190, 191, 196, 209, 214, 224, 232, 239, 258, 261, 273, 278, 285, 293, 298, 302, 321
Bianchi, Edward 253, 254, 255, 256, 257, 258
Biehn, Michael 253, 258
Blood and Lace 187–192, 196, 197, 214, 220, 224, 232, 233, 239, 258, 272, 273, 277, 278, 298, 302, 304, 321
Bochner, Lloyd 77, 79
Buono, Victor 26, 27, 30, 59

Caan, James 51, 52, 53, 108, 285, 288
Castle, William 42, 43, 44, 45, 46, 47, 75, 76, 77, 79, 80, 82, 83, 84, 85, 86, 94, 100, 110, 179
Chaffey, Don 223, 224, 225, 226, 227, 228
Collins, Max Allan 295, 296, 297, 298, 299, 307, 308, 310
Cotten, Joseph 58, 63, 79, 107, 214
Crawford, Joan 1, 3, 8, 9, 12, 13, 14, 15, 16, 24, 25, 28, 29, 30, 31, 35, 40, 42, 43, 44, 45, 46, 47, 48, 54, 57, 62, 63, 64, 65, 79, 82, 85, 86, 110, 112, 113, 114, 119, 120, 121, 135, 151, 152, 153, 154, 155, 164, 171, 179, 188, 190, 210, 286, 293, 313
Cry of the Banshee 3, 167–172, 183, 217, 220, 233, 272, 277, 304

Dalle, Beatrice 1, 323, 324, 325
Davis, Bette 1, 8, 9, 12, 13, 14, 15, 16, 24, 25, 26, 27, 28, 29, 30, 31, 33, 34, 36, 38, 46, 57, 58, 59, 61, 62, 63, 64, 65, 72, 79, 88, 89, 90, 91, 92, 121, 139, 149, 210
Dead Ringer 32–40, 67, 76, 124, 139, 163, 206, 217
De Havilland, Olivia 1, 50, 54, 55, 58, 59, 62, 63, 64, 65, 79, 107, 120, 214

Deneuve, Catherine 1, 261, 267
Dennis, Sandy 1, 144, 149
Die! Die! My Darling! 66–73, 76, 77, 83, 96, 101, 105, 106, 112, 120, 131, 140, 145, 158, 163, 190, 191, 196, 206, 209, 214, 217, 232, 239, 242, 245, 258, 261, 272, 273, 276, 278, 283, 284, 285, 291, 298, 302, 303, 320, 321
Dietrich, Marlene 12, 107
Dukakis, Olympia 303, 305

Epitaph 3, 275–279, 284, 291, 298, 302, 303, 304, 316, 321, 322
Eye of the Cat 3, 130–136, 140, 145, 158, 163, 164, 190, 191, 196, 200, 214, 223, 224, 232, 239, 245, 258, 261, 273, 278, 284, 290, 298, 302, 321

The Fan 251–258, 261, 269, 283, 285
Farmer, Frances 12, 47
Flesh Feast 156–160, 190, 196, 232
Fontaine, Joan 1, 64, 99, 100, 101, 102, 121, 257
A Fool There Was 6
Francis, Freddie 151, 153, 154
Frankel, Cyril 99, 101
Frightmare 3, 216–221, 233, 237, 239, 258, 272, 273, 277, 278, 298, 302, 304, 321

Games 103–108, 112, 118, 126, 131, 140, 141, 145, 158, 163, 175, 177, 183, 184, 190, 191, 196, 197, 200, 203, 214, 218, 224, 232, 239, 245,

258, 273, 278, 291, 298, 302, 321
Gilbert, Philip S. 188, 189, 190, 191, 192
Girard, Bernard 124, 138, 139, 140, 141, 142
Gordon, Ruth 127, 128, 135, 235
Grahame, Gloria 1, 188, 192
Grauman, Walter 50, 52, 53, 54
Grinter, Brad F. 157, 158, 159

Hardin, Ty 111, 114
Harrington, Curtis 94, 95, 96, 97, 104, 105, 106, 107, 108, 175, 176, 177, 178, 179, 180, 182, 183, 184, 185, 186, 199, 200, 201, 202, 203, 237, 238, 239, 240, 241, 242, 243
Hessler, Gordon 168, 169, 170, 171, 172
Hitchcock, Alfred 16, 17, 57, 61, 67, 71, 76, 78, 80, 94, 96, 101, 102, 112, 114, 120, 136, 253, 256, 272, 278, 284, 285, 314, 323
Holt, Seth 88, 89, 90, 91, 92, 287, 292
Homebodies 229–235, 239, 261, 272, 277, 284, 285, 304
Hopkins, Miriam 1, 116, 118, 120, 121, 122, 135, 139, 164, 257, 291, 293
The Hunger 94, 259–267, 269, 273, 278, 285, 298, 302, 321
Hunnicutt, Gayle 134, 135
Hush...Hush Sweet Charlotte 56–65, 69, 76, 77, 78, 83, 85, 89, 91, 106, 107, 124, 127, 141, 148, 164, 175, 177, 196, 197, 203, 206, 214, 217, 220, 233, 237, 270, 272, 277, 304, 313, 315, 320
Hutton, Brian G. 206, 207, 208, 209, 210, 291

I Saw What You Did 3, 81–86, 94, 96, 105, 112, 113, 114, 131, 140, 141, 145, 158, 163, 164, 168, 171, 190, 191, 196, 209, 214, 217, 224, 232, 239, 258, 261, 273, 278, 285, 293, 298, 302, 321
Inside 319–325

Katzin, Lee H. 124, 126, 127, 128
Keith, Sheila 1, 3, 220, 221
Kelly, James 162, 163, 164
The Killing Kind 197, 199–204, 212, 214, 217, 223, 224, 237, 239, 245, 258, 273, 278, 282, 291, 297, 298, 302, 315, 320, 321
A Knife for the Ladies 211–215, 261, 285

Ladd, Diane 1, 301, 303, 305
Lady in a Cage 49–55, 63, 68, 69, 77, 83, 101, 105, 106, 107, 112, 118, 120, 131, 140, 145, 147, 158, 163, 184, 190, 191, 196, 203, 209, 214, 224, 232, 239, 258, 261, 272, 273, 278, 283, 285, 291, 298, 302, 321
Lake, Veronica 1, 157, 159, 160
LaLoggia, Frank 301, 302, 303, 304
The Landlady 312–318, 320
Laurie, Piper 1, 237, 241, 242, 243

The Mad Room 124, 137–142, 145, 158, 163, 164, 176, 177, 197, 203, 209, 239, 258, 273, 278, 298, 302, 315, 321
Malenfant, Robert 313, 314, 315, 316, 317, 318
Marly, Florence 1, 3, 97
McCormack, Patty 1, 295, 296, 298, 299, 307, 308, 309, 310
Merhi, Joseph 276, 277, 278
Misery 280–288, 290, 291, 292, 293, 303, 322
Mommie Dearest 12, 46, 112, 279
Mommy 294–299, 302, 307, 308, 309, 310, 321
Mommy's Day 306–311
Moorehead, Agnes 58, 60, 61, 63, 65, 177, 179
Mother 300–305, 310, 320, 321

The Nanny 87–92, 145, 152, 182, 190, 224
Narizanno, Silvio 67, 68, 70, 71, 72, 73
Nascar, Delores 3, 276, 277, 278, 279

The Night Walker 74–80, 82, 83, 94, 96, 105, 112, 131, 140, 145, 158, 163, 176, 190, 191, 196, 202, 206, 214, 217, 232, 239, 245, 258, 261, 270, 273, 278, 285, 291, 298, 302, 313, 320, 321
Night Warning 268–274, 277, 278, 284, 287, 291, 292, 298, 302, 303, 304, 313, 315, 320, 321, 322
Night Watch 205–210, 217, 261, 285

O'Connolly, Jim 110, 112, 113, 114

Page, Geraldine 1, 124, 127, 129
Paradis, Alysson 24
Parker, Eleanor 1, 134, 135, 136, 164
Persecution 222–228, 237, 245, 291, 302, 320
Post, Ted 194, 196, 197
Powers, Stefanie 68, 69, 70, 72, 120
Psycho 5, 11, 16–19, 22, 26, 30, 38, 42, 45, 50, 62, 70, 72, 76, 82, 83, 84, 89, 94, 101, 110, 116, 119, 120, 124, 126, 127, 183, 188, 189, 196, 203, 214, 238, 253, 255, 256, 265, 272, 278, 283, 286, 297, 304, 309, 310

Queen of Blood 3, 93–97, 104, 145, 158, 183, 264

Raymond, Ruth 1, 290, 291, 292, 293
Reid, Beryl 164, 165
Reiner, Rob 282, 283, 284, 285, 286, 287
Reynolds, Debbie 1, 175, 178, 179, 180, 189
Rich, David Lowell 131, 132, 133, 134, 136
Robson, Flora 1, 162, 165
Roman, Ruth 1, 194, 195, 197, 198, 202, 212, 214, 215
Ross, Katharine 104, 105, 106, 107, 108
Ruby 236–243, 246, 258, 261, 270, 273, 278, 284, 298, 302, 313, 320, 321

Sarandon, Susan 263, 265, 266, 267
The Savage Intruder 4, 115–122, 125, 136, 139, 141, 148, 158, 163, 164, 184, 190, 197, 202, 203, 206, 209, 220, 224, 232, 233, 239, 257, 261, 272, 277, 284, 285, 291, 293, 304, 315
Scott, Tony 261, 262, 263, 264, 265, 266, 267, 303
Shire, Talia 1, 313, 316, 317, 318
Signoret, Simone 1, 104, 105, 107, 108
Sothern, Ann 1, 51, 199, 200, 203, 204, 212, 282
Spangler, Larry G. 212, 213, 214
Stanwyck, Barbara 1, 63, 76, 77, 79, 80
The Star 2, 12–14, 19, 22, 24, 28
Stevens, Stella 138, 140, 141, 176
A Stolen Life 33–34, 38
Strait-Jacket 16, 35, 41–48, 63, 68, 76, 77, 83, 85, 94, 96, 105, 112, 114, 131, 140, 145, 148, 158, 163, 169, 184, 188, 189, 190, 191, 196, 197, 214, 220, 224, 232, 233, 237, 239, 258, 270, 272, 273, 277, 278, 298, 302, 304, 313, 320, 321

Sunset Boulevard 9–11, 19, 22, 26, 27, 60, 62, 96, 117, 118, 119, 122, 136, 159

Taylor, Elizabeth 1, 206, 207, 209, 210
Taylor, Robert 77, 78, 79, 80
That Cold Day in the Park 143–149, 200, 277, 302, 304
Trog 150–155, 163, 223, 272, 273, 276, 284, 291, 303
Trueman, Paula 234, 235
Turner, Lana 1, 39, 223, 225, 227, 228
Tyrrell, Susan 1, 269, 273, 274

Vincent, Chuck 290, 291, 292

Walker, Pete 217, 218, 219, 220, 221
What Ever Happened to Aunt Alice? 123–129, 135, 158, 190, 197, 203, 206, 224, 232, 239, 284
What Ever Happened to Baby Jane? 1, 4, 8, 14, 15, 16, 19, 21–31, 33, 34, 35, 36, 40, 42, 45, 46, 57, 58, 60, 62, 63, 69, 70, 77, 83, 92, 101, 119, 120, 121, 124, 125, 126, 127, 135, 141, 158, 163, 164, 175, 176, 177, 179, 190, 197, 202, 203, 214, 224, 232, 237, 239, 242, 270, 272, 276, 283, 284, 286, 291, 292, 302, 313, 315, 316, 320
What's the Matter with Helen? 173–180, 185, 189, 197, 200, 202, 203, 209, 214, 237, 245, 261, 285, 291, 302, 320
Whoever Slew Auntie Roo? 181–186, 190, 191, 214, 224, 272, 277, 304
Willis, Gordon 245, 246, 247, 248, 249
Windows 244–250, 253, 261, 269, 285, 291, 302, 313, 317, 320
Winters, Shelley 1, 138, 139, 140, 141, 175, 179, 180, 182, 185, 186
The Witches 98–102, 105, 112, 121, 131, 169, 170, 200, 237, 245, 257, 261, 285, 291, 302, 320
Wolfe, Donald 116, 117, 118, 119, 120, 121, 122

Yust, Larry 230, 231, 232, 233, 234

www.ingramcontent.com/pod-product-compliance
Lightning Source LLC
Chambersburg PA
CBHW080758300426
44114CB00020B/2748